Philadelphia
Restaurants
2011

LOCAL EDITOR
Michael Klein

LOCAL COORDINATOR
Marilyn Kleinberg

STAFF EDITOR
Yoji Yamaguchi

Published and distributed by
Zagat Survey, LLC
4 Columbus Circle
New York, NY 10019
T: 212.977.6000
E: philadelphia@zagat.com
www.zagat.com

ACKNOWLEDGMENTS

We thank Fran and Joe Alberstadt, Charlotte Ann, Dick and Ann-Michelle Albertson, Cindy and Richard Blum, Suzanne and Norman Cohn, Paul and Tim DiIorio, Hugh E. Dillon, Jack and Mia Dorazio, Pete Dorazio, Ali VanGorden and Gregg Dorazio, Marcia Gelbart, Ellen and Steve Goldman, Lisa and Tom Haflett, Loretta and Tom Jordan, Donna and Larry Kane, Jodi and Alan Klein, Diane Klein, Jennifer, Rachel and Lindsay Klein, Karen and Dan McFaul, Carol and Ben Preston, Sybil Rothstein, Doris and Joe Segel, Devon Segel and Sean Perry, Justin Wineburgh and the Philadelphia Inquirer's food crew: Maureen Fitzgerald, Craig LaBan and Rick Nichols, as well as the following members of our staff: Christina Livadiotis (associate editor), Brian Albert, Sean Beachell, Maryanne Bertollo, Danielle Borovoy, Jane Chang, Sandy Cheng, Reni Chin, Larry Cohn, Caitlin Eichelberger, Alison Flick, Jeff Freier, Matthew Hamm, Justin Hartung, Garth Johnston, Natalie Lebert, Mike Liao, Becky Ruthenburg, Jacqueline Wasilczyk, Art Yaghci, Sharon Yates, Anna Zappia and Kyle Zolner.

Maps © Antenna Audio

Contents

Ratings & Symbols

	Zagat Top Spot	Name	Symbols		Cuisine	Zagat Ratings			
						FOOD	DECOR	SERVICE	COST

Area, Address & Contact	**☒ Tim & Nina's ◗** *Deli* ▽ 23 | 9 | 13 | $15 **Port Richmond** | 11104 Walnut St. (Zagat Blvd.) | 215-555-1234 | www.zagat.com
Review, surveyor comments in quotes	"Yo Rocky!" – join the Iggles and Phils fans at this "run- down" 24-hour joint for its "belly-busting" cheesesteaks and "five-pound" hoagies served up proudly with a side of "sass" by "Port Richmond girls" dripping with "atti- tude"; though your cardiologist may describe the "clas- sic" grub as a "heart attack on a plate", you'll probably find him in line looking for patients and bargains.

Ratings   **Food, Decor** and **Service** are rated on the Zagat
0 to 30 scale.

0	– 9	poor to fair
10	– 15	fair to good
16	– 19	good to very good
20	– 25	very good to excellent
26	– 30	extraordinary to perfection
	▽	low response | less reliable

Cost   Our surveyors' estimated price of a dinner with one drink
and tip. Lunch is usually 25 to 30% less. For unrated **newcomers** or **write-ins,** the price range is shown as follows:

I	$25 and below	E	$41 to $65
M	$26 to $40	VE	$66 or above

Symbols
- ☒   highest ratings, popularity and importance
- ◗   serves after 11 PM
- ☒   closed on Sunday
- Ⓜ   closed on Monday
- ⊘   no credit cards accepted

Maps   Index maps show restaurants with the highest Food ratings in those areas.

About This Survey

Here are the results of our **2011 Philadelphia Restaurants Survey,** covering 1,038 eateries in the greater Philadelphia metropolitan area. Like all our guides, this one is based on input from avid local consumers – 5,551 all told. Our editors have synopsized this feedback and highlighted representative comments (in quotation marks within each review). You can read full surveyor comments – and share your own opinions – on **ZAGAT.com,** where you'll also find the latest restaurant news plus menus, photos and more, all for free.

OUR PHILOSOPHY: Three simple premises underlie our ratings and reviews. First, we've long believed that the collective opinions of large numbers of consumers are more accurate than the opinions of a single critic. (Consider that, as a group, our surveyors bring some 711,000 annual meals' worth of experience to this Survey. They also visit restaurants year-round, anonymously – and on their own dime.) Second, food quality is only part of the equation when choosing a restaurant, thus we ask surveyors to separately rate food, decor and service and report on cost. Third, since people need reliable information in a fast, easy-to-digest format, we strive to be concise and to offer our content on every platform. Our Top Ratings lists (pages 10–16) and indexes (starting on page 196) are also designed to help you quickly choose the best place for any occasion.

ABOUT ZAGAT: In 1979, we started asking friends to rate and review restaurants purely for fun. The term "user-generated content" had not yet been coined. That hobby grew into Zagat Survey; 31 years later, we have over 375,000 surveyors and cover airlines, bars, dining, fast food, entertaining, golf, hotels, movies, music, resorts, shopping, spas, theater and tourist attractions in over 100 countries. Along the way, we evolved from being a print publisher to a digital content provider, e.g. **ZAGAT.com, ZAGAT.mobi** (for web-enabled mobile devices), **ZAGAT TO GO** (for smartphones) and **nru** (for Android phones). We also produce customized gift and marketing tools for a wide range of corporate clients. And you can find us on Twitter (twitter.com/zagatbuzz), Facebook and other social media networks.

JOIN IN: To improve our guides, we solicit your comments; it's vital that we hear your opinions. Just contact us at **nina-tim@zagat.com.** We also invite you to join our surveys at **ZAGAT.com.** Do so and you'll receive a choice of rewards in exchange.

THANKS: Special thanks go to our local editor, Michael Klein, a features columnist at the *Philadelphia Inquirer,* who has written its restaurant-news column, "Table Talk," since 1993. We also sincerely thank the thousands of surveyors who participated – all of our content is really "theirs."

New York, NY
August 25, 2010

Nina and Tim

Nina and Tim Zagat

What's New

For Philadelphia restaurant-goers, the recession wasn't *all* bad. Fifty-five percent of Survey participants say they're finding better meal deals while 38% feel their business is more appreciated. And though service remains a weak point – cited by 69% as the top dining-out irritant – that's an improvement over our last Survey, when 75% named it their No. 1 gripe. Still, the picture was hardly rosy for restaurateurs. Thirty-five percent of surveyors report dining out less frequently due to the economy, and Philadelphians again rank last among surveyed markets for average number of meals eaten out per week (2.5, vs. Zagat's U.S. average of 3.2). When they do dine out, 36% are more mindful of prices and 28% are choosing less costly places. That helps explain the host of value-conscious newcomers.

BISTRO INFERNO: Several bistro-ish arrivals are playing small ball, offering solid, affordable fare in modest surroundings. Three BYO examples: **Fond,** a New American in a South Philly storefront; **Hoof + Fin,** a rustic Argentinean in Queen Village; and **Koo Zee Doo,** a mom-and-pop Portuguese in Northern Liberties. In Wash West, **Zavino** is packing in scenesters with its pizza/wine bar formula.

BURGERS & BREWS: Burgers are still on a roll. Bobby Flay chose University City for a branch of **Bobby's Burger Palace,** and the folks behind Rittenhouse's **Rouge** are now offering praiseworthy patties at nearby storefront **500°.** Beer lovers, meanwhile, welcomed **City Tap House** (University City) and **Kraftwork** (Fishtown).

BIG GUNS: The alpha dogs also made their mark. Stephen Starr expanded his empire with **El Rey,** a casual Mexican cantina in Rittenhouse, and **Pizzeria Stella** in Society Hill. Jose Garces extended beyond Latin America with **Garces Trading Company,** an American cafe/wine shop/grocery in Wash West, and the burger-centric **Village Whiskey** in Rittenhouse. Marc Vetri, whose lofty Wash West Italian **Vetri** is No. 1 for Food in this Survey, added the somewhat less pricey trattoria **Amis** nearby. **Pod** and **Buddakan NYC** alum Michael Schulson, who owns Atlantic City's **Izakaya,** launched the slick Wash West Pan-Asian **Sampan.** And Daniel Stern closed **Rae** and **Gayle** to open **R2L,** a swanky New American on Two Liberty Place's 37th floor, and regional American specialist **MidAtlantic** in University City.

SURVEY STATS: The average meal cost is $34.17, up just 0.7%, annualized, from two years ago and slightly below the national average of $35.34 ... Despite the plethora of celeb chefs, only 32% of surveyors are drawn by a big name in the kitchen ... 41% book tables online, up from 25% two years ago.

Philadelphia, PA   Michael Klein
August 25, 2010

Most Popular

Plotted on the map at the back of this book.

1. Amada | *Spanish*
2. Buddakan | *Asian*
3. Le Bec-Fin | *French*
4. Osteria | *Italian*
5. Vetri | *Italian*
6. Zahav | *Israeli*
7. Prime Rib | *Steak*
8. Alma de Cuba | *Nuevo Latino*
9. Capital Grille | *Steak*
10. Fountain | *Continental/Fr.*
11. Morimoto | *Japanese*
12. Parc | *French*
13. Tinto | *Spanish*
14. Chifa | *Chinese/Peruvian*
15. Barclay Prime | *Steak*
16. Lacroix | *Eclectic*
17. Fork | *American*
18. El Vez | *Mexican*
19. Bibou | *French*
20. Estia | *Greek*
21. Distrito | *Mexican*
22. Gilmore's | *French*
23. 10 Arts | *American*
24. Matyson | *American*
25. Cuba Libre | *Cuban*
26. Pat's | *Cheesesteaks*
27. Yangming | *Chinese/Continental*
28. Savona | *Italian*
29. Dmitri's | *Greek*
30. Devon | *Seafood*
31. Palm | *Steak*
32. Davio's | *Italian*
33. Butcher & Singer | *Steak*
34. Continental Mid-town | *Eclectic*
35. Blackfish | *Seafood*
36. Melograno | *Italian*
37. Sabrina's | *Eclectic*
38. Fogo de Chão | *Brazilian/Steak*
39. Kanella | *Greek*
40. Birchrunville Store | *Fr./Italian*
41. White Dog Café | *Eclectic*
42. Sang Kee | *Chinese*
43. Reading Term. Mkt. | *Eclectic*
44. Modo Mio | *Italian*
45. Morton's | *Steak*
46. Jim's Steaks | *Cheesesteaks*
47. Tony Luke's | *Cheesesteaks*
48. Monk's Cafe | *Belgian*
49. Cheesecake Factory | *American*
50. Honey's | *Jewish/Southern*

It's obvious that many of the above restaurants are among the Philadelphia metropolitan area's most expensive, but if popularity were calibrated to price, we suspect that a number of other restaurants would join their ranks. Thus, we have added two lists comprising 90 Best Buys on page 17 as well as Prix Fixe Bargains on page 18.

KEY NEWCOMERS

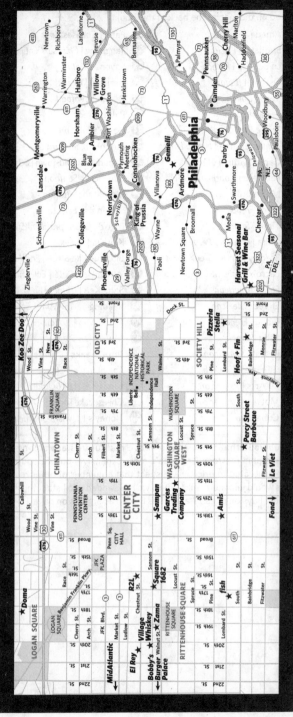

Menus, photos, voting and more - free at ZAGAT.com

Key Newcomers

Our editors' take on the year's top arrivals. See page 246 for a full list.

Amis | *Italian* | Roman treats in Wash West from Marc Vetri and crew

Bobby's Burger Palace | *Burgers* | Bobby Flay grills to thrill in University City

Doma | *Japanese/Korean* | Japanese BYO with panache in Logan Square

El Rey | *Mexican* | Stephen Starr goes south of the border in Rittenhouse

fish | *Seafood* | Stylish seafood in Graduate Hospital

Fond | *American* | New American BYO in South Philly

Garces Trading Co. | *American* | Jose Garces' BYO cafe in Wash West

Gemelli | *Italian* | French-influenced Italian BYO in Narbeth

Harvest Seasonal | *American* | Low-cal dining near West Chester

Hoof + Fin | *Argentinean* | Rustic South American BYO in Queen Village

Koo Zee Doo | *Portuguese* | Homespun Portuguese in Northern Liberties

Le Viet | *Vietnamese* | High-polish Vietnamese in South Philly

MidAtlantic | *American* | Daniel Stern focuses on local in U-City

Percy Street Barbecue | *BBQ* | 'Cue on South Street

Pizzeria Stella | *Pizza* | Stephen Starr's pizzeria in Society Hill

R2L | *American* | Daniel Stern's 37th-floor aerie in Two Liberty Place

Sampan | *Asian* | Slick Asian in Wash West

Square 1682 | *American* | Bold New American at The Palomar in Rittenhouse

Village Whiskey | *Amer.* | Jose Garces' take on a Rittenhouse public house

Zama | *Japanese* | Japanese from a former Pod chef in Rittenhouse

---

Coming down the Philly restaurant pipeline are new projects from Stephen Starr (**Il Pittore,** a Queen Village Italian with chef Chris Painter) and Jose Garces (**JG Domestic,** a Regional American in the Cira Centre, plus the beer-and-brat spot **Frohmans Wursthaus** in Washington Square West). Valerie Safran and Marcie Turney of Washington Square West's **Bindi** and **Lolita** are planning a summer opening of **Barbuzzo,** a Med lounge that will be located on the same block. **Tria,** the wine-cheese-beer lounge duo, will get a sibling, **Biba,** in University City, while **Tiffin**'s Munish Narula plans an upscale Indian this winter at 777 South Broad Street. Sating the city's beer mania will be the new **Hop Angel Brauhaus** in Northeast Philly as well as a Starr-produced *biergarten* in Fishtown, which will also be home to **Fathom Seafood Bar,** a casual bar from the **fish** crew.

Top Food

28 Vetri | *Italian*
Fountain | *Continental/French*
Birchrunville Store | *Fr./Italian*
Amada | *Spanish*
Gilmore's | *French*
Bluefin | *Japanese*
Morimoto | *Japanese*

27 Talula's Table | *European*
Bibou | *French*
John's Roast Pork | *Sandwiches*
Le Bec-Fin | *French*
Lacroix | *French*
Sovana Bistro | *French/Med.*
Horizons | *Vegan*
Capogiro | *American/Dessert*
Savona | *Italian*
Prime Rib | *Steak*
Le Bar Lyonnais | *French*
Fond | *American*
Matyson | *American*

Restaurant Alba | *Amer.*
Tinto | *Spanish*
Barclay Prime | *Steak*
James | *American*
Sola | *American*
Osteria | *Italian*

26 Blue Sage | *Vegetarian*
Swann Lounge | *Amer./French*
Nam Phuong | *Vietnamese*
Umai Umai | *Asian*
High St. | *Cajun/Creole*
Buddakan | *Asian*
Zento | *Japanese*
Le Virtù | *Italian*
L'Angolo | *Italian*
Pumpkin | *American*
Caffe Casta Diva | *Italian*
Modo Mio | *Italian*
Capital Grille | *Steak*
Carman's Country | *Eclectic*

BY CUISINE

AMERICAN (NEW)

27 Fond
Matyson
Restaurant Alba
James
Sola

AMERICAN (TRAD.)

25 Kimberton Inn
General Warren
24 Resurrection Ale House
Friday Sat. Sun.
23 Café Estelle

ASIAN

26 Umai Umai
Buddakan
25 Oishi
24 Nectar
Bunha Faun

BARBECUE

24 Sweet Lucy's
23 Bomb Bomb BBQ
21 El Camino Real
20 Percy Street Barbecue
Smokin' Betty's

CHEESESTEAKS

26 Tony Luke's
23 Dalessandro's
Campo's Deli
Steve's Prince/Steaks
Jim's Steaks

CHINESE

25 Yangming
Lee How Fook
24 Han Dynasty
Marg. Kuo's Media
Duck Sauce

CONTINENTAL

28 Fountain Restaurant
25 Duling-Kurtz House
22 Farmicia
20 William Penn Inn
Seven Stars Inn

ECLECTIC

27 Lacroix
26 Carman's Country
24 Reading Terminal Market
Sabrina's Café
Umbria

Excludes places with low votes.

FRENCH

28 Fountain Restaurant
   Birchrunville Store
   Gilmore's
27 Le Bec-Fin
   Swann Lounge

FRENCH (BISTRO)

27 Bibou
   Sovana Bistro
   Le Bar Lyonnais
25 Bistrot La Minette
24 Spring Mill

GREEK

25 Kanella
   Estia
24 Dmitri's
23 Olive Tree Med. Grill
22 South St. Souvlaki

INDIAN

25 Tiffin
24 Bindi
23 New Delhi
   Tiffin etc.
22 Palace of Asia

ITALIAN

28 Vetri
   Birchrunville Store
27 Savona
   Osteria
26 Le Virtù

JAPANESE

28 Bluefin
   Morimoto
26 Zento
25 Oishi
   Raw Sushi

LATIN/S. AMERICAN

25 Chifa
   Alma de Cuba
24 Tierra Colombiana
   Fogo de Chão
21 Chima

MEDITERRANEAN

27 Sovana Bistro
24 Valanni
23 Arpeggio
   Audrey Claire
   Figs

MEXICAN

26 Lolita
25 Tequila's Restaurant
   Distrito
24 Las Cazuelas
   Las Bugambilias

MIDDLE EASTERN

25 Zahav
   Bitar's
24 Alyan's
23 Konak
   Maoz Vegetarian

PIZZA

27 Osteria
25 Tacconelli's
24 Celebre's
23 Mama Palma's
22 Cooper's Brick Oven

SEAFOOD

25 Blackfish
   fish
   Radicchio
24 Dmitri's
   Creed's

SOUL/SOUTHERN

25 Honey's Sit 'n Eat
22 Warmdaddy's
21 Geechee Girl
   Marsha Brown
19 Jack's Firehouse

STEAKHOUSES

27 Prime Rib
   Barclay Prime
26 Capital Grille
   Morton's Steak
25 Davio's

THAI

26 Nan
25 Chabaa Thai
   Chiangmai
24 Thai Orchid
   White Elephant

VIETNAMESE

26 Nam Phuong
25 Vietnam
24 Vietnam Café
23 Vietnam Palace
22 Pho 75

BY SPECIAL FEATURE

BREAKFAST

25 Honey's Sit 'n Eat
24 Sabrina's
Famous 4th St. Deli
21 Winnie's Le Bus
18 Marathon Grill

BRUNCH

28 Fountain Restaurant
27 Lacroix
26 Swann Lounge
Carman's Country Kitchen
25 Kimberton Inn

BYO

28 Birchrunville Store
Gilmore's
27 Talula's Table
Bibou
Fond

CHILD-FRIENDLY

27 Capogiro
24 Ooka Japanese
Sweet Lucy's
23 Mama Palma's
Campo's Deli

CLASSIC PHILLY

25 Tacconelli's Pizzeria
24 Famous 4th St. Deli
23 Dante & Luigi's
19 City Tavern
18 Little Pete's

HOTEL DINING

28 Fountain Restaurant
    (Four Seasons)
27 Lacroix
    (Rittenhouse Hotel)
Prime Rib
    (Radisson Warwick)
26 Swann Lounge
    (Four Seasons)
25 Duling-Kurtz House

LATE DINING

27 Capogiro
Tinto
26 Swann Lounge
Tony Luke's
24 Valanni

MEET FOR A DRINK

28 Bluefin
27 Horizons
Prime Rib
Tinto
Osteria

OFFBEAT

28 Morimoto
26 Carman's Country Kitchen
25 Tacconelli's Pizzeria
Bitar's
Honey's Sit 'n Eat

PEOPLE-WATCHING

28 Amada
Morimoto
27 Lacroix
Prime Rib
Fond

POWER LUNCH

28 Fountain Restaurant
Amada
Morimoto
27 Le Bec-Fin
Lacroix

PRIVATE ROOMS

23 Pod
Upstares & Sotto Varalli
21 Dettera
Table 31
20 William Penn Inn

QUICK BITES

27 John's Roast Pork
26 Zento
Tony Luke's
25 Bitar's
Tiffin

QUIET CONVERSATION

28 Fountain Restaurant
Birchrunville Store
Gilmore's
27 Talula's Table
Bibou

SLEEPERS

24 Las Bugambilias
23 Bistro 7
Gemelli
Gables at Chadds Ford
22 Rose Tattoo

SMALL PLATES

27 Lacroix
26 Modo Mio
   Honey
25 Distrito
24 Valanni

TEEN APPEAL

26 Tony Luke's
24 Naked Chocolate Café
23 Pod
22 Continental Mid-town
19 Max Brenner

TRANSPORTING EXPERIENCES

28 Vetri
   Birchrunville Store

Gilmore's
Morimoto
27 Le Bec-Fin

TRENDY

28 Vetri
   Amada
   Morimoto
27 Tinto
   Barclay Prime

WINNING WINE LISTS

28 Vetri
   Fountain Restaurant
   Amada
27 Le Bec-Fin
   Lacroix

BY LOCATION

AVENUE OF THE ARTS

26 Capital Grille
   Morton's
25 Estia
24 Palm
   Fogo de Chão

BUCKS COUNTY

26 Blue Sage
   Honey
25 Oishi
   Inn at Phillips Mill
24 Duck Sauce

CHESTER COUNTY

28 Birchrunville Store
   Gilmore's
27 Talula's Table
   Sovana Bistro
26 High St. Caffé

CHESTNUT HILL

23 Osaka
   CinCin
20 Bocelli
   Cake
   Cafette

CHINATOWN

25 Vietnam
   Lee How Fook
24 Reading Terminal Market
   Charles Plaza
23 Rangoon

DELAWARE COUNTY

24 Marg. Kuo's Media
23 Charlie's Hamburgers
   Teikoku
   Gables at Chadds Ford
   Azie

FAIRMOUNT

26 Umai Umai
24 Sabrina's Café
   Trio
23 Figs
   L'Oca

LANCASTER/BERKS

24 Lily's on Main
23 Gibraltar
   Haydn Zug's
22 El Serrano
   Five Guys

LOGAN SQUARE

28 Fountain Restaurant
26 Swann Lounge
21 Chima
   Table 31
19 Aya's Café

MAIN LINE

27 Savona
   Restaurant Alba
   Sola
25 General Warren
   Yangming

MANAYUNK

- 25 | Jake's
- | Chabaa Thai
- 23 | Bella Trattoria
- | Cooper's Brick Oven
- 22 | Derek's

MONTGOMERY COUNTY

- 28 | Bluefin
- 26 | Rist. San Marco
- 25 | Blackfish
- | Chiangmai
- | Tiffin

NORTHEAST PHILLY

- 24 | Sweet Lucy's
- 23 | Steve's Prince of Steaks
- | Jim's Steaks
- 22 | Pho 75
- 21 | Moonstruck

NORTHERN LIBERTIES/ OLD CITY

- 28 | Amada
- 26 | Buddakan
- | Zento
- | Modo Mio
- | Chlöe

QUEEN VILLAGE/ SOUTH STREET

- 27 | Horizons
- 26 | Cochon
- 25 | Marrakesh
- | Southwark
- | Bistrot La Minette

RITTENHOUSE

- 27 | Le Bec-Fin
- | Lacroix
- | Capogiro
- | Prime Rib
- | Le Bar Lyonnais

SOUTH PHILLY

- 27 | Bibou
- | John's Roast Pork
- | Fond
- | James
- 26 | Nam Phuong

UNIVERSITY CITY

- 26 | Nan
- 25 | Distrito
- 24 | Marigold Kitchen
- | Rx
- 23 | Sang Kee Noodle

WASHINGTON SQUARE WEST

- 28 | Vetri
- | Morimoto
- 26 | Lolita
- 25 | Mercato
- | Kanella

NEW JERSEY

- 27 | Fuji
- | Sagami
- 26 | Siri's
- | Giumarello's
- | Capital Grille

DELAWARE

- 26 | Moro
- 25 | Mikimotos
- | Krazy Kat's
- | Harry's Seafood
- 24 | Green Room

Top Decor

28	Fountain Restaurant Union Trust	25	Bridgetown Mill Inn at Phillips Mill Marrakesh City Tavern Tequila's Restaurant Duling-Kurtz House Alma de Cuba Firecreek Parc Dettera Kimberton Inn Azie Davio's
27	R2L Nineteen Lacroix Water Works Buddakan Le Bec-Fin Simon Pearce		
26	Morimoto Dilworthtown Inn Nectar Prime Rib Savona Swann Lounge Moshulu Barclay Prime Butcher & Singer Del Frisco's General Warren	24	Cuba Libre Estia Positano Coast Chifa Distrito Black Bass Hotel Golden Pheasant

OUTDOORS

27	Water Works	21	Coyote Crossing
26	Moshulu		Bay Pony Inn
23	Parc Bistro	20	333 Belrose
22	Chart House	-	Hoof + Fin

PRIVATE ROOMS

27	Water Works	24	Estia
25	Duling-Kurtz House		Pod
	Alma de Cuba	23	10 Arts
	Dettera	22	Upstares & Sotto Varalli

ROMANCE

27	Nineteen	26	Dilworthtown Inn
	Lacroix		Savona
	Water Works	25	Alma de Cuba
	Le Bec-Fin	24	Estia

SIDEWALK SCENES

25	Parc		Devon Seafood
21	Rouge	17	Bridget Foy's
	Snackbar		Pizzeria Stella
	Derek's		Chestnut Grill

VIEWS

27	R2L		Simon Pearce
	Nineteen	26	Moshulu
	Lacroix	25	Inn at Phillips Mill
	Water Works	22	Chart House

Top Service

28	Fountain Restaurant

27	Vetri
	Birchrunville Store
	Gilmore's
	Lacroix
	Swann Lounge
	Le Bec-Fin

26	Mr. Martino's
	Prime Rib
	Horizons
	Fond
	Savona
	Talula's Table
	Bibou
	Dilworthtown Inn
	Barclay Prime

25	Le Bar Lyonnais
	Morimoto
	Honey
	General Warren

Davio's
Morton's
Capital Grille
James
Amada
Fogo de Chão
Kimberton Inn

24	Koo Zee Doo
	August
	Caffe Casta Diva
	Osteria
	Restaurant Alba
	Tequila's Restaurant
	Abacus
	Cafe Preeya
	Chifa
	Buddakan
	Sola
	Butcher & Singer
	Sovana Bistro

Menus, photos, voting and more – free at ZAGAT.com

Best Buys

In order of Bang for the Buck rating.

1. La Colombe
2. Capogiro
3. Charlie's Hamburgers
4. Maoz Vegetarian
5. John's Roast Pork
6. Brew HaHa!
7. Bonté Wafflerie
8. Naked Chocolate Café
9. Shank's Original
10. Campo's Deli
11. Bitar's
12. Five Guys
13. Steve's Prince of Steaks
14. Dalessandro's
15. Nifty Fifty's
16. Jim's Steaks
17. Reading Terminal Market
18. Alyan's
19. Tony Luke's
20. Tampopo
21. Giwa
22. Qdoba
23. Pho 75
24. Pat's Steaks
25. Celebre's
26. El Fuego
27. Taq. La Veracruzana
28. Baja Fresh Mex.
29. AllWays Café
30. Geno's Steaks
31. Day by Day
32. Hank's Place
33. Carman's Country
34. La Lupe
35. Sidecar
36. Morning Glory
37. Ardmore Station
38. SLiCE
39. Honey's Sit 'n Eat
40. More Than Ice Cream

OTHER GOOD VALUES

Abacus
Abyssinia
Adode Cafe
Banana Leaf
Beijing
Ben & Irv Deli
Cafe de Laos
Café Estelle
Charles Plaza
Chiangmai
Dahlak
Darling's
Dining Car
El Camino Real
Famous 4th St. Deli
Good Dog
Grace Tavern
Grey Lodge
Han Dynasty
Issac's
Jamaican Jerk Hut
Kibitz Room
Little Pete's
Mama Palma's
Mayfair Diner
McGillin's
Melrose Diner
Memphis Taproom
Minar Palace
My Thai
Nam Phuong
New Delhi
New Harmony
Pattaya Grill
Resurrection Ale House
Royal Tavern
Ruby's
Sabrina's Cafe
South St. Souvlaki
Sweet Lucy's
Tacconelli's
Taq. La Michoacana
Tiffin
Trolley Car
Urban Saloon
Vientiane Café
Vietnam
Vietnam Café
Vietnam Palace
Winnie's Le Bus

PRIX FIXE BARGAINS

DINNER ($35 & UNDER)

A La Maison $32	La Locanda/Ghiottone 35
Avalon 31	Limoncello 28
Bay Pony Inn 20	Little Café/NJ 30
Bella Tori 29	Little Marakesh 28
Bona Cucina 11	Majolica 25
Brick Hotel 21	Manon/NJ 25
Caribou Cafe 29	Marigold Kitchen 30
Catelli/NJ 30	Marrakesh 25
Cedars 25	Meridith's 30
CinCin 30	MidAtlantic 30
DeAnna's/NJ 20	Miller's Smorgasbord/LB 23
Derek's 33	Modo Mio 33
Dream Cuisine/NJ 35	Moonstruck 29
Fayette Street Grille 34	My Thai 18
Fez Moroccan 25	Prime Rib 35
Filomena/NJ 20	Privé 25
Firecreek 30	PTG 30
fish 28	Resurrection Ale House 25
General Warren 30	Ritz Seafood/NJ 35
Gilmore's 35	Roller's at Flying Fish 20
Gnocchi 30	Rx 25
Good 'N Plenty/LB 20	Salento 27
Green Hills Inn/LB 30	Slate Bleu 34
Harry's Savoy/DE 25	Sonata 31
High St. Caffé 30	Spring Mill 25
Il Cantuccio 28	Supper 35
Italian Bistro 20	Ted's on Main/NJ 30
Joseph Ambler 35	Time 30
Keating's 30	Toscana Kitchen/DE 30
Konak 25	Zacharias Creek Side Cafe . . . 26
Lacroix 35	Zinc 30

LUNCH ($25 & UNDER)

Bay Pony Inn $17	Jack's Firehouse 21
Bistro St. Tropez 20	Joseph Ambler 25
Bliss 19	King of Tandoor 11
Blue Bell Inn 20	Lacroix 24
Caribou Cafe 16	Lemon Grass 9
Cedars 25	Mamma Maria 20
Davio's 25	Mikado/NJ 9
Derek's 23	Nectar 13
Epicurean 22	Nineteen 19
Estia 17	Palm 19
Franco's Osteria 10	Paradigm 12
Harry's Savoy/DE 15	Pattaya Grill 9
Haydn Zug's/LB 20	Sweet Basil Thai 11
Il Cantuccio 11	Thai Singha 9

All restaurants are in the Philadelphia area unless otherwise noted
(LB=Lancaster/Berks Counties; NJ=New Jersey Suburbs;
DE=Wilmington/Nearby Delaware).

RESTAURANT
DIRECTORY

Philadelphia

Abacus ☑ *Chinese* | 24 | 19 | 24 | $25 |

Lansdale | North Penn Mktpl. | 1551 S. Valley Forge Rd.
(Sumneytown Pike) | 215-362-2010

"You can count" on this "affordable" strip-mall BYO in Lansdale for "lovingly prepared" Chinese cuisine and a "one-man comedy show" (aka manager Joe Chen), whose "cheeky recitation of specials" is "something to look forward to"; but seriously, folks, "attentive" service and a "stylish" setting featuring a large display fish tank help make it a "soothing experience" for suburbanites out on a "date night."

Abbaye ◑ *Belgian* | 20 | 16 | 18 | $23 |

Northern Liberties | 637 N. Third St. (Fairmount Ave.) | 215-627-6711

This "chill", "gritty" Belgian bar is one of Northern Liberties' designated hangouts for the "hipster set", thanks to the ever-changing local artwork on the walls and "scrumptious", "vegetarian"-friendly fare from the kitchen; whether you "place your order" at the copper-top bar or sit outside on the sidewalk, be prepared for "slow" service, caution critics, for it appears to be "understaffed."

Abyssinia ◑ *Ethiopian* | 23 | 11 | 15 | $18 |

University City | 229 S. 45th St. (Locust St.) | 215-387-2424

A "feast for all your senses" can be had at this "inexpensive" University City Ethiopian, where dishes with lots of "big spice" come in "large portions" that you tuck into using the "yeasty injera" as flatware, served in a "small" space some describe as a "modern hovel"; many gripe at the "glacial" service as well, but it does come "with a smile" from the "earnest" staff; P.S. you can "make a night" of it at the upstairs bar, which is open until 1 AM.

Adobe Cafe *Southwestern* | 20 | 16 | 20 | $23 |

Roxborough | 4550 Mitchell St. (Leverington Ave.) | 215-483-3947
South Philly | 1919 E. Passyunk Ave. (Mifflin St.) | 215-551-2243
www.adobecafephilly.com

You get that "whole warm-body feeling" (it could be the "cheap and lethal sangria" or "killer margaritas" kicking in) at these "quirkily decorated" cantinas in Roxborough and South Philly, where omnivores, "vegetarians who aren't into health food" and others go for Southwestern fare "without the f/x" at "reasonable prices"; even if some sniff that "food is not the star of the show", most agree that the "delicious waiters", outdoor seating and "party atmosphere" "will make you want to say 'ole.'"

NEW Adsum *American* | - | - | - | M |

South St. | 700-702 S. Fifth St. (Bainbridge St.) | 267-888-7002 |
www.adsumrestaurant.com

In a setting that's equal parts laboratory and library, this slick New American bistro is fronted by Lacroix at the Rittenhouse alum Matthew Levin, who's outfitted a Queen Village corner with antique beakers, flasks and microscopes – befitting his reputation as a mad scientist in the kitchen; the bar, featuring vintage cocktails and assorted housemade pickles, overlooks an outdoor patio.

Aki *Japanese* ∇ 21 | 19 | 19 | $31

Washington Square West | 1210 Walnut St. (S. 12th St.) | 215-985-1838 | www.akiphilly.com

Cronies calculate "sake + all-you-can-eat sushi = fantastic" at this Japanese in Washington Square West, where many satisfy their "urge to indulge" with "well-prepared" dinner selections for $24.95 (complemented by "tasty mixed drinks"), while various "meal deals" make it a solid "lunch spot" too; the "fashionable" yet "comfortable" space and "knowledgeable servers" also help make it "well worth a visit."

NEW A La Maison ⊠ *French* - | - | - | E

Ardmore | 53 W. Lancaster Ave. (Ardmore Ave.) | 484-412-8009 | www.alamaisonbistro.com

The "simple" French bistro–style dishes are "well above-average" and come in "ample servings" at this "casual" BYO in Ardmore; the staff is "friendly", the room "spacious" and there's "easy, free parking in the back", all of which make it a "date-night-worthy" option to those in-the-know.

Al Dar Bistro *Mediterranean* 19 | 16 | 19 | $34

Bala Cynwyd | 281 Montgomery Ave. (Levering Mill Rd.) | 610-667-1245 | www.aldarbistro.com

"After all these years" (more than 30), "you know what you are getting" at this Main Line Med "standby" – a "solid" menu that "incorporates many ethnic touches from elsewhere" and makes it easy to "eat healthy" ("Michelle Obama would be proud") and "interested, but not pushy service" "with a smile"; though a few quibble about the "dark" interior and find the "prices a little high for what you get", for most it's a "risk-free choice."

Alfa ◑ *American* 17 | 20 | 19 | $29

Rittenhouse | 1709 Walnut St. (S. 17th St.) | 215-751-0201 | www.alfa-bar.com

"Witty bartenders" mix "'80s-themed drinks at happy hour" for a "young, beautiful, professional crowd" at this midpriced New American off Rittenhouse Square, where the vibe is somewhere "between a hip bar and college dive"; the "creative" menu gets mixed marks, however, ranging from "passable" to "nothing to shout about", which is why most recommend sticking to "light fare" like the signature "sliders."

AllWays Café, The ⊠ *Eclectic* 23 | 10 | 17 | $15

Huntingdon Valley | Beth Ayres Shopping Ctr. | 634 Welsh Rd. (Huntingdon Pike.) | 215-914-2151 | www.allwayscafe.com

Your "tipping goes to charity" at this "bohemian lunch spot" in Huntingdon Valley that's "green without being self-righteous", where you "order at the counter" off the "blackboard menu" of affordable Eclectic fare that "packs a big punch", and servers bring it to your table – "if you can get one"; though a few grouse that the ambiance is

	FOOD	DECOR	SERVICE	COST

"zilch" and the service can be "zombielike", most agree the "awesome cookies" and "butternut squash soup" make it "worth a return visit."

Z Alma de Cuba *Nuevo Latino*   25 | 25 | 23 | $51

Rittenhouse | 1623 Walnut St. (bet. 16th & 17th Sts.) | 215-988-1799 | www.almadecubarestaurant.com

"What embargo?" scoff supporters of Stephen Starr's "hip" Nuevo Latino off Rittenhouse Square, which "Castro himself would envy" thanks to the "beautiful people" who go to "see and be seen" over "signature mojitos" in the "sexy" lounge where it always "feels like a party's going on"; Douglas Rodriguez's amply portioned *comida* (the "best vaca fritas", "stellar" ceviche) means there's "plenty to go around" for dinner with friends, and the "doting" staff keeps pace in the "fantastic" tri-level space.

Almaz Café *Ethiopian*   ∇ 21 | 11 | 23 | $14

Rittenhouse | 140 S. 20th St. (Walnut St.) | 215-557-0108 | www.almaz-cafe.com

Solomon Getnet's affordable "Ethiopian hideaway" off Rittenhouse Square offers "homey" African flavors, as well as "Western hot breakfasts and sandwiches" "without pretension" in a "tiny", bi-level space; throw in "knowledgeable" service "with a smile", and it's easy to see why so many regard it as a "breath of fresh air."

Alyan's *Mideastern*   24 | 10 | 20 | $14

South St. | 603 S. Fourth St. (South St.) | 215-922-3553

"There's really no decor" (unless you count the "back greenhouse") at this "authentic" South Street Middle Eastern BYO, but that's no matter to fans hooked on its "amazing" baba ghanoush, shawarma and other treats served by what "seems to be a never-ending rotation of pretty foreign exchange students"; what's more, it's so "cheap" most "never leave here unhappy."

Z Amada *Spanish*   28 | 24 | 25 | $53

Old City | 217 Chestnut St. (bet. 2nd & 3rd Sts.) | 215-625-2450 | www.amadarestaurant.com

"Ama-zing!" is how amigos describe Jose Garces' "contemporary" Spaniard, voted Philly's Most Popular restaurant thanks to "magnificent", "elegantly presented" tapas that "make your taste buds swoon", and while the tabs can add up, many agree the "tasting menu is the best deal in Old City"; "knowledgeable", "gracious" service and a "beautiful" ("perhaps too dark") space add to the "incredible experience" you can share with a "hot date" or "several friends" – just be sure to book "months in advance."

America Bar & Grill *American*   18 | 17 | 18 | $35

Chester Springs | Shops at Lionville Station | 499 E. Uwchlan Ave. (Lionville Station Rd.) | 610-280-0800
Glen Mills | Shoppes at Brinton Lake | 981 Baltimore Pike (Brinton Lake Rd.) | 610-558-9900
www.americabargrill.com

"Cheerful" service and a "warm, friendly" atmosphere make for "comfortable" dining at these midpriced western suburban strip-mall twins serving a "vast" menu of American and pub fare ranging from "tapas to burgers"; a "lovely" $16.95 Sunday brunch and $3.95 meal deals for kids 10-and-under keep families happy, and while a few critics find the staff "inexperienced" and the decor in need of "updating", most consider them "nice local options for a quickie meal."

NEW American Pub
at Centre Square ⊠ *American*

∇ | 15 | 15 | 17 | $21

Avenue of the Arts | 1500 Market St. (15th St.) | 267-639-6104 | www.theamericanpub.com

Seems only "commuters" who frequent the concourse across from City Hall know about this "basic", "dependable" multiple-TV-ed Avenue of the Arts sports bar ("don't go looking to find it from street level"), so "there's always a table available"; expect "decent" lunches and "happy-hour specials" of Traditional American grub at "reasonable prices", even if some cynics liken it to "an airport hotel bar."

NEW Amis ● *Italian*

24 | 22 | 24 | $51

Washington Square West | 412 S. 13th St. (Waverly St.) | 215-732-2647 | www.amisphilly.com

Just around the corner from his eponymous flagship, Marc Vetri's "unpretentious" Washington Square West newcomer "stays true to the smaller-scale concept of a Roman trattoria" and loyalists gladly brave the "general din" and "rock" soundtrack in the industrial setting to savor "fried artichokes" and other "insanely flavorful" "small-plates options" from chef Brad Spence's "open kitchen"; "innovative drinks" from the bar and "seamless service" add to its allure, but even admirers admit this "foodie" destination is "not for the famished or the cheap."

NEW Amuse *French*

- | - | - | M

Avenue of the Arts | Le Méridien Philadelphia | 1421 Arch St. (Broad St.) | 215-422-8222 | www.starwoodhotels.com

Contemporary accents in the grand Horace Trumbauer–designed Le Méridien hotel create a chic setting for this French arrival in the shadow of Philadelphia City Hall; the moderately priced menu includes brasserie staples (onion soup, salade niçoise, steak frites), while the bar in the hotel lobby dispenses a wide list of specialty cocktails, 22 wines by the glass and 60 bottles from all over, including 10 champagnes.

Anastasi Seafood ⊠Ⓜ *Seafood*

23 | 10 | 19 | $29

South Philly | Italian Mkt. | 1101 S. Ninth St. (Washington Ave.) | 215-462-0550 | www.anastasiseafood.com

"Forget the location or decor" advise afishionados, "there's a reason" this seafood "classic" "hidden away" in an Italian Market "fish store" has "been around for ages" – namely, "generous" portions of "no-nonsense" grub and a "family-friendly feel"; while the servers "straight from South Philly" may be as "fresh" as the fin fare, they're also "friendly and helpful", which is why "no one leaves here crabby."

	FOOD	DECOR	SERVICE	COST

NEW Apollinare *Italian* — — — M

Northern Liberties | 1001 N. Second St. (Germantown Ave.) |
215-923-2014 | www.apollinarerestaurant.com

Two restaurateurs fresh from Umbria, Italy, have set up this romantic, white-tablecloth branch of their Spoleto trattoria in the scenic
Piazza at Schmidt's in Northern Liberties, importing their own chefs
to make pastas and pizzas as well as hearty, refined meats and
fishes; tableside prep (including gelato made to order with liquid
nitrogen) is a specialty.

Aqua ⌧ *Malaysian/Thai* 21 17 19 $27

Washington Square West | 705 Chestnut St. (7th St.) | 215-928-2838

"If you value taste over glitz and glitter", "what's not to like" about this
"affordable" Malaysian-Thai BYO near Washington Square, which
offers "superb" soups and noodles and "speedy", "eager-to-please"
service (plus weekday-only delivery) in an "inviting", "no-frills setting"; it's dawned on more than a few this is "the age of aqua(rius)."

Arbol Café ⊄ *Paraguayan* ∇ 17 19 17 $14

Northern Liberties | 209 Poplar St. (2nd St.) | 215-923-3150 |
www.arbolcafe.com

The spacious, shaded outdoor garden is "larger than the cafe itself" at
this mom-and-pop, cash-only Paraguayan BYO, a "delightful" mag-
net for Northern Liberties folk with its affordable menu of sandwich
de lomito, empanadas and more, served in a "wonderfully relaxing"
setting; a few critics, though, find it "overpriced" and "inflexible."

Ardmore Station Cafe *Diner* 18 10 18 $15

Ardmore | 6 Station Ave. (Anderson Ave.) | 610-642-2683

It's "hard to be underdressed" at this "always packed", "dinerlike"
Main Line "joint" across from the SEPTA train line, where it's "like
eating in your friend's kitchen – if your friend makes decadent
French toast" and serves "divine" coffee; a few cynics shrug at the "ok"
eats and "plain" digs, but the staff's "speed and smiles" lead many
others to conclude that "the tip should be as large as the check."

Ariana *Afghan* 22 16 21 $28

Old City | 134 Chestnut St. (bet. Front & 2nd Sts.) | 215-922-1535 |
www.restaurantariana.com

"Be prepared to have your senses delighted" at this "lovely little"
Afghan BYO in Old City with "tasty", "well-priced" kebabs, "light,
flavorful" aashak (ravioli) and more; though it's "intimate", it's also
"accommodating" to "large groups", which are handled with aplomb
by "helpful" servers as you settle into pillows on the floor; it has a
newer (though still old-fashioned) branch in Voorhees, which offers
table seating only.

Arpeggio *Mediterranean* 23 17 22 $27

Spring House | 542 Spring House Village Ctr. (Bethlehem Pike) |
215-646-5055 | www.arpeggiobyob.com

Partisans promise you "can't go wrong" at this moderately priced
mid-Montco Med BYO, a neighborhood "staple" that's "always

crowded" thanks to "fabulous" "hummus and pita appetizers", "inventive pizzas" and more, as well as "personal attention" from people who seem "happy to work there"; given the "close seating", "be prepared for some extended conversation" with nearby tables.

Athena ⓜ *Greek/Seafood*   22 | 14 | 21 | $27

Glenside | 264 N. Keswick Ave. (Easton Rd.) | 215-884-1777 | www.athena-restaurant.net

For a "tzatziki" fix "before a show" at the Keswick Theatre in Glenside, fans tout this "no-frills" BYO Greek, where an "attentive" staff guides you through the "authentic" menu that features a popular "sampler platter" of apps; the interior is "simple" and many find the outdoor deck a "nice" touch, though a few grouse that it "borders a parking lot."

Audrey Claire ⓢ *Mediterranean*   23 | 18 | 20 | $36

Rittenhouse | 276 S. 20th St. (Spruce St.) | 215-731-1222 | www.audreyclaire.com

With the "windows open" and "sidewalk seating" in full swing, Audrey Taichman's "cosmopolitan" BYO bistro near Rittenhouse Square serving "sophisticated", "artfully prepared" Med fare makes you "feel like you are in a city more exotic than Philly"; meanwhile, "attentive" service helps make up for the "shoulder-to-shoulder" seating and "thunderously loud" acoustics in the "minimalist" dining room; P.S. the prices are "reasonable", but remember, "cash only."

August ⓜⓢ *Italian*   25 | 20 | 24 | $38

South Philly | 1247 S. 13th St. (Wharton St.) | 215-468-5926 | www.augustbyob.com

Fans aver this "precious little" Italian BYO "hideaway" on a South Philly corner "would charm even your *nona*" with a "limited" but "well-executed" menu of "creative" dishes "prepared with panache" and served by a "friendly", "attentive" staff in surroundings that are "sophisticated" "without being pretentious" and "conducive to conversation"; insiders rave about the "tapas-style $10 options" that are meant to be "shared", and advise "saving room for the homemade desserts."

August Moon *Japanese/Korean*   20 | 14 | 18 | $31

Norristown | 300 E. Main St. (Arch St.) | 610-277-4008 | www.augustmoonpa.com

This "unassuming" "family-run" Japanese-Korean hybrid "brightens up" the Downtown Norristown dining scene with "many good options" from both countries, including "interesting" sushi and "authentic" bibimbop, doled out by an "accommodating" staff; ratings slippage in all three categories since the last Survey, however, suggests a "redo" may be in order.

Augusto's ⓜ *Eclectic*   - | - | - | E

Warminster | 530 Madison Ave. (Nemoral St.) | 215-328-0556 | www.augustocuisine.com

"You're in for a treat" at Augusto Jalon's "off-the-beaten-path" Eclectic BYO (sibling of Huntingdon Valley's Tavolo), tucked into an "unlikely" neighborhood in a restaurant-starved slice of Bucks County; insiders are "extremely satisfied" by the "huge portions" of "amazing" global flavors served in a cozy, art-filled space by a "fabulous", "professional" staff.

Auspicious *Chinese*   19 | 17 | 18 | $26

Ardmore | 11 Cricket Ave. (Lancaster Ave.) | 610-642-1858 | www.mastersofkungfood.com

Loyalists laud this "sleek", affordable Chinese BYO in Downtown Ardmore as a "step or two up from the usual", thanks to "creative" Middle Kingdom fare, including "make-your-own stir fry", served by a "friendly" staff in an interior bedecked with "dark warm woods"; more than a few detractors, however, describe it as an "inconsistent" "P.F. Chang's wannabe" that "needs to determine" whether to be a "nice neighborhood spot" or go "upscale."

Avalon Ⓜ 🏂 *Italian*   25 | 22 | 22 | $43

West Chester | 312 S. High St. (Dean St.) | 610-436-4100 | www.avalonrestaurant.net

At his "rustic" Northern Italian BYO in Downtown West Chester, chef-owner John Brandt-Lee appeals to "adventurous" eaters with his "innovative" fare, including a "bargain" $31 "tour of the menu" and "unusual touches" such as "outstanding" charcuterie (with occasional comp beer tastings), served by a "professional" staff; it's "fabulous" by the fireplace or on the "romantic", "beautiful hidden patio", but along with your appetite, be sure to bring cash.

NEW Avenida Ⓜ *Pan-Latin*   ▽ 22 | 19 | 20 | $36

Mount Airy | 7402 Germantown Ave. (Gowen Ave.) | 267-385-6857 | www.avenidarestaurant.com

A "solid" menu of "fresh, healthy choices" is complemented by "excellent" mojitos and margaritas at Edgar and Kim Alvarez's "colorful", "cozy" Mount Airy Latin set in an 18th-century stone building boasting a laid-back patio and bar; the neighborhood regards it as a "date-night" "destination", and partisans promise "you'll be recognized" by the staff "by your second visit."

NEW Avril Ⓜ *Italian/French*   14 | 16 | 17 | $38

Bala Cynwyd | 134 Bala Ave. (Highland Ave.) | 610-667-2626 | www.avrilbyob.com

Supporters call this high-ceilinged, but "homey", Italian-French BYO bistro across from the movie theater in Bala Cynwyd a "sorely needed addition to the neighborhood", where you can enjoy "interesting" fare and the "lovely" hospitality of the "eager-to-please" husband-and-wife owners "without spending too much"; a post-Survey change in concept to more casual fare and all-day dining may outdate the Food score.

Aya's Café 🈺 *Egyptian*   19 | 18 | 21 | $31

Logan Square | 2129 Arch St. (22nd St.) | 215-567-1555 | www.ayascafe.net

When you want to "eat like an Egyptian", fans tout this "low-key", "atmospheric den" near Logan Square as a "neighborhood cafe" worth "going back" for its "friendly" service and "large portions" of "delicious", "eclectic" Med eats (though a few purists "can't understand the Italian food on the menu"); "sharing makes it fun" and BYO makes it "affordable."

Azie *Asian*
`23` `25` `21` `$43`

Media | 217-219 W. State St. (Orange St.) | 610-566-4750 | www.azie-restaurant.com

Azie on Main *Asian/Japanese*

NEW Villanova | 789 E. Lancaster Ave. (I-476) | 610-527-5700 | www.azieonmain.com

"Inventive" Asian fusion fare, including "super-tasty, outside-the-box sushi", "beautiful" rooms and a "modern" "Center City" "vibe" are the hallmarks of Win Somboonsong's "trendy", mid-priced twins in Media and Villanova; the "staff literally anticipates your needs" and "bartenders stay on track" with "unique drinks", but DIYers advise "don't miss cooking your own appetizer of Kobe beef on a hot rock."

Bahama Breeze ● *Caribbean*
`17` `18` `18` `$27`

King of Prussia | 320 Goddard Blvd. (Mall Blvd.) | 610-491-9822 | www.bahamabreeze.com

"You can almost smell the coconut oil" at these "upbeat" "tropical oases" in KoP and Cherry Hill, where the waits are "long" for "tasty island-inspired chain food with a Caribbean flair", washed down with "sweet" Bahama-Ritas; put on "your hula skirt" and "meet a friend" at the "fire pit" over "live steel drum music" and "faux fun in the sun", and you'll "wish there was a beach outside instead of a parking lot."

Baja Fresh Mexican Grill *Mexican*
`17` `10` `14` `$12`

King of Prussia | 340 W. DeKalb Pike (bet. Henderson Rd. & Pennsylvania Tpke.) | 610-337-2050

Abington | Abington Shopping Ctr. | 1437 Old York Rd. (Rte. 2017/ Susquehanna Rd.) | 215-885-4296

Conshohocken | Plymouth Square Shopping Ctr. | 200 W. Ridge Pike (Butler Pike) | 610-828-4524

North Wales | 110 Garden Golf Blvd. (Bethlehem Pike) | 215-412-5693

www.bajafresh.com

Fans of this "fast-food" Mexican chain "love the salsa bar" and want to "figure a way to smuggle out an entire bowl of their pico de gallo"; expect "quick", "decent" burritos at a "fair price", and amigos advise "just concentrate on the food" and not the "sterile" environs.

Banana Leaf ● *Malaysian*
`21` `14` `19` `$20`

Chinatown | 1009 Arch St. (bet. 10th & 11th Sts.) | 215-592-8288 | www.phillybananaleaf.com

You get "Malaysian spice for a nice price" at this BYO in the "heart of Chinatown", decorated in a "jungle" of "bamboo panels and palm fronds" reminiscent of *"Gilligan's Island"*; if you're confused by the "endless" menu of "vibrant", "unique dishes", "just ask the table next to you" or one of the "responsive" servers.

	FOOD	DECOR	SERVICE	COST

☑ Barclay Prime *Steak*   27 | 26 | 26 | $76

Rittenhouse | The Barclay | 237 S. 18th St. (Locust St.) | 215-732-7560 |
www.barclayprime.com

Carnivores feel as if they "died and went to steak heaven" at this
"celeb"-heavy meatery in the Barclay hotel, where signature "Kobe
sliders" and "melt-in-your-mouth" beef are proffered with "a selection of spectacular, but quite unnecessary, steak knives" ("I could
have cut the filet with a butter knife") in "retro library" digs with all
the "Stephen Starr trimmings" (alas, "unisex bathrooms"); though it
"can make your accountant cry", this "splurge" is "why the Lord
created expense accounts."

Bar Ferdinand ◑ *Spanish*   23 | 23 | 20 | $40

Northern Liberties | Liberties Walk | 1030 N. Second St. (bet. Girard Ave. &
Poplar St.) | 215-923-1313 | www.barferdinand.com

"Interesting ingredient combinations" make for "outstanding" tapas
at this "arty", bull mural–bedecked Northern Liberties Spanish, and
cognoscenti caution the "delicious" sangria can lead to "a night of
debauchery" (or two); the "knowledgeable" staff is able to keep
even "large groups" happy, and while a number complain about the
"atrocious" "noise level", most prefer to "eat outside for the maxi-
mum festive experience", anyway.

Bay Pony Inn Ⓜ *American*   21 | 21 | 21 | $39

Lederach | 508 Old Skippack Rd. (Salfordville Rd.) | 215-256-6565 |
www.bayponyinnpa.com

It's like taking a "step back into time" at this Traditional American in
central Montco, where "old-school-good" "comfort food" is
served by a "friendly", "efficient" staff amid "warm surroundings" graced with "colonial antiques"; $19.95 prix fixe dinners
and an $18.95 Sunday buffet help make the experience all
the more "relaxing."

Beau Monde Ⓜ *French*   23 | 22 | 21 | $30

Queen Village | 624 S. Sixth St. (Bainbridge St.) | 215-592-0656 |
www.creperie-beaumonde.com

For a taste of Breton "without the inconvenience of air travel", it's
tough to top this "booshie-boho" bistro off South Street in Queen
Village offering "expertly crafted", "savory or sweet" crêpes that
pair well with "Bloody Marys" or selections from a "great wine list";
the staff is "friendly" (even if it "seems to be perpetually involved in
a best-dressed-hipster competition"), the "fireplace" is "so-o romantic" and the patio is "nice" in warm weather; P.S. for some
"dancing at L'Etage upstairs is the real reason to go."

Beige & Beige Ⓜ *Eclectic*   17 | 18 | 14 | $41

Huntingdon Valley | 2501 Huntingdon Pike (bet. Philmont Ave. &
Red Lion Rd.) | 215-938-8600 | www.beigebeige.com

Sentiment on this "intimate" Eclectic BYO in Huntingdon Valley is all
over the map – proponents praise its "downtown" ambiance and "interesting variety of unusually flavored and sauced dishes", while detractors deride the food as "spotty" and the service as "snooty"

	FOOD	DECOR	SERVICE	COST

wags point out that at least you'll "enjoy private dining" here, as you may almost "have the place to yourself."

Beijing *Chinese* — 17 | 8 | 16 | $16
University City | 3714 Spruce St. (bet. 37th & 38th Sts.) | 215-222-5242 | www.beijingatpenn.com

"The bill practically comes with the dish" at this "cheap" Chinese "staple" "catering" to the "Penn and CHOP lunch crowds" in University City, thanks to the "friendly staff" that seems to follow a mantra of "order, pay and scram"; most agree the chow is "dependable", albeit "nothing spectacular", and the "massive" portions often wind up as "tomorrow's lunch."

Belgian Café, The ● *Belgian* — 19 | 16 | 17 | $26
Fairmount | 601 N. 21st St. (Green St.) | 215-235-3500 | www.thebelgiancafe.com

"You have to be ambitious to take on even the small order of mussels" at this "neighborhood" Belgian tap in Fairmount, a "comfortable alternative" to sibling Monk's; a "knowledgeable staff" will "guide you through the beer bible" and menu of "sophisticated" pub fare (which includes "fabulous" "vegetarian options"), and there's also "cool" "outside dining", but insiders warn it can be "difficult to get a table because patrons have a tendency to stay awhile."

Bella Cena *Italian* — ∇ 20 | 15 | 20 | $36
(fka Trattoria Primadonna)
Rittenhouse | 1506 Spruce St. (15th St.) | 215-790-0171 | www.bellacena-philly.com

Before a show at the Kimmel Center across the street, many head to this "simple" Italian for "classic, understated" eats, including "homemade" pastas and a whole bronzino that's filleted tableside, served by a "helpful" staff eager to get you to the curtain; best of all, although it has a liquor license, you can still BYO without a corkage fee.

Bella Tori — 18 | 23 | 20 | $48
at the Mansion 🅜 *Italian*
Langhorne | 321 S. Bellevue Ave. (bet. Gilliam & Maple Aves.) | 215-702-9600 | www.bellatori.com

"Prompt", "courteous" service wins special praise for this Italian set in a "beautifully remodeled old mansion" in Lower Bucks; while the cuisine is "consistent", some foodies feel it's better suited to "diners who prefer not to venture far from the tried and true" – i.e. "nothing special, but nothing to fear either."

Bella Trattoria *Italian* — 23 | 19 | 21 | $32
Manayunk | 4258 Main St. (bet. Rector St. & Roxborough Ave.) | 215-482-5556 | www.bellatrattoriapa.com

There's "nothing too fancy" but "plenty to bring you back" to this "low-key" red-gravy house in the heart of Manayunk, where the menu includes some "imaginative" items and the kitchen is "happy to accommodate" requests; a few frown at the "sparse" decor, but weather permitting, there's sidewalk seating, and the "friendly" staff will let you "sit outside with your pups and people-watch" along Main Street.

Bellini Grill *Italian*

21 | 16 | 20 | $31

Rittenhouse | 220 S. 16th St. (bet. Locust & Walnut Sts.) | 215-545-1191 | www.bellinigrill.com

There's "no pretense" about this "dependable" Italian "charmer" near the Kimmel Center, but it "can surprise you" nonetheless, thanks to a chef who's "willing to stray outside the menu" and deliver "solid", "nicely presented" fare that "won't break the bank"; the digs are "cozy enough so you get to know the next table" and "professional" staffers make "you feel like their favorite guest" – while BYO helps make it "affordable."

Ben & Irv Deli Restaurant *Deli*

19 | 10 | 18 | $18

Huntingdon Valley | Justa Farm Shopping Ctr. | 1962 County Line Rd. (Davisville Rd.) | 215-355-2000 | www.benandirvs.com

For some "matzo ball soup and the latest gossip", fans head to this "quintessential" "Jewish-style deli" fixture in a shopping center in Eastern Montco that's been slinging "all the cholesterol you could ever want" ("just check for the defibrillator") from a "mammoth menu" for what seems like a "zillion years"; expect "sweet, surly service" and a line that looks like the "early-bird special in Boca."

Beneluxx

20 | 14 | 20 | $26

Tasting Room ●⚅Ⓜ *Belgian*

Old City | 33 S. Third St. (Market St.) | 267-318-7269 | www.beneluxx.com

"Graze" from a "fine array of cheeses, wines, beers and desserts" served in "tasting portions" without "emptying your pocketbook" at this Old City "monastery-meets-European brewpub" from the staff of Eulogy; though the semi-subterranean space may look "like your uncle's basement", he probably didn't have one of the "city's biggest selections of draught Belgian beers", "drinks served in Erlenmeyer flasks" or "fountains in the middle of the tables to rinse your glass."

Benihana *Japanese*

19 | 18 | 20 | $35

Plymouth Meeting | Plymouth Meeting Mall | 508 W. Germantown Pike (Plymouth Rd.) | 610-832-5924 | www.benihana.com

At these links in the "original" "teppanyaki" chain, "swift knives" and "decent showmanship" from the chefs make for "entertaining" "celebration dinners" with the kids, but while the flying food may find its mark, many describe the flavors as "hit-or-miss"; "there is no intimate dining here", but some point out that the "distracting" "floor show" can be a "good thing" "if you don't like the person you're with."

Bensí *Italian*

17 | 16 | 17 | $29

North Wales | The Shoppes at English Vill. | 1460 Bethlehem Pike (Welsh Rd.) | 215-283-3222 | www.bensirestaurants.com

The Italian "classics" are "generally fresh" at this "nicely appointed" NJ-based chain, but the fare "doesn't stand out" in the eyes of critics who deem it only "three or four steps above Olive Garden"; as for service – "well, they try", but many say the staff can get "overwhelmed" at "peak times."

☑ Bibou ☒⇗ *French*   27 | 18 | 26 | $50

South Philly | 1009 S. Eighth St. (Kimball St.) | 215-965-8290 | www.biboubyob.com

The "only thing missing is the Seine" at this cash-only BYO "jewel box" in South Philly from Le Bec-Fin alum Pierre Calmels, who creates "beautifully rendered" French "masterpieces", and his "charming" wife Charlotte, who oversees "efficient" though "leisurely" service in an "informal" setting; the "snug" space seats only 32, so before you "dust off a great bottle of wine", keep in mind it's "hard to get a reservation" – especially for the $45 Sunday tasting dinners – now that the secret is out.

Bindi ☒⇗ *Indian*   24 | 18 | 21 | $36

Washington Square West | 105 S. 13th St. (bet. Chestnut & Sansom Sts.) | 215-922-6061 | www.bindibyob.com

"It's not Indian food as you know it" at this "elegant" "boutique" in a Washington Square West storefront across from sibling Lolita, but rather "sophisticated" "riffs" with "bold flavors" that "stretch your palate", served by a "knowledgeable" staff ; BYO vodka or rum to pair with "excellent juice mixers", which may help you overlook digs that some find "boring", and while you're at it, "don't forget to stop at the ATM" for cash (no plastic).

☑ Birchrunville   28 | 24 | 27 | $54
Store Cafe ☒☒⇗ *French/Italian*

Birchrunville | 1403 Hollow Rd. (School House Ln.) | 610-827-9002 | www.birchrunvillestorecafe.com

Francis Trzeciak's "quaint" Franco-Italian BYO "hideaway" in a circa-1892 Chester County store wows city folk and others with "magical" cuisine that yields an "ah-hah with every bite", served in a "relaxed" setting that exudes a "hands-on family-ownership feel"; it's a "little piece of heaven" all right – and some quip "you will think you drove that far" to get there (even the restroom is a "schlep") – but nearly all agree it's "more than worth" the trip (as long as you bring cash; no plastic).

Bistro La Baia ⇗ *Italian*   19 | 13 | 17 | $29

Graduate Hospital | 1700 Lombard St. (17th St.) | 215-546-0496 | www.bistrolabaia.com

"Generous portions" of "tasty" Italian "comfort food" at "low prices" explain why this cash-only BYO in Graduate Hospital is frequently "overrun with Penn students"; grumbling over "intolerable" "noise levels" in what can be "generously described as cramped" quarters is smoothed over by "a smile from the staff", whose accents make you feel like you're in a "popular touristy spot in Italy."

Bistro La Viola ☒⇗ *Italian*   24 | 16 | 21 | $32

Rittenhouse | 253 S. 16th St. (bet. Locust & Spruce Sts.) | 215-735-8630

If you "want to see a dropped jaw", "take a visiting NYer" to this cash-only Rittenhouse Square Italian BYO, a popular "pre-concert" "go-to" spot and arguably "the biggest bang for the buck" around, thanks to "amazing" *mangiare* at "affordable prices"; despite the "astounding speed" of the service, it "can be challenging to get a table" in the "cramped", "buzzing" room, but most agree it's "worth the wait"; sibling La Viola Ovest is across the street.

Bistro Romano *Italian* 22 | 22 | 22 | $39

Society Hill | 120 Lombard St. (bet. Front & 2nd Sts.) | 215-925-8880 | www.bistroromano.com

For a "reliable night out that won't break the bank", fans tout this "romantic" Society Hill Italian, "one of the originals from Philly's restaurant renaissance", where the "staff can't do enough for you" in the "old-fashioned", "European"-style "grotto" setting (tip: "call ahead for a table in the wine cellar"); the fare is "enjoyable" and the "table-side" Caesar salad "is worth every bite" and ensuing "garlic breath", "so go with someone who loves you."

Bistro 7 Ⓜ *American* 24 | 17 | 23 | $42

Old City | 7 N. Third St. (Market St.) | 215-931-1560 | www.bistro7restaurant.com

"Fresh", "local" ingredients go into the "sublime", "well-prepared" New American fare at Michael O'Halloran's "contemporary" BYO in Old City; though some grouse that the "decor is limited by the small size" of the "casual" "storefront", "über-friendly" service and $35 tasting menus that are a "steal" more than "cornpensate", which is why many vow to "return again and again."

Bistro St. Tropez *French* 19 | 19 | 17 | $42

Rittenhouse | Marketplace Design Ctr. | 2400 Market St., 4th fl. (23rd St.) | 215-569-9269 | www.bistrosttropez.com

"Only the decorators" seem to know of Patrice Rames' "low-key" country French bistro "hidden deep" at the top of the Marketplace Design Center in Rittenhouse, where the owner is redoubling efforts since closing sibling Patou; praise for the "interesting" menu, "stunning" views of the "Schuylkill at night" and special deals outweigh quibbles about "consistency issues" and "long waits."

Bistrot La Minette *French* 25 | 23 | 24 | $49

Queen Village | 623 S. Sixth St. (Bainbridge St.) | 215-925-8000 | www.bistrotlaminette.com

"Cheaper than a trip to Paris", this "sweet" Queen Village bistro is a "must-go" for its "sumptuous" Gallic "country" fare, served in "simple" yet "elegant" surroundings "without pretense" or "attitude" – "it's just like home, if mom was French and could cook like a chef"; "handmade" chocolates provide a sweet coda to the meal.

Bitar's Ⓧ *Mideastern* 25 | 8 | 19 | $12

South Philly | 947 Federal St. (10th St.) | 215-755-1121 | www.bitars.com

"Excellent hummus" and "incomparable falafel" come out of this "half of a Lebanese grocery store" in South Philly, where a "friendly family" serves up low-cost Middle Eastern specialties "without

frills" in the "tiny", 12-seat space; you can also find a "super selection of authentic, hard-to-find" nosh to take home.

Black Bass Hotel *American*   21 24 19 $53

Lumberville | Black Bass Hotel | 3774 River Rd. (Old Carversville Rd.) |
215-297-9260 | www.blackbasshotel.com

"Feel like a Colonial while dining on superb modern dishes" at
this Upper Bucks New American housed in a "refurbished",
18th-century inn with a "gorgeous" view of the Delaware; it's an
experience filled with "romance", and eight suites allow you to
sleep off too many cocktails if you can't call on a "chauffeur to
drive" you home.

Blackfish ☒ *American/Seafood*   25 17 22 $50

Conshohocken | 119 Fayette St. (bet. 1st & 2nd Aves.) | 610-397-0888 |
www.blackfishrestaurant.com

"Foodies" dub Chip Roman's "stark", "itty-bitty" nautical New
American BYO a "suburban" "nirvana" for its "inventive" midpriced
fare, including "excellent" seafood, served by a "competent" staff;
while some gripe about "close quarters", "skimpy" portions and
"Manhattan" attitude, the majority considers this one of "the best
things to come out of Conshohocken since, well . . . ever."

Black Sheep Pub ● *Pub Food*   17 16 17 $23

Rittenhouse | 247 S. 17th St. (Latimer St.) | 215-545-9473 |
www.theblacksheeppub.com

Just off Rittenhouse Square, this "neighborhood" Irish pub is a
fine "retreat" from the hustle and bustle of other local haunts,
suitable for "get-togethers with friends" (and "coeds") over
"good sports TV" and "respectable versions" of "specialties"
from "both sides of the pond"; some cynics, though, sniff that it
"looks like a bar, smells like a bar, tastes like a bar", and berate the
staff for being "too relaxed."

Bliss ☒ *American*   21 21 22 $50

Avenue of the Arts | 220-224 S. Broad St. (bet. Locust & Walnut Sts.) |
215-731-1100 | www.bliss-restaurant.com

"Imaginative" cuisine, an "unpretentious" yet "sophisticated"
setting and "friendly" service make this midpriced New American a
"sleeper tucked away in plain sight" on the Avenue of the Arts;
while a few feel it's "slipped" since the days of the "original
chef-owner", most consider it an "easy" pick as a destination
"before or after the theater", or "for a business meal [when] power
is not an issue."

Blue Bell Inn ☒ *American*   20 18 21 $46

Blue Bell | 601 Skippack Pike (Penllyn-Blue Bell Pike) | 215-646-2010 |
www.bluebellinn.com

Family-operated since 1945, this "reliable old-timer" in a "historic
tavern" (circa 1745) in central Montco is still the "bee's knees" to
loyalists who "came here as kids and now bring their own children"
for steak and prime rib, as well as some surprisingly "inventive"
twists on Traditional American cuisine; the service is "friendly", and

the bartenders "know how to mix a good cocktail"; a mid-Survey redo may not be reflected in the Decor score.

Z Bluefin Z *Japanese* | 28 | 14 | 21 | $39 |

Plymouth Meeting | 1017 Germantown Pike (Virginia Rd.) | 610-277-3917

"Don't just show up and hope for a table, it's not going to happen" at this "quality" Japanese BYO in a "dumpy" Plymouth Meeting strip mall, where suburban sushi "snobs" "fill themselves to the gills" with "spicy tuna sundaes" and other "phenomenal" offerings, served by an "over-the-top friendly" staff; most agree it's one of the "best around", and some lament "maybe if we hadn't told so many people, it would be easier to get a reservation."

Blue Pear Bistro Z *American* | 23 | 23 | 22 | $43 |

West Chester | 275 Brintons Bridge Rd. (Old Wilmington Pike) | 610-399-9812 | www.bluepearbistro.com

The "casual side" of the Dilworthtown Inn in West Chester wins praise for its "thoughtfully presented" New American "bistro" fare at a "fraction of the price you would pay next door", as well as "attentive" servers and "friendly" "bartenders"; the "old general store" "off Route 202" in West Chester exudes "pure Chester County atmosphere", making it a "gathering place" for locals who especially enjoy dining on the "outdoor porch."

Z Blue Sage
Vegetarian Grille Z M *Vegetarian* | 26 | 16 | 23 | $28 |

Southampton | 772 Second St. Pike (Rte. 132/Street Rd.) | 215-942-8888 | www.bluesagegrille.com

"Even guy's guys" are down with this affordable, "unpretentious" BYO "veg with an edge" located in a Bucks "strip mall", where Mike Jackson's kitchen "extracts amazing flavors out of vegetables, beans and grains" ("no tofu or mock meats") and turns them into "rich" creations, which come in "generous portions"; the "professional" waiters help you "forget any preconceptions" about meatless eats, and the "only downsides" reported are the "noise level" and "crowds."

Bobby Chez M *Seafood* | 22 | 11 | 18 | $23 |

Avenue of the Arts | The Lofts | 1352 South St. (Broad St.) | 215-732-1003 | www.bobbychezcrabcakes.com

See review in the New Jersey Suburbs Directory.

NEW Bobby's
Burger Palace *Burgers* | - | - | - | I |

University City | The Radian | 3925 Walnut St. (39th St.) | 215-387-0378 | www.bobbysburgerpalace.com

Food Network celeb Bobby Flay has rolled into Philly with a boldly decorated branch of his upscale burger joint housed in a bustling building in University City; between the sandwiches (potato-chip lovers can get them 'crunchified' for free) and an assortment of spiked shakes, this one's got the Penn kids more than covered.

Bocelli *Italian*
20 | 15 | 19 | $35

Chestnut Hill | 8630 Germantown Ave. (Bethlehem Pike) | 215-248-1980
Gwynedd | 521 Plymouth Rd. (Evans Rd.) | 215-646-9912
www.bocellidining.com

Fans of this "cozy" BYO duo located "at the top of the hill" in Chestnut Hill and inside the Gwynedd Valley SEPTA station predict you'll be "smacking your lips and licking your fingers" over "reliably prepared" Italian dishes with some "interesting flourishes" – but you won't be "paying an arm and a leg"; the service is "attentive", and the complimentary "homemade limoncello" when the check comes is a nice touch.

Bomb Bomb Bar-be-que Grill ⑤ *BBQ/Italian*
23 | 13 | 21 | $30

South Philly | 1026 Wolf St. (Warnock St.) | 215-463-1311 |
www.bombbomb-restaurant.com

There's plenty of bang in the "finger-lickin' good ribs" and "mussels" at this "kitschy", "old school" Italian "red-sauce" and BBQ tap in a "converted" "row house" that "looks like something out of *Rocky*", where "real South Philly waitresses" make "you feel like you're part of the family"; the consensus is that it truly is da "bomb"; P.S. "be sure to ask about the origin of the name."

Bona Cucina Ⓜ⑤ *Italian*
▽ 23 | 14 | 22 | $29

Upper Darby | 66 Sherbrook Blvd. (Marshall Rd.) | 610-623-8811

It "might not look like much", but aficionados assert "you can tell" "everything is made to order" at this "traditional", midpriced Northern Italian BYO, the go-to spot of Upper Darbyites for "excellent food, Sinatra music and Delaware County service" in a "charming" setting; in sum, most agree it's a "*bona*-fide gem" (just be sure to get a res for the weekend).

Bonefish Grill *Seafood*
21 | 19 | 20 | $35

Exton | 460 W. Lincoln Hwy. (bet. Rte. 100 & Ship Rd.) | 610-524-1010
Newtown Square | 4889 West Chester Pike (Providence Rd.) |
610-355-1784
Willow Grove | Regency Sq. | 1015 Easton Rd. (Fitzwatertown Rd.) |
215-659-5854
www.bonefishgrill.com

The majority have "no bones" to pick with this "midlevel" Outback offshoot and "forget it's a chain", thanks to "fresh" fin fare, including the signature "Bang Bang shrimp", and "friendly" service (management "clearly sends" the staff to "Server U") in "warm" environs; though some report "crowded", "chaotic" scenes on weekends, for most it remains a solid option "without going broke" for nights you "don't feel like cooking."

Bonjung Japanese *Japanese*
▽ 26 | 21 | 20 | $34

Collegeville | Collegeville Station | 50 W. Third Ave. (Walnut St.) |
610-489-7022 | www.bonjungsushi.com

Those in-the-know call this "contemporary" BYO in Collegeville "one of the best" Japanese choices "in the suburbs" for its "delicious sushi" and "sukiyaki the way mom used to make it", plus a number of "authentic" "Korean dishes" on a "varied" menu; though it's housed in a "dismal building", the interior is "beautiful", and "fast service" "impresses" as well, but a few cynics attribute its luster to the "lack of competition" in the area.

Bonté Wafflerie & Café *Coffeehouse*   21 14 17 $11

Rittenhouse | 130 S. 17th St. (bet. Sansom & Walnut Sts.) | 215-557-8510
Washington Square West | 922 Walnut St. (bet. 9th & 10th Sts.) | 215-238-7407
www.bontewaffles.com

Enthusiasts of these "European-style" Center City cafes are "in heaven" over the "scrumptious" "handheld" "Belgian *gaufré* (waffles)" washed down with "La Colombe coffee", as well as "interesting" salads and sandwiches; the staff "couldn't be any friendlier", but a few technophobes grouse that the "wireless Internet keeps the loungers from giving up their seats."

Bourbon Blue *Cajun/Creole*   18 19 19 $35

Manayunk | 2 Rector St. (Main St.) | 215-508-3360 | www.bourbonblue.com

Surveyors are split over this "festive" Cajun-Creole housed in a renovated stable by the Manayunk Canal – the "young partying" crowd touts "generous portions" of "very good New Orleans–influenced fare" (as well as signature "cheesesteak eggrolls") and "bands" blowing forth in the basement on weekends; more skeptical sorts report "uneven" experiences, and dismiss it as ultimately "forgettable."

Brandywine Prime *Steak*   22 23 20 $48

Chadds Ford | Chadds Ford Inn | 1617 Baltimore Pike (Rte. 100) | 610-388-8088 | www.brandywineprime.com

"Tasty" steaks, a "decadent Sunday brunch" and more are backed by "zinger drinks" and a "sensible" wine program at Dan Butler's "upscale casual" meatery in the "beautifully restored" Chadds Ford Inn; the "down-to-earth setting" "captures the Brandywine/Wyeth area", while the service is "friendly" and "professional"; P.S. regulars recommend the weeknight "low-cost specials" in the bar.

Branzino *Italian/Seafood*   23 19 21 $43

Rittenhouse | 261 S. 17th St. (bet. Locust & Spruce Sts.) | 215-790-0103 | www.branzinophilly.com

"Melt-in-your-mouth" "artichoke hearts", "risotto" and of course the "signature branzino" "filleted tableside" – "what more could you ask for in a BYO?" posit partisans of this "white-linen" Italian between the Avenue of the Arts and Rittenhouse Square; the "outstanding", "old-world" staff will get you to your curtain on time ("you'll waltz through dinner, but then they'll hustle you out"), and if it's "too crowded" in the "intimate" interior, there's always the "secret garden."

Brasserie 73 *French*   22 22 21 $45

Skippack | 4024 Skippack Pike (Mensch Rd.) | 610-584-7880 | www.brasserie73.net

"French bistro cooking" in the "boonies" of central Montco? – "you bet" assure aficionados of this "cozy, romantic" "find" in "lovely"

Skippack Village, which doubles down as a "sophisticated, elegant wine bar"; the staff is "well versed in the menu", and regulars report "you can't beat a table by the fire" or on the "outdoor patio."

Brauhaus Schmitz ● *German*   19 20 18 $32

South St. | 718 South St. (7th St.) | 267-909-8814 | www.brauhausschmitz.com

Freunden shout *"wunderbar"* for the "impressive" beer list and "tasty" Teutonic "staples" at this "boisterous" "Bavarian theme park" on South Street, where it's "fun" to "relax with friends and knock a few back" as the "noise level" rises (*aber "nicht so laut!"*), but some "can't help but pity" the staff *"frauleins"* in "hilariously over-the-top", "low-cut" dirndls; if you escape to the second floor, watch the low ceiling, for clunking your *kopf* is the "wurst."

Brew HaHa! *Coffeehouse*   17 15 20 $11

Washington Square West | 212 S. 12th St. (bet. Locust & Walnut Sts.) | 215-893-5680 | www.brew-haha.com

See review in the Wilmington/Nearby Delaware Directory.

Brick Hotel, The *American*   16 20 17 $39

Newtown | The Brick Hotel | 1 E. Washington Ave. (State St.) | 215-860-8313 | www.brickhotel.com

This stalwart New American draws mixed opinions – proponents tout the $26.95 "brunch buffet", as well as the $21 dinner prix fixe Sundays-Thursdays, "lovely" decor and "charming glassed-in patio" with a "great view" of "bucolic" Newtown; critics condemn the cooking as "unpredictable" and the service as "inefficient", concluding it "just shows that it's 'location, location, location.'"

NEW Brick House Tavern & Tap *American*   ▽ 17 19 16 $24

Willow Grove | 2402 Easton Rd. (Pennsylvania Tpke.) | 215-675-5767 | www.brickhousetavernandtap.com

"Big-boy appetites" will feel right at home at this branch of a "comfy" "sports bar"/man cave in Willow Grove; "good" burgers and salads are served to a "20s and 30s crowd" by waitresses in "short skirts" with a "tongue-in-cheek attitude", and many describe it as a "bargain-basement" version of "Hooters."

Bridget Foy's ● *American*   19 17 20 $31

South St. | 200 South St. (2nd St.) | 215-922-1813 | www.bridgetfoys.com

An "oasis" in the "epicenter of the madness" of South Street, this "classy", "casual" New American is a fun place to "watch" the "street life" from the patio, while its "well-thought-out" cuisine "raises simple to something special" and offers "good value"; with the "feel of a comfortable neighborhood pub" and "warm" service, "it's been around for ages for a reason."

Bridgetown Mill House 🗷 M *American*   24 25 22 $59

Langhorne | 760 Langhorne-Newtown Rd. (Bridgetown Pike) | 215-752-8996 | www.bridgetownmillhouse.com

The "country setting" at this "quiet, sedate" Bucks B&B in a circa-1791 Federal-style mansion is "just as good for a one-on-one business dinner as for a romantic evening" (the latter especially by the "roaring fireplace on a cold winter night" or on the "fantastic patio in summer"); the New American–Continental fare is "expensive, but worth it", and while a few grouse the service is "a bit slow", others counter that it's only because the "friendly, helpful" staff "allows you to slowly dine and enjoy" the experience.

Bridget's Steakhouse ● Ⓜ *American/Steak*

23	21	21	$50

Ambler | 8 W. Butler Pike (Main St.) | 267-465-2000 |
www.bridgetssteak.com

For "destination dining" in "hip" (?) Ambler, fans tout this upmarket, high-ceilinged steakhouse serving "awesome" steaks and "wonderful" New American dishes; though it's "pricey", the $27 three-course early-bird specials help ease the sting, and "yummy apps" served in the expanded bar area make for a "nice night out", especially when "they open the huge windows and you almost feel like you're out-side"; "friendly" service and "complimentary valet parking" are the "icing on the cake."

Bridgid's *Eclectic*

20	16	20	$28

Fairmount | 726 N. 24th St. (Meredith St.) | 215-232-3232 |
www.bridgids.com

"Get to know your Fairmount neighbors on a more intimate basis" at this "quaint", "cozy" ("verging on claustrophobic") Euro-centric "joint" serving a "fantastic" selection of "Belgian" and "out-of-the-ordinary" beers and "decent portions" of "hearty" Eclectic fare that goes "beyond bar food"; "decent prices", "friendly" service and a "happy atmosphere" help make it a "great first-date place."

Broad Axe Tavern ● *American*

16	18	17	$36

Ambler | 901 W. Butler Pike (Skippack Pike) | 215-643-6300 |
www.broadaxetavern.com

"Reborn" "from the ground up", this "busy", "beautiful" stonewalled New American tavern in central Montco is "a lot better" "than be-fore" according to "locals", who laud the "spectacular renovation" as well as its "excellent choice of reasonably priced small plates" and "full-size dinners"; a like number of critics, however, report "hit-or-miss" experiences and a "confused young" staff, and suspect it's "not sure what kind of restaurant it wants to be."

Buca di Beppo *Italian*

16	17	18	$29

Rittenhouse | 258 S. 15th St. (bet. Latimer & Spruce Sts.) |
215-545-2818
Exton | 300 Main St. (Bartlett Ave.) | 610-524-9939
www.bucadibeppo.com

You can sit by the "pope's head" or under a portrait of "Frank and Dean" at this "over-the-top" "schmaltzy" Italian chain, where "am-ple portions" of "basic" "classics", "guaranteed" to fill a "to-go box", are served "family-style" by a "bubbly" staff; fans advise "come hun-gry" in "loose clothing" with "a lot of friends", while purists sneer "stay home and open a can of Chef Boyardee" instead.

	FOOD	DECOR	SERVICE	COST

☑ Buddakan *Asian* — 26 | 27 | 24 | $56

Old City | 325 Chestnut St. (bet. 3rd & 4th Sts.) | 215-574-9440 | www.buddakan.com

The "beautiful, cool people" expect a "sublime" experience and "get it every time" at Stephen Starr's "tried-and-true", "loud, loud, loud" Pan-Asian "winner" in Old City, where the "amazing" fare can "send you into a food coma", served by a "top-notch" staff in a "handsome", "trendy" setting; a few suggest "Buddha would be offended", for "there is nothing in moderation" here – including the prices, though most agree "taste trumps budget" at this "awesome" "wonder."

NEW Bull Durham's *BBQ* — - | - | - | I

West Chester | 1347 Wilmington Pike (Dilworthtown Rd.) | 484-315-8039 | www.bulldurhams.com

A family with Texas ties has settled into the outskirts of West Chester with this Southwestern steakhouse serving inexpensive fare in a (kid-friendly) roadhouse setting; after dinner, it's aimed at the more mature crowd, with nightly entertainment including line dancing.

Bunha Faun *Asian/French* — 24 | 13 | 20 | $36

Malvern | 152 Lancaster Pike (Conestoga Rd.) | 610-651-2836

An "old standby" in Malvern, this "reliable", "underrated" French-Asian BYO in an "old Dairy Queen" offers "beautifully" prepared "fusion" specialties and "helpful" service to a mostly "older" clientele, and many marvel at "how they have maintained the low prices"; a few regulars who've "memorized" the bill of fare suggest "it might be nice to have a change in the menu from time to time", however.

Butcher & Singer *Steak* — 24 | 26 | 24 | $70

Rittenhouse | 1500 Walnut St. (15th St.) | 215-732-4444 | www.butcherandsinger.com

It's fun to "go back in time" and dine *Mad Men*"-style at Stephen Starr's "retro" steakhouse-cum-"supper club" on Walnut Street's Restaurant Row, where the "secretive, yet sexy, yet dangerous" atmosphere is "sure to class up your evening"; eating "meat may be murder, but they make it oh-so-tasty here" rationalize regulars who are also "wowed" by "pro" service that's "on the money" – of which you'll need plenty, by the way, to cover the "large bill."

Byblos ☻ *Mediterranean* — 18 | 16 | 16 | $30

Rittenhouse | 114 S. 18th St. (bet. Chestnut & Sansom Sts.) | 215-568-3050 | www.byblosphilly.com

"Holy hookah, Batman!" – after serving "amazing shish kebabs" and other "authentic" Med eats at dinner, this "cozy" Rittenhouse Square "find" goes "nightlife", with DJs spinning to a crowd of "twenty-somethings"; belly dancing on Sunday nights adds to the "fun."

Cactus ☻ *Southwestern* — ∇ 17 | 18 | 18 | $19

Manayunk | 4243 Main St. (Rector St.) | 267-385-6249 | www.cactusphilly.com

The "margaritas" are a "delight" at this "casual" Manayunk Southwestern, where daily "food and drink specials" help make it

FOOD | DECOR | SERVICE | COST

"affordable"; while fans praise the "heartwarming meals", they are balanced by critics who complain of "inconsistent execution" and a pervasive "meat-market" vibe in the restored storefront setting.

Café Con Chocolate ☑ *Japanese/Mexican*

- | - | - | I

South Philly | 2100 S. Norwood St. (Snyder Ave.) | 267-639-4506 | www.cafeconchocolate.com

Those "craving Mexican favorites or Japanese noodles" can choose either – or both – at this "lovely little" "neighborhood cafe" on a South Philly corner where chef-owner Yoshiko Yamasaki pays homage to her dual ancestry with *"muy autentico"* south-of-the-border grub (including "fabulous" "Oaxacan hot chocolate") as well as teppanyaki fare prepared with "skill and love", and all served by a "nice staff"; open Thursdays–Sundays, it's "also good for brunch."

Cafe de Laos *Laotian/Thai*

24 | 17 | 22 | $25

South Philly | 1117 S. 11th St. (bet. Ellsworth St. & Washington Ave.) | 215-467-1546

The "delicious variety" of "high-quality" Thai and Laotian cooking "always delivers" at this "charming" BYO near the Italian Market, so aficionados "go with an open mind"; while decor may be "minimal", "reasonable prices", "lovely" service and a "calm, serene" vibe are additional reasons most deem it "worth the trip to South Philly."

Café Estelle ☑ *American*

23 | 14 | 21 | $21

Northern Liberties | 444 N. Fourth St. (Spring Garden St.) | 215-925-5080 | www.cafeestelle.com

"Get in line early" for "delightfully presented", "well-crafted" "brunches" and "lunches" "that you would never make at home" at Marshall Green's "kitschy", "hipster gone up(per) scale" American cafe in an "industrial-looking setting" in a Northern Liberties apartment building; a staff that "aims to please", "bottomless" "self-serve coffee bar" and "environmentally responsible" "takeout" help make up for "excruciating waits."

Café L'Aube *Coffeehouse*

∇ 25 | 17 | 19 | $14

Graduate Hospital | 1512 South St. (15th St.) | 215-546-1550 | www.cafelaube.com

Jean-Luc Fanny makes you "feel like family" at his art-nouveau cafe located on a "growing commercial block" in Graduate Hospital, where Brussels-style waffles and "delicious" "crêpes" in any "combination" are served "fresh" and "hot", along with some of the "best coffee in town"; though service can be "slow", Gallic music in the background and piles of "French magazines" make it a place for the "true Francophile."

Cafe Preeya ☑ *Eclectic*

21 | 16 | 24 | $34

Huntingdon Valley | Village Ctr. | 2651 Huntingdon Pike (Red Lion Rd.) | 215-947-6195 | www.cafepreeya.com

Even "after all these years", this "cute", Thai-influenced Eclectic BYO in a Huntingdon Valley strip mall is still a "favorite" of many, delivering "fresh fish" and other "innovative" fare "that is large on

	FOOD	DECOR	SERVICE	COST

the satisfaction scale", including "fabulous" specials during the week; the staff is arguably more "gracious" than ever, judging from a spike in the Service score.

Cafette *Eclectic*
20 | 14 | 19 | $27

Chestnut Hill | 8136 Ardleigh St. (Hartwell Ln.) | 215-242-4220 | www.cafette.com

Chestnut Hillers who want to "get away from it all" flock to this "funky '60s-style" "hidden treasure" in a "backstreet" "cottage" for "awesome" "hippy-dippy" New American–Eclectic "comfort food", including "fried chicken [that] beats the rest" and lots of "fresh local produce" for the "vegheads"; the prices are "reasonable", and there's "no pretense" in the "friendly" service or "cute", "inviting" setting; P.S. the "outside garden" is a good bet in warm weather.

Caffe Casta Diva 🛇 Ⓜ ⇗ *Italian*
26 | 20 | 24 | $41

Rittenhouse | 227 S. 20th St. (Locust St.) | 215-496-9677

Rock-solid ratings reflect how Stephen Vassalluzzo "puts a lot of effort" into his "unsung", midpriced Italian BYO near Rittenhouse Square, where diners feel "transported" to "an apartment somewhere in Rome" over the "veal chop" and other "outstanding" options (the "desserts are off the charts"), served "graciously" in a "simple" room exuding a "soupçon of elegance"; the only quibbles are over the "cash-only" policy and the challenge of making "reservations on weekends."

Caffe Valentino *Italian*
∇ 22 | 15 | 19 | $41

South Philly | 1245 S. Third St. (Wharton St.) | 215-336-3033

In the "sea" of "basic red-gravy" joints in South Philly, this "neighborhood" BYO Italian in Pennsport is buoyed by a "reliable" kitchen that'll "take requests" and cook up something that's "not on the menu"; the atmosphere is "pleasant", but despite a 2009 renovation and expansion, it still can't shake perceptions of *Miami Vice*-inspired" decor and "no wow factor."

Cake Ⓜ *Bakery*
20 | 21 | 18 | $25

Chestnut Hill | 8501 Germantown Ave. (Highland Ave.) | 215-247-6887 | www.cakeofchestnuthill.com

"Dine amid the flowers" at this "sunny", "unpretentious" bakery-cafe in a "greenhouse setting" in Chestnut Hill, where you can "wake up" to "rich, delicious" breakfasts and savor "creative" lunches (as well as BYO dinners on Thursdays and Fridays), served by "attentive" folks; "save room" for dessert because you can "burn the calories" by strolling the hill afterward – thereby "having your cake and eating it too."

California Cafe *Californian*
20 | 19 | 19 | $35

King of Prussia | Plaza at King of Prussia Mall | 160 N. Gulph Rd. (bet. DeKalb Pike & Mall Blvd.) | 610-354-8686 | www.californiacafe.com

"Not your mother's mall food" is how fans describe the "creative" Californian "seasonal selections" and "small-plates possibilities", backed by a "great wine by-the-glass list", at this "comfortable" sit-down "refuge" in the Plaza at King of Prussia that's "worth putting up with the shopping bags"; "reasonable" prices, an "attractive" setting and "fun staff" make it a "pleasant surprise" that "definitely beats the food court."

California Pizza Kitchen *Pizza* 19 | 15 | 18 | $24

Wynnefield | 4040 City Ave. (Old Lancaster Rd.) | 215-473-7010
King of Prussia | King of Prussia Mall | 470 Mall Blvd. (DeKalb Pike) | 610-337-1500
Plymouth Meeting | 514 W. Germantown Pike (Hickory Rd.) | 610-828-8232
www.cpk.com

Fans confess to the "guilty pleasure" of this "tried-and-true" pizzeria chain where you can "eat out with kids and still feel like a grown-up", thanks to a lineup of "creative" pies in "permutations" that'll make your "head spin", and "outrageous desserts" that add a "dose of caloric delight"; the service is "friendly" and the "price is right", but be sure to "wear your sunglasses", for the digs are "bright, bright, bright."

Campo's Deli ⊅ *Cheesesteaks* 23 | 11 | 19 | $12

Old City | 214 Market St. (Strawberry St.) | 215-923-1000 | www.camposdeli.com

This "superb" Old City sandwichery is often "overrun" by visitors to Philly's historic district who come to experience its "yummy" "cheesesteaks, hoagies" and "other" "requisite" "Philadelphia specialties" (including "chocolate chip cookies" that some "could eat for dinner – oh, wait, I have"); still, the staff has it "under control" with "fast-paced" but "not rude" service in the "basic" storefront setting.

Cantina Los Caballitos ❂ *Mexican* 21 | 18 | 20 | $25

South Philly | 1651 E. Passyunk Ave. (Morris St.) | 215-755-3550 | www.cantinaloscaballitos.com

Cantina Dos Segundos ❂ *Mexican*

Northern Liberties | 931 N. Second St. (W. Laurel St.) | 215-629-0500 | www.cantinadossegundos.com

"Awesome", "frontera"-style Mex and "delicious margaritas in all sorts of flavors" are served by "good-looking, fun" servers in a "lively atmosphere" at these cantinas in South Philly and Northern Liberties that are usually "packed to the gills with hipsters" and "pretty young things"; "dangerously cheap" specials result in "lines" on "weekends."

⊠ Capital Grille, The *Steak* 26 | 24 | 25 | $66

Avenue of the Arts | 1338 Chestnut St. (Broad St.) | 215-545-9588 | www.thecapitalgrille.com

"Although it's a chain", when it comes to "entertaining business clients" who "want to be seen" – or enjoying a night out with your "rich uncle"– it's tough to beat this "man-cave" hailed by "carnivores on expense accounts" as the "mac daddy" of "top-notch" steaks, which are complemented by killer "Stoli dolis", near-"flawless" service and a "clubby", "contemporary" setting; while some gripe that "if you're not A-list here, you're invisible", the majority sees "Capital Thrill" as the steakhouse "gold standard."

Ⓩ Capogiro ☀ *American/Dessert*   27 | 15 | 20 | $9

Rittenhouse | 117 S. 20th St. (Sansom St.) | 215-636-9250
South Philly | 1625 E. Passyunk Ave. (Morris St.) |
215-462-3790
University City | Radian | 3925 Walnut St. (40th St.) |
215-222-0252
Washington Square West | 119 S. 13th St. (Sansom St.) |
215-351-0900
www.capogirogelato.com

Some of the "best gelato this side of the Atlantic" can be found at this "trendy" dessertery chain where "Willy Wonka sensibilities meet Italy", producing "heavenly" confections with some "surprising" flavors ("avocado and fennel", anyone?), dished out by "patient scoopers" who "cave to endless demands for samples"; it's "great for finishing off a big dinner" "nearby", "prices" be damned", and while it also serves good "panini" and a "mean" cup of coffee, many wonder "why waste the calories"?

Caribou Cafe *French*   21 | 19 | 20 | $37

Washington Square West | 1126 Walnut St. (bet. 11th & 12th Sts.) |
215-625-9535 | www.cariboucafe.com

"Berets are welcome" at this "French, French, French" Washington Square West bistro near the theaters on Walnut Street, where you can "let your arteries revolt" as you dive into Olivier de Saint Martin's "consistently wonderful" cuisine, including lunch and dinner prix fixe menus that are "always a pleaser", served in an "elegant" room or on the "nice" sidewalk cafe; "efficient, un-fussy" service completes the picture.

NEW Carluccio's Ⓜ *Italian*   ▽ 25 | 15 | 24 | $32

South Philly | 932 S. 10th St. (Carpenter St.) | 215-574-5000
For a "true taste of South Philly", "venture out of the suburbs with a great bottle of wine" to this "intimate" BYO "newcomer" and prepare to be "floored" by chef-owner Carlo Nigro's "high-quality", "perfectly cooked" *mangiare*, delivered by "Italian servers" who make you "feel like you're in their home"; the fare's "inexpensive" and comes in "real portions", which make it something of a "problem for waistline watchers."

Carman's Country Kitchen ⊅ *Eclectic*   26 | 15 | 23 | $20

South Philly | 1301 S. 11th St. (Wharton St.) | 215-339-9613
Brunch "prepared with love" and served "with attitude" is the main attraction of this "one-of-a-kind" South Philly Eclectic (open Fridays–Mondays, 8 AM-2 PM, only) where Carman Luntzel is at her "creative" best "doling out delicious flapjacks and bone-chilling up-and-down appraisals" of customers, while ceramic "phalluses" pop up everywhere in the "hole-in-the-wall" space, which includes a

FOOD DECOR SERVICE COST

table in the bed of a pickup truck; almost all agree the "crazy" "experience is totally worth it" – "unless you have a heart condition."

Carversville Inn Ⓜ Southern   ▽ 25 | 22 | 23 | $55

Carversville | 6205 Fleecydale Rd. (Aquetong Rd.) | 215-297-0900 | www.carversvilleinn.com

"Set your GPS and if you're lucky" you'll find this "authentic" Upper Bucks County "inn" in charming Carversville for a "getaway dinner"; though the "star of the house" is the "wonderful" Southern fare, it's supported by "terrific" service and a setting as "quaint" as all get-out, and regulars recommend you "sit by the fire" or out on the patio for the "ultimate atmosphere."

Cascade Lodge Ⓜ Continental   ▽ 20 | 17 | 23 | $47

Kintnersville | 5065 Lehnenberg Rd. (Rte. 611/Easton Rd.) | 610-346-7484 | www.cascadelodge.com

The "home-grown trout" caught from a nearby spring and "great Caesar salad prepared tableside" are highlights of this "legendary", "family"-run Continental set in a pre-Revolutionary War farmhouse in "bucolic" Upper Bucks; city slickers say the "*en plein air*" experience of dining on the terrace in spring and summer is "worth the ride."

Catherine's at the General Store Ⓜ American   ▽ 28 | 24 | 24 | $47

Unionville | General Store | 1701 W. Doe Run Rd. (Rte. 162) | 610-347-2227 | www.catherinesrestaurant.com

"Outstanding" New American food prepared with "great care and obvious love" and "friendly" service from a "wonderful" staff in a "beautiful" setting make this "intimate" mom-and-pop BYO housed in an old country store "worth the ride through Chester County"; so what if the *feng shui*-influenced, candlelit room can be "dark", even "with the menu-reading flashlights" – most agree it's the "best catch in town."

Cedar Hollow Inn American   17 | 17 | 19 | $40

Malvern | 2455 Yellow Springs Rd. (Rte. 29) | 610-296-9006 | www.cedarhollowinn.com

Fans of this "little hideaway" in a "peaceful country setting" in Malvern find the New American fare "good, if not exciting", the "local" "bar crowd" "interesting" and the space (think white linens, hardwood floors) "comfy"; detractors, though, dismiss the cuisine as "edible, but nothing more" and the "noisy" bar scene as somewhat "less than desirable"; there's live music and dancing Fridays–Saturdays.

Cedars Lebanese   ▽ 22 | 16 | 23 | $24

South St. | 616 S. Second St. (bet. Bainbridge & South Sts.) | 215-925-4950 | www.cedarsrestaurant.com

For "fresh" Middle Eastern food "and lots of it", regulars recommend the "great-value" $25 prix fixe sampler at this Lebanese "nook" just off South Street; while the space is "small", it's "not noisy" and the "family"-proprietors "make you feel like an invited guest."

	FOOD	DECOR	SERVICE	COST

Celebre's Pizzeria ❶ *Pizza*
| 24 | 10 | 18 | $15 |

South Philly | Packer Park Shopping Ctr. | 1536 Packer Ave. (Broad St.) | 215-467-3255

"Forget the chains", piezani promise "you can't go wrong" at this "no-frills", "no-nonsense" South Philly pizza "favorite" near the stadiums, where Gloria the waitress, who "should be a national landmark", slings beer and "amazing" pies such as the signature "Pizzaz" (American cheese and sliced tomatoes); so what if some think it "looks like a beauty shop with patio furniture", the eats are "worth it."

Centre Bridge
Inn, The Ⓜ *American*
| ▽ 22 | 23 | 21 | $53 |

New Hope | The Centre Bridge Inn | 2998 N. River Rd. (Upper York Rd.) | 215-862-9139 | www.centrebridgeinn.com

A "fireplace and summer patio overlooking" the Delaware boost the "charm" quotient at this "beautiful" "stone inn" in New Hope that was spruced up post-Survey (which is not reflected in the Decor score); respondents say it's a "delightful stop" for New American creations, notably the $24.95 lobster special on Wednesdays–Thursdays, and encounter "nice people" among the staff.

Chabaa Thai Bistro *Thai*
| 25 | 20 | 22 | $29 |

Manayunk | 4371 Main St. (Grape St.) | 215-483-1979 | www.chabaathai.com

The "ultimate when-in-doubt spot" of many for "first dates", "group" dining and "everything in between", this "pleasant", "relaxed" Thai BYO "destination" in Manayunk showcases the "authentic", "consistently excellent" cuisine of chef Moon Krapugthong (of Mango Moon down the block), served with "genuine care" in a "lovely space" that's due to expand in late 2010; "reasonable prices" and a "kid-friendly" atmosphere add to its allure; there's a $3 corkage fee.

Charles Plaza *Chinese*
| 24 | 12 | 22 | $22 |

Chinatown | 234-236 N. 10th St. (Vine St.) | 215-829-4383

"Do not hesitate" to "leave your appetite in the hands" of chef-owner Charles Chen, the "host with the most" at this "best-kept secret" BYO situated at the "edge of Chinatown", where "delicious and reasonably healthy" Mandarin dishes (including "magnificent" tilapia) come with "a smile and a story"; insiders suggest "taking a group", so he'll be "likely to remember you the next time you visit."

Charlie's Hamburgers ⌗ *Burgers*
| 23 | 7 | 18 | $10 |

Folsom | 336 Kedron Ave. (MacDade Blvd.) | 610-461-4228

The "best messy burgers you can buy" come off the grill of this "throwback" joint in Delco, where there are "no wraps, yuppie salads" or "pretense", "just good old American hamburgers, fries and shakes", served in a "cool" "hole-in-the-wall"; it's a "great place to bring kids" and "reminisce" about "the way it used to be"; it's closed Tuesdays.

	FOOD	DECOR	SERVICE	COST

Chart House *Seafood*   20 | 22 | 19 | $47

Delaware Riverfront | Penn's Landing | 555 S. Columbus Blvd.
(Spruce St.) | 215-625-8383 | www.chart-house.com

The "wonderful views" of the Delaware make "you feel like you're on a cruise ship" at this chain seafooder on Penn's Landing, where most deem the fare "better than average", though dissenters sniff that it's merely "pricey" and "nothing special"; still, it's a "nice Sunday brunch treat for the out-of-town aunt" who'll appreciate the "polite" service and "impressive" location.

Cheeseburger in Paradise ● *Burgers*   14 | 16 | 16 | $21

Langhorne | 750 Middletown Blvd. (Lincoln Hwy.) | 215-757-3179 | www.cheeseburgerinparadise.com

"Don't miss" the "sweet potato fries" and "frozen cocktails" at this Jimmy Buffett-themed "tiki" "chain"-cum-hamburger specialist, "an island getaway in your own backyard", albeit one that runs "a bit on the loud side"; "if this is the food they serve in paradise, count me out" jeer detractors who deem the eats "subpar" and the scene "cheesy", with all the appeal of a "reality show casting call."

Cheesecake Factory ● *American*   20 | 19 | 19 | $29

King of Prussia | Pavilion at King of Prussia Mall | 640 W. DeKalb Pike (Allendale Rd.) | 610-337-2200

Willow Grove | Willow Grove Park Mall | 2500 W. Moreland Rd. (Easton Rd.) | 215-659-0270
www.thecheesecakefactory.com

With a "menu as big as a phonebook" and "ridiculously large portions" that mean de rigueur "doggy bags", this "high-energy" New American "fancy diner" chain is "crowded every hour of the day", so be sure to bring along "your pocket *War and Peace*" for the "ridiculous" wait; "nothing is too much trouble" for servers who urge you not to skip the "yummy rich cheesecake" 'cause "that's what you really came for" ("oh my hips").

Chestnut Grill & Sidewalk Cafe *American*   17 | 17 | 20 | $27

Chestnut Hill | Chestnut Hill Hotel | 8229 Germantown Ave. (Southampton Ave.) | 215-247-7570 | www.chestnuthillgrill.com

As comfortable as a "pair of khakis", this "family-friendly" Traditional American "staple" in Chestnut Hill is a "pleasant" stop for "great burgers and salads" at "reasonable" prices; most prefer to "sit outside on the porch" and watch the "traffic streaming by", with some declaring the "subterranean room" downright "unappealing."

Chez Colette *French*   20 | 17 | 19 | $47

Rittenhouse | Sofitel Philadelphia | 120 S. 17th St. (Sansom St.) | 215-569-8300 | www.sofitel.com

Supporters of this "underappreciated" New French bistro off the lobby of the Sofitel near Rittenhouse Square commend it as a good bet for a "quiet" "business" meal or "Sunday brunch", citing "solid" fare, "sincere" service and "lively" decor; *non*-sayers demur at the "plain, basic" eats and "doubt the staff could find France on a map."

Chiangmai *Thai*
25 | 17 | 22 | $26

Conshohocken | 108 Fayette St. (1st Ave.) | 610-397-1757 |
www.mychiangmaicuisine.com

"Authenticity and a mélange of exotic flavors" are the hallmarks of the "excellent food at a good price" on offer at this "tiny", "family-operated" Thai "jewel" (sibling of Blue Bell's Thai Orchid) in Conshohocken; while the surroundings are "nothing extravagant", the "polite" staff takes pains "not to rush you", and the "Conshy crowd" is usually "on its best behavior", making for a "pleasant environment" all around.

Chiarella's *Italian*
∇ 22 | 14 | 21 | $37

South Philly | 1600 S. 11th St. (Tasker St.) | 215-334-6404 |
www.chiarellasristorante.com

"Now that's Italian" exclaim aficionados of this white-tablecloth BYO on the "bustling" East Passyunk "dining corridor", where South Philadelphia locals who "really know how to eat" can be seen "socializing" over "wonderful", "affordable" eats served "with confidence" by "super-friendly" folks; for those in a hurry, it now serves pizza through a take-out window.

Chickie's & Pete's Cafe ❶ *Pub Food*
18 | 16 | 17 | $25

Northeast Philly | Roosevelt Plaza | 11000 Roosevelt Blvd. (bet. Red Lion & Woodhaven Rds.) | 215-856-9890
Northeast Philly | 4010 Robbins Ave. (Robbins St.) |
215-338-3060 ⊡
South Philly | 1526 Packer Ave. (15th St.) | 215-218-0500
www.chickiesandpetes.com

"Love those Crab Fries" exclaim enthusiasts of these "landmark" sports bars, whose "boisterous" boosters from "all walks of life" gather over "calorically incorrect" "pub grub" served on "paper plates" while they "get" their "game on"; but some detractors snarl "youse gotta be kiddin' me" over what they see as "ordinary" eats, "laughable" waits and bartenders who couldn't "care less about their customers."

Chick's Café & Wine Bar Ⓜ *Eclectic*
21 | 19 | 21 | $33

South St. | 614 S. Seventh St. (Kater St.) | 215-625-3700 |
www.chickscafe.com

"Creative cocktails" and Jim Piano's "exciting", "well-crafted" Eclectic "small plates" make this "neighborhood" bar off South Street a good spot for a "romantic rendezvous" or "drink and some conversation after work"; there's a "strong hipster undercurrent" and the bartenders "know their wine", while the "outside tables are nice in summer" and the "lack of televisions" is a "definite plus" for some; it's no surprise so many "walk away happy."

ⓩ Chifa *Chinese/Peruvian*
25 | 24 | 24 | $52

Washington Square West | 707 Chestnut St. (7th St.) | 215-925-5555 |
www.chifarestaurant.com

Iron Chef Jose Garces' "exotically delicious" Chinese-Peruvian fusion cuisine makes this "trendy" Washington Square West storefront a "winner", especially for "those jaded by the usual" – expect "drool-worthy" "pork-belly buns" and other "adventurous" fare delivered by "sincere" servers who "enjoy what they're doing" in a setting replete with "beautiful" cabanas and "semiprivate" booths in the downstairs bar (good for "making out"); while a few quibble over the abundance of "cream sauce" in some dishes and warn the tab can be "dangerous to your wallet", it's "definitely on the repeat list" of most.

Chima Brazilian Steakhouse *Brazilian/Steak*

21 | 20 | 23 | $54

Logan Square | 1901 JFK Blvd. (20th St.) | 215-525-3233 | www.chimasteakhouse.com

"Bring your appetite" to this "gut-busting, guilt-inducing" Brazilian rodizio situated in "modern" quarters near Logan Square, where "attentive""gauchos" "keep coming" with "quality" "meat on skewers" and you can visit the "fresh and varied salad bar"; purists who point out that "quantity is not the same as quality" see it more as a "fun night out with friends" than "fine dining."

Chinnar Indian Cuisine *Indian*

∇ 23 | 13 | 23 | $25

Berwyn | Swedesford Plaza | 416 W. Swedesford Rd. (Contention Ln.) | 610-251-2526 | www.chinnarindian.com

"Outstanding" "ingredients" go into the "authentic" Indian treats, including "chicken tikka masala" and "thick, delicious" mango lassis, at this BYO in a Berwyn shopping center off Route 202, where the "pleasant" staff provides "excellent" service in the airy room; regulars recommend the "fresh and busy" $8.95 lunch buffet.

Chlöe ⊠Ⓜⵄ *American*

26 | 17 | 23 | $39

Old City | 232 Arch St. (bet. 2nd & 3rd Sts.) | 215-629-2337 | www.chloebyob.com

Though it's been on the Old City map for a decade, this "intimate" BYO "date place" is one of its "best-kept secrets" according to adherents who'd "go again in a heartbeat" for its "memorable" "creations" featuring "local, organic" ingredients ("Chlöe salad", "bread pudding"), served by a "friendly, accommodating" staff in a "quaint", "homey" space across from the Betsy Ross House; the only "downsides" – you have to "wait outside" until your party is complete and it's cash-only with no reservations.

Chops *Steak*

21 | 19 | 22 | $56

NEW Washington Square West | 700 Walnut St. (bet. S. 7th & 8th Sts.) | 215-922-7770

Bala Cynwyd | 401 City Ave. (bet. Monument Rd. & Presidential Blvd.) | 610-668-3400

www.chops.us

Owner Alex Plotkin and staff "know how to do it right" at this Bala Cynwyd meatery (and its new, dramatic Washington Square sibling) where "big portions" of "delicious" "comfort food", "good-size drinks" and an "excellent" wine list make it a "nice oasis of assured dining"; although some wallet-watchers wail that it "chops up your wallet", most agree "you get what you pay for."

	FOOD	DECOR	SERVICE	COST

Christopher's ◑ *American* | 16 | 14 | 17 | $24 |

Wayne | 108 N. Wayne Ave. (Lancaster Ave.) | 610-687-6558 | www.christophersaneighborhoodplace.com

While it's a "super place to bring the kids", providing "free balloons and crayons", this New American on the Wayne Avenue strip is also popular with "preppy Main Liners" for a "casual lunch or dinner", thanks to "solid bartenders" and a "reasonably priced menu"; the "high-ceilinged" space is "comfortable" (but "don't be surprised if someone at the table next to you is screaming"), and for most it's a "welcome alternative to franchise eateries."

Chun Hing *Chinese* | 22 | 10 | 22 | $24 |

Wynnefield | Pathmark Shopping Ctr. | 4160 Monument Rd. (Conshohocken Ave.) | 215-879-6270

Sinophiles swear "no one can beat the dumplings" at this "old standard" in Wynnefield, where Cantonese "goodies" served by a "helpful" staff are "a cut above" most, and help you overlook the "shopping-mall" "setting" that appears to be "from the 1950s"; though the location makes a few "uncomfortable", media mavens report you're bound to see local "newscasters from Channels 6 and 10" "ordering from Columns A and B."

CinCin *Chinese* | 23 | 18 | 21 | $35 |

Chestnut Hill | 7838 Germantown Ave. (Springfield Ave.) | 215-242-8800 | www.cincinrestaurant.com

"Creative", "sumptuous" dishes and "consistent" service from a staff that's "been there for years" add up to a "superb eating experience" at this "upscale" "French-inspired" Chinese "staple" in Chestnut Hill; some report "noise" issues, "scant parking" and long "waits", especially on "weekends", and note that it's a "little on the expensive side", but most agree it's "worth a drive."

NEW City Tap House ◑ *American* | – | – | – | M |

University City | The Radian | 3925 Walnut St., 2nd level (40th St.) | 215-662-0105 | www.citytaphouse.com

With 60 arcane and accessible beers on tap, plus refined New American gastropub fare from Al Paris of the now-closed Mantra – everything from pizzas to suckling pig – this newcomer in University City's Radian is hopping with college students and staff; the sprawling, ski lodge–like environs include five fire pits on a balcony overlooking Walnut Street, making for a convivial nighttime destination.

City Tavern *American* | 19 | 25 | 22 | $44 |

Old City | 138 S. Second St. (Walnut St.) | 215-413-1443 | www.citytavern.com

You can "picture Ben, Tom and John hanging out to discuss their place in history" at this "quaint" re-created 1773 tavern in Old City, "Philly's answer to Colonial Williamsburg", which has the mien of a "playful theme dinner party" with "engaging", "period-garbed" waiters serving "quality" Traditional American victuals; many locals put aside the "snobbery" and "tourist-trap" raps and "bring out-of-towners" for some "tri-cornered fun."

Clam Tavern *Seafood*

▽ 22 | 15 | 21 | $26

Clifton Heights | 339 E. Broadway Ave. (Edgemont Ave.) | 610-623-9537 |
www.clamtavern.net

Delco "locals" are happy as clams taking a "nostalgic trip" back to a simpler time at this ancient mariner in an "unexpected" location, where chef-owner Tony Blanche "greets and meets" and "still gets it done", preparing "baked clams to die for" and other seafood staples; if you're "looking for food and not decor", cronies confirm "you're in the right place."

Cochon Ⓜ⇗ *French*

26 | 18 | 22 | $41

Queen Village | 801 E. Passyunk Ave. (Catharine St.) | 215-923-7675 |
www.cochonbyob.com

Chef Gene Giuffi pays "homage to the other white meat" at this "un-assuming" French BYO in Queen Village, where diners go whole hog on his "mouthwatering" "piggy delights" in an "elbow-to-elbow" space evoking "everything you'd expect to find in rural France"; "personal" service comes "without the pretense" (thanks to wife Amy), and the consensus is that it's a "truly oink-credible value"; P.S. it doesn't take credit cards, so be sure to bring along the "bacon."

Cock 'n Bull *American*

18 | 18 | 19 | $34

Lahaska | Peddler's Vill. | 164 Peddlers Vill. (bet. Rtes. 202 & 263) |
215-794-4010 | www.peddlersvillage.com

"It's all about the prime rib" at this "tried-and-true", "reasonably priced" Traditional American in Peddler's Village, where there are "never any surprises" in the "yummy" "comfort food" or "pleasantly old-fashioned" setting; some dismiss the fare as "acceptable", but "nothing special", and the experience "over-touristed", but deals such as the Sunday brunch ($21.95) and Thursday seafood buffet ($36.95) "keep packing them in."

NEW Con Murphy's *Eclectic*

▽ 17 | 21 | 20 | $25

Logan Square | Windsor Suites | 1700 Ben Franklin Pkwy. (17th St.) |
267-687-1128 | www.conmurphyspub.com

It's "like stepping into a pub in Dublin" at this Eclectic newcomer a block from Logan Square, where "great drinks" and "perfectly decent" grub, including Irish breakfasts, are served by "friendly" waitresses in a "pretty" bi-level space "conducive to conversation" and "people-watching"; while some cynics find "nothing remarkable" about the fare, many others commend it as a "fun place for happy hour."

Continental, The *Eclectic*

22 | 19 | 20 | $35

Old City | 138 Market St. (2nd St.) | 215-923-6069 |
www.continentalmartinibar.com

Eclectic "upscale modern diner fare" is the star at Stephen Starr's "martini bar" "classic" in Old City, and whether you're out with a "five-year-old" or on a "date", "there's something for everyone" on the "interesting" menu; a few complain of "snooty" service, but for most, the "chill", "jazzy" "vibe" and "speared olive chandeliers" in the "snappy" retro-style digs "never get old", even after 15-plus years.

	FOOD	DECOR	SERVICE	COST

Continental Mid-town *Eclectic*
22	23	20	$36

Rittenhouse | 1801 Chestnut St. (18th St.) | 215-567-1800 |
www.continentalmidtown.com

It's a veritable "grown-up Barbie dream" at Stephen Starr's "ultra-cool" Rittenhouse Square Eclectic "diner-cum-nightclub", where fans dig the "enormous range" of menu choices and wash them down with "girlie drinks", all served "with a smile"; the "swinging" "birdcage" chairs on the balcony add to the "funky", "retro" vibe (just "wear earplugs"), and "young, hip" folk and the "girls'-night-out" crowd can also be seen getting "kicky" on the "rooftop deck."

NEW Cooperage *Southern*
-	-	-	M

Washington Square West | Curtis Ctr. | 601-45 Walnut St. (7th St.) |
215-226-2667 | www.cooperagephilly.com

This minimalist, industrial-looking whiskey bar, located in the Curtis Center on Washington Square, offers a tight Southern-inspired dinner menu of five main plates, accompanied by assorted sides and 40 whiskeys from around the globe (plus two dozen wines by bottle and glass); an adjacent grab-and-go cafe offers budget breakfasts and lunchtime sandwiches.

Cooper's Brick
Oven Wine Bar *American*
22	21	22	$33

Manayunk | 4367 Main St. (bet. Grape & Levering Sts.) |
215-483-2750 | www.jakesrestaurant.com

Manayunkers who "long for a little class" in their gastropubs head to this adjoining sidekick to Jake's, whose beer- and wine-oriented concept is "brilliant", offering the "best of both" eateries' menus – a "mix of plates" for "sharing" and for "singles" – and if you find it a "little tricky to navigate", the "helpful" staff is there to explain; the atmosphere is "festive" and "kid-friendly", and if it gets "too noisy" for you, it's "easy to request seating on the Jake's side."

Copabanana ● *American/Mexican*
17	12	15	$24

Northeast Philly | Grant Plaza | 1619 Grant Ave. (Welsh Rd.) |
215-969-1712
South St. | 344 South St. (4th St.) | 215-923-6180
University City | 4000 Spruce St. (40th St.) | 215-382-1330
www.copabanana.com

An order of "Spanish fries", a "pitcher of margaritas" and "thou" – "sometimes that's exactly what you need" attest amigos of these separately owned "south-of-the-border" bars, which nonetheless share a number of common elements – "above-average wacky bar food" , "optimum people-watching" and "kick-ass" drinks; while a number of critics cite housekeeping issues and "spotty" service, for most this trio is a "solid neighborhood pick."

Core De Roma Ⓜ *Italian*
▽ 25	20	23	$35

South St. | 214 South St. (2nd St.) | 215-592-9777

"Papa Gigi" Pinti "makes you feel as if you're old friends" at his "jewel" of a trattoria on South Street, where he presides over "reasonably priced" "Roman-style feasts of the highest order" (including "heavenly" "artichokes" and "Bolognese gravy par excellence"), served in a "pleasant", family-friendly setting; even though it's in the "heart of the tourist area", it's the "go-to authentic Italian" of many locals.

Coyote Crossing *Mexican*
21 | 21 | 18 | $36

Conshohocken | 800 Spring Mill Ave. (8th Ave.) | 610-825-3000 | www.coyotecrossing.com

"It doesn't get more romantic" than dining on the "awesome patio" on a "warm summer night" at this "engaging" Mexican off the main drag of Conshohocken, where the "strong margaritas" can "sneak up on you" and the "consistently good" *comida* is more than "just tacos and enchiladas"; most shrug and simply "accept" the merely "fair" service, but many warn that the scene can get "really loud", especially on "weekends."

Creed's Seafood & Steaks ☒ *Seafood/Steak*
24 | 19 | 24 | $52

King of Prussia | 499 N. Gulph Rd. (Pennsylvania Tpke.) | 610-265-2550 | www.creedskop.com

A "go-to" spot for "expense-account types" and the "fine-dining crowd", this "old-fashioned" King of Prussia surf 'n' turfer is recommended by regulars for "special occasions" or whenever you want to "paint the town red", thanks to a menu that's "strong across the board", "great wine list" and "attentive" service; the atmosphere is "formal", yet "comfortable" and "laid-back", and while it's "pricey", most agree it's "well worth it."

Criniti *Italian*
18 | 14 | 19 | $33

South Philly | 2611 S. Broad St. (Shunk St.) | 215-465-7750 | www.crinitirestaurant.com

"South Philly friends" testify that this "family-style" red-gravy house in a "converted church" on South Broad "still produces the goods" after a quarter-century – namely, "good", "basic" and "cheap" Southern Italian favorites served with "just the right attitude"; while a few skeptics sniff that, the formerly hallowed digs notwithstanding, the "flavors are more mundane than heavenly", it remains the "favorite" of many.

¡Cuba! ⓜ *Cuban*
▽ 16 | 19 | 19 | $33

Chestnut Hill | 8609 Germantown Ave. (bet. Bethlehem Pike & Evergreen Ave.) | 215-242-4422 | www.mycubanrestaurant.com

Two lines of thought emerge about this Cuban at the top of the hill in Chestnut Hill – proponents insist "Castro's loss is our gain" as they talk up "helpful" servers dishing out "enjoyable" "ethnic eats" (including a $15.95 three-course early-bird) on the "back patio"; detractors lament that it "doesn't live up to its promise" and see "no zing, zip or life."

☒ Cuba Libre *Cuban*
22 | 24 | 21 | $43

Old City | 10 S. Second St. (Market St.) | 215-627-0666 | www.cubalibrerestaurant.com

"Awesome" Latin food comes with a "creative twist" and the "legendary" mojitos can make you "forget where you are" at this "vibrant", "upscale" Old City Cuban, where "terrific" decor complete with "lush plantings" conjures up the "cool vibes" of "pre-Castro" "Havana"; this "mini-vacation" can be "loud but never out of control", the service is "congenial" and "salsa dancing" will help "work off dinner."

Cucina Forte Italian
26 | 17 | 24 | $36

South Philly | 768 S. Eighth St. (Catharine St.) | 215-238-0778
True to her name (which means 'strong'), Maria Forte's "kitsch"-filled South Philly "row-house" BYO delivers "lovingly authentic" fare that's "strong on flavor", including her "pillowy gnocchi that drift in from your dreams", at "too-good-to-be-true prices"; "friendly", "personal" service creates a "family feel", and while a few complain that it can get "crazy noisy", defenders insist it's just the "lively sound of happily contented diners."

Daddy Mims
Creole BYOB Ⓜ Creole
23 | 17 | 20 | $33

Phoenixville | 150 Bridge St. (bet. Church Ave. & Main St.) | 610-935-1800 | www.daddymims.com
Chef John Mims is "not afraid to turn up the spice" in the "quality" Creole cuisine at his BYO on Phoenixville's main drag, "highly recommended" by many for the "perfectly sized four-course meal for $30"; the servers are "friendly" and the toque can be seen "roaming the floor most nights" in the "sophisticated", contemporary space.

Dahlak Eritrean
22 | 13 | 19 | $19

Germantown | 5547 Germantown Ave. (Maplewood Ave.) | 215-849-0788 Ⓜ
West Philly | 4708 Baltimore Ave. (bet. 47th & 48th Sts.) | 215-726-6464 www.dahlakrestaurant.com
Learn the "real meaning of finger food" at this duo in West Philly and Germantown, where "savory", "exotic" Ethiopian and Eritrean specialties are served "family-style" and "sopped up" with "yeasty injera" and washed down with "cheap" wine and beer; while a few grouse that the seating "can be hard on the back" and the "service is so slow, you wonder if [your order is] being shipped from Africa", most agree the "quality of the food" and "smiling" staff "make up for it."

Dalessandro's
Steaks ◑⇔ Cheesesteaks
23 | 7 | 17 | $11

Roxborough | 600 Wendover St. (Henry Ave.) | 215-482-5407 | www.dalessandros.com
"Forget" "Ninth and Passyunk", this "no-frills" sandwich "nirvana" in Roxborough is the "real thing" boast boosters, who declare its "mouthwatering" cheesesteaks "some of the best" around; though there's "no atmosphere" and you'll "feel like a sardine" "jammed" against the "old-fashioned counter" while waiting for your order, fans assert you won't be able to "resist the mountains of onions and mushrooms" and free "homemade" peppers.

	FOOD	DECOR	SERVICE	COST

D'Angelo's Ristorante Italiano ● Ⓢ *Italian*   24 | 17 | 21 | $47

Rittenhouse | 256 S. 20th St. (bet. Locust & Spruce Sts.) | 215-546-3935 |
www.dangeloristorante.com

"A heady mix of old-timers with a healthy sprinkling of young professionals" gets "treated like family" at this "old-school" Italian
"classic" near Rittenhouse Square, and while it may not be for those
"seeking sleek and trendy", it's nonetheless a good choice for "family gatherings" or entertaining "out-of-town friends", thanks to
"consistent" fare "done right, not fancy"; it's "a lot of fun" "after
dark" when the "35–60 crowd" hits the floor to DJs spinning in the
"disco ball dance room."

Dante & Luigi's Ⓜ☞ *Italian*   23 | 17 | 21 | $41

South Philly | 762 S. 10th St. (Catharine St.) | 215-922-9501 |
www.danteandluigis.com

"As steady as Gibraltar", this "old-world" "red-gravy South Philly
Italian landmark" "can whisk you back to the '50s, in a good way",
with "solid classics" "without frills" from a "menu you can't refuse",
served by "chatty waiters" amid "candlelight" in a "comfortable"
100-year-old row home; the prices make it a "very good value", and
"they don't murder you for a glass of wine" – just remember to
"bring cash or your check book (no credit cards)."

Dark Horse Pub ● *Pub Food*   19 | 18 | 19 | $23

Society Hill | 421 S. Second St. (Pine St.) | 215-928-9307 |
www.darkhorsepub.com

"Perfect for a laid-back evening", this "neighborhood" English pub on
Head House Square provides "European sports" on the telly,
"Guinness" on tap and plates of decent "fish 'n' chips" and other
"basic" fare, as well as American staples, including "super-juicy"
burgers; the "cavelike" environs have "lots of space" and "just
enough rooms to confuse" "you after a few pints" ("will you find the
bathroom in time?").

Darling's *American*   17 | 14 | 16 | $18

Logan Square | 2100 Spring St. (21st St.) | 215-496-9611 |
www.darlingscheesecake.com
Northern Liberties | Piazza at Schmidt's | 1033 N. Second St.
(Germantown Ave.) | 267-239-5775 | www.darlingsdiner.com ●
Rittenhouse | 404 S. 20th St. (Pine St.) | 215-545-5745 |
www.darlingscheesecake.com

While these "unassuming" "coffee-shop" twins in Rittenhouse and
Logan Square are popular stops for a "quiet break" over free Wi-Fi and
"awesome cheesecake", the Northern Liberties "diner" sibling garners
mixed opinions – fans laud the "delicious" breakfasts, late weekend
hours (until 5 AM), "spacious" digs and waitresses who "treat you
like family"; critics, though, are cool to the "ominously large" setting
and carp over "inconsistent" chow and "clueless" service.

Dave & Buster's ● *American*   12 | 16 | 14 | $25

Delaware Riverfront | Pier 19 N. | 325 N. Columbus Blvd.
(bet. Callowhill & Spring Garden Sts.) | 215-413-1951

(continued)

Dave & Buster's

Northeast Philly | Franklin Mills Mall | 1995 Franklin Mills Circle
(Woodhaven Rd.) | 215-632-0333
Plymouth Meeting | Plymouth Meeting Mall | 500 W. Germantown Pike
(bet. Hickory & Plymouth Rds.) | 610-832-9200
www.daveandbusters.com

"If you don't mind" a "circus" of "screaming" kids, "gamers" or
"bachelor/bachelorette parties", this "interactive" "arcade" chain
dishes out "upgraded" American "bar food" at a "fair price", and even
many "adults" insist the "entertainment value is top-notch"; cynics,
though, sniff "to work up an appetite, try getting a server's attention."

Davio's   *Italian/Steak*   25 25 25 $58

Rittenhouse | Provident Bank Bldg. | 111 S. 17th St. (bet. Chestnut &
Sansom Sts.) | 215-563-4810 | www.davios.com
A "wonderful respite" from "busy" Rittenhouse, this "primo" Northern
Italian steakhouse is the "epitome of class" and worth the "splurge"
thanks to "scrumptious", "well-prepared" food and an "extensive
wine list" in a historic bank building with "soaring ceilings" and an
"elegance only found in 1940s musicals"; the staff makes you feel
"like royalty" and helps you "impress" clients, rounding out an
altogether "awesome" experience.

Day by Day   ☑ *American/Eclectic*   23 14 20 $18

Rittenhouse | 2101 Sansom St. (21st St.) | 215-564-5540 |
www.daybydayinc.com
The "creative", "fresh" American-Eclectic breakfasts, lunches,
weekend brunches and "in-house desserts" are a "bargain" at this
"casual", longtime Rittenhouse BYO where an "efficient" staff ensures
that you get "back to work on time"; many say the "new decor" un-
veiled in spring 2010, featuring butcher-block tabletops, art photos
and a wall-size chalkboard, "rises to the level of the clever menu."

Del Frisco's   20 26 20 $69
Double Eagle Steak House   *Steak*

Avenue of the Arts | 1426-28 Chestnut St. (15th St.) | 215-246-0533 |
www.delfriscos.com
The "magnificent", high-ceilinged "old bank" building with "red
drapes", "marble columns" and "towering wine display" creates the
"wow factor" at this "macho" meatery chain link off the Avenue of
the Arts, where waitresses in "short skirts" deliver "buttery-tender
steaks that'll cost you a mint" to a "power crowd"; some dissenters
would rather "keep their money" in a "real bank" and lament "glitz
and glam come first", but for many, the "late-night" "fashion show
in the bar area" alone is a "reason to go."

Delmonico's Steakhouse   *Steak*   25 22 23 $63

Wynnefield | Hilton Philadelphia City Ave. | 4200 City Ave. (Stout Rd.) |
215-879-4000
Carnivores counsel "don't overlook" this "traditional" steakhouse in
the "recently remodeled" Hilton in Wynnefield, where "flavorful

FOOD DECOR SERVICE COST

steaks" and "tasty" sides are complemented by "fast service with a Disney smile" amid "relaxing", "modern" environs; the "bar menu" is a "great value", making it a favorite of many "locals."

Derek's *American* | 22 | 21 | 22 | $37 |

Manayunk | 4411 Main St. (bet. Gay & Levering Sts.) | 215-483-9400 | www.dereksrestaurant.com

Derek Davis' "reliably good", midpriced New American in Manayunk keeps rolling along with an "uncomplicated", yet "creative" menu featuring "fresh local ingredients" as well as "happy-hour specials" offered in the upstairs martini bar (the "place to be on a Saturday night") or on the sidewalk on a "warm summer night"; it all adds up to a "winning combination" that many deem a "must-return."

NEW Dettera *American* | 21 | 25 | 20 | $48 |

Ambler | 129 E. Butler Ave. (bet. Lindenwold & Ridge Aves.) | 215-643-0111 | www.dettera.com

"Ambler meets the 21st century" at this "*très chic*" "hot spot", "an oasis of sophistication" with "upscale", "imaginative" New American fare (at "$$$" "prices"), "interesting" wine list and "romantic" ambiance in the "upstairs" lounge (downstairs, the "high ceiling" may make it "difficult to hear your dining partners"); most laud the "first-rate" service, though a few find it "a little too stuffy for its own good."

Devil's Alley *BBQ* | 19 | 17 | 18 | $24 |

Rittenhouse | 1907 Chestnut St. (19th St.) | 215-751-0707 | www.devilsalleybarandgrill.com

For "a little hellish comfort food", fans descend on this "casual", "not-too-intimate" "joint" near Rittenhouse Square for its "unique spin on BBQ" ("hot damn") and other "reliably tasty" eats, and it's also a "great hangover breakfast option after a night from hell"; while some report that "down-to-earth" service runs "fast" or "slow", depending on the day ("guess the devil's in the details"), many recommend it for "brunch" or "happy hour."

Devil's Den ● *American* | 19 | 19 | 19 | $25 |

South Philly | 1148 S. 11th St. (Ellsworth St.) | 215-339-0855 | www.devilsdenphilly.com

"Oh, my, the beer" exclaim enthusiasts of this "downright chummy" South Philly "watering hole" offering "one of the greatest tap lists in the neighborhood" (plus an "impressive" bottle lineup) and "knowledgeable" service in a "cozy" space with exposed-brick walls and a working fireplace; the mid-Survey arrival of chef Alex Ureña (ex Pamplona of NYC) and his American gastropub menu may address demands for more "consistent" food, and perhaps outdate the Food score.

Devon Seafood Grill *Seafood* | 23 | 21 | 21 | $46 |

Rittenhouse | 225 S. 18th St. (bet. Locust & Walnut Sts.) | 215-546-5940 | www.devonseafood.com

"Straightforward seafood" at "reasonable prices" in a "spacious dining room" reels finatics into this Rittenhouse Square "favorite", a "safe" option with "helpful" service and a "good bar scene"; it's owned by Houlihan's but lacks a "chain feel", and though it "gets a little noisy at times", the "delicious" fin fare and "addictive" biscuits "quickly refocus your attention to where it should be."

Dilworthtown Inn *American* 25 | 26 | 26 | $63

West Chester | 1390 Old Wilmington Pike (bet. Brintons Bridge Rd. & Wilmington Pike) | 610-399-1390 | www.dilworthtown.com

Chester County's "go-to for significant events", this "old-fashioned" New American in a "beautiful" inn "setting" "out in the country" "has stood the test of time", as staffers "who care" deliver "perfectly prepared" cuisine in a "lovely", "dress-up" setting sans "kitsch"; though a few detect a "stuffy attitude" and warn that "you'll never forget the bill", most consider it a "wonderful dining experience" that's "worth the trek."

DiNardo's Famous Seafood *Seafood* 19 | 11 | 18 | $36

Old City | 312 Race St. (bet. 3rd & 4th Sts.) | 215-925-5115 | www.dinardos.com

"Crab freaks" and others "get down and dirty with hard-shell" crustaceans and "fried seafood" "basics" at this "family-friendly" maritimer in Old City, where it's "not fancy but they make you feel welcome"; some crabby critics blast the "tacky" "shack" and sniff "eh, not so famous anymore", but most feel it's "worth another trip."

Dining Car ●∅ *American* 19 | 13 | 16 | $17

Northeast Philly | 8826 Frankford Ave. (bet. Academy Rd. & Pennypack St.) | 215-338-5113 | www.thediningcar.com

Though it's set in an art deco–style "train dining car" in Northeast Philly, this 24-hour "classic" "feels like home, sweet home" to fans, offering "diner food" with a "modern twist" from a menu that "has something for everyone", "gut-busting treats" from the on-site bakery, "strong drinks" and "friendly" service; a few credit-worthy critics "don't like [the] cash-only policy", while others warn of long queues for "Sunday breakfast", but regulars report the "line moves fast."

Z Distrito *Mexican* 25 | 24 | 22 | $44

University City | 3945 Chestnut St. (40th St.) | 215-222-1657 | www.distritorestaurant.com

Iron Chef Jose Garces' "modern Mexican" "magnet" in University City delivers "out-of-this-world" *comida* in a "hyper-kinetic" "funhouse" setting on "two floors", complete with a "VW Bug" booth and wall of professional "wrestling masks"; groups of "Penn students" and others "go back again and again" to have their "eardrums shattered" over "creative signature drinks" and "inventive" tapas, which are brought to you by "outstandingly beautiful" servers; P.S. the $35 tasting menu is a "steal."

Divan Turkish Kitchen *Turkish* 20 | 16 | 18 | $29

Graduate Hospital | 918 S. 22nd St. (Carpenter St.) | 215-545-5790 | www.divanturkishkitchen.com

The "flavorful" "tastes of Istanbul" come in "generous" portions at this "unpretentious" Turkish-Med "off the beaten track" on a "residential corner" in G-Ho; the staff is "very good with youngsters", while the prices are "reasonable" – and those paying with cash get a "substantial discount" – plus, there's no corkage if you BYC Sundays–Thursdays, making it a good option for entertaining "out-of-town guests."

☑ Dmitri's *Greek*   24 | 13 | 19 | $33

NEW **Northern Liberties** | 944 N. Second St. (Laurel St.) | 215-592-4550 ⊄
Queen Village | 795 S. Third St. (Catharine St.) | 215-625-0556 ⊄
Rittenhouse | 2227 Pine St. (23rd St.) | 215-985-3680

Dmitri Chimes' "unpretentious" and "affordable" Hellenic tavernas are in a "league of their own", serving "simply prepared" "grilled seafood" and "Greek salads that would make Greece jealous"; claustrophobes quip that the "attentive" servers must be "size five or less" to navigate the "tight tables", and some grouse about "noise" that "reaches airport runway levels", but the "consistently fresh" fare "keeps 'em coming back for more", the Northern Liberties branch and Queen Village flagship are cash-only BYOs, while Fitler Square takes credit cards and serves wine and beer.

Dock Street ☒ *Pub Food*   21 | 17 | 15 | $23

University City | 701 S. 50th St. (Baltimore Ave.) | 215-726-2337 | www.dockstreetbeer.com

The "awesome" "brick-oven pizzas" and "trio fries" are "upstaged" only by the "innovative" microbrews "brewed on the premises" at this "little treasure" in West Philly; though some critics pan the service as "scattered" and clamor over the "noise" in the "warehouse"-like setting of the former firehouse, most agree it's "worth it for the food and casual atmosphere."

Doc Magrogan's Oyster House *Seafood*   17 | 20 | 19 | $33

West Chester | 117 E. Gay St. (bet. Matlack & Walnut Sts.) | 610-429-4046 | www.docmagrogans.com

The jury's hung on this "lively", "publike" downtown West Chester seafooder from the Kildare's orbit – fans are happy to "belly up to the bar" to "slurp" "excellent" oysters and laud the "buck-a-shuck" Monday night special as a "great deal"; foes find the fare "ho-hum", the service "mechanical" and the ambiance reminiscent of an "upscale Bennigan's."

NEW Doghouse *American*   - | - | - | I

Downingtown | 24 E. Lancaster Ave. (bet. Manor & Wallace Aves.) | 610-269-9381 | www.doghouseburgers.com

Craft beers and wine complement a "decent" menu of "good ol'" gourmet burgers at this modern American joint on the bank of the Brandywine River in Downingtown (adjacent to sister restaurant Firecreek), and though it's maybe "not a place where you want to sit and talk", it is "clean", and the stools that swing out from the counter are a novel touch; a hot-dog menu and park across the street make it more kid-friendly.

Dolce ⓈⓂ *Italian*   17 | 19 | 15 | $40

Old City | 241 Chestnut St. (3rd St.) | 215-238-9983 | www.dolcerestaurant.com

Fans wax "positive" about the "decent" Italian fare at this Old City eatery where the servers are "helpful, when they're able to hear you over the music" in the "glitzy", "floor-lit" space; critics, however, feel a "makeover" is in order, and lament that while "it was hot when it opened", it's now a "weekend" "scene" for the "bridge-and-tunnel crowd", with "underwhelming" eats and "poor" service.

NEW Doma *Japanese/Korean*   - | - | - | M

Logan Square | 1822 Callowhill St. (18th St.) | 215-564-1114

There's much to choose from at this tranquil BYO located in Logan Square, where the midpriced menu mixes Japanese specialties (uni appetizers, bento boxes), Korean staples (kimchi, kalbi) and combinations of the two cuisines – e.g. bibimbop rolls; the staff is well versed in the copious varieties of sushi prepared by two chefs working the counter.

Down Home Diner *Southern*   17 | 11 | 16 | $18

Chinatown | Reading Terminal Mkt. | 51 N. 12th St. (Filbert St.) | 215-627-1955

Jack McDavid's "reliable" "chow-down" is a "must stop for breakfast or lunch" at Reading Terminal Market, and his Southern "comfort food" ("scrapple, anyone?") and "creamy milkshakes" at "reasonable prices" are a "sinfully delicious" "reward" for shoppers "stocking up on fresh fruit and vegetables"; the "retro" setting with "cozy booths" is "family-friendly", and while a small chorus of negativists decry the "wildly inconsistent" fare, most feel it's "holding up well" after more than two decades.

Drafting Room *American*   16 | 14 | 19 | $30

Exton | Colonial 100 Shops | 635 N. Pottstown Pike (Ship Rd.) | 610-363-0521 | www.draftingroom.com

"So many beers and so little time" lament fans of this "totally suburban" New American tavern in Exton offering "lots of unusual" varieties, plus "pretty good" New American pub grub and "friendly" service, amid "utilitarian" surroundings; a few decry the "spotty execution" and "drab" decor, but it remains a "keeper on the casual dining rotation" of many "western suburbanites."

Duck Sauce Ⓜ *Chinese*   24 | 16 | 21 | $28

Newtown | 127 S. State St. (bet. Mercer & Penn Sts.) | 215-860-8873

Though Tony Huang's Bucks BYO might be "a little pricey" for some, fans attest the "broad menu" of "carefully prepared" Chinese and Pan-Asian cuisine "spoils you for the rest" of the Sino spots around; "friendly" service helps make up for the "tiny parking lot", "dark" lighting and "often long waits", and while a few cynics sniff that because "it's Newtown", it's "judged on a different scale", for most it is a "special place."

Du Jour
Cafe & Market *American*   18 | 15 | 16 | $26

NEW **Logan Square** | Commerce Sq. | 2001 Market St. (bet. 20th & 21st Sts.) | 215-735-8010 🗷
Haverford | Haverford Sq. | 379 Lancaster Ave. (bet. Station & Woodside Rds.) | 610-896-4556
www.dujourmarket.com

Main Line matrons in "Dior shades", "stay-at-home moms" and others head to this "cavernous" New American cafe/market in Haverford (while folks "working nearby" Logan Square patronize its weekday-only outlet) where there's "something for everyone", including "mouthwatering" salads, sandwiches and "naughty desserts"; the "museum cafeteria ambiance" works "if you're not looking for fancy", and though a few find it "a few dollars too expensive", the majority "leave satisfied."

Duling-Kurtz House &
Country Inn *Continental*   25 | 25 | 24 | $53

Exton | Duling-Kurtz House & Country Inn | 146 S. Whitford Rd. (Commerce Dr.) | 610-524-1830 | www.dulingkurtz.com

The "charming" "ambiance is king" at this Exton "country" inn "mainstay" in the "far western suburbs", which offers "consistently excellent" (and "pricey") Continental cuisine and "gentle" service in an "old-world" setting, "appropriate" for a "romantic" evening or "family special occasions", such as "grandma's birthday"; in sum, it's a "complete dining experience" – but, a few qualify, maybe "not an exciting one."

Earth Bread +
Brewery 🅼 *American*   21 | 17 | 18 | $23

Mount Airy | 7136 Germantown Ave. (Durham St.) | 215-242-6666 | www.earthbreadbrewery.com

"Delicious flatbread pizzas", a "list" of "great" "handcrafted" "brews" that's "longer than the menu" and "reasonable" prices are the signatures of this "crunchy" "green" brewpub "destination" in Mount Airy, where a "good attitude and atmosphere are every-where" in the "funky" space decorated with "salvaged furnishing"; the scene is "all families" at dinnertime before it morphs into a "grown-up" spot, and a few regulars lament that its growing "popu-larity" now means "ungodly" waits.

East Cuisine *Chinese/Japanese*   ▽ 21 | 13 | 19 | $27

Ambler | Broad Axe Shopping Ctr. | 851 W. Butler Pike (Skippack Pike) | 215-283-9797 | www.eastcuisine.com

"Solid" "sushi" and "consistently good" Chinese at "modest prices" can be found "under one roof" at this "multicultural" BYO "secret" in the Broad Axe Plaza strip mall; the "super-friendly" staff is "always obliging", and if some are turned off by the "wide-screen TV" in the dining room, there's always "takeout."

	FOOD	DECOR	SERVICE	COST

Effie's Ⓜ *Greek*

21 | 16 | 20 | $31

Washington Square West | 1127 Pine St. (Quince St.) | 215-592-8333 |
www.effiesrestaurant.com

You'll "get to know" your "seatmates" at this "tiny" Greek BYO in a
"quaint house" in Wash West, but that's ok because the "friendly"
servers treat you like "one of the family" while dishing out "down-
home goodness" that tastes like "someone's grandma is cooking in
the kitchen"; those who might chafe at the forced intimacy can "sit
outside" in the "cute courtyard."

Ekta *Indian*

- | - | - | I

Fishtown | 250 E. Girard Ave. (Marlborough St.) | 215-426-2277
NEW **Bryn Mawr** | 1003 W. Lancaster Ave. (Warner Ave.) |
610-581-7070 Ⓜ
www.ektaindianrestaurant.com

These BYO twins owned by a Tiffin alum win over "converts to Indian
food" with "delicious" takes on chicken tikka, vegetable samosas
and more; the Fishtown original is known primarily for delivery and
takeout (witness fans who "double park" out front), while the more
refined offshoot in Bryn Mawr draws with $8.95 buffet lunches.

El Azteca I Ⓩ *Mexican*

20 | 10 | 17 | $20

Washington Square West | 714 Chestnut St. (bet. 7th & 8th Sts.) |
215-733-0895

The prices are "so low, you feel like you're spending pesos" at this
plain-Jane Mexican cantina in Wash West, where the "above-
average" "standards" come in "huge" portions, and you can now
order drinks from a "limited" cocktail list or "BYO tequila and they
will make margaritas"; skeptics, though, sneer that their "Polish
grandmothers could make better" *comida* and liken the setting to a
"high school cafeteria."

El Camino Real ◑ *BBQ/Mexican*

21 | 18 | 19 | $23

Northern Liberties | 1040 N. Second St. (bet. Girard Ave. & Poplar St.) |
215-925-1110 | www.bbqburritobar.com

Enthusiasts explain that this Northern Liberties joint is "always
crowded" because owner Owen Kamihira (Bar Ferdinand) was
"smart enough to combine" Texas BBQ and Mexican border fare on
the menu – thus, "melt-in-your-mouth" "brisket" and "burritos"
(plus "vegetarian" items) can be washed down with "beers" and
"margaritas"; "low prices" make it "popular with the young", notwithstanding some gripes that "you'll starve to death" before the
"quirky" "hipster" servers "take your order."

Elephant & Castle ◑ *Pub Food*

11 | 13 | 13 | $26

Rittenhouse | Crowne Plaza Philadelphia Center City | 1800 Market St.
(18th St.) | 215-751-9977 | www.elephantcastle.com

Regulars recommend "stick with the fish 'n' chips or beef dip" at this
"workingman's" English-style pub in the Crowne Plaza on Market
Street, while detractors quip "eat before you get here", reflecting
the ambivalent response to the "ordinary" bar fare; many also pan
the service as "hit-or-miss", but defenders deem it "ok for a beer"

and a "game on one of the big-screen TVs", or cocktails "on the sidewalk in warm weather."

El Fuego *Californian/Mexican*　　　19 | 12 | 17 | $14

Rittenhouse | 2104 Chestnut St. (21st St.) | 215-751-1435
Washington Square West | 723 Walnut St. (8th St.) | 215-592-1901 ⊠
www.elfuegoburritos.com

The "flavorful", "healthy" Californian-Mexican grub is an "incredible
value" at these storefronts in Wash West (serving beer and wine)
and Rittenhouse Square (margaritas and sangria) where the counter
service is "fast", with "no hassle", and there's "great people-watching"
in the "fun, modern" digs; while some lament the "long lines" at
lunchtime, most say *gracias* to the chef for fare that's "infinitely
better" than many chain options.

NEW **El Rey** / *Mexican*　　　- | - | - | M

Rittenhouse | 2013 Chestnut St. (bet. 20th & 21st Sts.) | 215-563-3330 |
www.elreyrestaurant.com

Stephen Starr has raided Southern Californian and Mexican flea
markets to decorate this casual cantina in a former Rittenhouse
Square diner; the menu features Veracruz-style plates from chef
Dionicio Jimenez (ex Xochitl), the space throbs with an eclectic mix
of rock and blues, and the dim, sexy speakeasy in back, Ranstead
Room, boasts a drink lineup by NYC mixologist Sasha Petraske.

El Sarape *Mexican*　　　23 | 18 | 21 | $36

Blue Bell | 1380 Skippack Pike (DeKalb Pike) | 610-239-8667 |
www.elsarapebluebell.com

Los Sarapes *Mexican*

Chalfont | 17 Moyer Rd. (E. Butler Ave.) | 215-822-8858 |
www.lossarapes.com Ⓜ

Horsham | Horsham Center Sq. | 1116 Horsham Rd. (Limekiln Pike) |
215-654-5002 | www.lossarapeshorsham.com

Boosters rate this "upper-crust" suburban trio "top-shelf" for its
"authentic", "traditional" fare – "not the typical tacos and
burritos" – backed by an "astounding choice of tequilas"; there's a
"family feeling" in the "cozy" environs, and though Horsham and
Blue Bell are "small", "accommodating" staffers "manage to move
people in and out quickly."

Z **El Vez** *Mexican*　　　23 | 24 | 20 | $38

Washington Square West | 121 S. 13th St. (Sansom St.) |
215-928-9800 | www.elvezrestaurant.com

Holy guacamole cry fans of Stephen Starr's Mexican "ode to Elvis"
in Wash West that "knocks your socks off" with "excellent varia-
tions" on "traditional" foods plus margaritas that "sneak up on you
quickly" and have you taking "goofy pics at the photo booth" before
you know it; it's "hard to hold a conversation" (especially on a Friday
night) in the "theme-park" setting complete with a glittery "motor-
cycle on display over the bar", and while a few foes find it "tacky"
and "overpriced", it's the "favorite" option of many "for a fun
get-together with friends."

	FOOD	DECOR	SERVICE	COST

Epicurean, The *American*

20 | 16 | 19 | $33

Phoenixville | Village at Eland | 902-8 Village at Eland (Kimberton Rd.) | 610-933-1336 | www.epicureanrestaurant.com

"Solid, reliable" New American fare "without a bunch of hype", served by a "friendly" staff, is how fans describe this "old standard" in Phoenixville's Village at Eland, which has "jumped on the small-plates bandwagon" while still offering "real entrees" in "ample portions"; critics see it differently, deeming the fare just "average", the service "uneven", and warn that the tapas-style offerings can "add up to pricey meals."

Ernesto's 1521 Cafe 🅢 🅜 *Italian*

19 | 17 | 21 | $40

Rittenhouse | 1521 Spruce St. (bet. 15th & 16th Sts.) | 215-546-1521 | www.ernestos1521.com

It "feels like home" at this "reliable" Italian in a roomy "brownstone" across from the Kimmel Center, where owner Ernesto Salandria "oversees everything", and the service is "so efficient you never feel rushed" to make the curtain; it's easy to "relax" in the "quiet, calm environment", and the "tasty" fare is "well prepared", even if a few feel it "never quite wows"; BYO is allowed with a $5 corkage.

🆉 Estia *Greek*

25 | 24 | 23 | $53

Avenue of the Arts | 1405-07 Locust St. (bet. Broad & 15th Sts.) | 215-735-7700 | www.estiarestaurant.com

Choose from the "absolute freshest fish" that's "on display" in the "beautifully appointed" space at this Hellenic destination off the Avenue of the Arts, which transports you to a "taverna" in a "lovely" "Greek village" with "wonderful" fare and "powerful" ouzo, "dramatic", "rustic" decor and live bouzouki music on weekends; the "friendly" staff with "exotic" accents sets "the bar very high" as well, but euro-counters warn that "you pay for the freshness" of the food with tabs approaching "first-class airfare."

Eulogy Belgian Tavern ➊ *Belgian*

19 | 13 | 17 | $27

Old City | 136 Chestnut St. (2nd St.) | 215-413-1918 | www.eulogybar.com

At this Belgian "crowd-pleaser", the brew menu (300 bottles, 22 drafts) is "mind-boggling" to "serious and non-serious beer drinkers alike", but "knowledgeable" staffers are on hand to help you "wade through the tome", while the "tasty", "cost-effective" "pub fare" is "not a mere afterthought"; the "comfy dive" setting has a religious theme, including a second-floor "coffin" room, and while a few sniff that it's "more bar than restaurant", the majority agrees it's "worth a trip to Old City."

Fadó Irish Pub ➊ *Pub Food*

17 | 19 | 18 | $25

Rittenhouse | 1500 Locust St. (15th St.) | 215-893-9700 | www.fadoirishpub.com

Fans wish they "could sleep over" to enjoy an "Irish brunch" after a night of drinking at this "traditional" Rittenhouse Square pub, whose hours vary to accommodate early AM soccer games; you can "nestle" in one of the "dark-wood nooks" in the "mazy" space with your "decent" "Celtic" grub and "pint" of "Guinness", though regulars report that "it turns into a loud disco club Friday and Saturday nights."

Famous 4th Street Delicatessen *Deli*   24 | 14 | 19 | $22
South St. | 700 S. Fourth St. (Bainbridge St.) | 215-922-3274
NEW **Rittenhouse** | 38 S. 19th St. (Chestnut St.) | 215-568-3271
www.famous4thstreetdelicatessen.com
"Unless you can unhinge your jaw like a snake", the "obscenely" "awesome" sandwiches "can't fit in your mouth" claim cronies of this "politico"-heavy, "NYC"-style Queen Village deli institution and its Rittenhouse Square branch, where "glossy white subway tiles" line the "cramped" digs and the "humongous" helpings "piled higher than heaven" come with a "dose of attitude"; a few kvetch about the prices, but c'mon, you're guaranteed "leftovers."

Farmicia Ⓜ *Continental*   22 | 20 | 20 | $35
Old City | 15 S. Third St. (bet. Chestnut & Market Sts.) | 215-627-6274 | www.farmiciarestaurant.com
There are "lots of options for every type of eater", from "locavores" to "omnivores", at this Old City Continental from the Metropolitan Bakery folks, whose "commitment to sustainability" is reflected in the "well-prepared", "wholesome" "comfort food", which can be washed down with some "tasty tonics"; a "young, hip" staff mans the "bright", "airy" room, with windows that "open to the street in nice weather", and the atmosphere is at once "romantic and child-friendly"; it's BYO-friendly, except for parties of 11 or more.

NEW Fat Salmon *Japanese*   - | - | - | M
Washington Square West | 719 Walnut St. (Seventh St.) | 215-928-8881 | www.fatsalmonsushi.com
Popular, shoebox-size Wash West sushi haven Shinju has grown up, moving just off the square into a larger storefront – and rebranding with a new fish-friendly name; Jack Yoo's signature rolls and other midpriced fare are dished up in a modern dining room with white furnishings and a roomy sushi bar, and a pending liquor license will allow a sake selection.

Fayette Street Grille Ⓜ *American*   23 | 16 | 22 | $36
Conshohocken | 308 Fayette St. (bet. 3rd & 4th Sts.) | 610-567-0366 | www.fayettestreetgrille.com
Conshy cognoscenti commend the "delicious", "well-prepared" New American chow as "well worth the price" at this "low-key" "storefront" BYO on the "main drag", whose $34 prix fixes are "always a great value"; the digs are "adorable", and most agree the "only downside is how small it is", which means it "can get noisy" and "reservations are a good idea."

Fellini Cafe *Italian*   19 | 12 | 16 | $25
Ardmore | 31 E. Lancaster Ave. (bet. Cricket Ave. & Rittenhouse Pl.) | 610-642-9009 | www.fellini-cafe.net
"Expect to wait for a table" at this "little" Italian BYO in Ardmore that offers Main Liners a "huge menu" of "affordable" eats in "generous portions", served in "close quarters" with a "Brooklyn base-

ment" motif; critics compare the fare to "supermaket takeout", and slam the "silly" policy of "one entree per person" – "even two-year-olds" – but most agree it's one of the "best values" around, which is why it's "always crowded."

Fellini Cafe Newtown Square ⓜ *Italian*   22 | 13 | 19 | $31

Newtown Square | St. Albans Shopping Ctr. | 3541 West Chester Pike (Rte. 252) | 610-353-6131 | www.fellinicafenewtownsquare.com

"Large amounts" of "flavorful" food at "reasonable prices" mean there's usually a "line out the door" of this Italian BYO in Newtown Square, which is so snug "you can eat off the plate on the table next to you" (though the interior was recently "updated"); surveyors report that the once "brusque" service has become "more pleasant" and "kid-friendly."

Fergie's Pub ☻ *Pub Food*   16 | 13 | 16 | $23

Washington Square West | 1214 Sansom St. (bet. 12th & 13th Sts.) | 215-928-8118 | www.fergies.com

To its "dedicated followers", this "stalwart" Irish tap (run by a "hoot" of an owner) in Wash West is a far cry from "the many Disney-fied" pubs nearby, with "surprisingly good" grub and a "smart, low-key" staff pulling "pints of Guinness" and sparking interesting "chats because of the no-TV policy" in a setting with "no pretentions"; "excellent live music" on weekends seals the deal for many.

Fez Moroccan Cuisine *Moroccan*   19 | 20 | 20 | $41

South St. | 620 S. Second St. (bet. Bainbridge & South Sts.) | 215-925-5367 | www.fezrestaurant.com

"Take a trip to Morocco" at this "romantic" spot off South Street offering vegetarian-friendly seven-course prix fixe dinners ($25), "hookahs", "low seats" and "weekend belly dancers"; detractors find the fare "underwhelming", the service "slow" and the room "too dark", but defenders declare it a "great value."

Field House *American*   ▽ 12 | 13 | 13 | $22

Chinatown | 1150 Filbert St. (12th St.) | 215-629-1520 | www.fieldhousephilly.com

You can have a "field day" of "social interaction" at this "lively" sports bar with "TVs everywhere" across from Reading Terminal Market, touted by fans as a "great place to watch a game" or just "gather with friends"; while many find the fare "nothing special" and chide a staff that seems to "think rudeness is a plus", at least the "prices are not out of this world."

Figs ⓜ⇋ *Mediterranean*   23 | 16 | 20 | $31

Fairmount | 2501 Meredith St. (25th St.) | 215-978-8440 | www.figsrestaurant.com

A "delightful" stop before or after the Museum of Art, this "inviting", cash-only Moroccan-style BYO on a "sun-drenched corner" of Fairmount offers an "affordable menu" of Med fare "oozing with flavor", including what some say is the "best brunch in the city", served by "personable" folks; the "unassuming" space is "small", and aficionados advise it's "impossible to park", so "walk or take a taxi."

	FOOD	DECOR	SERVICE	COST

Fiorello's Café *Italian*   ▽ 17 | 11 | 16 | $36

West Chester | 730 E. Gay St. (bet. N. Bolmar St. & Westtown Rd.) |
610-430-8941 | www.fiorellosinwestchester.com

"Families" "with kids" groove on the "pastas", "brick-oven pizzas"
and other Southern Italian fare at this Downtown West Chester
cafe, where the $13.95 "lunchtime buffet is a terrific deal"; although
the surroundings are "a bit tight" and some say the eats can be "inconsistent", the suspense "only adds to the fun" for many.

NEW Firecreek *American*   20 | 25 | 18 | $46

Downingtown | 20 E. Lancaster Ave. (Brandywine Ave.) | 610-269-6000 |
www.firecreek-restaurant.com

A "trendy" interior in an "architecturally interesting" "converted old
mill" by the Brandywine River sets the stage for "tasty" fare from an
"open kitchen" at this Downingtown New American, where many
"look forward to spring and sitting outside"; a number grouse that
you "shell out a lot of coin" for a "limited" menu that "doesn't light
any fires" and "enthusiastic but amateurish" service, and surmise
that "if the food catches up to the surroundings, it will be outstanding."

NEW fish *Seafood*   25 | 19 | 22 | $50

Graduate Hospital | 1708 Lombard St. (17th St.) | 215-545-9600 |
www.fishphilly.com

Mike Stollenwerk's "creative" preparations of fin fare are "beyond
compare" at his "adorable" "boutique" seafooder in a Graduate
Hospital storefront; in addition to offering some of the "best-tasting
fish in the city", he reels in afishionados with "reasonable wines by
the glass", "knowledgeable" service and a "relaxed" vibe in the
"sparsely decorated", "candlelit" setting.

Five Guys *Burgers*   22 | 9 | 16 | $11

Rittenhouse | 1527 Chestnut St. (15th St.) | 215-972-1375
Warminster | 864 W. Street Rd. (York Rd.) | 215-443-5489
Clifton Heights | 500 W. Baltimore Ave. (Delmar Dr.) | 610-622-5489
Glen Mills | Keystone Plaza Shopping Ctr. | 1810 Wilmington Pike
(Woodland Dr.) | 610-358-5489
Bala Cynwyd | 77 E. City Ave. (Monument Rd.) | 610-949-9005
Wayne | 253 E. Swedesford Rd. (W. Valley Rd.) | 610-964-0214
www.fiveguys.com

"The greasier, the better" say fans of this national "made-to-order"
chain where "anything more than a single patty with fixings" (which
are free, "so take advantage") is "gluttony", and when you add
"enormous" portions of "thick-cut" "fries" and "free peanuts", your
"cholesterol count" may go up "by 40 points"; there's "no atmosphere", but most agree "you can't beat the prices or fast service."

NEW 500º *Burgers*   - | - | - | I

Rittenhouse | 1504 Sansom St. (15th St.) | 215-568-5000 |
www.500degrees.com

Philly's burgeoning burger craving has another enabler with this
Rittenhouse storefront from the folks behind Square landmark Rouge;
the simple menu includes topped burgers, three kinds of fries and

milkshakes made from locally sourced Bassetts ice cream, and crowds sit at long, wooden tables in an industrial-vibe seating area.

Flavor *Thai*   ∇ 19 | 15 | 18 | $31

Wayne | 372 W. Lancaster Ave. (Conestoga Rd.) | 610-688-5853 | www.flavorwayne.com

Fans can "always find something" on the menu at this "reliable" Thai BYO in "pleasant", "modern" quarters in Wayne; though a few say "service can be slow", "lunch is a good deal" and, after all, it's "something different" in this part of the Main Line.

Fleming's Prime Steakhouse *Steak*   24 | 23 | 24 | $62

Radnor | 555 E. Lancaster Ave. (Radnor-Chester Rd.) | 610-688-9463 | www.flemingssteakhouse.com

"Discerning" "carnivores" come for "flawless steaks" at this "leathery masculine steakhouse" chain link where "top-notch servers will help when you "get lost just reading" the "wine list"; the "large, but not impersonal" space is "always crowded" and "noisy", and there's a "good bar scene after work"; P.S. "bring lots of money", unless you opt for the "happy-hour specials" or Sunday prime rib deal.

Fogo de Chão *Brazilian/Steak*   24 | 22 | 25 | $60

Avenue of the Arts | Widener Bldg. | 1337 Chestnut St. (bet. Broad & Juniper Sts.) | 215-636-9700 | www.fogodechao.com

For a "meatfest worthy of a full month's penance", carnivores recommend this "upscale" Avenue of the Arts Brazilian rodizio-style steakhouse where "gauchos" are "always at your elbow" offering "deliciously cooked meats", which are complemented by an "immense salad bar", an "astonishingly deep selection of wines" and "tasty desserts, for those who still have room left"; most concur it's "an experience foodies need to try at least once" – except "vegans."

⊠NEW Fond ⊠Ⓜ *American*   27 | 18 | 26 | $44

South Philly | 1617 E. Passyunk Ave. (Tasker St.) | 215-551-5000 | www.fondphilly.com

Virtually all agree this "bright" BYO "star" in a "high-end storefront" on South Philly's "ever-growing East Passyunk strip" is a "can't-miss experience", thanks to Le Bec-Fin alum Lee Styer's "creative", "excellent" New American cuisine and Jessie Prawlucki's breads and desserts, for which "your mouth will keep thanking you"; "superb" service helps make up for the "noise", but "space is limited", so be sure to snag a reservation.

⊠ Fork *American*   24 | 21 | 23 | $48

Old City | 306 Market St. (bet. 3rd & 4th Sts.) | 215-625-9425 | www.forkrestaurant.com

The good tines roll at Old City's "go-to" "crown jewel", where Terence Feury's "delectable", "highly satisfying" New American cuisine, including "house-cured charcuterie" and "jaw-dropping" Wednesday night $40 "feasts", is served by a "knowledgeable" staff in a "fashionably chic" setting with "just enough noise"; fork etc. next door has a "wonderful array" of "take-out selections", as well as tables for casual noshing.

🡲 Fountain Restaurant *Continental/French* 28 | 28 | 28 | $89

Logan Square | Four Seasons Hotel | 1 Logan Sq. (Benjamin Franklin Pkwy.) | 215-963-1500 | www.fourseasons.com

"When you want to impress" someone, the Four Seasons' "swish" main room (No. 1 for Decor and Service in this Survey) is the "gold standard" for "luxurious" "power" dining, where Rafael Gonzalez's Continental-French cuisine will "blow you away", as will the "unparalleled" service "fit for a king and queen"; jackets are required and it'll "cost you more than three coins" in Logan Square's fountain outside, but most agree it's "worth every penny" and "calorie."

Fountain Side *American/Italian* 20 | 15 | 20 | $34

Horsham | 537 Easton Rd. (Meetinghouse Rd.) | 215-957-5122 | www.fountainsidegrill.com

Ignore the "statutes that greet you" at this Italian-American BYO in a Horsham strip mall, offering "huge portions" of "AAA" seafood and other *mangiare* from an "extensive menu"; "friendly" service and a "roomy, brightly lit" space are pluses, and while a few cynics find "nothing outstanding" about it, many others attest it's "nice enough for the neighborhood."

Four Dogs Tavern *American* 20 | 19 | 20 | $28

West Chester | 1300 W. Strasburg Rd. (Telegraph Rd.) | 610-692-4367 | www.marshaltoninn.com

You might need a bloodhound to "find" this "rustic" "countryside" bar outside of West Chester, where there's "something for just about anyone" on the "varied", yet "unpretentious" New American menu; the "bartenders" are "always ready to help out" and "really chill" airs are conducive to a "hangout", whether there's "laughter dancing off the copper ceiling tiles" or "music on the back patio during the summer" (where you can "bring your dog").

Four Rivers *Chinese* ▽ 26 | 7 | 20 | $21

Chinatown | 936 Race St. (bet. 9th & 10th Sts.) | 215-629-8385

Devotees declare "you have no excuse for getting mediocre Chinese" with this "reasonably priced" Chinatown BYO around, serving "authentic" Sichuan fare "flowing with flavor" at "reasonable prices"; the service is "not overwhelming", and regulars learn to "ignore the decor", but almost all agree it's "well worth a drive from the suburbs."

Fox & Hound ❶ *Pub Food* 11 | 11 | 12 | $23

Rittenhouse | 1501 Spruce St. (15th St.) | 215-732-8610
King of Prussia | Plaza at King of Prussia Mall | 160 N. Gulph Rd. (bet. DeKalb Pike & Mall Blvd.) | 610-962-0922
www.totent.com

With "more TVs than your average Best Buy", these "warehouse-y" sports bars in Rittenhouse and KoP are "always jumpin'" during games and become "a sea of red" during baseball season; scores of boo birds, though, bash the grub as "hit-or-miss", suggest "ordering beers two at a time" because service can be "slow" and wonder what a "Steelers bar" is doing in Philly.

	FOOD	DECOR	SERVICE	COST

NEW Franco's Osteria *Italian*
- | - | - | M

Wynnefield | Presidential City Apts. | 3900 City Ave. (I-76) | 215-473-3900
Franco Faggi has set up shop on the ground floor of the Presidential in Wynnefield (across the Schuylkill from his former spot, Franco's Trattoria) with this warmly decorated Italian; besides modest-priced eats – and a wood-fired oven in the dining room – there's a civilized, grown-up-friendly bar catering to the Bala Cynwyd business crowd.

Franco's Trattoria *Italian*
22 | 19 | 22 | $39

East Falls | 4116 Ridge Ave. (Kelly Dr.) | 215-438-4848 | www.francostrattoria.net
Nestled in East Falls, this "old-school Italian" is a "great meeting place between Center City and the suburbs", offering "fabulous" fare at "reasonable prices" and "accommodating" service; a "change of ownership" has fans hoping the new team "doesn't change anything."

Freight House, The *American*
16 | 20 | 15 | $48

Doylestown | Doylestown SEPTA Station | 194 W. Ashland St. (Clinton Ave.) | 215-340-1003 | www.thefreighthouse.net
"Swanky for Doylestown", this "energetic" New American in the SEPTA station tries to "appeal to the masses" with an "enjoyable" vibe and bar scene, but many find the fare "underwhelming" and feel the service doesn't "live up to the setting"; late Thursdays–Saturdays it goes the "pickup joint" route, drawing a "blend of hot young things and dirty old men" that "makes it great" for "people-watching."

Friday Saturday Sunday *American*
24 | 19 | 22 | $43

Rittenhouse | 261 S. 21st St. (bet. Locust & Spruce Sts.) | 215-546-4232 | www.frisatsun.com
A "standby with staying power", Weaver Lilley's circa-1973 "quaint" and "quirky" Traditional American "institution" near Rittenhouse Square still "delivers" "old standards" such as the "lip-licking good" cream of mushroom soup, a "well-priced" wine list and "efficient" service from a staff with "character"; drinks in the "sexy, intimate" tank bar upstairs are a "must" for many.

From the Boot *Italian*
21 | 15 | 19 | $29

NEW Ambler | 110 E. Butler Ave. (York St.) | 215-646-0123
Lafayette Hill | 517 Germantown Pike (Kerper Rd.) | 610-834-8680
www.fromtheboot.com
"Put your name" on the waiting list and brace yourself for "daunting" waits at these "hopping" Montco "red-sauce" Italians where "everything "tastes homemade" and "no one leaves hungry"; many recommend the "down-home" Lafayette Hill "strip-center" original (which is BYO without corkage) over the somewhat "barren" (but convenient to theaters) Ambler outpost.

Fuji Mountain ● *Japanese*
20 | 17 | 19 | $30

Rittenhouse | 2030 Chestnut St. (bet. 20th & 21st Sts.) | 215-751-0939 | www.fujimt.com
This "bare-bones" Japanese near Rittenhouse Square is the "go-to" sushi house of many, thanks to "friendly" "cooks" who deliver

"huge", "yummy" "rolls" "made with care", and while it's not the "cheapest", cronies contend that's "not where you'd want to get raw fish", anyway; though a minority claims it's "not worth going out of your way", they're outnumbered by those who think it "delivers value for the price."

Full Plate Café, A *Eclectic* ∇ 19 | 17 | 21 | $17

Northern Liberties | 1009 Bodine St. (George St.) | 215-627-4068 | www.afullplate.com

"Show up hungry" advise aficionados at this Southern-accented Eclectic BYO in Northern Liberties, which dishes out "really full plates" of "fresh", vegetarian-friendly "comfort food" at "great prices"; the "unpretentious" setting may not "impress a date", but the "relaxed", "hippieish" airs make it a fine spot "to chill with friends over a long meal."

Funky Lil' Kitchen ⑤Ⓜ *American* ∇ 25 | 16 | 21 | $46

Pottstown | 232 King St. (Penn St.) | 610-326-7400 | www.funkylilkitchen.com

Michael Falcone's "quirky" BYO destination "tucked away" in Pottstown "never ceases to amaze and amuse" fans willing to make the "drive" from "Center City" for his "bold", "innovative" New American creations emphasizing "farm-fresh ingredients"; it occupies a small space decorated with antique pie plates and a curtain of silverware, so "be sure to have a reservation", and tote your own loaf because "they don't do bread", even though "his sauces are worth sopping up to the last drop."

FuziOn Ⓜ *Asian* 21 | 16 | 20 | $31

Worcester | Center Point Shopping Ctr. | 2960 Skippack Pike (Valley Forge Rd.) | 610-584-6958 | www.fuzion-restaurant.com

"Reliable", "well-prepared" French-influenced Asian fusion cookery is the hallmark of this BYO located in a "strip mall" near Skippack, where "friendly" staffers "never miss a beat" in the "roomy", high-ceilinged space featuring a wrought-iron chandelier; there's also "nice dining on the patio", plus "plenty of on-site parking", making it a "solid dinner selection" for suburbanites.

Gables at Chadds Ford, The Ⓜ *American* 23 | 22 | 22 | $45

Chadds Ford | 423 Baltimore Pike (Brintons Bridge Rd.) | 610-388-7700 | www.thegablesatchaddsford.com

Jack McFadden's "got the magic touch" at his "atmospheric" New American housed in a "retrofitted" circa-1897 dairy barn in the Brandywine Valley, where "fresh choices" abound on the "fabulous" menu and the wine program is aided by a BYO option at only $5 a bottle; for many, the "alfresco" patio, "enclosed within an old stone wall" and boasting a waterfall, is "in a league of its own."

NEW Garces Trading Company *American* - | - | - | I

Washington Square West | 1111-13 Locust St. (11th St.) | 215-574-1099 | www.garcestradingcompany.com

This latest American concept from Jose Garces (Amada, Chifa, Distrito, Tinto, Village Whiskey), located in Washington Square

West's Western Union Building, combines a cafe, wine shop and grocery store all under one roof; patrons can dine casually in a center seating area or browse the cases for charcuterie, oils, coffee, bread and prepared foods for takeout.

Gaya *Korean*

| - | - | - | M |

Blue Bell | 1002 Skippack Pike (Valley Rd.) | 215-654-8300 | www.gayarestaurant.com

Lots of "Korean families" and others head to this kalbiteria in Blue Bell, where you cook your own meats on a tabletop "smokeless BBQ" or order "authentic" dishes from the kitchen, and the "extensive" array of "banchan" (sides) leads some to eschew "appetizers"; while a few feel "like outsiders" amid the mostly "Asian" clientele, the "exemplary" staff "tries to make you feel comfortable", and a "nice, unusual selection of spirits" can also help break the ice.

Geechee Girl Rice Café Ⓜ *Southern*

| 21 | 16 | 20 | $32 |

Germantown | 6825 Germantown Ave. (Carpenter Ln.) | 215-843-8113 | www.geecheegirlricecafe.com

"Enjoyable", "authentic" "Low Country" cooking with an emphasis on "locally grown" ingredients attracts fans to Valerie Erwin's "spare" Germantown BYO that's bursting with a "down-home feel", thanks to "family photos" gracing the walls and "warm, welcoming" service (albeit at a "slow" pace more in tempo with the "Carolina coast"); most find the "unique" experience "great for the heart and soul."

NEW Gemelli 🅾❧ *Italian*

| 23 | 17 | 20 | $38 |

Narberth | 232 Woodbine Ave. (Iona Ave.) | 610-660-0160 | www.gemellinarberth.com

A "true bistro with personality", this "tiny" French-influenced Italian "gem" in Narberth from Clark Gilbert (ex Taquet) rises "head and shoulders above" the Main Line BYO "competition" according to fans, who fete the "solid, well-done" fare and "warm, friendly" hospitality offered in a "comfortable", "informal" setting; despite a few grumbles about the "noise" and "long waits", most concur that it's "a neighborhood joint worth going to."

General Lafayette Inn & Brewery *American*

| 18 | 20 | 18 | $28 |

Lafayette Hill | The General Lafayette Inn | 646 Germantown Pike (Church Rd.) | 610-941-0600 | www.generallafayetteinn.com

"Step back into Colonial times" at this "period inn and brewpub" in Lafayette Hill, where "it's all about" the "fabulous ales brewed on-site" and "ok" grub served in an "old-world" setting with a "big old fireplace" that makes it "cozy in the winter" and, legend has it, a "resident ghost"; while a few sniff it's the "kind of place you might bring your aunt or grandmother", for most, the "friendly vibe", "reasonable" prices and "awesome brews" make it "worth a trip."

General Warren Inne 🅾 *American*

| 25 | 26 | 25 | $53 |

Malvern | General Warren Inne | Old Lancaster Hwy. (Warren Ave.) | 610-296-3637 | www.generalwarren.com

Whether you're getting "romantic" with your "spouse" or feting your "grandmother on her birthday", fans tout this "elegant special-occasion" spot in Malvern set in a "beautiful Revolutionary War building" full of "Colonial charm", where "interesting preparations" of Traditional American fare (including "beef Wellington" that "kicks the proverbial booty") and a "great" "wine selection" are served by a "caring" staff; the consensus is "you won't be disappointed."

Geno's Steaks ●≢ *Cheesesteaks*
| 18 | 7 | 13 | $12 |

South Philly | Italian Mkt. | 1219 S. Ninth St. (Passyunk Ave.) | 215-389-0659 | www.genossteaks.com

An eclectic crowd that includes "tourists", "clubgoers" and "EMTs" heads to Joey Vento's "garishly lit" 24-hour Ninth and Passyunk "sangwitch" "mecca"; "read the sign" and order "in English", then stand among the "star pics" to snarf cheesesteaks "wit 'wiz'" or "wit provolone", and wind up with "sauce dripping" down your sleeve; "service with a snarl" is "part of the Brotherly Love experience", and while a few contrarians say *"otras mejor"*, for many devotees it's as "serious as communion."

Georges' Ⓜ *Eclectic*
| 22 | 22 | 20 | $52 |

Wayne | 503 W. Lancaster Ave. (Conestoga Rd.) | 610-964-2588 | www.georgesonthemainline.com

For those seeking "Center City" dining in a Main Line shopping center, Le Bec-Finner Georges Perrier's "clubby" Eclectic in an "airy" faux-farmhouse setting is "just the ticket", offering "well-prepared, but not daring" fare served by a "knowledgeable" staff that runs like a "well-oiled machine"; the mood is "pleasant" in the three "small" dining rooms, while the "more casual", "friendly-feeling" bar is a "bargain" and home to "one of the best burgers in the suburbs."

ⓩ Gilmore's ⓏⓂ *French*
| 28 | 24 | 27 | $56 |

West Chester | 133 E. Gay St. (bet. Matlack & Walnut Sts.) | 610-431-2800 | www.gilmoresrestaurant.com

You "always feel well cared for and well fed" at Peter Gilmore's "plush" French BYO "destination" in West Chester, where his "exquisite" "epicurean delights" and "solicitous" service from a "professional" staff "add up to a first-rate" experience that transports you to "France" and "that little place in the valley that everyone whispers about"; it takes "three to four weeks' advance notice" to book a table in the "compact" townhouse space, but almost all agree it's "well worth the wait"; P.S. the $35, four-course feast served Tuesday–Thursdays is a "genuine bargain."

Girasole *Italian*
| 21 | 21 | 22 | $55 |

Avenue of the Arts | 1410 Pine St. (Broad St.) | 215-732-2728 | www.girasolephilly.com

Fans of this "family-operated" Italian just off the Avenue of the Arts call it an "unsung" "hero" that's "never crowded and deserves to be", for dishes such as the "wonderful salt-baked bronzino", "splendid" crudos and "to-die-for homemade pastas"; an "efficient" staff mans the "over-the-top" room dripping with "Versace", and while a few dissenters find it "too pricey", the $35 nightly early-bird makes it a "perfect pre-theater venue" for many.

	FOOD	DECOR	SERVICE	COST

Giwa 🖼 *Korean*   23 | 13 | 19 | $16

Rittenhouse | 1608 Sansom St. (bet. 16th & 17th Sts.) |
215-557-9830

Seoulmates swear the "bibimbop is the thing to order" at this
"shoebox-size" Korean "fast-food stop" in Rittenhouse, where "long
lines" form at "lunch" for "healthy, delicious" fare that "won't blow
your budget", served by a "friendly" staff at the counter; because it
"feels like eating in a Cosi", many cognoscenti opt for "takeout",
while others "come for dinner, when it's fairly empty."

Gnocchi ⇱ *Italian*   19 | 15 | 20 | $30

South St. | 613 E. Passyunk Ave. (bet. Bainbridge & South Sts.) |
215-592-8300

"Bring a big appetite" to this "small", "cozy" Italian BYO off South
Street where the "yummy" "namesake food" is some of the "best in
Philly", and the rest of the "reasonably priced", "old-school" menu
(including $30 four-course prix fixes) is "above average"; it's usually
"loud and crowded", and while it saw a slip in ratings, it's still the
"go-to any day of the week" for many.

Golden Pheasant Inn 🅜 *French*   23 | 24 | 23 | $47

Erwinna | Golden Pheasant Inn | 763 River Rd. (Dark Hollow Rd.) |
610-294-9595 | www.goldenpheasant.com

Some say the ride along "one of the most beautiful stretches" of
River Road alone is "worth the trip" to this "secluded" Erwinna
French, but "foodies" come for the Faure family's "skillfully
prepared" "old-time standards" (including the bargain $22,
three-course prix fixe Sunday brunch), which come with a side of
"romantic" ambiance in a "quaint", "historic inn" setting; it's "not
the easiest place to get to", but "you can stay the night" in one
of six guestrooms.

Gold Standard Café *American*   ▽ 17 | 16 | 20 | $19

West Philly | 4800 Baltimore Ave. (48th St.) | 215-727-8247 |
www.abbracciorestaurant.com

"All guests are warmly welcomed" at this "neat" BYO revival of a
West Philly institution, which now puts out "reasonably priced" New
American "comfort food" and "addictive sweets" in "homey" digs
with a fireplace from morning until dinnertime; while middling
scores reflect the sentiment that it's "fine, not great", many nonetheless appreciate its "commitment" to the neighborhood, and insist its "sincerity makes up for what glitches there are."

Golosa 🖼🅜⇱ *Dessert*   ▽ 26 | 21 | 27 | $16

South Philly | 806 S. Sixth St. (Catharine St.) | 215-925-1003 |
www.golosacafe.com

"Unique" "artisanal bon bons", "cups of rich chocolate" and
other "decadent" treats at this "tiny but adorable" South Philly
dessertery are the "perfect way to end an evening" for many
chocoholics; Tuscan-born owner Fabio Scarpelli is "happy to chat
with you" as he provides "doting" service, the "cherry on top" of
a "delightful experience."

	FOOD	DECOR	SERVICE	COST

Good Dog ❶ *Pub Food* — 22 | 14 | 18 | $22

Rittenhouse | 224 S. 15th St. (bet. Locust & Walnut Sts.) |
215-985-9600 | www.gooddogbar.com

A "mix of suits and messengers" comes, sits, stays for the "unbelievable" "burgers" with "Roquefort cheese oozing out of the middle"
and the "wonderful selection of draughts" at this tri-level
Rittenhouse Square "watering hole" ("dive bar" to some) where
wags surmise the "staff must have a tattoo requirement"; it doesn't
take reservations, so cognoscenti counsel "go for lunch", for "you'll
never squeeze in for dinner or later", and keep in mind that after
9 PM, no one under 21 is permitted.

Grace Tavern ❶ *American* — 21 | 13 | 18 | $21

Graduate Hospital | 2229 Grays Ferry Ave. (23rd St.) | 215-893-9580 |
www.gracetavern.com

A "chill hangout" that many recommend "for lunch or dinner when you
don't have a lot of cash", this "nicely cleaned and buffed" "old"
"neighborhood pub" in G-Ho is "one of the city's best-kept secrets",
serving New American grub with a Big Easy accent (including "addictive" blackened green beans), as well as an "excellent beer list"; the
"interesting" staff has time to "regale you" with "witty comments" and
tales of "bad life choices" because it's "rarely crazy busy."

NEW Green Eggs Café *American* — ∇ 26 | 23 | 21 | $20

South Philly | 1306 Dickinson St. (Clarion St.) | 215-226-3447 |
www.greeneggscafe.net

You won't find any green eggs (or Sam-I-Am) at this South Philly
cafe, but you will see a "neighborhood crowd" that's "fun to watch"
tucking into inexpensive, "fresh, tasty" American breakfast, brunch
and lunch fare daily until 4 PM (though coffee sippers can linger
until 7 PM) in a "cute", airy dining room featuring comfy sofas, a
flat-screen and a fireplace; a few report it's still "working out the
kinks in service", but most "welcome" its arrival on the scene.

Grey Lodge Pub ❶ *Pub Food* — 19 | 15 | 18 | $20

Northeast Philly | 6235 Frankford Ave. (bet. Harbison Ave. &
Robbins St.) | 215-825-5357 | www.greylodge.com

"With "lots of malty winners", this bi-level American tap in the
Northeast is all about the "phenomenal beer selection", although it
also gets props for "good pub grub", including "great mussels", tasty
"tomato pie" and "cheesesteaks", which can be ordered in the "casual" first-floor space or the "more refined" upstairs room; though a
few sniff at the "stereotypical" scene, most applaud the "committed
ownership" for bringing this "oasis" to a neighborhood that
lacks "quality pubs."

Gullifty's ❶ *American* — 15 | 14 | 17 | $26

Rosemont | 1149 Lancaster Ave. (bet. Franklin & Montrose Aves.) |
610-525-1851 | www.gulliftys.com

"Family place" by "day", "college bar" by "night", this "sprawling"
Main Line "staple" is known for its "plentiful beer selection", "solid,
above-average bar food", cool "outside bar" and "hit-or-miss" ser-

vice from "peppy" "college girls" ("Go, 'Nova"); after more than 35 years, many say it's "in need of a face-lift", but all agree that as long as you "don't look for gourmet here", "you'll be fine."

Gypsy Saloon *American/Italian*

| 22 | 17 | 18 | $37 |

West Conshohocken | 128 Ford St. (1st Ave.) | 610-828-8494 |
www.gypsysaloon.com

Regulars "keep coming back" for the "delicious" "specialty" "lobster mac 'n' cheese" and other "reliably good" eats at this "colorful" Italian-American in West Conshy; "friendly and comfortable", it "rocks" for "lunch" as well as "happy hour", when martinis in "huge glasses" fuel the "energy" that entertains "without making you crazy."

Half Moon Saloon ☒ *American*

| 20 | 17 | 18 | $31 |

Kennett Square | 108 W. State St. (Union St.) | 610-444-7232 |
www.halfmoonrestaurant.com

This "funky" Kennett Square New American "hangout" is a "pleasant surprise" to many, serving "exotic" "game" for "adventurous" palates as well as more "traditional" fare to complement an "incredible beer selection"; the skies are visible from the "lovely gardenlike" rooftop greenhouse, which works for a "date" or "girls' night out."

Ha Long Bay *Vietnamese*

| ∇ 21 | 11 | 17 | $21 |

Bryn Mawr | 816 W. Lancaster Ave. (Bryn Mawr Ave.) |
610-525-8883

Phonatics get their "pho fix" at this "plain" BYO next to the Bryn Mawr cinema, where the "carefully made" Vietnamese cuisine "does the job" for a "reasonable price"; though some say it lacks "pizzazz" and fault the staff for "forgetful" lapses, most agree it's a "very good value" and a "great place before or after a movie."

Han Dynasty *Chinese*

| 24 | 17 | 20 | $24 |

NEW **Old City** | 108 Chestnut St. (S. Front St.) | 215-922-1888
Exton | 260 N. Pottstown Pike (Waterloo Blvd.) | 610-524-4002
Royersford | Limerick Square Shopping Ctr. | 70 Buckwalter Rd.
(Rte. 422) | 610-792-9600
www.handynasty.net

"Quirky" "raconteur" Han Chiang and crew will discourage you from ordering off the "American" side of the Chinese menus at his "tasteful, modern" BYO trio, so "be brave" and let them "steer" you to "divine" Taiwanese and Sichuan delights with varied degrees of spiciness – if you want, they'll make it "so hot it makes a towering inferno look like a matchstick"; purists praise it as the "real thing" – and a "welcome alternative to a sea of fortune cookie-cutter" competitors.

Hank's Place ⊄ *Diner*

| 21 | 13 | 20 | $17 |

Chadds Ford | 1410 Baltimore Pike (Creek Rd.) | 610-388-7061 |
www.hanks-place.net

"Interesting local folk", "Wyeth"-seeking tourists and others head to this Chadds Ford "landmark" for what many call the "best breakfast in the Brandywine Valley" – "yummy", "down-home cooking" with a Greek diner touch but "without the stainless steel"; a few grouse about "too many high-end vehicles" in the "parking lot", but most agree it offers a "bang for the buck like nowhere else", and a recent enlargement may alleviate notorious weekend lines.

Happy Rooster ⊠ *Pub Food* 18 | 15 | 18 | $42

Rittenhouse | 118 S. 16th St. (Sansom St.) | 215-963-9311 |
www.thehappyrooster.com

This "divine dive" bar on a "corner" near Rittenhouse Square underwent a mid-Survey chef change (which may outdate the Food score), and loyalists hope Jason Goodenough and his "innovative" Franco-American fare will provide the "wake-up call" some critics say it needed; the "great drinks" might "keep you there all night", anyway.

Hard Rock Cafe *American* 13 | 21 | 15 | $29

Chinatown | 1113-31 Market St. (12th St.) | 215-238-1000 |
www.hardrock.com

"Awesome" "music" memorabilia is the main lure for many at this Chinatown outpost of the "loud" "tourist" haven; while "kids enjoy" the "loud", "fun" atmosphere, most grown-ups shrug "seen one, seen 'em all" and are left to wonder why "overpay" for "hardly rockin' food" (aside from "good" "burgers") when "Reading Terminal Market is right next door"?

Haru *Japanese* 20 | 20 | 19 | $40

Old City | 241-243 Chestnut St. (3rd St.) | 215-861-8990 |
www.harusushi.com

This "bright", "modern" Japanese offshoot of the Benihana chain in Old City "feels like a NYC restaurant" (though "with better service"), serving "generous pieces" of "high-quality" sushi and "creative" cooked fare (including specials that "rock"), and even better for sake-phants, it's one of the few in the area that "serves alcohol"; the "upstairs lounge" "plays at trendy for the see-and-be-seen" set, and while a "disappointed" few feel it "suffers from high expectations", most take it as a "good sign" that it's "always packed."

Harusame ● *Japanese* ∇ 22 | 12 | 19 | $28

Ardmore | 2371 Haverford Rd. (Wynnewood Rd.) | 610-649-7192 |
www.harusamerestaurant.com

Many Main Line afishionados "pass three other sushi places on the way" to this storefront Japanese in Ardmore, a "diamond in the rough" serving "inventive rolls", "dependably delicious" "noodles in all their incarnations" and an "amazing selection of beer" – all at "reasonable prices"; a few find the digs "nothing special" and the service "spotty", but for most the "hardest part" is "parking" in the train station lot across the street.

NEW Harvest Seasonal - | - | - | M
Grill & Wine Bar *American*

Glen Mills | Glen Eagle Sq. | 549 Wilmington West Chester Pike (Marshall Rd.) | 610-358-1005 | www.harvestseasonalgrill.com

'Local and low-cal' is the mantra at this cozy, moderately priced New American in Glen Mills from the team behind Kildare's and Doc Magrogan's; menu selections take advantage of nearby farms and

	FOOD	DECOR	SERVICE	COST

weigh in at under 500 calories each, while the green-minded setting, heavy on earth tones and natural elements, includes reclaimed wood flooring and recycled glass bar tops.

Havana *American/Eclectic*

	18	16	19	$34

New Hope | 105 S. Main St. (bet. Mechanic & New Sts.) | 215-862-9897 | www.havananewhope.com

Your meal "comes with a show" when you sit outside at this longtime Eclectic–New American on New Hope's Main Street; most find the "trendy" fare just "ok", but many assert "you forget what you are eating" when the "strange" parade of motorcycles and people gets going, and though the tropical-themed interior boasts a granite bar, all agree "outside is where it's at"; P.S. there's "great (live) music at night" Tuesdays–Sundays.

NEW Hawthornes *American*

	▽ 22	19	19	$20

South Philly | 738 S. 11th St. (Fitzwater St.) | 215-627-3012 | www.hawthornecafe.com

Fans fete the "fantastic concept" of this "comfy" cafe on a South Philly corner, where you go to "the fridge for beer" (with 1,000 bottles to choose from) to pair with "inventive" sandwiches and "notable" brunch items; the "owners" "make you feel like you are at their house", and though a few suggest "they just have to work out a few little things" on the service end, the majority revels in the "awesome neighborhood feel" of the place.

NEW HeadHouse 🅢🅜 *American*

	-	-	-	I

Society Hill | 122 Lombard St. (2nd St.) | 215-625-0122 | www.headhousephilly.com

Beer, beer everywhere – 20 on tap, 100 by the bottle and cocktails made from the stuff (plus sangria on tap) – is the lure of this sleek pub that comes to Head House Square in Society Hill via caterer and Philly Beer Week co-founder Bruce Nichols; designed for brew pairings, the easy-on-the-bank-account menu runs the gamut from bar snacks to sandwiches to mussels sold by the kilo, with a few entrees for heartier appetites.

NEW Healthy Bites to Go *American*

	-	-	-	I

South Philly | 2521 Christian St. (Stillman St.) | 215-259-8646 | www.healthybitestogo.com

Everything is good for you (and the staff is eager to talk nutrition) at this shoebox-sized corner cafe in South Philly, where Katie Cavuto Boyle (from *The Next Food Network Star*) serves wholesome but filling breakfasts and midday sandwiches; although the name highlights its appeal as a takeaway option, there are a few tables inside and out.

Hibachi *Japanese*

	18	17	20	$29

Delaware Riverfront | Pier 19 N. | 325 N. Columbus Blvd. (Callowhill St.) | 215-592-7100 | www.pennslandingbanquet.com
Springfield | 145-147 S. State Rd. (bet. Bobbin Mill Rd. & Dora Dr.) | 610-690-4911
Berwyn | 240 W. Swedesford Rd. (Valley Forge Rd.) | 610-296-4028

(continued)

(continued)

Hibachi

Downingtown | 985 E. Lancaster Ave. (Rte. 30) | 610-518-2910
Jenkintown | Benjamin Fox Pavillion | 261 Old York Rd.
(Township Line Rd.) | 215-881-6814

"Bring your coupons", your "group" of family or friends, and your sense of humor to this midpriced Japanese teppanyaki chain where "hibachi chefs flip your soon-to-be dinner around" and commit random acts of "comedy at the grill"; though it's a "fun place" for "kids' birthdays", some adults deem the culinary experience "unspectacular" and suggest copious amounts of sake may be "required."

HighNote Cafe Ⓜ *Italian*   ▽ 23 | 20 | 23 | $42

South Philly | 1549 S. 13th St. (Tasker St.) | 215-755-8903 |
www.highnotecafe.com

If you're lucky you'll hear the "staff burst into opera" at Franco Borda's street corner Italian trattoria in South Philly, which hits a "high note" with "large servings" of "better-than-expected", "traditional" cooking and "helpful", "fast-paced" service; there's also live music nightly, rounding out a "truly enjoyable evening"; P.S. it has a liquor license but you can BYO for $10 a bottle (tip: make it a "Chianti").

Ⓩ High Street Caffé Ⓜ *Cajun/Creole*   26 | 18 | 23 | $38

West Chester | 322 S. High St. (Dean St.) | 610-696-7435 |
www.highstreetcaffe.com

It's like a "Mardi Gras party" in full swing at this "terrific" Cajun-Creole in Downtown West Chester where fans attest you "cannot go wrong" with the "unusual", "top-notch" chow ("alligator", "wild boar", anyone?), while $30 prix fixes Sundays–Thursdays and BYO (with $5 corkage) also make it a "rock star"; the staff "aims to please" even when things are "jarringly loud" from live bands in the "sexy" "purple" environs that "would give Prince a run for his money."

Hikaru *Japanese*   20 | 15 | 20 | $34

Manayunk | 4348 Main St. (Grape St.) | 215-487-3500
South St. | 607 S. Second St. (bet. Bainbridge & South Sts.) |
215-627-7110

"Affordable", "consistently fresh sushi and sashimi", "solid" cooked fare and "always friendly" service make this "dependable" Japanese duo shine; Queen Village is a popular option for a "pleasant" meal "before the theater", and while critics say Manayunk "needs some serious updating", fans recommend its *tatami* room for a more "authentic" experience.

H.K. Golden Phoenix ◑ *Chinese*   20 | 9 | 15 | $22

Chinatown | 911 Race St. (bet. 9th & 10th Sts.) | 215-629-4988

"Dim sum paradise" is what many fans call this "no-frills" Chinatown Chinese where it's "best to go with a crowd so you can taste more" "piping hot" delights, whether it's on a midday Sunday or when a "late-night" "Cantonese" craving strikes; the "extensive menu" and "reasonable" prices – "not the ambiance" or service – are "why you go."

	FOOD	DECOR	SERVICE	COST

Hokka Hokka *Japanese* ▽ 23 | 20 | 21 | $38

Chestnut Hill | 7830 Germantown Ave. (bet. Moreland & Willow Grove Aves.) | 215-242-4489 | www.restauranthokka.com

They do a lot "with a square room and a fireplace" at this "hip but comfortable" Chestnut Hill Japanese, where "you won't mind the trouble" parking in return for "fresh", "yummy" sushi "nicely served" by "friendly" servers; there's a small wine and drink list, and Sundays and Mondays are BYO with no corkage.

Honey 🅢 *American* 26 | 22 | 25 | $41

Doylestown | 42 Shewell Ave. (Main St.) | 215-489-4200 | www.honeyrestaurant.com

Joe and Amy McAtee's "tiny", "quaint date-night destination" in Downtown Doylestown is "worth a detour" for "creative, inspiring" New American "small plates" with "big tastes" that you'll "find yourself fighting over", backed by a "wonderful list of local microbrews"; "attentive", "helpful" service adds to the "classy" vibe, and while a few find the "flea-size portions" "too expensive", most "want to return again and again"; lunch is served Thursdays–Saturdays.

Honey's Sit 'n Eat 🍴 *Jewish/Southern* 25 | 15 | 19 | $21

Northern Liberties | 800 N. Fourth St. (Brown St.) | 215-925-1150 | www.honeys-restaurant.com

"NoLibs hipsters" and others "hooked" on this "kitschy", "comforting" "Southern-Jewish combo" endure parking "hassles", "painful" waits and a cash-only policy in order to enjoy "outrageous" breakfasts and "shockingly good" brunches, lunches and dinners of "phenomenal" nosh (e.g. "grits or a latke with your omelet") served in "sparse" surroundings; a few find the "hip" servers lacking in "social graces", but many others think they're "sweet", and just about everyone leaves "with a smile and a stuffed belly."

🆕 Hoof + Fin *Argentinean* - | - | - | M

Queen Village | 617 S. Third St. (Bainbridge St.) | 215-925-3070

The name doesn't lie at this casual Argentinean BYO in Queen Village serving a midpriced menu of steaks and seafood plus fresh pastas and even Latin-inspired appetizers (empanadas, grilled sardines); the setting's rustic style (butcher block tables, hanging lightbulbs and Jersey Shore–related knickknacks) befits its positioning as a neighborhood drop-in place, complete with secret garden/patio out back.

🆉 Horizons 🅢Ⓜ *Vegan* 27 | 23 | 26 | $40

South St. | 611 S. Seventh St. (Kater St.) | 215-923-6117 | www.horizonsphiladelphia.com

Rich Landau and Kate Jacoby "delete the meat" from the "complex" "haute" vegan cuisine at their "unpretentious" bistro off South Street, proving that "you don't need to kill your food to have a killer menu"; "fabulous" "margatinis" and an "interesting", all-vegan wine list complement the "incredible" fare, served by a "fantastic" staff in "serene", "romantic" surroundings – in sum, it's a "superb dining experience" for "vegetarians" and "carnivores" alike.

Hostaria Da Elio Ⓜ *Italian*   23 | 16 | 21 | $35

South St. | 615 S. Third St. (bet. Bainbridge & South Sts.) | 215-925-0930

Cronies quip "you have to pull in your stomach just to fit into" this lovely Italian BYO "jewel" off South Street, which "transports diners to the mother country" with "excellent homemade pastas", "tons of specials" and a staff that's "willing to accommodate"; it feels like "you're having dinner with your rather eccentric but fun family."

Hotel du Village Ⓜ *French*   23 | 24 | 24 | $54

New Hope | Hotel du Vill. | 2535 River Rd. (Phillips Mill Rd.) | 215-862-9911 | www.hotelduvillage.com

At this "charming" "inn" "tucked away on a country road" in New Hope, the "solid", "traditional" country French cooking is "rarely creative", but that's "exactly how" many boosters like it; the "wonderful owners" and "professional" staff provide "attentive" service in the "beautiful" Tudor-style space, where regulars "try to get a table by the back window in nice weather" or "by the fireplace" in the winter; P.S. insiders advise "leave the kids home."

Hunan *Chinese*   ∇ - | - | - | M

Ardmore | 47 E. Lancaster Ave. (Rittenhouse Pl.) | 610-642-3050

Closing in on its 40th anniversary, this snug Main Line landmark has returned all fired up after a blaze shut it down, updating its Downtown Ardmore environs from traditional to contemporary and its culinary approach, augmenting the homespun Chinese menu with dishes from its titular home province; the BYO policy and family-friendly approach haven't changed, however.

Hymie's Merion Deli *Deli*   19 | 10 | 15 | $20

Merion Station | 342 Montgomery Ave. (Levering Mill Rd.) | 610-668-3354 | www.hymies.com

"Hon'", "your bubbe will love you forever" if you bring her some nosh from this Main Line "deli" "institution", where "diet-busting" delights such as "corned beef" on "wonderful rye bread" are "worth the extra cholesterol" ("oy, my arteries") – and don't miss a trip to the "classic" pickle bar; it's "always crowded", and if the staff acts as if it's "doing you a favor by serving you", well, "that's part of the charm."

Il Cantuccio Ⓢ⇄ *Italian*   21 | 13 | 18 | $33

Northern Liberties | 701 N. Third St. (Fairmount Ave.) | 215-627-6573

"They take a lot of pride in their food" at this "family-owned", cash-only Tuscan BYO in Northern Liberties, where the "wonderful, rustic" "no-frills" fare (including $11 lunch and $28 dinner prix fixes) and "friendly" service will "impress" your "first-date" companion; though some find the space "a little drab" and "tight", few feel that it "detracts from the experience."

Illuminare *Italian*   15 | 19 | 17 | $35

Fairmount | 2321 Fairmount Ave. (bet. 23rd & 24th Sts.) | 215-765-0202 | www.illuminare2321.com

To some, it feels like a "ski chalet" inside this storefront Fairmount Italian where many stop for "decent" "brick-oven pizzas" after a visit to the "Art Museum"; management is "forgiving of kids" in the "inviting" space with a cathedral ceiling, and the back patio is a "fun surprise", but some lament that the "food doesn't match the ambiance."

Il Portico *Italian*   21 | 19 | 20 | $48
Rittenhouse | 1519 Walnut St. (bet. 15th & 16th Sts.) | 215-587-7000 | www.il-portico.com

Surveyors are split on this "classic" expense-account Italian near Rittenhouse Square – proponents praise the "delicious, made-to-order pastas" and "exceptional service" in a "lovely" setting; detractors demur at the "adequate" hospitality and "ho-hum" food that appears to be "priced more for its address rather than what it has to offer" (prix fixes start at $50.95); the lounge Club Adesso occupies the second floor.

Il Tartufo ⊄ *Italian*   ∇ 21 | 18 | 19 | $45
Manayunk | 4341 Main St. (Grape St.) | 215-482-1999

For a "nice lunch alfresco", those in-the-know tout Il Portico's "more reasonably priced", cash-only sibling in Manayunk, where "fabulous" "Jerusalem artichokes" and other Tuscan treats are served "without the attitude" in a "quaint", classic northern Italian setting; a few, however, fret that the "small" wine list "does not do justice to the menu."

Imperial Inn ◑ *Chinese*   20 | 11 | 17 | $22
Chinatown | 146 N. 10th St. (bet. Cherry & Race Sts.) | 215-627-5588

The "top-notch, piping hot" dim sum at this Chinatown "favorite" "should be put in a hall of fame somewhere" boast boosters, who counsel "get there early" to avoid crowds and "don't be afraid to try new things" from the "expansive menu"; while most find the "worn" dining room "comfy", some say it "needs a refresh", and the "service could be friendlier."

Inn at Phillips Mill ⊄ *French*   25 | 25 | 23 | $51
New Hope | Inn at Phillips Mill | 2590 River Rd. (Phillips Mill Rd.) | 215-862-9919 | www.theinnatphillipsmill.com

"Dining on the patio is like being in Paris" at this "charming", "quintessential" New Hope country French BYO housed in an antiques-filled "old stone building", where the "wonderful" cooking "always delights"; "doting" service and a "no-rush", "romantic" atmosphere make it "perfect" for an "anniversary or even a proposal", and devotees declare "if your evening doesn't end well", it's probably "your fault" – just don't forget to bring your billfold (no plastic).

Iron Hill Brewery & Restaurant *American*   19 | 19 | 20 | $28
Phoenixville | 130 E. Bridge St. (Church Ave.) | 610-983-9333
West Chester | 3 W. Gay St. (High St.) | 610-738-9600 ◑
Media | 30 E. State St. (bet. Jackson & Monroe Sts.) | 610-627-9000
North Wales | Shoppes at English Vill. | 1460 Bethlehem Pike (Welsh Rd.) | 267-708-2000
www.ironhillbrewery.com

"Beers, beers everywhere" at this local micro-brewpub chain, which boasts "plenty of choices" of "top-shelf" "suds" that even a "wine chick" can love, as well as a "diverse" selection of "well-prepared" New American "comfort food"; while the portions are "man-size", it's a "kid-friendly" scene, and "knowledgeable" servers are "happy" to provide brew samples, so "don't let the cold, hard name throw you."

Isaac Newton's *American*   17 | 14 | 17 | $25

Newtown | 18 S. State St. (Washington Ave.) | 215-860-5100 | www.isaacnewtons.com

"All hail Sir Isaac" at this "informal" "brass railing" in Bucks, "a mecca" for "beer fans" with 19 brews on tap plus 200 by the bottle, where aficionados advise "stick with the basics" on the "dependable" "diner-style" American "menu" and excuse the "slow" service; whether you sit in the "cozy" bar area or outside garden, you'll see why locals "gravitate" to this spot "like an apple to the earth."

Isaac's Restaurant & Deli *Deli*   17 | 12 | 16 | $17

Exton | Crossroads Sq. | 630 W. Uwchlan Ave. (Pottstown Pike/Rte. 100) | 484-875-5825

West Chester | Commons at Thornbury | 1211 Wilmington Pike (Rte. 202) | 610-399-4438
www.isaacsdeli.com

"The early bird gets a great sandwich" at this "simple" deli chain that's "popular with the young crowd" for its "interesting" avian-themed creations, "housemade soups" and especially the "pretzel rolls – enough said"; while a few dismiss it as an "unremarkable", "sorta sandwich shop", most find it "satisfactory for a quick stop."

Italian Bistro *Italian*   17 | 15 | 17 | $30

Avenue of the Arts | 211 S. Broad St. (bet. Locust & Walnut Sts.) | 215-731-0700

Northeast Philly | 2500 Welsh Rd. (Roosevelt Blvd.) | 215-934-7700
www.italianbistro.com

This pair of independently owned Italians is a "safe" (if "not exciting") choice for "affordable", "decent" eats – the "casual" Avenue of the Arts branch is "convenient" to theaters and its $20 nightly specials are a "good value"; the Far Northeast outpost is a popular venue for "family celebrations", with a staff that takes "good care of you."

Izumi ⓜ *Japanese*   ▽ 25 | 23 | 23 | $35

South Philly | 1601 E. Passyunk Ave. (Tasker St.) | 215-271-1222 | www.izumiphilly.com

"Unusual" "selections" of "fresh, well-prepared" sushi and "great people-watching" come together at this "hip" Japanese BYO on South Philly's East Passyunk strip, from the owners of Paradiso; "creative" cooked fare and "amazing" specials also win praise, as does the "knowledgeable" staff, and complaints of "tight" quarters are addressed by "open windows" that make sidewalk dining possible.

Jack's Firehouse *Southern*   19 | 20 | 20 | $37

Fairmount | 2130 Fairmount Ave. (bet. 21st & 22nd Sts.) | 215-232-9000 | www.jacksfirehouse.com

Serving "real down-home food with twists that take it above your expectations" (and "most everything is local"), this "tried-and-true"

	FOOD	DECOR	SERVICE	COST

Southern-fried "staple" in Fairmount is an "adventure", and fans insist "you won't get hosed" when the bill comes; the bartenders are "quick" and the servers "friendly", and regulars recommend dining on the "outdoor courtyard" – the "[Eastern] State Penitentiary" across the street is a "real conversation starter" – or checking out the "sculling shell that hangs from the ceiling."

Jake's *American* | 25 | 21 | 22 | $53 |

Manayunk | 4365 Main St. (bet. Grape & Levering Sts.) | 215-483-0444 | www.jakesrestaurant.com

Bruce Cooper keeps it "consistent and exciting" at his Manayunk New American "classic", which has become a "bargain" after going the BYO route with the opening of adjoining Cooper's Brick Oven Wine Bar (where there's a $5 corkage); it still offers the "best crab cakes" and other "outstanding" eats, plus lighter fare from next door, served by an "attentive" staff in an "attractive" setting that's "right" for "business entertaining" "without being too pretentious."

Jamaican Jerk Hut *Jamaican* | 19 | 13 | 16 | $19 |

Avenue of the Arts | 1436 South St. (15th St.) | 215-545-8644

"Reggae music, spicy Jamaican jerk and a bucket of ice-cold Red Stripes" in a "backyard BBQ atmosphere" make it easy to "enjoy life" at this Caribbean BYO off Broad Street; though a few critics claim the fare "doesn't quite hit the mark" and the service is so "laid-back" it's "in reverse", many others insist it's "worth the adventure."

☑ James Ⓜ *American* | 27 | 24 | 25 | $59 |

South Philly | 824 S. Eighth St. (bet. Catharine & Christian Sts.) | 215-629-4980 | www.jameson8th.com

"Long live King James" – aka Jim Burke, who gives a "lesson" in "daring", "imaginative" food featuring "sustainably sourced ingredients" at his "fab, fab, fab" New American in South Philly, which exudes a "touch of class" at every turn thanks to wife Christina, who "runs a very tight ship"; the "hip", yet "intimate" setting "puts you at ease" (though some find it "too dark") and is one of the "best places for a romantic evening" in town, albeit an "expensive" one.

J.B. Dawson's *American* | 18 | 17 | 20 | $29 |

Langhorne | Shoppes at Flowers Mill | 92 N. Flowers Mill Rd. (Rte. 213) | 215-702-8119

Drexel Hill | Pilgrim Garden Shopping Ctr. | 5035 Township Line Rd./ Rte. 1 (Fairway Rd.) | 610-853-0700
www.jbdawsons.com

Dawson's *American*

Plymouth Meeting | 440 Plymouth Rd. (Germantown Pike) | 610-260-0550 | www.michaelsfamilyofrestaurants.com

"Families" and others are fond of these "reliable" Traditional Americans for their "immense" portions of "simple", "tasty" fare that come "without a jolt to the wallet"; "team service produces quick results" and the "large booths provide a feeling of privacy", though many complain the lighting is "barely bright enough to read the menu"; Plymouth Meeting is independently owned.

	FOOD	DECOR	SERVICE	COST

Jim's Steaks ● *Cheesesteaks*   23 | 10 | 15 | $12

Northeast Philly | Roosevelt Mall | 2311 Cottman Ave. (Bustleton Ave.) | 215-333-5467

South St. | 400 South St. (4th St.) | 215-928-1911 ⊟

West Philly | 431 N. 62nd St. (bet. Callowhill St. & Girard Ave.) | 215-747-6615 ⊟

Springfield | Stony Creek Shopping Ctr. | 469 Baltimore Pike (Sproul Rd.) | 610-544-8400

www.jimssteaks.com

"Fresh meat being shaved", "globs of Cheez Whiz" and the "aroma of fried onions" inspire "dreams" at these "classic" sandwich stands whose "contribution to the culinary arts" is measured in "long, long lines"; "fast service" eases the waits, however, and most agree "wit or wit out", this is the "real deal" – "no attitude, no phony show."

Joe Pesce Ⓜ *Italian/Seafood*   21 | 16 | 19 | $42

Washington Square West | 1113 Walnut St. (11th St.) | 215-829-4400

"Fresher-than-fresh seafood" and service with a "warm smile" make this pair of budget-friendly Italians in Philly and South Jersey a "keeper" for many afishionados; Collingswood is BYO, while Wash West is a "chic" spot for "drinks after work", even though some warn the "noise level" can be "a bit deafening."

Johnny Brenda's ● *American/Eclectic*   21 | 16 | 19 | $25

Fishtown | 1201 Frankford Ave. (Girard Ave.) | 215-739-9684 | www.johnnybrendas.com

"Hot and tasty" Traditional American and Eclectic "gastropub" grub and a "good variety of local brews" "on tap" attract "neighborhood hipsters, Center City yuppies" and others to this swell "hang" in Fishtown that only looks like a "campy dive bar"; staffers go "out of their way" to make you "feel welcome", and the pool table is conducive to "conversation", until live music kicks in on the second floor.

🅉 John's Roast Pork Ⓧ⊟ *Sandwiches*   27 | 7 | 17 | $11

South Philly | 14 E. Snyder Ave. (Weccacoe Ave.) | 215-463-1951 | www.johnsroastpork.com

The top-rated sandwich shop in town occupies a "cramped", "nondescript" shack hidden behind a South Philly Lowe's, where groupies solve the "impossible decision" between the "best cheesesteak in town" and "equally outstanding" roast pork "with greens and provolone" by "getting both"; "surly service adds to the experience", and the only drawbacks are the "long lines" and "short hours" (until 3 PM or whenever the "bread runs out").

Jones ● *American*   20 | 21 | 20 | $32

Washington Square West | 700 Chestnut St. (7th St.) | 215-223-5663 | www.jones-restaurant.com

Stephen Starr's "sophisticated" "'70s" "flashback" off Washington Square generates "feel-good" American comfort food that tastes "better than the home cooking you remember" (and "without the guilt trip"), which can be washed down with microbrews and "specialty cocktails"; a "chill" staff waits on you in a "kid-friendly" setting that's part "ski lodge", part *Brady Bunch* living room", where "all you need is an ottoman and a remote control."

Jong Ka Jib *Korean* ▽ 25 | 17 | 21 | $17
East Oak Lane | 6600 N. Fifth St. (66th Ave.) | 215-924-0100
If you don't speak *pyojuneo* you might "feel like a fish out of water" at this BYO Korean BBQ in East Oak Lane, but "once you have figured out how the service works", it's "the place to go" for spareribs, bibimbop and any "food originating from near the 38th parallel"; the "friendly" staff brings your order "quickly" in the storefront space, and proponents ponder "can you think of a better way to spend $10?"

Joseph Ambler Inn *American* 21 | 23 | 23 | $53
North Wales | Joseph Ambler Inn | 1005 Horsham Rd. (bet. Stump & Upper State Rds.) | 215-362-7500 | www.josephamblerinn.com
"Somewhat formal" and full of "country charm", this "perennial favorite" housed in a North Wales "historic inn" is "always" on locals' lists for New American fare "prepared and presented" with "artistry" and served by a "top-notch" staff; insiders recommend dining on the "gorgeous" summer patio, as well as the $35 three-course prix fixe dinners; a post-Survey chef change may outdate the Food score.

José Pistola's ● *Mexican* 15 | 12 | 18 | $22
Rittenhouse | 263 S. 15th St. (Spruce St.) | 215-545-4101 | www.josepistolas.com
They "get spicy right" at this "dark", "hip" bar in Rittenhouse, where "Mexican pizzazz" means "craft" beer and "burritos together like they were meant to be"; the "friendly" staff acts "like your friends", but the less-enthused see it as merely a "fallback" "joint" or a place to "watch a game", with "nothing spectacular" to offer.

Joy Tsin Lau ● *Chinese* 20 | 12 | 15 | $22
Chinatown | 1026 Race St. (bet. 10th & 11th Sts.) | 215-592-7226
"Chaos at its finest" is how fans describe this Chinese "parlor" in Chinatown, where "rolling carts" laden with "awesome" "dim sum" are pushed by "efficient" waiters in a "red-and-gold" setting that causes some to experience "sensory overload"; many marvel at "how much food can be served in such a short time" – and be so "cheap" – just hope you "don't mind waiting for a table on the weekends."

Kabobeesh *Pakistani* ▽ 26 | 8 | 15 | $18
University City | 4201 Chestnut St. (42nd St.) | 215-386-8081 | www.kabobeesh.com
Take a tip from "Philly's taxi drivers" and head to this "no-frills" "retrofit" of a "diner" in University City for "bountiful platters" of Pakistani staples served by "delightful" folks; "don't judge the place by its cover" – just "pick your sides, pay a pittance and enjoy."

Kabul *Afghan* 21 | 17 | 19 | $27
Old City | 106 Chestnut St. (bet. Front & 2nd Sts.) | 215-922-3676 | www.kabulafghancuisine.com
"Succulent rice dishes" and anything "with pumpkin" are among the standouts at this "pleasantly exotic" Afghan BYO in Old City, an "in-

teresting change of pace" for treating "out-of-town guests"; while opinions are split on the surroundings – "romantic" vs. "travel-agency decor" – just about everyone agrees it's a "great deal for your money."

Kanella ⓜ Greek
25 | 18 | 22 | $38

Washington Square West | 266 S. 10th St. (Spruce St.) | 215-922-1773 | www.kanellarestaurant.com

"Culinary heaven" is what fans are calling Konstantinos Pitsillides' "bustling" Greek-Cypriot BYO in Wash West, which offers "creative", "rustic" dishes "not for the unadventurous eater" and "spot-on" service that "feels like family"; it's often so "noisy" in the "small" room that some regulars recommend getting a table "before 5 PM, unless you and your dining companions know sign language"; P.S. it also serves a "first-rate" weekend brunch.

Karma Indian
21 | 16 | 16 | $28

Old City | 114 Chestnut St. (bet. Front & 2nd Sts.) | 215-925-1444 | www.thekarmarestaurant.com

There's a lot of "spicy" going on at this Old City Indian serving "inexpensive", "above-average" fare, including an "extra-special" lunch buffet deal, in a "pleasant" contemporary setting with a "high-end" feel; the karma chameleon is service, which a few say swings "from good to poor", though most insist it's usually "friendly."

Kaya's Fusion Cuisine ⓈⓂ American
∇ 19 | 16 | 24 | $35

Havertown | 5 Brookline Blvd. (Darby Rd.) | 610-446-2780 | www.kayascuisine.com

Cognoscenti claim this "small", family-run storefront BYO in Havertown "deserves a whole lot more attention" for its "well-thought-out" New American menu from a "creative chef", "accommodating" service and a "lively scene"; a few complain there's "not enough decor to absorb the noise" and find it "a little too pricey", but most others deem it a "real find."

K.C.'s Alley ☾ Pub Food
16 | 14 | 17 | $22

Ambler | 10 W. Butler Pike (Main St.) | 215-628-3300 | www.kc-alley.com

"Fab burgers any way you like them" and "great daily specials" are backed by "good vibes", "beer, TV and noise" at this "fun pub in the heart of Ambler", boasting a "rustic" interior and a "little alleyway with cozy tables"; though some sniff it's "nothing special", it's "always consistent" and the service is "friendly."

Keating's American
∇ 18 | 18 | 18 | $44

Delaware Riverfront | Hyatt Regency at Penn's Landing | 201 S. Columbus Blvd. (Dock St.) | 215-521-6509 | www.keatingsrivergrill.com

On a clear day you can see New Jersey across the Delaware from the deck of this Traditional American in the Hyatt Regency at Penn's Landing, where the interior has a nautical theme, complete with a captain's table and sails for window curtains; the "well-prepared" business meals and "nice breakfasts" are "more than" you "usually get in a hotel", but don't expect to find many locals here.

	FOOD	DECOR	SERVICE	COST

Khajuraho *Indian*
| 20 | 13 | 15 | $32 |

Ardmore | Ardmore Plaza | 12 Greenfield Ave. (Lancaster Ave.) |
610-896-7200 | www.khajurahoindia.com

Loyalists laud the "high-quality Indian" chow with a "taste of authenticity" served in a "serene", "informal" "atmosphere" at this
Ardmore BYO, popular for its "bargain" lunch and brunch "buffets";
critics, though, clamor that it "needs a makeover", from the staff's
"attitude" to the "R-rated" photos (which others find "interesting")
on the walls, and hope the introduction of "new competition" in the
area will provide the needed impetus.

Kibitz Room *Deli*
| 21 | 9 | 15 | $18 |

Rittenhouse | 1521 Locust St. (16th St.) | 215-735-7305 |
www.thekibitzroom.com

See review in the New Jersey Suburbs Directory.

Kildare's ❶ *Pub Food*
| 16 | 20 | 17 | $26 |

Manayunk | 4417 Main St. (Green Ln.) | 215-482-7242
West Chester | 18-22 W. Gay St. (High St.) | 610-431-0770
King of Prussia | 826 DeKalb Pike (N. Gulph Rd.) | 610-337-4772
www.kildarespub.com

"Begorra" is the password at this mini-chain that reminds some of an
"Irish Disney World", serving "traditional faves" that pair well "with
your Guinness" in spaces graced with "authentic decorations"; most
agree it's a "blast" for drinks, but "going there for dinner is not gonna
happen" for many who find the grub "predictable" and "average."

Kimberton Inn Ⓜ *American*
| 25 | 25 | 25 | $50 |

Kimberton | 2105 Kimberton Rd. (Hares Hill Rd.) | 610-933-8148 |
www.kimbertoninn.com

Set in an "elegant" 18th-century inn, this Chester County Traditional
American has "stood the test of time", and city folk deem it "worth
the drive" for a "fine-dining experience" that does not "disappoint"
(especially "by the fireplace" "on a cold winter's night"), featuring
"thoughtfully prepared" cuisine and "superior" service; while it's
"expensive", the majority agrees "you get your bang for the buck here";
P.S. the $23.95 "Sunday brunch" comes "highly recommended."

Kingdom of Vegetarians *Chinese/Vegetarian*
| ▽ 25 | 11 | 22 | $17 |

Chinatown | 129 N. 11th St. (bet. Arch & Race Sts.) | 215-413-2290

"New owners" have "improved" the vegetarian offerings at this "little" Chinese "oasis" in Chinatown, whose "mock meat dishes can
fool a carnivore"; if you skip the $12 buffet, note "super-fast" ser-
vice from a staff that's "happy to accommodate special requests" –
which makes it easier to "forgive" the "fake floral arrangements."

King of Tandoor *Indian*
| ▽ 23 | 17 | 21 | $28 |

Fairmount | 1824 Callowhill St. (19th St.) | 215-568-0750 |
www.kingoftandoor.com

"When you ask for spicy", "you better mean it" at this "lovely"
Fairmount Indian BYO, whose eponymous oven turns out "delicious"

"tandoori" dishes, while "warm" servers "recommend their favorites"; though it's "a bit more expensive than most", most agree "you can tell the difference" in the "higher-quality" fare.

Kingyo *Japanese*
(fka Genji)

- | - | - | M

Rittenhouse | 1720 Sansom St. (bet. 17th & 18th Sts.) | 215-564-1720
At this storefront Japanese in Rittenhouse Square, regulars recommend you "sit at the sushi bar", "ask" the "friendly" chefs "what's fresh" and watch the action", for there's "not much reason to sit" in the "nondescript" dining room; it's "pricey", but "very delicious."

Kisso Sushi Bar *Japanese*

∇ 25 | 18 | 25 | $40

Old City | 205 N. Fourth St. (Race St.) | 215-922-1770
"Killer" "house-invented sushi rolls" are the "superstars" at this "quiet" but "spunky" Japanese BYO in Old City, while the "shumai are nothing to sneeze at, either", and regulars report there's "none of the pretention" you find at the "hipper" places, just chef-owner Alex Park's "personable" hospitality; sure, the "room is simple", "but it suits the food", and you "can always carry on an audible conversation."

Kite & Key ❶ *American*

16 | 15 | 20 | $26

Fairmount | 1836 Callowhill St. (19th St.) | 215-568-1818 | www.thekiteandkey.com
"Better-than-average bar food" and 16 "craft beers" on tap attract a "25- to 35-year-old" "after-work crowd" from the "neighborhood" to this Fairmount pub; the "acoustics have all the subtlety of an aircraft hangar", adding to the "frat-party" atmosphere, but "helpful service" and a "large outdoor patio" make it a "keeper" for many.

Knight House 🚫🅼 *American*

∇ 23 | 20 | 18 | $45

Doylestown | 96 W. State St. (Clinton St.) | 215-489-9900 | www.theknighthouse.com
Whether it's the "outstanding burgers", small plates or "seafood", the "eclectic" menu at this Doylestown New American can "surprise" you according to fans, although a few detractors find it "kinda pricey for what it is"; still, all agree that the "patio in back really rocks when the weather is warm."

Knock *American*

∇ 16 | 19 | 18 | $42

Washington Square West | 225 S. 12th St. (Locust St.) | 215-925-1166 | www.knockphilly.com
There's a "sexy" quality to this "quaint" New American in the Wash West "gayborhood" that transforms into a weekend nightspot after 10 PM, complete with a "secret back room" with "piano bar"; while the service is "appropriately attentive" and the "quiet" setting "comfortable", and the only knock on it is for merely "average" fare.

Konak 🅼 *Turkish*

23 | 21 | 22 | $33

Old City | 228 Vine St. (bet. 2nd & 3rd Sts.) | 215-592-1212 | www.konakturkishrestaurant.com
"Check out the fresh fish selections on your way to your seat" at this "family-run" Turkish in Old City, where a "polite" staff is "happy to

help make a selection" from the "large menu" of "beautifully prepared" eats in a space with 20-ft. ceilings "tastefully decorated" to "resemble" a residential "courtyard"; throw in entertainment on Fridays and Saturdays and no-corkage BYO on Sundays, and you have a spot "every foodie should experience."

NEW Koo Zee Doo *Portuguese*   25 | 20 | 24 | $39

Northern Liberties | 613 N. Second St. (Spring Garden St.) | 215-923-8080 | www.koozeedoo.com

"Magnificent", "rustic" Portuguese cuisine perfect for "sharing" comes forth from the center-stage "open kitchen" of this "homey" mom-and-pop BYO "find" for "adventurous foodies" in Northern Liberties ("don't miss the chicken gizzards" and "sensational" breads); the staff "clearly explains everything" on the "value-priced" menu, so tote a "good bottle" of Iberian wine and get ready for a "wonderful dining experience."

Kotatsu *Japanese*   ∇ 24 | 14 | 24 | $32

Ardmore | 36 Greenfield Ave. (bet. Lancaster & Spring Aves.) | 610-642-7155 | www.kotatsusteakhouse.com

There's "heavy enthusiasm in the air" at this "cozy" Japanese BYO (with a $2.50 corkage) located in an Ardmore "strip mall", where "entertaining chefs" "prepare a tasty meal" at the teppan grills and the "guys behind the sushi bar" turn out "delicious, fresh" fin fare (including "all-you-can-eat" for $25.95 on Mondays–Wednesdays), while the "decor is what you'd expect"; still, most recommend it as a "good value" for a "family night out."

NEW Kraftwork 🅢Ⓜ *American*   - | - | - | I

Fishtown | 541 E. Girard Ave. (Montgomery Ave.) | 215-739-1700 | www.kraftworkbar.com

Artist-quality metalwork and woodwork fill this Fishtown American gastropub, a sibling of G-Ho's Sidecar, providing a workmanlike atmosphere to enjoy the 24 brews on tap (a 25th is available to-go in growlers); the budget-friendly, beer-focused fare is unapologetically rich – how about a pork 'krispy' treat (pork rinds, marshmallow, bacon fat and bacon) for dessert?

NEW Kumo Asian Bistro *Asian*   - | - | - | M

North Wales | The Shoppes at English Vill. | 1460 Bethlehem Pike (Welsh Rd.) | 215-283-6066 | www.kumojapanesebistro.com

This "chic", "sleek" Pan-Asian BYO "looks like it belongs in town or New York" rather than the Shoppes at English Village in North Wales, but locals are glad to have such a "great addition to the 'burbs"; "beautifully presented", "always fresh" sushi and "tasty appetizers" are served in a mod setting boosted by thumping music.

La Belle Epoque   ∇ 21 | 18 | 21 | $33
Wine Bistro Ⓜ *French*

Media | 38 W. State St. (Olive St.) | 610-566-6808 | www.labellebistro.com

You "feel like" you just "stepped off the Metro" at this "pleasant" French bistro in Media, known for "delicious and affordable" "crêpes" and "other light fare" for brunch or a "before-theater" bite; most applaud the "great wine flights", although a few preferred it "when it was a BYO" (still permitted, but now with $10 corkage).

La Collina 🗷 *Italian* 22 | 19 | 21 | $53
Bala Cynwyd | 37 Ashland Ave. (Jefferson St.) | 610-668-1780 | www.lacollina.us
Fans "cannoli say good things" about this "gussied-up" Northern Italian "throwback" on the Main Line, whose menu "has something for everyone", while "waiters dressed to the nines" provide "old-world-style service" and singers croon three nights a week; "Belmont Hills ain't Beverly Hills" but the "hilltop view" is "still nice."

⬚ La Colombe *Coffeehouse* 24 | 17 | 20 | $9
Rittenhouse | Rittenhouse Sq. | 130 S. 19th St. (bet. Sansom & Walnut Sts.) | 215-563-0860 | www.lacolombe.com
"It's all about the coffee" – "no stupid couches" or "glitz" – at this "homegrown" shop in Rittenhouse (voted Philly's No. 1 Bang for the Buck), where "helpful", "too-cool-for-school" "baristas take pride in their foam art" as they dispense "cappuccinos" and "espressos" with enough "pure octane" to "set your hair on fire"; the "cool hangout" is "always packed with laptop users" who linger over "heavenly" joe and "tasty baked goods."

⬚ Lacroix at The Rittenhouse *Eclectic* 27 | 27 | 27 | $76
Rittenhouse | Rittenhouse Hotel | 210 W. Rittenhouse Sq. (bet. Locust & Walnut Sts.) | 215-790-2533 | www.lacroixrestaurant.com
"Classy with a capital C", this "magnificent" Rittenhouse Hotel establishment is a "luxurious", "über-modern" showcase for chef Jason Cichonski's "inventive", "awesome" Eclectic tasting menus, which are "matched with amazing views" of the square and "attentive" service from a staff that's "sometimes a little too eager to please"; the "$59 Sunday brunch" buffet, $24 lunch and $35 dinner prix fixes, and the "new bar" are budget-friendlier slices of "foodie heaven."

La Famiglia 🗷 *Italian* 23 | 21 | 22 | $60
Old City | 8 S. Front St. (bet. Chestnut & Market Sts.) | 215-922-2803 | www.lafamiglia.com
After 35 years, the Sena family's "little jewel" in Old City is still living up to its "usual high standards" according to stalwarts who cite "impeccable" service, "wonderful" food and an "out-of-control" wine list of some 450 labels; the "formal" setting is "quite romantic", and while the majority agrees the "memorable" experience is "worth every penny", a few grumble that "the staff should remember who is paying and who is serving."

La Fontana Della Citta *Italian* 21 | 17 | 21 | $33
Rittenhouse | 1701 Spruce St. (17th St.) | 215-875-9990 | www.lafontanadellacitta.com
"If you are dining with a crowd" near Rittenhouse Square, boosters tout this "neighborhood" Italian that dishes up "large portions" of "all the staples necessary to appease picky eaters" plus specialties to make "foodies happy"; everything's "served with grace" by "effi-

cient", "heavily accented" servers who'll ensure you make your show at the Kimmel or Academy of Music on time.

Lai Lai Garden *Asian*

19 | 20 | 19 | $34

Blue Bell | 1144 DeKalb Pike (Skippack Pike) | 610-277-5988 | www.lailaigarden.com

Offering "something for everyone" and "helpful" service, this Pan-Asian in Blue Bell is a "solid" "banquet"-venue for "bar mitzvahs and sweet 16s"; a decline in the scores, however, reflects the sentiment that it's "slipped in quality" and "needs to work" on the food and hospitality to warrant the "pricey" tabs.

La Locanda del Ghiottone 🅼🖻 *Italian*

24 | 18 | 22 | $31

Old City | 130 N. Third St. (Cherry St.) | 215-829-1465

You can't get "more South Philly-ish" than this "boisterous" Italian BYO in Old City, where the "loud" vibe is "part of the charm"; you'll think you just "stepped into someone's kitchen" for "spectacular", "moderately priced" eats (the mushroom crêpes are a "must"), served by "smart alec" staffers who "make you feel at home" – but those "looking for a quiet night out" may want to "steer clear."

La Lupe ◑ *Mexican*

21 | 8 | 18 | $15

South Philly | 1201 S. Ninth St. (Federal St.) | 215-551-9920

"Enormous portions" of "authentic" Mexican fare at "reasonable prices" are the draw at this "airy", no-frills BYO "cantina" near the Pat's-Geno's intersection in South Philly; just "don't show up starving" or otherwise "in a hurry" warn many critics, who contend that staffers seem to "have no idea what they're doing sometimes."

La Na Thai-French Cuisine *French/Thai*

∇ 18 | 15 | 20 | $29

Media | 33 W. State St. (bet. Jackson & Olive Sts.) | 610-892-7787 | www.lanabyob.com

"Impeccable" service makes for a "relaxed" mood at this Media BYO that adds a "French infusion" to "well-presented" traditional Thai cooking (notably its "fish" "specials" and "high-quality desserts"); though it's "not much on decor", many local fans cheerfully bring their "out-of-town guests"; P.S. it's also a "great take-out spot."

Landing, The *American*

18 | 22 | 17 | $42

New Hope | 22 N. Main St. (Bridge St.) | 215-862-5711 | www.landingrestaurant.com

The outdoor dining is "delightful" at this "lovely", long-running New American in New Hope, but you can always take in "beautiful views" of the Delaware whether you sit inside or on the "pretty patio"; the "varied menu" runs the gamut from "burgers to salmon, with some tasty salads thrown in", and while a few critics complain that the "staff tends to get lost", all agree the "ambiance makes up" for any lapses.

L'Angolo 🅼 *Italian*

26 | 14 | 22 | $38

South Philly | 1415 W. Porter St. (Broad St.) | 215-389-4252 | www.salentorestaurant.com

You "walk through the kitchen" to get to the "sardine can" of a "dining room at this "inviting" South Philly BYO (from the owners of

Salento) where "stellar", "off-the-boat" "authentic" Italian dishes are served by "tip-top" waiters who "make each trip seem like a visit to Italy", while the kitchen "graciously accommodates special requests"; "reasonable" prices are another reason many recommend it "for your to-go list" – just be sure to "make a reservation."

Langostini Ⓜ Italian

| - | - | - | I |

(fka Langostino's)

South Philly | 100 Morris St. (Front St.) | 215-551-7709 | www.langostini.com

Insiders report "some of the best seafood plates" around, plus red-gravy classics and homemade desserts that shine at this "comfortable", white-tablecloth Italian BYO in South Philly run by "charming" chef-owner Irene Datsko; serving dinner only, it's a fave of those headed to the ballpark, and free parking across the street is a plus.

La Pergola Eastern Euro./Mideastern

| 19 | 13 | 17 | $25 |

Jenkintown | 726 West Ave. (Johnson St.) | 215-884-7204

Serving "always reliable" Middle Eastern "comfort" grub and "Eastern European soul food" at "reasonable prices", this Jenkintown BYO is a "longtime favorite" "with the older crowd", which is why "it gets busy early"; some grouse that the "presentation could be improved" and the room is "so bright it's almost painful", but even in the glare, the "food stands out."

Las Bugambilias Mexican

| 24 | 19 | 20 | $36 |

South St. | 148 South St. (2nd St.) | 215-922-3190 | www.lasbugambiliasphilly.com

If it's not the "best Mex in Philly", it "must be close" insist backers of this South Street "gem", where Carlos Molina can "make a palate sing" with his "spirited" "gourmet" cooking from "all regions", which can be washed down with "excellent" margaritas and selections from a "limited" but "well-priced" wine list; groupies gasp "boy, do they squeeze you" into the "snug" room decorated with "Mexican film star portraits", which also boasts a "cute bar", but "knowledgeable", "helpful" service helps make up for the "lack of elbow room."

LaScala's Old World Italian Italian

| 19 | 17 | 19 | $32 |

Washington Square West | 615 Chestnut St. (7th St.) | 215-928-0900 | www.lascalasphilly.com

This "low-key", "neighborhood" Italian in Wash West offers a "great value" for red-sauce specialties according to boosters who boast that there's "nothing that will disappoint" on the menu, but critics counter that there's "nothing exceptional", either; for many, the "people-watching" "in the heart of the historic district" trumps the fare (validated parking after 3 PM weekdays and on weekends helps too).

Las Cazuelas Ⓜ Mexican

| 24 | 20 | 22 | $28 |

Northern Liberties | 426 W. Girard Ave. (bet. 4th & Lawrence Sts.) | 215-351-9144 | www.lascazuelas.net

The "innovative", "authentic" Mexican cuisine from an open kitchen shines at this "enjoyable", "out-of-the-way" BYO in

Northern Liberties, where regulars recommend "bringing a great fruity red to balance the spice" or a "tequila" for the staff, which "knows how to have a good time", to mix "exceptional margaritas" for you; there's occasional live entertainment in the "small" space, and "outdoor seating" as well, though some warn that it "can be loud" from the street.

La Terrasse ⓩ *American/French* | 19 | 20 | 20 | $39 |

University City | 3432 Sansom St. (bet. 34th & 36th Sts.) | 215-386-5000 | www.laterrasserestaurant.com

Opinions are split over the New American cuisine at this "casual" spot in the "middle of Penn's campus", after a mid-Survey chef change and a shift in influence from French to Mediterranean – supporters claim "it just gets better", while negativists call it "generic" and "uninspired"; still, thanks to "relaxed" ambiance and "not too expensive" pricing, it remains a popular "standby" for "quiet business lunches" and "small private parties."

La Veranda *Italian* | 22 | 20 | 21 | $52 |

Delaware Riverfront | Penn's Landing, Pier 3 | 5 N. Columbus Blvd. (Market St.) | 215-351-1898 | www.laverandapier3.com

"Powerful people" and others gravitate to this "classic old-world Italian" "haunt" on Penn's Landing, where "special occasions" are abetted by "poised" personnel and "river views"; although some cavil that the "high prices" are "over the top", most say it's "worth the trip" for its "succulent" "seafood", "good bar" and "scenic" location.

La Viola Ovest ⑃ *Italian* | 23 | 17 | 21 | $34 |

Rittenhouse | 252 S. 16th St. (bet. Locust & Spruce Sts.) | 215-735-8630

A "brilliant pre-theater choice" in Rittenhouse, this "extremely affordable" Italian BYO can help you "fool your loved one into thinking you've splurged", with "fabulous eats" that are not "overly fussy or contrived" served by a "friendly" staff "straight from Italy" (or at least Bistro La Viola across the street); yes, it's "too" darn "small", "always crowded", they don't take cards and make you "wait, even with a reservation", but most still regard it as "one of Philly's hidden gems."

ⓩ Le Bar Lyonnais ⓩ *French* | 27 | 23 | 25 | $55 |

Rittenhouse | 1523 Walnut St. (bet. 15th & 16th Sts.) | 215-567-1000 | www.lebecfin.com

At Le Bec-Fin's subterranean spin-off in Rittenhouse, you can enjoy "true French cooking" and "excellent", "but not obtrusive" service in "intimate, sophisticated" environs, with Georges Perrier "always around to schmooze"; it's "half the price" of dining upstairs, and while it comes "without the elegance and drama" of the mother ship, "after two glasses of wine, you won't be able to tell the difference."

ⓩ Le Bec-Fin ⓩ *French* | 27 | 27 | 27 | $98 |

Rittenhouse | 1523 Walnut St. (bet. 15th & 16th Sts.) | 215-567-1000 | www.lebecfin.com

"Save your calories for days" before heading to Georges Perrier's "gorgeous", "sense-seducing" Rittenhouse "institution", where the dress code may have been "relaxed" but not the kitchen's standards: expect "sublime" French cuisine "prepared to perfection" and enhanced by an "amazing dessert cart" and "impeccable" service; if a few think "time has passed" this "legend" by and quip that you have to "sell your kids" to pay the bill, most agree it's "world-class dining" that "everyone should experience at least once."

Le Castagne ☒ *Italian*   25 | 22 | 23 | $52

Rittenhouse | 1920 Chestnut St. (bet. 19th & 20th Sts.) | 215-751-9913 | www.lecastagne.com

La Famiglia's Rittenhouse sibling has retained "all the good points" of its cross-town fratello – namely, "crowd-pleasing", "homemade pastas" and other "sophisticated" Italian cuisine delivered by "attentive, but not overbearing" servers in a "dignified", "austere" space with a "no-need-to-hurry" ambiance; though it's a "wee bit pricey", many recommend it for those times when you want to "really impress your date."

Lee How Fook Ⓜ *Chinese*   25 | 9 | 17 | $23

Chinatown | 219 N. 11th St. (Spring St.) | 215-925-7266 | www.leehowfook.com

"Nondescript" and "shoebox-size" it may be, but this Chinatown BYO is a "force to be reckoned with" say fans of its "superior", "authentic" Cantonese cooking and "reasonable prices"; the owners are "friendly" and, sure, there's "no atmosphere", but at least "no one will notice if your hair's not perfect."

Legal Sea Foods *Seafood*   19 | 18 | 19 | $41

NEW **South Philly** | Philadelphia International Airport | B/C Connector | 267-295-9300

King of Prussia | King of Prussia Mall | 680 W. Dekalb Pike (Mall Blvd.) | 610-265-5566

www.legalseafoods.com

"Consistency", "quality" and "good-sized portions" reel in finatics to this pair of "classy", "inviting" seafood chain links located in King of Prussia and the Philadelphia International Airport; service is another "strong" point, and while some detractors feel it's ventured "too far" from the "original Boston roots", and begrudge paying "big bucks" for "boring" fin fare, defenders insist it's "worth" the tabs and the "waits."

NEW **Leila Cafe** ☽ *Lebanese*   - | - | - | I

Washington Square West | 401 S. 13th St. (Pine St.) | 267-319-1903 | www.leilacafe.com

Rather than "mimic the set of *Aladdin*", this "true" Lebanese "cafe" keeps it real with a "small", "intimate" setting highlighted by exposed brick and a mosaic "glass mural", as well as sidewalk tables furnished with "hookahs", where "superb" "shawarma", "falafel", "Turkish coffee" and more are served at "very reasonable prices"; even when it gets "extremely busy" the "staff and owner still find time to be personable"; just keep in mind that no alcohol is permitted.

	FOOD	DECOR	SERVICE	COST

Lemon Grass Thai *Thai*

20 | 15 | 17 | $24

University City | 3626-30 Lancaster Ave. (36th St.) |
215-222-8042
King of Prussia | Henderson Sq. | 314 S. Henderson Rd.
(Pennsylvania Tpke.) | 610-337-5986
www.lemongrassphila.com

"Bring on the chilis" clamor fans of these Thai triplets that make
their mark with "authentic, tasty morsels" and "can't-beat" three-
course "lunch specials", which "trump so-so service" (i.e. "speedy,
but rarely friendly") and "unobtrusive" digs; University City has
wine and drinks, while the King of Prussia branch and separately
owned Lancaster location are BYO.

NEW Le Viet *Vietnamese*

- | - | - | M

South Philly | 1019 S. 11th St. (bet. Kimball St. & Washington Ave.) |
215-463-1570 | www.levietrestaurant.com

Modern environs meet old-fashioned, midpriced Vietnamese
home cooking at this slick-looking South Philly bistro tucked behind a CVS drugstore near the Italian Market; chefs behind the
glass partition are keen on presentation and are not above plat-
ing their dishes in hollowed-out fruits; it's BYO for now, until the
liquor license arrives.

Ƶ Le Virtù *Italian*

26 | 20 | 22 | $47

South Philly | 1927 E. Passyunk Ave. (bet. McKean & Mifflin Sts.) |
215-271-5626 | www.levirtu.com

Even though chef Luciana Spurio "does not seek to dazzle", her
"hands of gold" still create "beautiful", "homemade" dishes that
exemplify "the special charm of the Abruzzese table" at this
"spectacular" Italian that "rises above South Philly expectations"; the service is "friendly", and though the "unassuming"
decor "lets you know you're in the neighborhood", the patio is "wonderful" in "warm weather."

Limoncello *Italian*

23 | 18 | 20 | $38

West Chester | 9 N. Walnut St. (Gay St.) | 610-436-6230 |
www.limoncellowc.com

The erstwhile "little BYO that could" is now the "spot to see and
be seen in Downtown West Chester" according to fans of this
"family-owned" Italian where "Mama and her staff consistently
churn out amazing pastas and grilled specialties" for the nightly
"hordes"; the "fantastic" fare and "reasonable cost" will "make
you forget the noise" in the "cramped" space; P.S. the $9.95
lunch buffet and Sunday- Monday BYO (with no corkage) ramp
up its "affordability."

Little Marakesh Ⓜ *Moroccan*

- | - | - | M

Dresher | 1825 S. Limekiln Pike (Twining Rd.) | 215-643-3003 |
www.littlemarakesh.com

An "exotic escape for suburbanites", this traditional Moroccan BYO in
a Dresher strip mall offers "an experience beyond the food" for "small
to medium parties", complete with "hookah pipes" and "belly dancers"

that complement the seven-course, $27.95 feasts of "unique" offerings; still, a few critics grouse about the "limited" bill of fare.

Little Pete's *Diner*   18 | 9 | 18 | $16

Fairmount | The Philadelphian | 2401 Pennsylvania Ave. (bet. 24th & 25th Sts.) | 215-232-5001
Rittenhouse | 219 S. 17th St. (Chancellor St.) | 215-545-5508 ●↩

"No airs" or "surprises", just "huge portions" of "solid", "basic" chow and "low prices" at this "quintessential" "dive" diner duo; the "habitués vary" at the 24/7 Rittenhouse Square original (everyone from "cops" to "drunkards") while the sibling in the Philadelphian sometimes resembles a "Florida early-bird" scene, and all served by "sassy", "old-school" waitresses who act like they've "seen it all."

L'Oca *Italian*   23 | 16 | 18 | $36

Fairmount | 2025 Fairmount Ave. (Corinthian Ave.) | 215-769-0316 | www.locafairmount.com

"See the sizzle, smell the sauce and chat" with the "talented" chef in the "open kitchen" while you wait for your meal at this "sophisticated" BYO "tucked away" in Fairmount, serving a Northern Italian menu with a "focus on wild game" and "fantastic" rustic pastas; although some critics accuse the toque of displaying "too much pretense" and "temper", many recommend it especially "in summer" when you can sit "outdoors" or near one of the "windows" for "ample people-watching" from its "nice corner spot."

Local 44 ● *American*   16 | 15 | 17 | $20

West Philly | 4333 Spruce St. (44th St.) | 215-222-2337 | www.local44beerbar.com

"Local is the key word" at this "all-purpose" pub and "Penn grad student hangout" in West Philly where lagerheads recommend you "try the wings" and a brew from "one of the best beer lists in the city"; you can "expect a wait for a table", and regulars report the usually "friendly" vibe is "sometimes marred by snotty undergraduates."

Lolita ↩ *Mexican*   26 | 19 | 21 | $36

Washington Square West | 106 S. 13th St. (bet. Chestnut & Sansom Sts.) | 215-546-7100 | www.lolitabyob.com

There are "long waits" "for a reason" at this "haute", "trendy" cash-only "BYOT(equila)" in Wash West, which takes "Mexican to a new level" with "original flavors and combinations" and not "a chimichanga in sight", while "fantastic" "margarita mixers" will "change your perception of the drink"; though the "open kitchen" and "lively" scene cause a few to grouse that "some soundproofing would go a long way", "friendly, efficient" service helps smooth things over.

London Grill *American*   17 | 16 | 17 | $34

Fairmount | 2301 Fairmount Ave. (23rd St.) | 215-978-4545 | www.londongrill.com

This "charming" Fairmount "neighborhood joint" has "proven itself over the years", with a "solid" New American "menu full of both reliables and novelties", "lovely" staff and "old-bar" ambiance that are all "tough to beat"; the middling ratings notwithstanding, many agree it's "the kind of place one can easily make a regular" stop.

Lourdas Greek Taverna Ⓜ 🛱 *Greek* | 21 | 14 | 20 | $38 |

Bryn Mawr | 50 N. Bryn Mawr Ave. (Lancaster Ave.) | 610-520-0288 | www.lourdasgreektaverna.com

Though the "delicious" seafood is the "standout" at this "vibrant" BYO taverna in Bryn Mawr, the other "Hellenic" specialties are "dependably good" as well, while the servers are "knowledgeable"; though some grumble that the "seats are a little too close for comfort" and find the cash-only policy "inconvenient", "reasonable" tabs that "won't leave you with a Greek-style financial crisis" silence most gripes.

L2 Ⓜ *American* | 19 | 18 | 23 | $39 |

Graduate Hospital | 2201 South St. (22nd St.) | 215-732-7878

"Top-notch" service and "excellent drinks" are the big sells of this "cozy", "eclectic" Traditional American in G-Ho, while the "nice selection" of "reasonable priced", "simple to sophisticated" dishes also add to its allure; exposed brick, old pictures and lots of candles highlight the eclectic space, and Thursday jazz is part of the "great gay-friendly bar scene late into the night."

🆕 Lucky 7 Tavern ◑ 🛱 *American* | ∇ 17 | 16 | 18 | $18 |

Fairmount | 747 N. 25th St. (Aspen St.) | 215-232-7736

"Reasonably priced" bar food and "friendly service" draw a "nice crowd of regulars to this New American in Fairmount, where the staff "tries to please"; a few hard chargers are peeved that it "doesn't take credit or debit" cards, but to most, this "comfortable neighborhood hangout" works just "fine" for a "sandwich or snack."

🆕 Mac's Tavern ◑ *American* | - | - | - | I |

Old City | 226 Market St. (bet. 2nd & 3rd Sts.) | 267-324-5507

If everyone seems a bit bright and cheery at this Old City watering hole, that might be because it's part owned by Rob McElhenney and Kaitlin Olson, stars of the TV comedy *It's Always Sunny in Philadelphia*; the look suggests 'Philly dive bar' but the menu runs more toward gastropub, offering a selection of sandwiches, wings and five kinds of topped fries, all to pair with 17 beers on tap and dozens by the bottle.

🆕 MaGerks ◑ *American* | 15 | 14 | 14 | $21 |
(fka Bent Elbo Tavern)

Fort Washington | 582 S. Bethlehem Pike (Rte. 73) | 215-948-3329 | www.magerks.com

"Ever-thirsty suburbanites" "pack" this "clean", "well-lit" Fort Washington "sports bar" for "basic pub fare" (including a "good kids' menu") and a scene of controlled "chaos", including 30 TVs and "live bands"; though it's "not a foodie destination", most agree the owners have "made the best" of the former site of the late Bent Elbo.

	FOOD	DECOR	SERVICE	COST

Maggiano's Little Italy *Italian* `20` `18` `19` `$34`
Chinatown | 1201 Filbert St. (12th St.) | 215-567-2020
King of Prussia | King of Prussia Mall | 205 Mall Blvd. (Gulph Rd.) |
610-992-3333
www.maggianos.com
"Mangia, mangia!" – you "get your money's worth and then some" at
this "vintage", "family-style" chain known for "humongous" "feasts"
of "commercial" "Italian standards done right", as well as "long
waits" and "noise"; while some purists would leave the "fake" "corporate" experience to "tourists and suburbanites", the majority considers it "generally a crowd-pleaser."

Maggio's *Italian/Pizza* `18` `16` `19` `$25`
Southampton | Hampton Sq. | 400B Second St. Pike (bet. Madison &
Rozel Aves.) | 215-322-7272 | www.maggiosrestaurant.com
"Good, basic Italian food with some unique extras" is the draw at
this "family"-friendly Bucks County "institution", where regulars
recommend checking out the "nightly specials"; though a few
carp that it can get "too noisy to hear yourself chew", to most it's
"ok for a cheapie night out" – which might include a brew at the
adjoining sports bar.

Majolica Ⓜ *American/French* `24` `19` `22` `$44`
Phoenixville | 258 Bridge St. (bet. Gay & Main Sts.) | 610-917-0962 |
www.majolicarestaurant.com
"Locavores rejoice" over the "imaginative" Franco-American fare
"made with fresh, local ingredients" at Andrew Deery and Sarah
Johnson's "contemporary" BYO "jewel" in Phoenixville, where the
"knowledgeable" staff treats you "as if you're their only customer";
photos by area artists adorn the otherwise "plain" space, where you
can "pack a good bottle of wine and join the cognoscenti", and if you
feel it's "a little pricey", the $25 three-course prix fixes on
Wednesdays, Thursdays and Sundays can reduce the bite.

Mama Palma's Ⓜ⇄ *Italian* `23` `14` `18` `$23`
(aka Mama Palma Gourmet Pizza)
Rittenhouse | 2229 Spruce St. (23rd St.) | 215-735-7357
Brick-oven pizzas "made in heaven" and "bedlam" complete with
"screaming kids" make this "reasonably priced" Italian near
Fitler Square feel like "Sunday dinner at home" to many; while
the owners are "nice folks", critics say the service sometimes
"leaves much to be desired", and further grumble that the "cash-
only" and "no-reservations" policies cause "more heartburn
than the pizza."

Mamma Maria *Italian* `22` `16` `20` `$52`
South Philly | 1637 E. Passyunk Ave. (bet. Morris & Tasker Sts.) |
215-463-6884 | www.mammamaria.info
Regulars "come hungry" to this "romantic" South Philly Italian,
where "mamma" will visit "your table and chat until you feel at
home" before serving up "multiple courses" of "excellent" fare and
plying you with "endless" wine and "after-dinner cordials" ("if only

your real mother encouraged you to drink so much"); it's $55 for seven courses, and it now offers à la carte dining on weeknights.

Manayunk Brewery & Restaurant ● *Pub Food*

17 | 17 | 19 | $27

Manayunk | 4120 Main St. (Shurs Ln.) | 215-482-8220 | www.manayunkbrewery.com

This "drinker's eatery" in Manayunk offers a "great array" of pub grub "to choose from" – including "sushi" – to complement its "wonderful selection of craft beers and cocktails", served by a "pleasant" staff; the "huge" "outdoor deck" overlooking the "picturesque" "canal" is a "fun place to hang out" in the summer, another reason it's become a popular "social spot" for "twentysomethings."

Mandarin Garden *Chinese*

22 | 15 | 20 | $25

Willow Grove | 91 York Rd. (Davisville Rd.) | 215-657-3993

"Loyal customers come back repeatedly" for "generous portions" of "consistently delicious" Chinese "comfort food" served by a "quick, efficient" staff at this eatery across from the Willow Grove SEPTA station; though it may look like "your typical suburban" drop-in, most deem it "uncommonly good", and a "great value" as well.

MangoMoon Ⓜ *Asian*

∇ 17 | 17 | 21 | $36

Manayunk | 4161 Main St. (Lock St.) | 215-487-1230 | www.mymangomoon.com

"Interesting" Asian with healthful ingredients and exotic drinks (including infused liquors made in-house) are the calling cards of this sexy, sumptuous lounge in Manayunk, where moderately priced plates come in assorted sizes, allowing patrons to share or go solo; "friendly" service contributes to the "great vibe", though a few rate it "second-best" compared to elder sibling Chabaa Thai up the street.

Manny's Place Ⓢ *Seafood*

∇ 20 | 7 | 16 | $21

Chestnut Hill | 8229 Germantown Ave. (Southampton Ave.) | 215-242-4600 Ⓜ

Bala Cynwyd | 140 Montgomery Ave. (Penbroke Rd.) | 610-771-0101 Ⓜ

Wayne | Gateway Shopping Ctr. | 251 E. Swedesford Rd. (Rte. 202, exit Valley Forge) | 610-688-1000
www.mannyscrabcakes.com

"Why cook at home?" when you can "take out" "excellent crab cakes", "shrimp puffs" and other "reasonably priced" seafood from these "pickup" piscatoriums that do sport a "few tables" (but "no waitress service") if you just can't make it home; "don't forget the garlic (or lobster) mashed potatoes."

Maoz Vegetarian *Mideastern/Vegetarian*

23 | 9 | 16 | $10

South St. | 248 South St. (3rd St.) | 215-625-3500 ●
Washington Square West | 1115 Walnut St. (11th St.) | 215-922-3409
www.maozveg.com

"McDonald's be damned", the South Street and Washington Square links of this Holland-based Mideast-vegetarian chain shows "how fast food should be done": "make your own" "healthy" falafel sandwich or salad with "fresh" ingredients amid "cheery" surroundings with "virtually no seating" – and don't forget the "amazing" Belgian fries; it's a perfect stop for lunch or "after the bars" "let out."

Marathon Grill *American* | 18 | 14 | 16 | $23 |

Avenue of the Arts | 1339 Chestnut St. (Juniper St.) | 215-561-4460
Rittenhouse | 121 S. 16th St. (Sansom St.) | 215-569-3278
Rittenhouse | 1818 Market St. (18th St.) | 215-561-1818 ⊠
University City | 200 S. 40th St. (Walnut St.) | 215-222-0100
Washington Square West | 927 Walnut St. (bet. 9th & 10th Sts.) | 215-733-0311 ◗
www.marathongrill.com

"Office workers" and others frequent this "family-run" local chain of "glorified" "diners" for its "diverse menu" "with lots of yummy" "quick-bite" American choices and "awesome daily specials" that pack "lots of bang for the buck"; cognoscenti caution that "snagging a table isn't easy" in the "noisy", "crowded" setting, while the service is charitably described as "organized chaos"; P.S. "late-night happy-hour specials make the bar a nice option."

Marathon on the Square *American* | 18 | 15 | 17 | $27 |

Rittenhouse | 1839 Spruce St. (19th St.) | 215-731-0800 | www.marathongrill.com

Devotees praise this "solid" "unsung hero" of Rittenhouse Square for its "crowd-pleasing", "eclectic" New American fare that generates "long lines and waits", especially at "brunch"; while some critics kvetch about "snobby" airs and an "abbreviated" menu that's "trying too hard to be fancy", it "always works" for fans when they "can't think of anywhere" else.

Marco Polo *Italian* | 20 | 15 | 20 | $39 |

Elkins Park | Elkins Park Sq. | 8080 Old York Rd. (Church Rd.) | 215-782-1950 | www.mymarcopolo.com

"Solid seafood" and "kibitzing" "waiters" who "have been there forever" are the hallmarks of this "comfortable" strip-mall Italian where Elkins Parkers know they'll "see the neighbors" (including a few who seem to be "professional complainers") out for a "weeknight" dinner; the fare is "well executed", if "not spectacular", and most deem it a "good old standby" in an "area with very few restaurants."

Margaret Kuo's *Chinese/Japanese* | 23 | 22 | 20 | $40 |

Wayne | 175 E. Lancaster Ave. (Louella Ave.) | 610-688-7200 | www.margaretkuos.com

Ambivalent Asiaphiles can choose from two concepts under one Main Line roof – "stylish" Japanese upstairs, "fancy, dress-me-up" Chinese with a "ginormous menu" downstairs – at Margaret Kuo's "elegant" Wayne establishment; the "gong" that sounds when "the Peking duck" "enters the dining room" makes it worthy of a "celebration", but surveyors are split on the servers – they're either "fast" or "constantly disappearing."

Margaret Kuo's
Mandarin *Chinese/Japanese*   22 | 18 | 21 | $29

Frazer | 190 Lancaster Ave. (Malin Rd.) | 610-647-5488 |
www.margaretkuos.com

This "inviting" Frazer BYO is a "winner", offering both Japanese and
Chinese cuisine and getting both "right" ("two words: Peking duck");
"everything tastes fresh" on the $8.95 lunch buffet, while "attentive,
friendly" service contributes to the "warm, inviting atmosphere",
but a few quip "don't forget your Chinese-English dictionary."

Margaret Kuo's
Media *Chinese/Japanese*   24 | 21 | 22 | $36

Media | 6 W. State St. (Jackson St.) | 610-892-0115 |
www.margaretkuos.com

"Be prepared to be treated like royalty" (and "spend cash") at
Margaret Kuo's "upscale" Sino-Japanese in Downtown Media for
"dependable" tastes "as real as dining in Chinatown" and some of
the "freshest sushi around"; most agree the "quality" justifies the
price and the service is "attentive", though a few think the staff
could stand to "smile" once in a while.

Margaret Kuo's
Peking *Chinese/Japanese*   ∇ 27 | 24 | 24 | $32

Media | Granite Run Mall | 1067 W. Baltimore Pike (Middletown Rd.) |
610-566-4110 | www.margaretkuos.com

While it's been in Media's Granite Run Mall for nearly four decades,
Margaret Kuo's eatery is "not your run-of-the-mill" shopper's stop,
but rather a "fine-dining" establishment offering a "wonderful"
"mix-and-match" of Chinese and Japanese dishes that are as "authentic" as they get; "helpful" service is another plus, and all agree
the "only sense of the mall is in the address."

Maria's Ristorante
on Summit Ⓜ *Italian*   ∇ 21 | 15 | 19 | $36

Roxborough | 8100 Ridge Ave. (Summit Ave.) | 215-508-5600
Maria keeps the "kitchen on its toes" at this Roxborough Italian,
which is "popular among locals and those lucky enough to have been
tipped off" about its "generous portions" of "simple", "consistent"
cuisine; "reasonable" prices and a "friendly" atmosphere make it a
"comfortable anytime restaurant" for many, even if the "limited
parking can be a real hassle."

Marigold Kitchen Ⓜ *American*   24 | 18 | 22 | $46
University City | 501 S. 45th St. (Larchwood Ave.) | 215-222-3699 |
www.marigoldkitchenbyob.com

At this "cozy" New American BYO in University City, chef Robert
Halpern "sets a very high bar" for "creative" cooking, and "every
course" on his tasting menu "features a sublime combination of flavors" ("a little foam goes a long way"), though a few think he's "trying
too hard" and question the "fascination with bubbles"; still, most all
are happy with the "attentive" service and the "sitting-in-someone's-
dining-room atmosphere" of the updated "Victorian mansion."

| | FOOD | DECOR | SERVICE | COST |

Marrakesh ⌀ *Moroccan*

| | 25 | 25 | 22 | $38 |

South St. | 517 S. Leithgow St. (South St.) | 215-925-5929

"Knock on a door in an alleyway" off South Street and "enter the mysterious Middle East" at this Moroccan serving "awesome" seven-course $25 feasts that are a "real-deal, eat-with-the-hands experience"; the vibe is "so relaxing" you may "fall asleep between courses", and keep in mind it's "a tourist spot that isn't a trap" (complete with belly dancers on weekends or upon request), so "go with a group and enjoy" – and "get a reservation, because they only have so much room."

Marra's Ⓜ *Italian*

| | 21 | 13 | 18 | $25 |

South Philly | 1734 E. Passyunk Ave. (Moore St.) | 215-463-9249 | www.marras1.com

Seems like they "turn the clock" back at this South Philly octogenarian "staple", where the "classic" "brick-oven pizzas" and "tried-and-true", "red-gravy" Italian chow "haven't changed a bit", attracting post-"game" patrons and locals entertaining "out-of-towners"; there's plenty of "attytood" as "brusque" "waitresses hurry patrons to turn the tables", and even though some claim it's "past its prime", many more regard it as one of the "best bargains in town."

Marsha Brown *Creole/Southern*

| | 21 | 24 | 21 | $58 |

New Hope | 15 S. Main St. (Bridge St.) | 215-862-7044 | www.marshabrownrestaurant.com

The "refurbished" "old church" in the middle of New Hope sets a "stunning" stage for Ms. Brown's "exquisite" (albeit "pricey") Creole-Southern cooking, including "sweet potatoes so good, you want to roll around naked in them"; a "stellar" staff waits on a clientele that "seems not to know if this place is jacket and slacks, or biker vest and boots", which means the "people-watching is always fun" in the "beautiful venue."

Mary Cassatt
Tea Room & Garden *Tearoom*

| | - | - | - | M |

Rittenhouse | Rittenhouse Hotel | 210 W. Rittenhouse Sq. (bet. Locust & Walnut Sts.) | 215-546-9000 | www.rittenhousehotel.com

"Elegant ladies" and others who are in "no hurry" "chat and gossip all afternoon" at this "elegant" tearoom off the lobby of the Rittenhouse Hotel, where from 2-5 PM you can choose the signature tea for $24.95 ($5 extra for champagne) featuring some of the "loveliest sandwiches" "this side of London"; "comfortable" sofas and an "extra-special" "garden view" add to its allure.

Masamoto Asian
Grill & Sushi Bar *Asian*

| | ▽ 26 | 14 | 23 | $33 |

Glen Mills | Keystone Plaza Shopping Ctr. | 1810 Wilmington Pike (Woodland Dr.) | 610-358-5538 | www.masamotosushi.com

Regulars recommend you "sit at the bar" and let chef-owner Johnny Cia "take care of you" with "original" sushi "works of art" and "delicious" Pan-Asian dishes at his "must-try" strip-mall BYO in Glen Mills; with "amazingly helpful" service and "great-value" pricing, it "rates with Center City" establishments in the eyes of many.

NEW Más Mexicali Cantina ● *Mexican*

— | — | — | I

West Chester | 102 E. Market St. (Walnut St.) | 610-918-6280 | www.mascantina.com

From the oversized portions to the high-energy rock soundtrack, more is more at this over-the-top arrival (from the Kildare's crew) in Downtown West Chester that offers a budget-friendly menu of Californian-style Mexican; various theme nights and drink specials ensure that it's always lively.

☑ Matyson ⊠ *American*

27 | 19 | 24 | $45

Rittenhouse | 37 S. 19th St. (bet. Chestnut & Ludlow Sts.) | 215-564-2925 | www.matyson.com

"Foodies" call this "classy" New American near Rittenhouse Square the "best BYO in the city", thanks to the "wonderful, creative" and "always changing" menu from Brian Lofink and Ben Puchowitz that is at once "consistent" and "refreshing"; the staff "feels like family", and while some chafe at the "forced intimacy" of the "small storefront" space and "noise" that'll have you "communicating in sign language", the majority deems it a "cut above the rest."

Max & David's *Mediterranean*

21 | 18 | 21 | $43

Elkins Park | Yorktown Plaza | 8120 Old York Rd. (Church Rd.) | 215-885-2400 | www.maxanddavids.com

"This is not your bubbe's cooking" kvell cronies of this stylish, "upscale kosher" Elkins Park Med bistro that stands in a "league" of its "own", offering "class" and "friendly service" along with "rib-eye" steaks that make your "taste buds dance"; it's BYO (kosher only) and keeps Sabbath.

Max Brenner ● *American*

19 | 20 | 20 | $29

Rittenhouse | 1500 Walnut St. (15th St.) | 215-344-8150 | www.maxbrenner.com

The "11-page dessert menu" says it all about this "*Willy Wonka*-like" "chocoholic's dream come true" located near Rittenhouse Square, where a "peppy staff" slings "out-of-this-world" "sweets" and a line of "reasonably priced" sandwiches; amid such "culinary decadence", you may want to bring along "a chaperone to avoid embarrassing yourself."

Mayfair Diner ● *Diner*

15 | 13 | 19 | $17

Northeast Philly | 7373 Frankford Ave. (bet. Bleigh Ave. & Tudor St.) | 215-624-4455

Proponents posit "what's not to like" about this "no-frills" diner "institution" in Northeast Philly, which appears to have maintained its "local following" despite a change in ownership; "sassy" waitresses who've "been there for longer" than you've been "alive" deftly dish up "down-home" "late-night meals" in the "classic" "railroad-car" space.

	FOOD	DECOR	SERVICE	COST

McCormick & Schmick's *Seafood*   21 | 21 | 21 | $47

Avenue of the Arts | 1 S. Broad St. (Penn Sq.) | 215-568-6888 |
www.mccormickandschmicks.com

The "high-quality" seafood almost "never disappoints" at this "comfortable" upscale-casual chain according to fans unperturbed by the "corporate feel", who praise it for "attentive, but not obtrusive" service and a "nice selection" of "fish" and "beef"; aficionados report the "happy-hour specials are a well-kept secret and well worth a visit."

McFadden's ❶ *Pub Food*   15 | 17 | 15 | $23

Northern Liberties | 461 N. Third St. (bet. Spring Garden & Willow Sts.) |
215-928-0630 | www.mcfaddensphilly.com
South Philly | Citizens Bank Park | 1 Citizens Bank Way (Pattison Ave.) |
215-952-0300 | www.mcfaddensballpark.com

"If you are over 30, you will feel old" at these "standard" "tavern-cum–dance party" chain links where the "atmosphere certainly adds to the dining experience" ("they serve food here?" quip critics) – think "young female coeds", "Jell-o shots", "ear-splitting music" and "drunken bachelor parties"; the Citizens Bank Park location is the "place to be" on "Phillies and Eagles game days" when, not surprisingly, it gets "really crowded."

McGillin's Olde Ale House ❶ *Pub Food*   16 | 20 | 18 | $22

Washington Square West | 1310 Drury St. (bet. Chestnut & Sansom Sts.) |
215-735-5562 | www.mcgillins.com

Regulars report it's often "standing room–only" at this "hopping", "historic ale house" near City Hall, where a "wide mix of people" head for "hearty, fresh" fare and "good drinks" "after work" and on "karaoke" nights; "you feel like you've stepped back in time" in the "homey" 150-year-old space with the beloved "wobbly tables", and most agree it's a "must-see for any visitor."

Melograno Ⓜ *Italian*   24 | 18 | 21 | $41

Rittenhouse | 2012 Sansom St. (20th St.) | 215-875-8116 |
www.melogranorestaurant.com

Like "Tuscany without paying the airfare" is how loyalists describe this "bustling" mom-and-pop "oasis" near Rittenhouse, "arguably the best Italian BYO" in town according to admirers who "love watching" Gianluca Demontis "do his magic" in the "open kitchen", creating especially "delicious" specials; the staff makes you "feel at home" in the "new larger quarters", but even with the added capacity, many wail "come on – no reservations?"

Melrose Diner ❶ *Diner*   15 | 11 | 18 | $17

South Philly | 1501 Snyder Ave. (15th St.) | 215-467-6644

"Everyone who knows goes" to this "old-fashioned" 24/7 South Philly diner for the "home cooking" and "stays for the 'tude", as well as "lots of people-watching"; while some call it a "sad", "mediocre" vestige of its old self (a bit like "the Who at the Super Bowl"), others insist this "classic" is "exactly what it should be"; P.S. after a post-Survey renovation, which may outdate the Decor score, you no longer have to "share your booth" with strangers.

	FOOD	DECOR	SERVICE	COST

Melting Pot *Fondue*
19 | 17 | 20 | $46

Chinatown | 1219 Filbert St. (bet. 12th & 13th Sts.) | 215-922-7002
King of Prussia | 150 Allendale Rd. (bet. Court Blvd. & DeKalb Pike) |
610-265-7195
www.meltingpot.com

Those who've "taken a dip" at these fondue chain links in Chinatown
and King of Prussia are of two opinions: fans find them "fantastic"
for a "fun date night" or "dinner with friends" or "adventurous kids",
and laud the "melt-in-your mouth" prix fixes and happy-hour options; some detractors dunk the idea of paying "$50 to cook your
own food", but even they concede that the "dessert fondue makes
up for everything."

Mémé *American*
23 | 15 | 22 | $45

Rittenhouse | 2201 Spruce St. (22nd St.) | 215-735-4900 |
www.memerestaurant.com

"So, what are you waiting for?" wonder backers of David Katz's
"charming" New American near Rittenhouse Square, as they
encourage their "neighbors" and others to try his "inventive, surprising" small-plates "combinations"; most agree the "down-to-
earth" staff is a "treasure" (a few fret that it's "overworked") and try
to keep an "open mind" about the "rock" soundtrack" and "spartan"
"storefront" space with "smooshy seating."

Memphis Taproom ◗ *American*
23 | 19 | 24 | $24

Port Richmond | 2331 E. Cumberland St. (Memphis St.) | 215-425-4460 |
www.memphistaproom.com

While loyalists agree that "beer is king" at this "hopping" "hipsters'"
tap in Port Richmond (from the owners of Resurrection Taproom and
Local 44), the "inventive" American gastropub grub comes in a
"very close second"; a "friendly" staff navigates the "rotating menu
of craft brews" and bill of fare that includes "good options for vegetarians and those with dietary restrictions", and while the scene can
get predictably "hectic", insiders recommend the "rear dining room"
as a "refuge from the noise and crowds."

Mendenhall Inn *American*
19 | 20 | 21 | $48

Mendenhall | Clarion Inn at Mendenhall | 323 Kennett Pike (Rte. 1) |
610-388-1181 | www.mendenhallinn.com

"Friendly" service, "delectable" New American fare (including one
of the "best" Sunday brunches around) and a "surprisingly good
bar" with a "stone fireplace" make this "elegant" eatery "worth the
drive" to Brandywine Valley; critics, however, find it "dated" and
"overrated", and say the food "misses the mark."

Mercato ✄ *American/Italian*
25 | 18 | 21 | $39

Washington Square West | 1216 Spruce St. (Camac St.) | 215-985-2962 |
www.mercatobyob.com

"Fresh, seasonal", "out-of-the-ordinary Italian" fare is the norm at
this cash-only Wash West BYO (from the owners of Valanni and
Varga Bar) that's "open both to the street and to the kitchen"; the
"familial, talk-across-the-tiny-tables atmosphere" ("noisy" to

	FOOD	DECOR	SERVICE	COST

some), "attentive" service and "flights of olive oil" are "memorable", but there are "no reservations", so "get there early."

Meridith's *American*   20 | 19 | 18 | $39

Berwyn | 575 Lancaster Ave. (Old Lancaster Rd.) | 610-251-9600 | www.meridiths.com

Thanks to its "new location" complete with a new bar, "parking is no longer a problem" outside this "upscale-casual" Berwyn New American, and fans report the "ambiance is much improved"; it's still a "great place" for a "terrific" breakfast, lunch with the "gals" or a "creative dinner", though a few feel the "snarky" service "needs work"; BYO is still allowed, with $7 corkage.

Meritage Philadelphia Ⓜ *American*   25 | 21 | 23 | $47

Graduate Hospital | 500 S. 20th St. (Lombard St.) | 215-985-1922 | www.meritagephiladelphia.com

This New American on a corner in G-Ho "merits regular visits" thanks to Susanna Foo alum Anne Coll's "wonderful, Asian-tinged" small and medium plates, which are "prettily served" in a newly "chic", "bright" setting, along with "affordable custom drinks" and a "great wine selection"; the "cute" servers are "attentive and helpful without being overbearing."

Mexican Post *Mexican*   16 | 14 | 16 | $24

Logan Square | 1601 Cherry St. (16th St.) | 215-568-2667
Old City | 104 Chestnut St. (Front St.) | 215-923-5233 ◑
www.mexicanpost.com

The "pitcher of margies" is the main attraction at this "standard", "affordable" Mex chain, where "recession-wary", "coupon"-toting regulars expect "nothing out of the ordinary, but nothing bad either" (unless you count "slow" service); the Old City flagship is an "unpretentious, dive-y" spot "Clint Eastwood would smoke a cheroot in, if there weren't a smoking ban."

NEW MidAtlantic Ⓢ *American*   20 | 23 | 23 | $36

University City | 3711 Market St. (38th St.) | 215-386-3711 | www.midatlanticrestaurant.com

At his moderately priced Regional American situated upstairs from the "research geeks" at University City's Science Center, R2L's Daniel Stern puts a "creative" "twist" on "traditional Pennsylvania treats" (pretzels, oysters, scrapple); "knowledgeable, engaging" servers are on hand to "explain the sometimes confusing menu" in the "urban-industrial" space, which has a surprisingly "warm", "homey" vibe.

NEW Miga *Korean*   - | - | - | M

Rittenhouse | 211 S. 15th St. (Walnut St.) | 215-732-1616 | www.migarestaurant.com

There's little flash at this quiet Korean BBQ in Rittenhouse, but the kitchen delivers "large portions" of "well-prepared" "banchan", "kalbi" and "bulgogi", and patrons can also get into the act with the tabletop grills; add a decent wine list and attentive service from a hands-on owner and staff, and you have an "excellent value."

Mikado *Japanese* | 20 | 17 | 21 | $30 |

Ardmore | 64 E. Lancaster Ave. (bet. Rittenhouse Pl. & Simpson Rd.) |
610-645-5592

Mikado Thai Pepper *Thai*
(fka Thai Pepper)

Ardmore | 64 E. Lancaster Ave. (Argyle Rd.) | 610-642-5951 |
www.mikadothaipepper.com

Once neighbors and now under the same roof, this "dependable"
Japanese-Thai in Ardmore is "usually crowded" with folks craving the
"wide variety" of "reasonably priced" choices served by a "friendly"
staff; though some characterize the cuisine as "schizophrenic"
("Thai? Japanese? who knows?"), it suffices "for the Main Line."

Mi Lah Vegetarian *Vegan/Vegetarian* | ∇ 21 | 15 | 18 | $25 |

Rittenhouse | 218 S. 16th St. (Walnut St.) | 215-732-8888 |
www.milahvegetarian.com

Omnivores, "don't let" the term "vegetarian" "keep you away" from
this "reasonably priced" white-tablecloth BYO "oasis" near
Rittenhouse Square, where the "creative" chef "uses vegetables to
their full potential" without relying on "faux meat" to create an
eclectic menu that is 99% vegan; while the staff seems "delighted to
have you", cognoscenti caution "don't go in a rush", for the tempo of
service can match the "calm" environs.

Minar Palace ⊠ *Indian* | 18 | 12 | 12 | $17 |

Washington Square West | 1304 Walnut St. (13th St.) | 215-546-9443 |
www.minarphilly.com

The "portions are big enough to get you through two meals" at this
"inexpensive" Indian BYO in Wash West, where "all the students" go
to "fill up" on "nicely spiced" fare (the "saag paneer rocks my world");
though it relocated to "fancy-feeling" digs, cronies quip that "they
haven't updated the tacky plastic plates", and the "usual indifferent
help" remains, but "the food is still the real thing" too.

Miraku *Japanese* | - | - | - | M |

Spring House | Spring House Vill. | 1121 N. Bethlehem Pike
(Chesterfield Dr.) | 215-643-0100

"Large" portions and "creative presentations" of "excellent" sushi
and other Japanese staples are served by a "friendly, helpful" staff
at this central Montco Japanese located "in a strip mall off Bethlehem
Pike" with "plenty of on-site parking"; the "quality" makes it easy to
overlook the "average" decor.

Mirna's Café *Eclectic/Mediterranean* | 22 | 16 | 21 | $34 |

Blue Bell | Village Sq. | 758 DeKalb Pike (Skippack Pike) | 610-279-0500
Jenkintown | 417 Old York Rd. (West Ave.) | 215-885-2046 Ⓜ
"No one leaves hungry" from these "attractive", "high" "noise-level"
Med-centric Eclectic BYOs in Montco where there's "something for
everyone" on the menu; Jenkintown lives up to its rep as a "great little
neighborhood gem" with "solid" eats in a "storefront" space, while the
Blue Bell strip-maller is more spacious and "comfortable", and many
report "efficient, but not very friendly" service at both.

Misconduct Tavern ● *Pub Food*   19 | 15 | 19 | $24

Rittenhouse | 1511 Locust St. (15th St.) | 215-732-5797 |
www.misconduct-tavern.com

"From architects to lawyers to Mummers to sports fans", this thoroughly "nautical" Rittenhouse Square "meeting place" "draws everyone in" for "fun" times complete with "plasma screens" lining the walls, "surprisingly good" "burgers" and "pub grub", and a "good variety of quality beers on tap"; it's a popular stop after the Kimmel Center or Academy of Music, or spending a "day watching whichever sport is in season."

Mission Grill ⬛ *Southwestern*   18 | 19 | 20 | $35

Logan Square | 1835 Arch St. (bet. 18th & 19th Sts.) | 215-636-9550 |
www.themissiongrill.com

Better suited for "people-watching" and "happy hour" than a "tête-à-tête", this "boisterous" Southwestern (from the crew behind City Tap House and Public House) is also a "satisfactory" stop for lunch, serving up "ok", if "not authentic" chow; cynics call it a "little too conceptual and froufrou", not to mention "too pricey", but most acknowledge its value to the neighborhood on the "outskirts" of Logan Square.

Mix *Italian*   ▽ 17 | 15 | 16 | $22

Rittenhouse | RiverWest Condominiums | 2101 Chestnut St. (21st St.) |
215-568-3355 | www.mixbrickovenpizza.com

"If you can overlook the crying toddlers", insiders insist this Italian "joint" on the ground floor of the RiverWest condos near Rittenhouse Square is a "pleasure", offering "original" "brick-oven pizzas", "plenty" of low-priced "wines by the glass" and "relaxed, casual" service from a "cute" staff; it's "heaven on Chestnut Street", especially "when the weather permits" you to "eat outside."

Mixto *Pan-Latin*   20 | 21 | 19 | $31

Washington Square West | 1141 Pine St. (bet. Quince & 12th Sts.) |
215-592-0363

A confluence of "wonderful mojitos", "divine" *comida* and a "fun vibe" makes this "elegant" Pan-Latin in a "great old building" in Wash West swell for a "date", "light bite or grand feast", and the prices make it the "bargain of the century" in the minds of many; "friendly" service, "warm, colorful" decor and "curbside umbrellas" that "beckon" on warm "brunch" days all add to its allure.

NEW MIXX *American*   ▽ 17 | 19 | 15 | $29

Villanova | 789 E. Lancaster Ave. (I-476) | 610-527-0700 |
www.mixxrestaurant.com

"The action and the deals are at the bar" at this "hopping" New American downstairs from Azie on Main in Villanova, where "decent" "sandwiches, burgers and pizza" are served in a "large", "brightly lit" "cafeteria-like" setting that resembles "Anywhere, Suburban USA"; while most agree the cuisine is "better than expected", some critics describe the service as "scattered" and "inattentive."

	FOOD	DECOR	SERVICE	COST

Mizu ☒ *Japanese* — 20 | 8 | 19 | $21

Old City | 220 Market St. (bet. 2nd & 3rd Sts.) | 215-238-0966
Rittenhouse | 133 S. 20th St. (Moravian St.) | 215-563-3100
University City | 111 S. 40th St. (bet. Chestnut & Sansom Sts.) |
215-382-1745
www.mizusushibar.com

"Well-prepared" sushi "standards" at "reasonable prices" make this Japanese trio appealing to those "on a budget"; the "small" spaces and "sparse" decor make them easy to "miss", but the "friendly" service and "delicious" fare make up for what they lack in looks (University City does not allow BYO).

Modo Mio ☒☞ *Italian* — 26 | 16 | 21 | $39

Northern Liberties | 161 W. Girard Ave. (Hancock St.) | 215-203-8707 |
www.modomiorestaurant.com

Foodies "swoon" over Peter McAndrews' "lusty", "spot-on" Italian cuisine (including "some of the best bread in town") at his "inviting" trattoria on the edge of Northern Liberties, which fans proclaim one of the city's "best" BYOs, "hands-down"; the cash-only $33 prix fixe 'turista' menu offers "Vetri quality at McDonald's prices", while staffers "care that you have a good meal", so "run, don't walk" (and "bring earplugs") for a "special experience."

Molly Maguire's ◐ *Pub Food* — ▽ 16 | 21 | 18 | $27

Phoenixville | 197 Bridge St. (Main St.) | 610-933-9550 |
www.mollymaguirespubs.com

"You don't have to be Irish to enjoy" the "expertly poured Guinness" at this "inviting" "interpretation" of a Dublin pub on Phoenixville's main drag, complete with "ornate bars on each floor" and "cool open-air deck upstairs"; a few say "blah" to the grub and grumble that "you'll need a microscope to see the portions", but most others are too busy "making new friends" and "people-watching" to notice.

🆕 Momiji Sushi & Grill *Japanese* — - | - | - | I

Society Hill | 522 S. Fifth St. (Lombard St.) | 215-574-1557
This Japanese cafe in a storefront off South Street keeps it tight, from the limited menu to the setting – a wee sushi bar and dinerlike booths, with a mural of a geisha adding interest; low-cost lunch options (including a few cooked dishes such as teriyaki, tempura and yakitori) are a plus, as are doors that open to the sidewalk and let in lots of light.

Monk's Cafe ◐ *Belgian* — 22 | 15 | 17 | $29

Rittenhouse | 264 S. 16th St. (bet. Latimer & Spruce Sts.) | 215-545-7005 |
www.monkscafe.com

Sure, this Belgian "institution" near Rittenhouse Square may look like a "leftover from the 1980s" (or a "Hogwarts for adults"), but who cares when you're perusing a "heavenly" "beer list as long as the Declaration of Independence", complemented by "mouthwatering" burgers, fries and mussels served with a "European flair"; but "you'll have to wait for a table", and a few grumble that management and staff are "becoming full of themselves."

| | FOOD | DECOR | SERVICE | COST |

Moonstruck *Italian*

21 | 22 | 22 | $44

Northeast Philly | 7955 Oxford Ave. (Rhawn St.) | 215-725-6000 |
www.moonstruckrestaurant.com

An "oldie but goodie", this "classy" Northeast Philly Italian "still
maintains a high standard" for "fine dining" according to fans who
laud the "elegant" space that "sparkles with etched glass and shin-
ing metal", where staffers "pamper you just right", whether you opt
for the $29 prix fixe "value" meal or go à la carte (which can get
"very pricey"); "BYO on Sundays and Wednesdays" also help to
keep the costs down.

More Than Just Ice Cream *Dessert*

20 | 13 | 17 | $18

Washington Square West | 1119 Locust St. (bet. Quince & 12th Sts.) |
215-574-0586

There's "fresh" "comfort food" and "enough sugar to summon the
tooth fairy" at this "reliable", "low-key" Traditional American/
dessertery in Wash West; while some gripe that the service can be
"flighty", most are forgiving when they decide to "drop the diet" and
have a hunk of "mile-high apple pie" or some "rich, creamy ice cream."

Moriarty's ◐ *Pub Food*

20 | 16 | 18 | $27

Washington Square West | 1116 Walnut St. (Quince St.) | 215-627-7676 |
www.moriartyspub.com

"Massive, spicy wings" and a "great beer list" (including some 30
drafts) make sojourners "stuck in hotels" "feel at home" and "satisfied" at this Wash West watering hole, a "genuine", "low-rent alternative" to the "uptight" pub "options" in the neighborhood; though
it's been labeled "frat boy heaven", many recommend it as a "cool"
stop before or after the theater or for Saturday karaoke, as long as
you're not "too adventurous" with the menu.

☒ Morimoto *Japanese*

28 | 26 | 25 | $76

Washington Square West | 723 Chestnut St. (bet. 7th & 8th Sts.) |
215-413-9070 | www.morimotorestaurant.com

"Amazing", "pristine sushi", a "fascinating array" of cooked dishes and
"top-notch" service all "dazzle" at this Japanese from Stephen Starr
and *Iron Chef* Masaharu Morimoto, set in a "luminescent", "post-
modern whale's belly of a space" in Wash West; besides maybe the
"trippy" "phallic lamps" on the tables, the "only hindrance comes at
the end" "on a little piece of paper" quip sticker-shocked surveyors,
but "rest assured" it's worth it – especially if you "jump off the deep
end" and try the "sublime" omakase tasting menu.

Morning Glory Diner ⌑ *Diner*

22 | 14 | 17 | $17

South Philly | 735 S. 10th St. (Fitzwater St.) | 215-413-3999 |
www.themorningglorydiner.com

"Go early" or "be prepared to wait" at this "diner-ish" Bella Vista
cash-only cafe "institution" where a mixed crowd ranging from "hipsters to hippies to yuppies" flock for "high-quality", "lumberjack"-size
"frittatas", "pancakes" and "waffles", in portions so big you can "take
half home and it's cheaper than buying groceries"; most condone the
staff's "surly" mien, insisting it gets "better" "the busier they are."

	FOOD	DECOR	SERVICE	COST

Morton's The Steakhouse *Steak* | 26 | 22 | 25 | $66 |

Avenue of the Arts | 1411 Walnut St. (Broad St.) | 215-557-0724
King of Prussia | Pavilion at King of Prussia Mall | 640 W. DeKalb Pike
(bet. Allendale & Long Rds.) | 610-491-1900
www.mortons.com

"There's no such thing as a small portion" at these "dark", "expense-account" steakhouse chain links (aka "carnivore central") on the Avenue of the Arts and in King of Prussia, where "service is always on" and devotees cheerfully indulge in "reliable", "high-quality" beef and "fantastic sides"; a few grumble that "they nickel and dime you to death", but the majority agrees "you can't go wrong taking an out-of-town guest", because they're simply a "cut above."

Moshulu *American* | 22 | 26 | 22 | $52 |

Delaware Riverfront | Penn's Landing | 401 S. Columbus Blvd.
(Spruce St.) | 215-923-2500 | www.moshulu.com

Many attest the "best water views" in Philly are here on this 100-year-old four-masted barque berthed at Penn's Landing, where it's full steam ahead for "awesome" Polynesian-influenced New American chow, served by a crew awash in "warmth and professionalism" in "romantic", "antique" nautical quarters complete with "curved bulkheads"; Sunday brunch has "everything you could want" and in summer, "the bar on the deck" feels like "somewhere in the Caribbean."

NEW M Restaurant 🖼️Ⓜ️ *Pan-Latin* | ▽ 21 | 20 | 22 | $52 |

Washington Square West | Morris House Hotel | 225 S. Eighth St.
(bet. Locust & Walnut Sts.) | 215-625-6666 | www.morrishousehotel.com

Pascual Cancelliere's "stellar" Argentinean small plates with an Italian flair are prepared with "grace and imagination" and served in a "charming" room at the boutique Robert Morris House in Wash West, but some insist it's the "Georgian garden" "oasis" "surrounded by beautiful historic buildings" that makes it a "dining experience for grown-ups"; some demur at the "limited menu" and recommend it for drinks instead (though lunch is now an option too).

Z Mr. Martino's Trattoria Ⓜ️🚫 *Italian* | 24 | 20 | 26 | $30 |

South Philly | 1646 E. Passyunk Ave. (bet. Morris & Tasker Sts.) |
215-755-0663

"Delicious homemade everything" explains the menu at this "old-world" husband-and-wife-run BYO housed in a former South Philly hardware store, where it's "like going to your Italian neighbor's for dinner" in the "tin-ceilinged" room brimming with "charm" and "contagious" "good cheer"; if it's "underappreciated", that's probably because it's open only Fridays–Sundays for dinner, and it's cash-only.

Ms. Tootsie's *Soul Food* | ▽ 25 | 21 | 20 | $32 |

South St. | 1314 South St. (13th St.) | 215-731-9045

Ms. Tootsie's Restaurant Bar Lounge ● *Soul Food*

South St. | 1312 South St. (13th St.) | 215-985-9001
www.kevenparker.net

"True" Southern staples such as "fried chicken", "catfish" and "mac 'n' cheese" ensure "you will leave full" from KeVen Parker's South

Street storefront soul fooders (restaurant/bar/lounge on one side, cafe on the other), where some devotees swear their "grandmother is cooking in the kitchen"; the digs are "lovely" but "tight", and critics quip the service can be as "slow as a lazy day by the fishing hole."

🆕 Munk & Nunn *Mediterranean* | - | - | - | M |
(fka Zesty's)

Manayunk | 4382 Main St. (Levering St.) | 215-483-6226 | www.munkandnunn.com

Tom Konidaris has revamped his Manayunk mainstay Zesty's into this Mediterranean offering a small-plates menu (which includes several favorites from its predecessor) in an intimate, modern monastic setting that's conducive to conversation; the 30-seat bar is stocked with signature cocktails, wines and microbrews.

Murray's Deli ⇨ *Deli* | 18 | 10 | 16 | $21 |
Bala Cynwyd | 285 Montgomery Ave. (Levering Mill Rd.) | 610-664-6995 | www.murraysdeli.com

The "wholesome Jewish soul food" at this Main Line deli "won't disappoint" as long as you "stick to the basics" say fans, who swear it's "still a great place" for a "schmooze over a cup of coffee" – especially since "nobody rushes to prepare or serve your food"; while a "remodeling" has boosted the Decor score, a contingent kvetches that the current owners "threw away all the charm."

Mustard Greens *Chinese* | 22 | 15 | 23 | $27 |
Queen Village | 622 S. Second St. (bet. Bainbridge & South Sts.) | 215-627-0833

Those who prefer their Chinese with "sweet, sticky sauces" may be disappointed in "gracious" chef-owner Bon Siu's "fresh", "delicately seasoned" takes on Cantonese cuisine at his "unpretentious" storefront off South Street, but few can find fault with the "great prices"; "clean, comfortable" digs are another plus, but as it approaches its 20th year in business, a few suggest "the menu needs an update."

My Thai *Thai* | 22 | 17 | 22 | $24 |
Graduate Hospital | 2200 South St. (22nd St.) | 215-985-1878

"Penn students, professors" and others on a budget pack this "cozy", "well-established" Thai "retreat" in Graduate Hospital for "killer" "weeknight three-course specials" of "reliable" eats served by a "friendly" staff; while the "small" room that feels like a "grandmother's" parlor may not be "as sprightly as some of the newer places", many fans attest there's "nothing more comforting" than this "warm neighborhood spot."

Naked Chocolate Café *Dessert* | 24 | 17 | 19 | $14 |
Avenue of the Arts | 1317 Walnut St. (13th St.) | 215-735-7310 | www.nakedchocolateonline.com

You're liable to "bounce off the walls with a sugar rush" at this "seductively named", "good-to-the-last-lick" Avenue of the Arts dessertery dishing out treats such as a liquid-cocoa specialty that's "pure happiness in a cup" and "cupcakes" that are a "splurge" well "worth the extta time on the treadmill"; it's manned by one of the "cheeriest staffs in the world", and there's also "fantastic" "live entertainment."

☑ Nam Phuong *Vietnamese*   26 | 11 | 17 | $19

South Philly | 1100-1120 Washington Ave. (11th St.) | 215-468-0410 | www.namphuongphilly.com

The "delicious" "grilled Vietnamese goodies with all the accompaniments" at this South Philly strip-mall fave are "super-cheap" and enable you to "eat adventurously" for less than the cost of "shopping next door at the supermarket"; the "food comes out extremely quickly", although gripes about "spotty" service are common, and while the digs may resemble an "institutional dining hall", what do you expect for such a "colossal bargain"?

Nan ☒ *French/Thai*   26 | 17 | 22 | $39

University City | 4000 Chestnut St. (40th St.) | 215-382-0818 | www.nanrestaurant.com

The "menu doesn't change often" at Kamol Phutlek's "unassuming" French-Thai "treasure" in University City, which is just fine for regulars who rhapsodize over his "insanely" "delicious" duck and "marvelous rack of lamb", and BYO makes it a "wonderful way to show off your own cellar without cooking"; although a few feel the digs could be "spruced up", many others appreciate the "subdued", "civilized" environs, and almost all agree the "reasonable" prices make it an "unbelievable value."

Nan Zhou   ▽ 23 | 5 | 12 | $11
Hand Drawn Noodles ⊟ *Noodle Shop*

Chinatown | 927 Race St. (bet. 9th & 10th Sts.) | 215-923-1550

"Cheap", "tasty", "fast" and "filling" – the paeans fly as quickly as the chefs "stretch" out and "smack" down the "freshly handmade noodles" that go into the "superlative soups" at this "no-frills", "atmosphere-free" shop in Chinatown; while neophytes cheerfully "slurp" and "gnaw on the bones" of the "authentic" fare, cognoscenti caution that some add-ins, such as "cooked pig ears", are "more of an acquired taste."

National Mechanics ❶ *Pub Food*   ▽ 18 | 18 | 16 | $25

Old City | 22 S. Third St. (Market St.) | 215-701-4883 | www.nationalmechanics.com

While many head to this "spacious" pub in the National Mechanics Building (circa 1837) for its "huge selection of beer", some find the "inexpensive" pub grub "tasty enough" to warrant "going back just for the food"; though it can get "noisy", the "great atmosphere" and "fun mix of events", including "quizzo, karaoke and DJs", make it a "good alternative to some of the more pretentious eateries in Old City."

Nectar *Asian*   24 | 26 | 21 | $52

Berwyn | 1091 Lancaster Ave. (Manchester Ct.) | 610-725-9000 | www.tastenectar.com

"Delicious" "nouveau" Pan-Asian fare, "techno music" and a "gleaming", "high-ceiling" space have a "transporting" effect on

FOOD DECOR SERVICE COST

Main Liners who park their "Bentleys in the parking lot" and go in to see "and be seen" by the "monster-sized Buddha"; by night, the "hopping bar scene" transforms it into "cougar city", while by day, the "two-course" prix fixe lunch is a bargain at $12.95.

New Delhi 🅼 *Indian* `23` `13` `18` `$19`
University City | 4004 Chestnut St. (40th St.) | 215-386-1941 | www.newdelhiweb.com

All-you-can-eat aficionados "need to be rolled out" after taking advantage of the "fantastic buffet" at this University City Indian ($7.95 lunch, $10.95 dinner, "dessert included"), while others insist the "cooked-to-order dishes can't be beat"; the service is "prompt and friendly", and though a redo created "more space for seating", the line can still "go out the door", so those in-the-know arrive "early."

New Harmony *Chinese/Vegetarian* `22` `10` `19` `$21`
Chinatown | 135 N. Ninth St. (bet. Cherry & Race Sts.) | 215-627-4520

"Even the hungriest carnivore" will find "delicious", "imaginative" vegetarian offerings, including "lots of mock meat selections" such as the "convincing steamed pork buns (not!)", at this Chinese BYO known for "impossibly cheap" tabs; it "isn't much to look at", but it is "family-friendly", and with the "new" name come Sunday buffets with "so many choices."

New Samosa *Indian/Vegetarian* `-` `-` `-` `I`
Washington Square West | 1214 Walnut St. (bet. 12th & 13th Sts.) | 215-546-2009

Boosters agree the "price is right" (i.e. $6.99 lunch, $9.99 dinner) at this "solid", "buffet-style" vegetarian Indian in Wash West; the meatless fare, including goods from its on-site bakery, is "good for a quick meal before or after a play or concert."

New Tavern, The 🅱 *American* ∇ `21` `19` `23` `$35`
Bala Cynwyd | 261 Montgomery Ave. (Levering Mill Rd.) | 610-667-9100 | www.thetavernrestaurant.com

For a "sudden attack" of "comfort-food" cravings, cronies recommend this "comfortable" taproom in Bala that dishes out "good-old American cuisine" and "Greek specialties" at a "fair price", while owner Nick Zarvalas "makes each guest feel welcome"; the majority describes it as a "warm neighborhood hangout" – just be "prepared to be the youngest person in there by 40 years if you go for lunch."

Newtown Grill *Italian/Steak* ∇ `19` `18` `19` `$40`
Newtown Square | 191 S. Newtown Street Rd. (½ mi. south of West Chester Pike) | 610-356-9700 | www.italiansteakhouse.com

An "impressive wine list" and "friendly bar" highlight this "cozy" Newtown Square Italian steakhouse, recommended by fans as a "nice place to bring the family" for "sophisticated" dining and "friendly" service in a "cozy" setting with a fireplace; though some critics pan it as "boring" and "overpriced", it remains the "neighborhood favorite" of many.

	FOOD	DECOR	SERVICE	COST

New Wave Café ● *American* `17` `14` `18` `$26`

Queen Village | 784 S. Third St. (Catharine St.) | 215-922-8484 |
www.newwavecafe.com

"You can give yourself whiplash people-watching" at this "upbeat"
neighborhood staple" on a Queen Village corner, whether you're
"outside" at "brunch "on a warm day" or "catching a game"; the New
American "gastropub" chow and "attractive" staff are a "treat", and
while a few dismiss it as a "paper-napkin place", most aver "you can
always find something good at virtually every price range."

Nicholas ▱ *American* `▽ 22` `19` `22` `$41`

South Philly | 2015 E. Moyamensing Ave. (Emily St.) | 215-271-7177 |
www.nicholasphilly.com

"Small in size but not in substance", this "elegant" New American
BYO is a "jewel in South Philly" where devotees find "sincere good
cooking" and "fresh flavors" on a "menu that changes weekly", cour-
tesy of the "friendly and accommodating" team of Nick and
Nicholas (or is that Nicholas and Nick?); the "elegant, warm" setting adds to what many describe as a "special dining experience";
it's open Thursdays–Sundays only.

Nifty Fifty's ♄ *Diner* `19` `19` `19` `$14`

Northeast Philly | 2491 Grant Ave. (Blue Grass Rd.) | 215-676-1950
Bensalem | 2555 Street Rd. (Knights Rd.) | 215-638-1950
Folsom | 1900 MacDade Blvd. (Kedron Ave.) | 610-583-1950
www.niftyfiftys.com

For a dose of "'50s nostalgia", fans head to these "loud", "eye-
blindingly" bright "throwback" diners where "you can feel your arteries
clogging as you enjoy juicy burgers" and pick from a "mind-boggling"
selection of "sodas" and "milkshakes" that "would even make the
Fonz say "aayyy"; a "wonderful" staff makes it easy to "bring the
kids", and the prices meet most "family budgets."

⊠ Nineteen (XIX) *American/Seafood* `23` `27` `23` `$55`

Avenue of the Arts | Park Hyatt at the Bellevue | 200 S. Broad St., 19th fl.
(Walnut St.) | 215-790-1919 | www.parkhyatt.com

"Exhilarating" views from the 19th floor of the Hyatt at the Bellevue
and elegant "strings of pearls" hanging over the "rotunda ceilings"
create a surefire "transporting" experience at this "fancy hotel" New
American; the "meticulously prepared" cuisine is complemented by
an "outstanding wine list" and served by a "courteous" staff, although a few feel the service sometimes "needs help"; P.S. don't
miss the "fabulous" $19 lunch specials Mondays–Saturdays.

Noble American Cookery ▱ *American* `20` `21` `19` `$45`

Rittenhouse | 2025 Sansom St. (bet. S. 20th & 21st Sts.) |
215-568-7000 | www.noblecookery.com

A "beautifully remodeled storefront" featuring an "incredible" bar
and a rooftop garden is the backdrop for "inventive" but "not overly
complicated" New American fare and "unexpectedly interesting"
wines at this rough-hewn Rittenhouse Square eatery; critics cavil
"come hungry, leave hungry" over "two-bite"-size portions that are

FOOD | DECOR | SERVICE | COST

"not cheap", while decrying the service as "a little snooty", but for most, "unique", "creative" fare makes it "worth a trip."

Nodding Head Brewery & Restaurant ● *Pub Food*
19 | 14 | 18 | $23

Rittenhouse | 1516 Sansom St., 2nd fl. (bet. 15th & 16th Sts.) | 215-569-9525 | www.noddinghead.com

Heads are bobbin' over the "world-class" beer selection at this "comfortable, low-key" and "slightly dumpy" second-floor Monk's offshoot in Rittenhouse Square; the "tasty" pub chow "exceeds the typical bar menu" and the "prompt and friendly" staff is full of "recommendations for those needing a little guidance."

Novità Bistro ⊘ *Mediterranean*
∇ 18 | 14 | 18 | $38

Graduate Hospital | 1608 South St. (16th St.) | 215-545-4665 | www.novitabistro.com

"Nicely prepared" "tagines" earn props for this "Moroccan-tinged" Med BYO set in a cozy, exposed brick–walled space, which is part of the "growing west South Street scene" in G-Ho; while most view it as a "reasonably priced" "change-of-pace from the ubiquitous Italian" joints nearby, a few report "uneven" food and "pedestrian" experiences, and "hopefully they'll continue to improve."

N. 3rd ● *American*
23 | 19 | 20 | $28

Northern Liberties | 801 N. Third St. (Brown St.) | 215-413-3666 | www.norththird.com

Peter Dunmire's "off-the-charts" "comfort food" and a selection of "superior beer and cocktails" attract an "interesting" assortment of "hipsters", "artists" and "young" spirits to this "cozy" Northern Liberties "gastropub" where the "bartenders' iPods provide the soundtrack"; the digs are "seriously without light", so bring a "small flashlight" at night to "read the menu" or view the painting of "boobs" in the "back room"; P.S. "check out the independent short films" screening on Tuesday nights.

Ocean Harbor *Chinese*
21 | 10 | 14 | $21

Chinatown | 1023 Race St. (bet. 10th & 11th Sts.) | 215-574-1398

The "long lines of Chinatown locals say it all" about this "basic" dim summery, where regulars recommend you "bring your appetite" for the carts "rolling through" the dining room laden with "always fresh", "awesome" treats, or you can "be adventurous" and order off the menu; complaints of "dingy" airs and "hit-or-miss" service notwithstanding, the consensus is it's "worth the chaos."

Oishi *Asian*
25 | 19 | 21 | $34

Newtown | 2817 S. Eagle Rd. (Durham Rd.) | 215-860-5511 | www.eatoishi.com

Some devotees think the path to "heaven" might be "lined" with the "cucumber rolls" from this Pan-Asian located in an "otherwise unremarkable strip mall" in central Bucks serving "world-class" "sushi", some of the "best" "bulgogi east of Seoul" and "hibachi" (teppanyaki) offerings; since it's a "secret no more", insiders report that service is "occasionally rushed" due to the crush of "local tweens/teens and their parents" "sitting cheek to cheek" in the "minimalist" digs.

Old Guard House Inn ☒ *American* | 22 | 22 | 24 | $53 |

Gladwyne | 953 Youngsford Rd. (Righters Mill Rd.) | 610-649-9708 | www.guardhouseinn.com

"You're back in the '50s" at this Main Line "mainstay" – but is it the 1950s, with Albert Breuer's "delicious" takes on retro Traditional American fare, or the 1750s, in a log-cabin setting where you "expect to see George Washington at the next table"?; "friendly, knowledgeable" service makes it "enjoyable" whichever era you prefer, even if some wiseacres quip that it's "not for the young and hip, but for the ones with hip replacements."

Olive Tree Mediterranean Grill ☒ *Greek* | 23 | 15 | 23 | $29 |

Downingtown | 379 W. Uwchlan Ave. (Peck Rd.) | 610-873-7911 | www.olivetreegrill.com

"Friendly" folks "take care of you" at this "modest" Greek BYO in Downingtown, where locals are "packed" in "wall-to-wall" for "authentic", "well-prepared" "house specialties" (gyros, moussaka, hummus) and "deliciously delightful desserts"; it "looks like a modern diner", so "don't go expecting to be charmed" by the atmosphere, but "what it lacks in decor, it makes up for with service."

Ooka Japanese *Japanese* | 24 | 21 | 21 | $35 |

Doylestown | 110 Veterans Ln. (Main St.) | 215-348-8185
NEW Montgomeryville | 764 Bethlehem Pike (Yeakel Ave.) | 215-361-1119
Willow Grove | 1109 Easton Rd. (Fitzwatertown Rd.) | 215-659-7688
www.ookasushi.com

"Delicious", "beautifully presented" sushi and "superior hibachi" (teppanyaki) keep "customers coming back for more" at this "trendy" Japanese trio with branches in Montgomeryville and Doylestown (small sake and Japanese beer list) and "off the turnpike" in Willow Grove (BYO); all told, "this is dinner and a show for the price of just dinner", and a "reasonable" one at that.

Orchard, The Ⓜ *American* | ▽ 27 | 24 | 25 | $65 |

Kennett Square | 503 Orchard Ave. (Rte. 1) | 610-388-1100 | www.theorchardbyob.com

Gary Trevisani's "fine, minimalist touch" on "creative" New American cuisine pleases patrons at his "special-occasion" "stunner" in Kennett Square; the "welcoming" staff "truly understands the art of BYO" and contributes to the "pleasant environment" in the "intimate" quarters, although a few critics jeer that you need to "practice being upscale and putting your nose in the air before you go."

Osaka *Japanese* | 23 | 18 | 22 | $39 |

Chestnut Hill | 8605 Germantown Ave. (Evergreen Ave.) | 215-242-5900 | www.osakachestnuthill.com
Wayne | 372 W. Lancaster Ave. (Strafford Ave.) | 610-902-6135

"Reliable sushi and sashimi" and "interesting", "well-prepared" cooked dishes are the stock in trade of these "effective", separately owned Japanese eateries in Wayne and Chestnut Hill; the "attentive" staff "makes you feel at home" in the "simple", modern settings, but some critics report "slow" service when it's "crowded on weekends."

Z Osteria *Italian*   27 | 24 | 24 | $56

North Philly | 640 N. Broad St. (Wallace St.) | 215-763-0920 | www.osteriaphilly.com

"Let your inhibitions go" at the Vetri gang's "industrial"-meets-"rustic" Italian in a "pioneering" North Philly location; it's "perfect" for a "date" or "celebratory night out" thanks to chef Jeff Michaud's "swoon-worthy" pizzas, charcuterie and pastas, which are backed by an "expansive" wine list and served by a staff that makes you feel "snuggled up in a warm, doughy embrace" in a room that's "full of energy"; while it's "not cheap", "easy street parking" (albeit in a "questionable" area) will save you some $$$.

Ota-Ya Ⓜ *Japanese*   23 | 13 | 20 | $34

Newtown | 10 Cambridge Ln. (Sycamore St.) | 215-860-6814 | www.ota-ya.com

Serving "fresh, pristine" raw fin fare at "very reasonable prices" (including "awesome" specials), this Japanese BYO in Lambertville and its Newtown "counterpart" are a "sushi lover's heaven" in areas "lacking in Japanese options"; "solicitous" service from a "friendly" staff creates a "warm" environment.

Otto's Brauhaus *German*   19 | 17 | 21 | $27

Horsham | 233 Easton Rd. (Pine Ave.) | 215-675-1864 | www.ottosbrauhauspa.com

"Tasty and filling" German dishes "paired" with "decent" beers highlight the "true" Teutonic "experience" at this Deutsch octogenarian in Horsham, where "nothing's fancy" but it's still a "great place for a date night"; in warm weather, the "beer garden's jumpin'" and "regulars" are happy to "lift a pint" to the $20.99 Sunday buffet (4-8 PM).

Oyster House ⓼ *Seafood*   23 | 20 | 21 | $39
(fka Sansom Street Oyster House)

Rittenhouse | 1516 Sansom St. (bet. 15th & 16th Sts.) | 215-567-7683 | www.oysterhousephilly.com

After a "180"-degree "transformation" at the hands of the Mink family, this "nostalgic" Rittenhouse seafooder has "risen" like a "Phoenix" and is "better than ever", with a revamped menu featuring "artfully presented" raw bar offerings and "sublime" "snapper soup", plus "buck-a-shuck" "happy-hour" specials that are "not to be missed"; "minimalist" white subway tiles and "colorful antique oyster plates" highlight the "nicely renovated" space, and "re-energized" service also helps makes it a "winner."

Pace One *American*   ▽ 21 | 23 | 22 | $41

Thornton | 341 Thornton Rd. (Glen Mills Rd.) | 610-459-3702 | www.paceone.net

The "personality" and "charming Colonial atmosphere" at this 18th-century farmhouse in the Brandywine Valley make it "a favorite of locals and tourists alike", and "good feelings abound" for "sophisticated preparations" of "reliably good" New American fare; the "warm, cozy" vibe is another reason many deem it a "restaurant worth seeking out."

Paddock at Devon *American*
15 | 16 | 15 | $33

Wayne | 629 W. Lancaster Ave. (Old Eagle School Rd.) | 610-687-3533 | www.devonpaddock.com

"They don't horse around" at this "always packed" Main Line "neighborhood" American where (a middling Food score notwithstanding) fans report a "high-quality brunch" served in the "über-horsey'd" setting, as well as "friendly" service; there's "a lot of action at the bar" from folks "hunting for husband/wife number two or three", but detractors deride the "over-the-hill" gang trying to sow its oats.

Palace of Asia *Indian*
22 | 14 | 18 | $27

Fort Washington | Best Western Inn | 285 Commerce Dr. (Delaware Dr.) | 215-646-2133 | www.palaceofasia.net

The $10.55 "weekday lunch buffet totally rocks" at this Indian "oasis" in Fort Washington's Best Western, where "foodies" fete the "extensive menu" of "consistently good" eats that go "above and beyond" the usual, served by a "gracious" staff; cognoscenti counsel ignore the "crappy hotel" setting, for it's "much better than you think it's going to be."

Palm, The *Steak*
24 | 20 | 24 | $64

Avenue of the Arts | The Bellevue | 200 S. Broad St. (Walnut St.) | 215-546-7256 | www.thepalm.com

It's "politico central" at this "classic", "top-tier" meatery in the Bellevue where many of the "celebs" on "the walls" show up in person for "shockingly high-quality" steaks and lobsters and to be "treated like kings" by servers who "seem to be there whenever needed, but are never in the way"; the high "noise" factor makes it a "great place to go with someone you don't want to talk to", and if you're the kind to beef about the bill, get a friend to "pick up the tab."

Paradigm ⓈⓂ *American*
20 | 22 | 20 | $42

Old City | 239 Chestnut St. (bet. 2nd & 3rd Sts.) | 215-238-6900 | www.paradigmrestaurant.com

Mixing a "laid-back" vibe with a "sleek and chic" setting complete with 40-ft.-long granite bar, this Old City Traditional American is "definitely more of a place for drinks", where a visit to the restrooms whose "glass doors" fog up only when locked is considered de rigueur; an $11.95 lunch prix fixe and $29.95 early-birds earn it "standby" status for hipsters on a budget.

Paradiso Ⓜ *Italian*
25 | 23 | 23 | $47

South Philly | 1627-29 E. Passyunk Ave. (Tasker St.) | 215-271-2066 | www.paradisophilly.com

"*Bellissimo!*" exclaim enthusiasts of Lynn Rinaldi's "delightful" Italian "charmer" in the "heart" of "the Avenue" in South Philly, where *paesani* promise "one bite and you'll sigh" over her menu of "classic" and "nontraditional" dishes, served in an "airy", "transporting" setting with "outdoor seating" that provides primo "people-watching"; "friendly bartenders" are there to help with the "broad, well-priced" wine list, which is supplemented by a BYO option on Sundays.

▤ Parc *French* | 22 | 25 | 21 | $46 |

Rittenhouse | Parc Rittenhouse | 227 S. 18th St. (Locust St.) | 215-545-2262 | www.parc-restaurant.com

Stephen Starr's "super-sexy" "slice of Paris" on Rittenhouse Square is a "well-oiled operation" dispensing "authentic bistro" fare and the "best bread basket in town", and though service can be authentically "aloof" and the "noise level" can "make you cringe" inside the otherwise "warm", "rustic" space, there's "excellent people- (and dog-) watching if you can snag a table" outside; while a few think it's "too crowded and hip for its own good", most simply exclaim *"quel plaisir!"*

Parc Bistro *American* | 23 | 23 | 23 | $39 |

Skippack | 4067 Skippack Pike (bet. Church & Store Rds.) | 610-584-1146 | www.parcbistro.com

An "innovative menu" highlighting "in-season ingredients" draws Central Montco foodies to this New American housed in a restored 19th-century roadside inn in Downtown Skippack, where "conviviality" is the word, whether it's at the "bar" over a "pizza" and wine or outside on the summer patio; while some find it "a little pricey" for the area, most regard it as a "dependable" option.

NEW Parker's Prime *Steak* | ∇ 21 | 23 | 18 | $55 |

Newtown Square | 4755 W. Chester Pike (Crum Creek Rd.) | 610-353-5353 | www.parkersprime.com

"Tender" "Kobe" beef, "well-done" sushi" and other offerings from a Morimoto alum (and *Iron Chef* Japan contestant) get high marks at this mod-looking steakhouse in a Newtown Square "strip center" from the crew behind Azie and Teikoku; while it might be "great for date night", critics gripe about "rough spots" in service and "Center City prices", and urge the operators to "decide what they are – Asian, steak, American, what?"

▤ Pat's King of Steaks ●♯ *Cheesesteaks* | 21 | 7 | 13 | $12 |

South Philly | 1237 E. Passyunk Ave. (9th St.) | 215-468-1546 | www.patskingofsteaks.com

"Still regal after all these years", this 24/7 South Philly "institution" and inventor of the cheesesteak "reigns" with "melt-in-your-mouth" sandwiches that come with a "side of rudeness", making for "entertaining" experiences "'witout' a cover charge"; it's "always busy" despite the "parking challenge" and seating "outside in the cold", and loyal subjects insist it's the "only place to be at 3 AM after the blue-blood debutante ball, without the debutante."

Pattaya Grill *Thai* | 20 | 15 | 20 | $22 |

University City | 4006 Chestnut St. (40th St.) | 215-387-8533 | www.pattayacuisine.com

"Reasonably priced specials" (including $8.95 lunches and $10.95 early-bird dinners) and "consistent, authentic" cooking make this "comfortable" Thai in University City a popular choice in the Penn community, whose denizens "love" to camp out in the "sunny room in the back"; "lots of healthy options" and "prompt" service also make it an "above-average" choice.

NEW Paul Ⓜ⌿ *American* ▽ 22 | 19 | 22 | $39

Washington Square West | 1120 Pine St. (Quince St.) | 215-238-0210 | www.paulphilly.com

They "go out of their way to accommodate you" at this "homey" Wash West New American (from the team at Effie's across the street) where "inventive", "well-prepared" dishes are served in a tiny, 28-seat room that feels like "your own restaurant"; despite the "intimate" arrangement, fans insist "you don't feel crammed at all"; a post-Survey chef change may outdate the Food score.

Penang ● *Malaysian* 21 | 16 | 18 | $26

Chinatown | 117 N. 10th St. (bet. Arch & Cherry Sts.) | 215-413-2531 | www.penangusa.com

There's "never a dull entree" at these "cool", "cheap" Malaysian mainstays, offering a "variety" of "bold", "soul-feeding" dishes ranging from "mainstream to yikes"; the wide-open "techno" setting is an "acquired" "taste" for many, but while you "may have to wait for a table", regulars report your "food comes fast."

Penne *Italian* 18 | 19 | 17 | $39

University City | Inn at Penn | 3611 Walnut St. (36th St.) | 215-823-6222 | www.pennerestaurant.com

Sit at the "pasta bar" and "watch" chefs make "phenomenal" dishes in the "open kitchen" at this "lovely" Italian in the Inn at Penn in University City, whose "decent wine selection" and "well-spaced" tables make it a "solid" fave among "Penn" parents (it's a stretch for "the usual student budget"); while the "cheerful" staff's "knowledge is impeccable", many grouse about the "funereal pace" of service.

NEW Percy Street Barbecue ⌿ *BBQ* 20 | 18 | 20 | $30

South St. | 900 South St. (Ninth St.) | 215-625-8510 | www.percystreet.com

"Even Texans in from out of town" "approve" pit mistress Erin O'Shea's "superb dry-rubbed brisket and ribs" and "wonderful sides" dished out "family-style" by an "attentive" staff at this "slightly upscale" South Street "smokehouse"-cum-"roadhouse" from the crew behind Xochitl and Zahav; most 'cuennoisseurs agree "you definitely get your money's worth" – plus, it's hard to "argue with beer by the gallon."

Persian Grill *Persian* 21 | 12 | 20 | $31

Lafayette Hill | 637 Germantown Pike (Crescent Ave.) | 610-825-2705 | www.persiangrille.net

"Bountiful" portions of "well-prepared" Persian fare (and an "unusual variety of homemade infused vodkas") are served with "authentic flair" by a "friendly" staff at this "neighborhood" mainstay occupying a former diner space in Lafayette Hill; it's a "tasty", "interesting" experience "where you'd never expect it."

	FOOD	DECOR	SERVICE	COST

P.F. Chang's China Bistro *Chinese* 20 | 20 | 20 | $31

Warrington | Valley Sq. | 721 Easton Rd. (Street Rd.) | 215-918-3340
Glen Mills | Shoppes at Brinton Lake | 983 Baltimore Pike
(Brinton Lake Rd.) | 610-545-3030
Plymouth Meeting | 510 W. Germantown Pike (Hickory Rd.) |
610-567-0226
www.pfchangs.com

Boosters boast there are "tons of tasty guilty-pleasures" at this "modern", "upscale" "ersatz-Chinese" chain where friends "love to get together here and pass the plates" in a "fun", "noisy" atmosphere; sure, the signature "chicken lettuce wraps" and other "flavorful" items are not "100% authentic", and the "waits are usually very long", but most agree it's a "cut above your local takeout" – if you can stand the "screaming kids."

Phillips Seafood *Seafood* 16 | 16 | 18 | $39

Logan Square | Sheraton City Center Hotel | 200 N. 17th St. (Race St.) |
215-448-2700 | www.phillipsseafood.com

While fans "can understand why" this Baltimore-based fish house chain's "crab cakes are famous", many others "expected more" from this link "conveniently located" in the Sheraton City Center near Logan Square; though some are "pleasantly surprised", most deem the fare "average" and the "prices high relative to the value of the meal."

Phil's Tavern ● *American* 18 | 12 | 19 | $24

Blue Bell | 931 Butler Pike (Skippack Pike) | 215-643-5664 |
www.thephilstavern.com

Insiders advise "bring your appetite" to this "great neighborhood" "pub"-slash-"family restaurant" in Blue Bell offering "thousands of choices" "put together well", and be prepared to "leave with a doggy bag"; it's "not the place to come for presentation, formality or small plates" – just a "haven" for "sports fans" who like to phil up on "awesome burgers and ribs" and "attentive" service.

Pho 75 ⇗ *Vietnamese* 22 | 6 | 15 | $12

Chinatown | 1022 Race St. (10th St.) | 215-925-1231
Northeast Philly | 823 Adams Ave. (Roosevelt Blvd.) | 215-743-8845
South Philly | 1122 Washington Ave. (12th St.) | 215-271-5866

"These guys do one thing – pho – and do it better than anywhere else" proclaim phonatics of these "inexpensive", bare-bones Viet noodle shops in Northeast Philly, South Philly and Chinatown; you can "throw darts" at the menu and "you'll enjoy" what you get, "even if you don't know the ingredients", and it comes to you "super-fast."

Pho Thai Nam Ⓜ *Thai/Vietnamese* ▽ 23 | 15 | 23 | $21

Blue Bell | Whitpain Shopping Ctr. | 1510 DeKalb Pike (Yost Rd.) |
610-272-3935 | www.phothainam.com

"Cheap", "awesome pho" at "wallet-friendly" prices makes this "reliable" Viet-Thai BYO a "special treat" in a Blue Bell "strip mall"; a "friendly" staff mans the "roomy, quiet" space, where the strains of music from both countries can be heard, while "plenty of on-site parking" also keep "regulars" happy.

Pho Xe Lua *Vietnamese* ▽ 24 | 6 | 15 | $17

Chinatown | 907 Race St. (9th St.) | 215-627-8883

"Take down a giant bowl" of "amazing" pho "under the neon train" in the window of this Vietnamese in Chinatown, where the tab "feels like larceny on your part" (which may help explain the "nonexistent" decor); aficionados advise the "relationship between food and service is inversely proportional", so if you need help choosing from the menu, "just order what they're having at the next table."

Piccolo Trattoria *Italian* 22 | 15 | 17 | $32

NEW Langhorne | Shoppes at Flowers Mill | 144 N. Flowers Mill Rd. (E. Maple Ave.) | 215-750-3639
Newtown | 32 West Rd. (Eagle Rd.) | 215-860-4247
www.piccolotrattoria.com

"Top-notch" "Brooklyn pies", "terrific" "salads" and "sandwiches" and "wonderfully prepared" Italian "favorites" generate "lines out the door" at these "solid", unassuming "jewels" in Bucks; while many laud the "courteous, prompt" service, a few caution that the "specials are marked up handsome" and they "don't tell you" the "prices" "unless you ask."

Pietro's Coal Oven Pizzeria *Pizza* 21 | 15 | 17 | $24

South St. | 121 South St. (bet. Front & Hancock Sts.) | 215-733-0675
Rittenhouse | 1714 Walnut St. (bet. 17th & 18th Sts.) | 215-735-8090
www.pietrospizza.com

Fans of this Philly South Street–based Italian chain declare "if you go home hungry, it is your own damn fault", what with its "killer" "thin-crust, sauce-heavy" pizzas and "shareable portions" of "amazing pasta dishes", while the "pleasant" environs make it "perfect for kids" as well as a "date/friend meet-up place"; some wallet-watchers warn that the "costs climb dramatically when you add toppings", but most agree it's "worth a visit" for an "easygoing meal."

Pietro's Prime *Steak* ▽ 23 | 22 | 23 | $58

West Chester | 125 W. Market St. (Darlington St.) | 484-760-6100 | www.pietrosprime.com

West Chester beef lovers think nothing of "grabbing a fork" and tucking into "big, thick, buttery steaks" at this meatery near the Chester County Courthouse, where the space is "cozy" enough for a "date night", and "yummy cocktails" can be had at the "super-fun" bar; regulars deem the service "excellent now", reflecting a spike in that score, and while a few feel it's "not worth the price", fans swear "if you like steak you'll like this place."

Pistachio Grille Ⓜ *American/Mediterranean* 20 | 14 | 19 | $35

Maple Glen | 521 Limekiln Pike (Norristown Rd.) | 215-643-7400 | www.thepistachiogrille.com

"Once you ignore the strip-mall" setting, this "roomy" New American BYO in Maple Glen is a "surprising find", where an "attentive" staff delivers "well-prepared" eats from a "diverse menu" that includes "delicious specials" in "inviting", "quiet" surroundings; a few cynics, however, sniff that "they're trying to be upscale, but fall short."

	FOOD	DECOR	SERVICE	COST

NEW **Pizzeria Stella** *Pizza* — 22 | 17 | 20 | $28

Society Hill | 215 Lombard St. (2nd St.) | 215-320-8000 |
www.pizzeriastella.net

Stephen Starr's "lively" but "surprisingly understated" "neighborhood boutique pizza shop" in Society Hill is "always packed" with piezanos hooked on the "quality" "personal-sized" pies served in a "bustling" "high school cafeteria"–like setting, complete with "communal tables" and rock soundtrack; there are "exciting visuals" from the seats "in front of the oven", where you can watch chefs "kneading" and "spinning", while less hectic dining options are found outside and in the adjacent bar that opened post-Survey.

Pizzicato *Italian* — 19 | 17 | 19 | $31

Old City | 248 Market St. (3rd St.) | 215-629-5527 |
www.pizzicatoristorante.com

Admirers attest this Old City Italian has "a lot of things to offer" besides "tasty", "reasonably priced" pizzas and pastas – such as a "city feel" and "always friendly" service; catering to crowds before or after shows at the Arden or Ritz, it sits on a "happening corner" and affords "great" "people-watching", while its branch in Marlton, NJ, benefits from its own "Promenade" location.

P.J. Whelihan's ◐ *Pub Food* — 16 | 15 | 16 | $23

Blue Bell | 799 Dekalb Pike (Skippack Pike) | 610-272-8919 |
www.pjspub.com

See review in the New Jersey Suburbs Directory.

Plate *American* — 14 | 15 | 15 | $35

Ardmore | Suburban Sq. | 105 Coulter Ave. (Anderson Ave.) |
610-642-5900 | www.platerestaurant.com

Fans of this "comfortable", "family-friendly" New American in Suburban Square say it "doesn't get the respect it deserves", despite a winning "formula" to "keep everyone happy" – i.e. "simple but well-prepared" food, "attentive" service, a stylish "outdoor" setup and some 20 bottles of wine under $30; cynics claim it thrives only "because there are so few choices on the Main Line."

Plough & the Stars *Pub Food* — 20 | 21 | 21 | $33

Old City | 123 Chestnut St. (2nd St.) | 215-733-0300 |
www.ploughstars.com

The bartenders at this "customer-focused" Irish pub in Old City pull the "best Guinness this side of the Atlantic" while the "reliable kitchen" puts out "hearty" grub; "impromptu" Sunday night "live music performances" generate a "touch of fun", and the fireplace in the main room of the high-ceilinged former bank creates a "cozy" vibe on a "cold winter's night."

Pod *Asian* — 23 | 24 | 21 | $45

University City | 3636 Sansom St. (bet. 36th & 37th Sts.) |
215-387-1803 | www.podrestaurant.com

"Bring your silver mylar suit and space goggles" to Stephen Starr's "spendy" Pan-Asian "spaceship" in University City, where the "all-

white, futuristic" surroundings (dotted by light-up dining "pods")
and "awesome" "sushi conveyor belt" are "still holding up"; insiders
insist the sci-fi "fun" "does not detract from fresh, creative food options", while the "helpful" service is worthy of "visiting" Penn "parents", but a few grouse that the "walls create an echo chamber
effect", and observe that "most people look terrible in purple light."

Porcini ☒ Italian
Rittenhouse | 2048 Sansom St. (bet. 20th & 21st Sts.) | 215-751-1175 |
www.porcinirestaurant.com

23 | 13 | 23 | $35

The Sansone brothers are "absolute dolls" at their "sweet" white-linen
Italian BYO "tucked away" near Rittenhouse Square, where they
"add to the vibe" by "welcoming" diners and offering menu "recommendations" in the "cramped" room; while the "delicious" fare "daz-
zles" most, some critics describe the portions as "impossibly small."

Portofino Italian
Washington Square West | 1227 Walnut St. (bet. 12th & 13th Sts.) |
215-923-8208 | www.portofino1227walnut.com

20 | 18 | 19 | $44

You're "treated like family" at this "classic", "old-school" Italian
"mainstay" going on 40 years in the same location near the theaters
in Washington Square West; *paesani* promise "decent food for a decent price", a "wonderful" atmosphere and "Beefeater martinis" to
help you "forget the miserable show" you just saw (the "20% discount" with your ticket stub helps too).

Positano Coast Italian
Society Hill | 212 Walnut St., 2nd fl. (2nd St.) | 215-238-0499 |
www.positanocoast.net

21 | 24 | 21 | $43

Sitting on "comfy couches" with the "girls" or a "date", you feel
"transported" "directly to the Positano Coast" at this "sexy", "airy"
"Mediterranean dream" in Society Hill, where "oh-so-charming bartenders" mix "addictive" drinks; "excellently prepared" Italian fare is
served in portions "adequate for sharing", and "cheerful" servers
won't allow you to "leave the table until you are positively stuffed."

Primavera Pizza Kitchen Pizza
Ardmore | 7 E. Lancaster Ave. (Cricket Ave.) | 610-642-8000 |
www.primaveraardmore.com

19 | 20 | 19 | $32

"First-rate thin-crust" pizzas and "well-executed" "pasta" offerings
draw Main Liners to this Italian housed in a "grandiose" former
"bank" in Downtown Ardmore, regarded by many as a "dependable", "child-friendly" option; some report the staff can get "overwhelmed" on weekends when it gets "hectic", and a few sniff that
"it's nothing to shout about", but the consensus is that it's "good to
have" and you certainly "won't feel ripped off"; it's unrelated to the
Downingtown restaurant with the same name.

☒ Prime Rib Steak
Rittenhouse | Radisson Plaza-Warwick Hotel | 1701 Locust St.
(17th St.) | 215-772-1701 | www.theprimerib.com

27 | 26 | 26 | $63

You "feel like you're in a movie" at this "special-occasion" steakhouse in the Warwick, where a "fancy-shmancy", "'40s nightclub"

tableaux sets the stage for "caveman cuts" of "primo" beef, "large cocktails" and "tuxedo-clad" waiters who are "true professionals" (even when serving the "bargain" $35 prix fixe special); add "unobtrusive", "romantic" live piano music to the mix, and fans insist it's "all you need to feel that things get better" in "tough economic times."

Privé ● *Mediterranean*   ▽ 21 | 22 | 18 | $48

Old City | 246 Market St. (3rd St.) | 215-923-8313 | www.priveoldcity.com

The "eclectic" Med menu is "creative" but "not over the top" at this "sexy, provocative" boîte in Old City, where it's "romantic" and "quiet" early in the evening amid the "cloth-draped" walls and "private booths", before the late-night lounge scene kicks in; the "$25 prix fixes" on Sundays and Mondays and $45 five-course tasting menus make up for service that surveyors say varies from "over-friendly" to "sour"; a post-Survey chef change is not reflected in the Food score.

Prohibition Taproom ● *American*   ▽ 22 | 17 | 21 | $20

North Philly | 501 N. 13th St. (bet. Buttonwood & Nectarine Sts.) | 215-238-1818 | www.theprohibitiontaproom.com

Those in-the-know call this "dark" "watering hole" tucked away in the "loft district" just north of Center City one of the town's "best-kept secrets", serving "lots of great beers and food that is not freezer-to-fryer" to the tunes from an "awesome jukebox"; "once you find it", "you can never go wrong" "meeting friends or a date" over "drinks", "quiet conversation" and the "grilled cheese of the day."

PTG Ⓜ *Italian*   ▽ 23 | 16 | 22 | $38

Roxborough | 6813 Ridge Ave. (Parker Ave.) | 215-487-2293 | www.ptgrestaurantandcaterers.com

This "small, feel-at-home" white-linen Italian BYO dinner house run by two earnest caterers in a Roxborough "storefront" is a "great family place" where you can bring everyone "from kids to grandparents" for "good, often excellent" grub and "service with a smile"; the $30 prix fixe dinners Tuesdays–Thursdays make it easy on the wallet.

Pub & Kitchen, The ● *European*   22 | 18 | 18 | $30

Graduate Hospital | 1946 Lombard St. (20th St.) | 215-545-0350 | www.thepubandkitchen.com

"Rub elbows" with a "great crowd" at this "cozy", "hip" Graduate Hospital "scene" (but "prepare to be eye-stripped by all the attractive, hunting singles") where Jonathan Adams' "well-thought-out", "locavore"-focused Euro-style pub menu, which includes a brunch "worth getting out of bed on the weekends", has earned it the nickname "The Pub & Better-Than-Mom's Kitchen"; despite reports of "uneven" service and the fact that it's "not cheap", it's a "winner" in most people's books.

Public House at Logan Square *American*   14 | 14 | 15 | $30

Logan Square | 1801 Arch St. (18th St.) | 215-587-9040 | www.publichousephilly.com

"Young" "professionals" "looking for boobs and muscles" head to this "after-work meat market" off Logan Square, where many "out-of-town bankers" "start" their evenings with "happy hour" at the 80-ft.-long bar; while it's probably "not for a date night", insiders insist it's a "decent" lunch option, as long as you "stick to the basics" on the somewhat "eclectic" New American menu.

Pub of Penn Valley Eclectic

19 | 13 | 20 | $29

Narberth | 863 Montgomery Ave. (Iona Ave.) | 610-664-1901 | www.pubofpennvalley.com

"Problem is, all the locals love" this Tudor-style "gastropub masquerading as a neighborhood joint" in Narberth lament foodies, so count on a "wait" to "snag a table" for "killer" Eclectic grub and "welcoming" service from staffers who "make you feel like family"; as you watch "sports on the tube" or just "hang out for a while", you'll probably "run into someone you know", so "be on your good behavior."

Pumpkin ☒ ⇗ American

26 | 18 | 23 | $41

Graduate Hospital | 1713 South St. (17th St.) | 215-545-4448 | www.pumpkinphilly.com

Ian Moroney's "knockout" New American "combinations" star at his "intimate" cash-only BYO in Graduate Hospital, where the staff is "friendly and knowledgeable" and the $35 five-course Sunday night prix fixe is "especially enticing"; the "matchbox-size" room is "not the most comfortable", but hey, "you can't eat decor."

Pura Vida ☒ ☒ ⇗ Pan-Latin

- | - | - | I

Northern Liberties | 527 Fairmount Ave. (6th St.) | 215-922-6433 | www.puravidaphilly.com

Still a "great little secret" on the edge of Northern Liberties, this "small" Pan-Latin on a quiet corner doles out "unbeatable burritos" and "Cubano sandwiches" at "great prices" in a rustic setting; the staff also makes "wonderful drinks" with your alcohol, so be sure to BYO (and cash, because no cards are accepted).

Q BBQ & Tequila BBQ

16 | 12 | 15 | $29

Old City | 207 Chestnut St. (bet. 2nd & Strawberry Sts.) | 215-625-8605 | www.qoldcity.com

There's "something for everyone" at this Old City BBQ, which caters to a "young crowd" with tasty "ribs", "homemade brisket" and "moist towelettes", plus a "fabulous beer list" to join the assortment of "designer tequilas"; despite "reasonable prices", many foes find it "forgettable", lamenting that it "doesn't live up to its potential."

Qdoba Mexican Grill Mexican

18 | 11 | 15 | $12

North Philly | 1600 N. Broad St. (W. Oxford St.) | 215-763-4090
Rittenhouse | 1528 Walnut St. (16th St.) | 215-546-8007
Rittenhouse | 1900 Chestnut St. (19th St.) | 215-568-1009
University City | 230 S. 40th St. (Locust St.) | 215-222-2887
Springfield | 1054 Baltimore Pike (Riverview Rd.) | 610-543-4104
Bala Cynwyd | Bala Cynwyd Shopping Ctr. | 33 E. City Ave. (Conshohocken State Rd.) | 610-664-2906
www.qdoba.com

"Huge burritos" and other "basic", "cheesy" Mexican eats come "custom-made" at this "inexpensive" "fast-food" chain, where the "spare" digs are built for speed; many regard it as "ok, but nothing to write home about – especially if home is Southern California."

Radicchio *Italian*   25 | 17 | 22 | $37

Old City | 402 Wood St. (N. 4th St.) | 215-627-6850 | www.radicchio-cafe.com

"Every dish smells like heaven on earth" at Luigi Basile's "rustic" Old City Italian BYO, where the "whole fish" "filleted tableside" and other "great" examples of "home cooking" are served by "friendly, informative" folks who maintain an "unhurried" pace; while most agree it's "definitely worth the schlep from the suburbs", regulars warn "go early or you will be out of luck", because space is "tight" and there are no "reservations."

Ralph's ⊅ *Italian*   23 | 15 | 20 | $35

South Philly | Italian Mkt. | 760 S. Ninth St. (bet. Catharine & Fitzwater Sts.) | 215-627-6011 | www.ralphsrestaurant.com

"You get the South Philadelphia–Ninth Street", "grandmom's-in-the-kitchen", "row-house" "experience" at this century-old "gravy-licious" Southern Italian, where a "mixture of locals and tourists" "muscle" their way into the "small" space for "mussels" and various "parm" dishes brought out by "old-time waiters"; sure, it's "crowded and noisy" and cash-only (though there's an ATM on premises), but "heaven may be like that too" (sans ATM, we think).

Rangoon *Burmese*   23 | 13 | 21 | $24

Chinatown | 112 N. Ninth St. (bet. Arch & Cherry Sts.) | 215-829-8939

"Thousand-layer bread" and other "sensational, delicious dishes seem to appear magically within minutes of ordering" at this "reliable" Chinatown Burmese; it may be "lacking in ambiance, but not flavor" according to "locals" and others who also praise "pleasant" staffers who "don't mind when you ask a million questions" about the cuisine, which aficionados describe as "the best of Indian and Thai cuisines in one delicious package."

Raw Sushi & Sake Lounge *Japanese*   25 | 22 | 21 | $40

Washington Square West | 1225 Sansom St. (bet. 12th & 13th Sts.) | 215-238-1903 | www.rawlounge.net

"Aficionados as well as newbies" applaud the "awesome sushi" and one of the city's "best sake selections", served by a "professional" staff at this "trendy", "modern" Japanese in Wash West; though it's "on the expensive side", it's definitely a "place to be seen", especially late in the "lounge" or in the "outdoor" area that's "designed to make you feel like you're eating poolside at a resort (sans pool)."

Ray's Cafe & Tea House ⊠ *Taiwanese*   ∇ 23 | 14 | 22 | $23

Chinatown | 141 N. Ninth St. (bet. Cherry & Race Sts.) | 215-922-5122 | www.rayscafe.com

If you need a "cozy place for rendezvous in Chinatown", look no further than this "small, deli-looking" Taiwanese tearoom, where the "dumplings" are "special" and the "siphon coffee is good and strong" (and its Rube Goldberg–like brewing contraption is good theater); fans call it a "find" and swear "owner-hostess" Grace's "name fits her" to a T.

Reading Terminal Market *Eclectic*   24 | 16 | 17 | $15
Chinatown | 51 N. 12th St. (Arch St.) | 215-922-2317 | www.readingterminalmarket.org

"A tempting tour of 10,000 indulgences" "under a common roof" awaits at this "vibrant", "quintessentially Philadelphian" "gastronomic bazaar" in Chinatown next to the Pennsylvania Convention Center, the city's "happy place" for "noshing" and "shopping" since 1893; you're forced to make "decisions, decisions, decisions" ("roast pork"? "Thai curry"? "Amish desserts"?) while you "wend through the stalls" and eat at picnic tables amid "masses of humanity", and though you may encounter "attitude" or a "cheerful" smile, all agree it's a "must", especially for "tourists."

Redstone American Grill ● *American*   20 | 21 | 20 | $38
Plymouth Meeting | Plymouth Meeting | 512 W. Germantown Pike (Hickory Rd.) | 610-941-4400 | www.redstonegrill.com

"You can feel the energy" at this "upscale" Traditional American chain whose "dark", rough-hewn environs with "romantic" fireplace, "solid grilled" fare (and signature "cornbread") and "eager-to-please" staff are "magnets" for suburban "date-nighters"; meanwhile, "young" professionals "hang" in the "vibrant" "outdoor bar area", where it's hard to believe you're in the "middle of a mall parking lot."

Rembrandt's *American*   19 | 16 | 19 | $34
Fairmount | 741 N. 23rd St. (Aspen St.) | 215-763-2228 | www.rembrandts.com

This "family-friendly" "neighborhood fixture" in Fairmount near the Art Museum "continues to surprise after all these years", the latest being "new owners" who came on board mid-Survey, "sprucing up" the "reasonably priced" Traditional American fare (which may not be reflected in the Food score) and adding a "constantly changing beer menu"; the "awesome views of Philadelphia's skyline" remain a constant, though.

☑ Restaurant Alba 🅂🅼 *American*   27 | 22 | 24 | $52
Malvern | 7 W. King St. (Warren Ave.) | 610-644-4009 | www.restaurantalba.com

A "mecca for seasonal locavores", Sean Weinberg's "open kitchen" in Malvern creates "amazingly creative" "Euro-style" New American "grill" dishes that are served by a "terrific staff" in a "micro"-sized, "rustic" setting; "you can't go wrong" with the "new" Italian wine list from "small producers", but some who find it "pricey" in general lament that it "now charges $10 corkage."

NEW Resurrection Ale House ● *American*   24 | 19 | 23 | $28
South Philly | 2425 Grays Ferry Ave. (Catharine St.) | 215-735-2202 | www.resurrectionalehouse.com

"Oh-so-tasty" Traditional American dishes ("twice-fried chicken", even "housemade pickles") and an "impressive", "uncommon" beer list combine at this "homey", "old-fashioned" "gastropub" from the

couple behind Local 44 and Memphis Taproom, who've "resur-
rected" a forgettable taproom located across from Naval Square in
South Philly; there's "always a friendly face" at the bar, and the rest
of the "knowledgeable" staffers do an "impressive" job.

Rib Crib ●🖾Ⓜ≉ *BBQ* ▽ 24 | 8 | 17 | $27

Germantown | 6333 Germantown Ave. (bet. Duval St. &
Washington Ln.) | 215-438-6793

"The place to go for ribs" is how many 'cuennoisseurs describe this
cash-only BBQ stand on Germantown Avenue that's been dishing out
some of the "best takeout in the city" since 1968; aficionados insist
it's also "worth" it just for "the experience of ordering and people-
watching"; it's open Thursdays–Saturdays.

Ristorante Castello *Italian* ▽ 17 | 18 | 19 | $36

North Wales | Montgomery Commons | 1200 Welsh Rd. (N. Wales Rd.) |
215-368-9400 | www.ristorantecastello.com

Looking "more upscale than the shopping center" it calls home, this
"nicely" "decorated" Central Montco Italian BYO offers a "broad
menu" of standards, though the kitchen is "willing to prepare customized dishes", while the rest of the staff is "polite" and "helpful";
still, some find it "pricey for the location."

Ristorante La Buca 🖾 *Italian* 22 | 17 | 21 | $52

Washington Square West | 711 Locust St. (bet. 7th & 8th Sts.) |
215-928-0556 | www.ristlabuca.com

Count on "superb" Italian classics, a "fairly priced, undersung" list
of Boot wines and "well-honed", "old-world" service from "tuxedoed
waiters who have worked for years" at Giuseppe Giuliani's "basement grotto" on Washington Square, a good bet for "romantic" or
"business-related dinners" for 30 years; a recent "face-lift" to the
lounge may address complaints about the "dingy setting."

Ristorante Panorama *Italian* 23 | 22 | 23 | $51

Old City | Penn's View Hotel | 14 N. Front St. (Market St.) |
215-922-7800 | www.pennsviewhotel.com

When you "want to impress someone", this Italian in the Penn's
View Hotel in Old City is a "fly-me-to-the-moon" "destination"
where "extremely knowledgeable" folks serve "superb" pastas in
the "lovely" "dining room" and 120 wines by the glass and 27 tasting
flights at the "busy bar"; the "boutique hotel right upstairs" is handy
if the vino kicks in.

Ristorante Pesto *Italian* ▽ 25 | 20 | 25 | $37

South Philly | 1915 S. Broad St. (bet. McKean & Mifflin Sts.) |
215-336-8380 | www.ristorantepesto.com

The "welcoming" staff "makes you feel like part of the family" at this
South Philly "classic" trattoria across from St. Agnes Medical Center,
and the kitchen puts a "creative spin on urban Italian" cuisine with
its "yummy pastas" and "standards"; wrought-iron chandeliers and
terra-cotta walls highlight the simple space where some report
"deafening" decibels "when it's crowded" and a new bar is a work in
progress (for now, it's BYO without corkage).

	FOOD	DECOR	SERVICE	COST

Ristorante Positano *Italian* ▽ 20 | 20 | 21 | $45

Ardmore | 21 W. Lancaster Ave. (bet. Ardmore & Cricket Aves.) | 610-896-8298 | www.positanoristorante.com

A "cozy" setting graced with "original oil paintings" from the Amalfi coast and "great food without a lot of flash" are the hallmarks of this Southern Italian in Ardmore, where "those in-the-know" drop in to sit at the bar or outside in the pretty "alley"; stirred, not shaken, surveyors describe the "lemon drop martini" as "heaven in a glass."

Ristorante Primavera *Italian* 20 | 15 | 20 | $40

Wayne | 384 W. Lancaster Ave. (Conestoga Rd.) | 610-254-0200

"You always feel at home" at this Wayne "staple", which has "only improved with time" according to fans (and supported by an uptick in the Food score), drawing Main Liners for more than two decades with "dependable" Italian cuisine served by an "accommodating" staff in a "pleasant" atmosphere (valet parking at dinner is a plus); while a few purists dismiss the fare as "sanitized" and "not exciting", it remains a "reliable" "standby" for many.

Ristorante San Marco ☒ *Italian* 26 | 23 | 22 | $53

Ambler | 504 N. Bethlehem Pike (Dager Rd.) | 215-654-5000 | www.sanmarcopa.com

"*Bellissimo!*" exclaim the "regulars" of this old-school "gem" set up in an old Ambler schoolhouse, where "you can't go wrong" with the "fresh-made pastas", seafood and other Italian dishes; a piano bar sets the mood in the white-tablecloth room where "you are treated like gold" by "various servers", making it worthy of a "special occasion."

Riverstone Café *American* ▽ 18 | 20 | 18 | $34

Exton | 143 W. Lincoln Hwy. (Rte. 100) | 610-594-2233 | www.riverstonecafe.com

It's "martini heaven" at this mod New American "oasis" in an "otherwise humdrum" Exton shopping center; you get to "soak up the alcohol" with "decent tapas" and "oyster-bar" selections (especially Wednesday's buck-a-shuck night), and the $16.95 Sunday brunch buffet is an "awesome" deal.

Roberto's Trattoria *Italian* ▽ 19 | 15 | 22 | $33

Erdenheim | 700 Bethlehem Pike (Montgomery Ave.) | 215-233-9955 | www.robertotrattoria.com

Roberto Toselli and wife Anne Gallagher "welcome you like a cherished friend" at their "charming" Southern Italian in Erdenheim, which draws "a younger crowd" with "interesting" fare and "prices within reason"; works by local artists adorn the homey space where you can listen to live music on occasion.

Rock Bottom
Restaurant & Brewery *Pub Food* 14 | 14 | 16 | $24

King of Prussia | Plaza at King of Prussia Mall | 160 N. Gulph Rd. (bet. DeKalb Pike & Mall Blvd.) | 610-337-7737 | www.rockbottom.com

"The beer is what it's all about" at this "corporate" brewpub "convenient to the mall" in KoP, popular for its "happy hour" featuring "inviting" specials and a "predictable" lineup of suds; though many find the fare "unremarkable", stoics shrug it's "good enough" for those times when "you're stuck in a mall."

Roller's at Flying Fish ⓂⓖⒹ *Eclectic*   19 | 13 | 16 | $37

Chestnut Hill | 8142 Germantown Ave. (bet. Abington Ave. & Hartwell Ln.) | 215-247-0707 | www.rollersrestaurants.com

"Old reliable" is what fans dub Paul Roller's "homey", "affordable" cash-only Eclectic in Chestnut Hill, where there's "enough variety" to keep "regulars" coming back "again and again" for his "creative cooking"; a decline in scores, however, reflects complaints about a "tired" menu, "worn" environs and staffers who "sometimes" "act like they don't care if you are there or not."

Rose Tattoo Cafe Ⓔ *American*   22 | 22 | 22 | $39

Fairmount | 1847 Callowhill St. (19th St.) | 215-569-8939 | www.rosetattoocafe.com

Going on 30 years, this "funky" New American "hideaway" near the Art Museum is a "veteran" "that knows how to do things right", "rewarding" patrons (especially "first-daters") with "dependable" fare and a "friendly" atmosphere; if you "sit on the second floor" "overlooking the rainforest" of a "fern bar", you might "expect to see Demi Moore and Rob Lowe", as it "transports" you "magically to 1983."

Rouge *American*   22 | 21 | 20 | $44

Rittenhouse | 205 S. 18th St. (bet. Locust & Walnut Sts.) | 215-732-6622 | www.rouge98.com

"Couples, cougars and the men who love them" pack "elbow-to-elbow" into this "cosmopolitan chic" New American bistro, where the "awesome view" of Rittenhouse Square and sidewalk cafe make it the "closest thing to stepping inside a Monet painting" (and with better "people-watching"); the "sharp kitchen" is heralded for "world-famous" burgers and more, and while the staffers may seem "terribly impressed with their 'in'-ness" to some, most praise them as "friendly and outgoing."

Rouget Ⓜ *American*   24 | 20 | 23 | $45

Newtown | 2 Swamp Rd. (Sycamore St.) | 215-860-4480 | www.restaurantrouget.com

If Brian Held "were in the city, he'd be a megastar" declare "foodies" who "flock" to his French-influenced New American BYO in a lovely Newtown "mansion" for "creatively prepared" meals worthy of a "special occasion", including $36 prix fixes on Fridays and Saturdays; a "pleasant" staff works in the "calm", "intimate" setting, which includes a "pretty porch that's often "crowded"; P.S. the name refers to the fish, not the dining room's "Pepto-Bismol-color walls."

Royal Tavern ◑ *American*   24 | 16 | 20 | $23

South Philly | 937 E. Passyunk Ave. (bet. Carpenter & Montrose Sts.) | 215-389-6694 | www.royaltavern.com

Go figure, a South Philly "hipster institution that actually knows how to make great food" marvel mavens of this Bella Vista "gastropub", which boasts an "adventuresome" menu backed by a "fantastic beer list";

| | FOOD | DECOR | SERVICE | COST |

"you're treated like royalty" in the "clean, well-lighted place" where the "noise level" soars off the charts from the "jukebox" and crowds of "vegetarians" and omnivores who gather amid the "year-round Christmas lights" – perhaps "not recommended for anyone over 40."

NEW Ro-Zu *Japanese* — | — | — | M

South Philly | 700 S. Seventh St. (Bainbridge St.) | 267-273-0885 | www.ro-zuphilly.com

This Japanese BYO in a Bella Vista storefront offers sushi presented with colorful garnishes, plus a few cooked options like seared seafood and teriyaki; seats fill up quickly in the spare, modern dining room, and there's also a seven-seat sushi bar and some outdoor tables.

☑ NEW R2L ☒ *American* 21 | 27 | 20 | $60

Rittenhouse | Residences at Two Liberty | 50 S. 16th St., 37th fl. (Chestnut St.) | 215-564-5337 | www.r2lrestaurant.com

A "private elevator" takes you up to the 37th floor and Daniel Stern's "swank", "romantic" New American yearling in Two Liberty Place, where you "can't beat" the "panoramic" view or "gracious" atmosphere; chefs in the "open kitchen" apply "creative twists" to "old standards", while a "busy lounge scene" teems with "thirtyome-things" and feels like a "throwback to *Wall Street*" ("I expected to see Gordon Gecko sitting at the bar").

Ruby's *Diner* 16 | 17 | 16 | $19

Glen Mills | Brinton Lake | 919 Baltimore Pike (Brinton Lake Rd.) | 610-358-1983
King of Prussia | Plaza at King of Prussia Mall | 160 N. Gulph Rd. (bet. DeKalb Pike & Mall Blvd.) | 610-337-7829
Ardmore | Suburban Sq. | 5 Coulter Ave. (Anderson Ave.) | 610-896-7829
www.rubys.com

These "old-school", chain diners "take you back to a simpler time" with burgers and milkshakes that are "worth the calories", served by a "competent" staff in "rocking" "retro" environs with the special appeal of a "toy train" that "chugs" "overhead"; still, some wonder would "anyone go without kids"?

Ruth's Chris Steak House *Steak* 23 | 22 | 23 | $61

Avenue of the Arts | 260 S. Broad St. (Spruce St.) | 215-790-1515 ◑
King of Prussia | 220 N. Gulph Rd. (DeKalb Pike) | 610-992-1818
www.ruthschris.com

When carnivores "hear that sizzling platter" they "know what to expect" at these links of the "expense-account" meatery chain – a "fabulous steak" with "no big surprises", served by "dedicated" staffers who "make sure they know your name and use it often"; ignore the "cattle decorating the walls" in the otherwise "cozy" digs and "just appreciate being at the top of the food chain."

Rx ☒ *Eclectic* 24 | 16 | 21 | $32

University City | 4443 Spruce St. (45th St.) | 215-222-9590 | www.caferx.com

For a "recommended dosage" of "creative", "delicious" Eclectic cooking, proponents prescribe this "reliable neighborhood" BYO "gem" in West Philly, where a "friendly" "hipster" staff dispenses "excellent" $25 prix fixe dinners Tuesdays–Thursdays in a "spare" setting; fans swear by the "amazing" brunch as a sure cure for tired taste buds – "side effects include delight and possible drowsiness."

Sabrina's Café *Eclectic*   24 | 15 | 20 | $22
Fairmount | 1804 Callowhill St. (18th St.) | 215-636-9061
South Philly | 910 Christian St. (bet. 9th & 10th Sts.) |
215-574-1599
www.sabrinascafe.com
"Gargantuan" portions of "amazing" "home cooking" ("can't beat the stuffed French toast") keep the weekend brunch line "out the door" at these "cramped", "hipster-y" Eclectic BYO twins in Fairmount and the Italian Market, which also offer "wonderful, handcrafted comfort food" at dinner; fans report a "dynamite experience" that "yells Philly" thanks to a "tattooed" staff that's quick to top off the "mismatched coffee cups", though a few are "not sure if (even) Audrey Hepburn could fit" inside the "cramped" digs.

NEW Saffron *Indian*   - | - | - | M
Bala Cynwyd | 145 Montgomery Ave. (bet. Bangor & Tregaron Rds.) |
484-278-4112
Ambler | 60 E. Butler Ave. (Ridge Ave.) | 215-540-0237
www.saffronofphilly.com
"Even the most unadventurous" diner will be "pleased" by these "small" but "vibrant" BYOs on Bala Cynwyd's and Ambler's traditionally "Indian-deprived" Restaurant Rows; early reports of "long lines attest" to the appeal of "authentic" fare "as it was meant to be", at prices that don't "break the bank."

Salento Ⓜ *Italian*   23 | 15 | 24 | $37
Rittenhouse | 2216 Walnut St. (23rd St.) | 215-568-1314 |
www.salentorestaurant.com
Behind a "modest storefront" this Italian BYO near Rittenhouse Square is "lovingly run" by the folks behind South Philly's L'Angolo, and devotees report being 'blown away" by Puglian-style fare and housemade pastas served by a "warm and friendly" staff in an "intimate yet casual" room that a few liken to a "white box"; frugal fans say the $27 prix fixe dinner (served Sundays, Tuesdays–Thursdays) is a "satisfying dinner experience" that's "oh so worth the trip."

Saloon *Italian/Steak*   24 | 21 | 23 | $61
South Philly | 750 S. Seventh St. (bet. Catharine & Fitzwater Sts.) |
215-627-1811 | www.saloonrestaurant.net
Regarded by many as the "gold standard" of Italian steakhouses after nearly 45 years, this "classic" South Philly "1970s old-boys club" is "good to its regulars", who take their "expense accounts" and "best clients" "upstairs" for "great steaks" and "veal chops", and the "people-watching" isn't bad either (including some of the "best-looking servers in town"); though most insist it's easy to "see the care taken to satisfy the customers", some retort that "tried-and-true" sometimes lapses into "tired-and-true."

	FOOD	DECOR	SERVICE	COST

Salt & Pepper 🍴Ⓜ *American*   25 | 13 | 22 | $36
South Philly | 746 S. Sixth St. (Fitzwater St.) | 215-238-1920 |
www.saltandpepperphilly.com

"You feel like you are sitting in a friend's kitchen" at this "tiny",
"spartan" BYO "gem" in Bella Vista, where "every bite" of Sean
Ford's "creative" New American fare is a "yummy joy"; "congenial"
owner Robert Reilly "takes care of his baby", and "chatting with him
is part of the charm", another reason this "keeper" is usually
"crowded and noisy – but in a happy way."

ⲚⲈⲊ Sampan *Asian*   21 | 21 | 19 | $39
Washington Square West | 124 S. 13th St. (bet. Sansom & Walnut Sts.) |
215-732-3501 | www.sampanphilly.com

"Inventive" Pan-Asian tapas are served in a "mod" setting complete
with "loud" rock soundtrack and a "color-changing" illuminated
"forest on the walls" at this "date" scene from Michael Schulson
(AC's Izakaya; ex Pod), which many laud as an "impressive" addition
to Wash West, though a few hope it becomes more "consistent" and
the staff will "drop the velvet rope attitudes"; at the indoor and outdoor bars, you can choose from a selection of sake or "funky fresh
cocktails" – just "beware the scorpion bowl."

Sang Kee Asian Bistro *Chinese*   23 | 12 | 19 | $23
Wynnewood | 339 E. Lancaster Ave. (Remington Rd.) | 610-658-0618 |
www.sangkeeasianbistro.com

Sang Kee Noodle House *Chinese*
ⲚⲈⲊ University City | Sheraton University City | 3549 Chestnut St.
(36th St.) | 215-387-8808 | www.sangkeenoodlehouse.com

Sang Kee Peking
Duck House 🥢 *Chinese*
Chinatown | 238 N. Ninth St. (Vine St.) | 215-925-7532
Chinatown | Reading Terminal Mkt. | 51 N. 12th St. (bet. Cuthbert &
Filbert Sts.) | 215-922-3930
www.sangkeephiladelphia.com

When you've "got to have" "delicious" noodle dishes, "wonderful"
dumplings or Peking duck that's "all it's quacked up to be", Michael
Chow's "ridiculously cheap" Chinese joints are all "without peer",
be it the "nothing fancy" Chinatown BYO and Reading Terminal
Market stand (both cash-only) or the "bustling" bistros; service
is "blazingly fast", but even so they're "always jammed" –
and "deservedly so."

🄯 Savona *Italian*   27 | 26 | 26 | $66
Gulph Mills | 100 Old Gulph Rd. (Rte. 320) | 610-520-1200 |
www.savonarestaurant.com

While Evan Lambert has freshened his "elegant" Italian "mainstay"
in Gulph Mills, shrinking the "special-occasion" dining room, boosting
the outside patio and expanding the bar, Main Liners still come for
chef Andrew Masciangelo's "Rolls-Royce" cuisine "at Kia pricing";
the "informative" staff provides "superb", "consistent" service,
while master sommelier Melissa Monosoff oversees a 1,000-bottle
list housed in a "really cool wine cellar."

Sazon ⓜ *Venezuelan*
▽ 22 | 15 | 19 | $23

Northern Liberties | 941 Spring Garden St. (10th St.) | 215-763-2500 | www.sazonrestaurant.com

"Amazing hot chocolate" is only one of the delights at this "friendly", "unpretentious" Venezuelan BYO in the loft district on the western fringe of Northern Liberties; groupies laud the "spectacular" *comida* that "even a native would love", served in a "colorful" former diner where, caution cognoscenti, "depending on who your server is", you'll get "South American hospitality or Philly grit."

Scannicchio's *Italian*
23 | 16 | 22 | $39

South Philly | 2500 S. Broad St. (Porter St.) | 215-468-3900 | www.scannicchio.com

"Big" red-gravy Italian food "like your grandmom might have made if she was creative" is the lure at this South Philly BYO near the sports complex (an outpost of the Atlantic City original), where you may need to "bring some WD-40 to squeeze into the tight quarters", which can fill up "after a game"; add "friendly" service, and you'll see why followers want "to keep it a secret" – so "forget you read this."

Scoogi's Classic Italian *Italian*
19 | 16 | 19 | $33

Flourtown | 738 Bethlehem Pike (Arlingham Rd.) | 215-233-1063 | www.scoogis.com

"Plentiful portions" of "reliable", "fairly priced" Italian "standards" suit "any mood" at this "comfortable" Flourtown bar/eatery that's "good with kids" and a popular "last-minute" option on nights when "you don't want to cook"; insiders opt for the 'sun room' when the "low-ceilinged" main dining room gets "too crowded" and "noisy."

Seafood Unlimited *Seafood*
21 | 12 | 19 | $29

Rittenhouse | 270 S. 20th St. (Spruce St.) | 215-732-3663 | www.seafoodunlimited.com

Offering "swimmingly fresh" fin fare "with no fuss" plus a "fish market" under the same roof, this "unpretentious" Rittenhouse Square sea-fooder is a "solid" choice for a "satisfying", "reasonably" priced meal (including $5 "happy hour" apps "all night" and BYO Wednesdays), albeit in "close" quarters; it "hasn't survived" 40 years "for no reason."

Seasons 52 *American*
- | - | - | M

NEW **King of Prussia** | 160 N. Gulph Rd. (Mall Blvd.) | 610-992-1152

You can count "calories" and still "have a wonderful meal" at these sophisticated, handsomely decorated chain outlets that belie their corporate ownership; a "knowledgeable", "efficient" "weight staff" guides patrons through a solid wine list and "interesting", health-conscious New American grill menu that "changes with the seasons" in an atmosphere that maintains a happy buzz.

Serrano *Eclectic*
21 | 18 | 21 | $36

Old City | 20 S. Second St. (bet. Chestnut & Market Sts.) | 215-928-0770 | www.tinangel.com

"International home cooking" with some "interesting twists" heads the bill at this "cozy" Old City Eclectic "fixture", which "defines comfort" thanks to a "roaring fire in the fireplace" and staffers who "treat you like you just came home from a long absence"; if you book dinner and order tickets for a "concert upstairs" at the Tin Angel, you get bumped up to a "front table."

Seven Stars Inn Ⓜ *Continental*
| 20 | 17 | 20 | $52 |

Phoenixville | Hoffecker Rd. & Rte. 23 (W. Seven Stars Rd.) | 610-495-5205 | www.sevenstarsinn.com

"Bring your appetite – it's on" at this "classic" Phoenixville Continental where fans get starry-eyed over "ginormous portions" of prime rib, "seafood and sides", backed by a moderately priced wine list and "served up" by a "great staff" in a "quaint", circa-1736 setting; perhaps it's "not gourmet" and it's been offering the "same menu for years", but most agree it's "worth the trip."

Shanachie *Irish*
| 13 | 15 | 17 | $28 |

Ambler | 111 E. Butler Ave. (Ridge Ave.) | 215-283-4887 | www.shanachiepub.com

It's "fun" to "pop in" at this Irish-themed pub in Downtown Ambler for some "Guinness" and "stick-to-your-ribs food from the old country" "before or after" a movie across the street; "friendly" owners "work the floor" of the "dimly lit" digs and "make you feel special", though a dip in ratings reflects the view that it's "average at best", "even with the live music."

Shangrila *Asian*
| ∇ 21 | 19 | 21 | $40 |

Devon | 120 W. Swedesford Rd. (Valley Forge Rd.) | 610-687-8838 | www.shangrila120.com

"Everything comes off quite well" at this "well-appointed" Asian fusion housed in a former Denny's in Devon, where you "can't help but marvel" at the "eclectic menu" that has "sushi sharing space with risotto", and the "attentive" staff that keeps everything straight; while a few find it "overpriced", most agree it's a "delightful" experience.

🆕 Shank's Original *Italian*
| 23 | 8 | 18 | $11 |

(fka Shank's & Evelyn's Luncheonette)

Rittenhouse | 120 S. 15th St. (bet. Market & S. Broad Sts.) | 215-629-1093 ⌴
South Philly | Pier 40 | 901 S. Columbus Blvd. (Christian St.) | 215 218-4000 Ⓢ
www.shanksoriginal.com

Now located in "tight" spaces in Rittenhouse and at Pier 40 along the Delaware, this "venerable" South Philly émigré still makes its mark with "fabulous" Italian sandwiches prepped by "amusing" cooks who have "snappy retorts down to a science" and "treat everyone like *la famiglia*"; though some say it's "lost its charm in the move", most agree it still serves "old-school" Philly food "done right"; 15th Street is cash-only.

Shiao Lan Kung ➍ *Chinese*
| 23 | 8 | 17 | $24 |

Chinatown | 930 Race St. (bet. 9th & 10th Sts.) | 215-928-0282
Satisfy your craving for "salt-baked seafood" and other Chinese "standards" at this "simple", "always crowded" Chinatown BYO,

which has "maintained" its "high standards" and "economical" price points for more than 25 years on the Race Street strip; there's "no atmosphere, but who cares" – especially since the kitchen takes "requests" and it's "open late" (until 1:30 AM or later).

Shiroi Hana *Japanese*   24 | 17 | 22 | $30

Rittenhouse | 222 S. 15th St. (bet. Locust & Walnut Sts.) | 215-735-4444 | www.shiroihana.com

So "it's not trendy" – devotees declare this "lovely", "traditional-as-it-gets" Rittenhouse Japanese (from the crew behind Doma) the "real deal" for its "great, straightforward sushi" and "hot pots" that are "definitely worth ordering", all at "reasonable prices"; "they don't rely on gimmicks", and purists insist that's why it's "been there forever."

Siam Cuisine *Thai*   22 | 15 | 21 | $27

Chinatown | 925 Arch St. (bet. 9th & 10th Sts.) | 215-922-7135
Buckingham | Buckingham Green Shopping Ctr. | 4950 York Rd. (Hwy. 202) | 215-794-7209
Newtown | Village at Newtown | 2124 S. Eagle Rd. (bet. Durham & Swamp Rds.) | 215-579-9399
www.siamcuisinepa.com

Fans of these "consistent" Thai triplets (Newtown is BYO) are always "satisfied" with the "fresh", "above-average" "standards" ("spring rolls", "special teas and coffees") served in the "quiet" digs located in a Chinatown storefront and two Bucks strip malls; although a few think an "overhaul" is needed, all agree they're "reasonably priced."

Sidecar *Eclectic*   23 | 17 | 22 | $20

Graduate Hospital | 2201 Christian St. (22nd St.) | 215-732-3429 | www.thesidecarbar.com

"Better than bar food", the Eclectic grub is "surprisingly excellent" at this "edgy" "gastropub" "sleeper" in G-Ho, where Brian Lofink adds a "shifting cast" of "adventuresome" dishes to his roster of "down-home American favorites", which are washed down by an "inspiring" "beer selection"; "knowledgeable" service, "reasonable prices" and a "near-perfect brunch menu" all add to its allure, and a planned expansion should address comments about its "dive-bar" appearance.

Silk City ◐ *American*   21 | 17 | 20 | $26

Northern Liberties | 435 Spring Garden St. (bet. 4th & 5th Sts.) | 215-592-8838 | www.silkcityphilly.com

"Not your classic" diner, this "totally hipster" Northern Liberties spot is "decorated with complete randomness" and lots of tile work, and the menu pops with "creative" American "comfort food", while a "quirky" staff makes you "feel at home"; youthful spirits groove to "DJs" spinning in the "cutting-edge" "dance space", and the "spacious" outdoor "beer garden" is "wonderful" "in the summer."

Silk Cuisine *Thai*   ▽ 21 | 15 | 21 | $24

Bryn Mawr | 656 W. Lancaster Ave. (bet. Lee Ave. & Penn St.) | 610-527-0590

Newcomers are "amazed at what comes out of the kitchen" at this "simple", "affordable" Thai BYO in Bryn Mawr, which has been drawing Main Liners "for years" with "consistently excellent" fare and "courteous service" in a quiet, low-key atmosphere; one caveat: "parking can be a problem", so "look carefully" for "tow signs."

Simon Pearce on the Brandywine *American* 22 | 27 | 21 | $47

West Chester | 1333 Lenape Rd. (Pocopson Rd.) | 610-793-0948 | www.simonpearce.com

Regulars report a "picture-perfect" experience at this "lovely" New American upstairs from Simon Pearce's glass factory near West Chester, where "every table has a view of the river" and "watching the glassblowers" and "shopping in their retail shop" pre- or post-meal is the "entertainment"; you get to "test-drive" the "glassware and pottery" on "arty", "simple, yet so good" chow that makes "ample use" of "local" products and is served by a "professional, efficient" staff.

Singapore Kosher ∇ 20 | 14 | 23 | $17
Vegetarian *Chinese/Vegetarian*

Chinatown | 1006 Race St. (bet. 10th & 11th Sts.) | 215-922-3288

This Chinese vegetarian in Chinatown will "make you happy without making any animals unhappy" say fans who praise the "scrumptious", "well-priced" fare that pleases even "carnivores"; chef-owner Peter Fong will "go out of his way for you", so if there's a "fake meat product" you want to try, go ahead and ask.

Sitar India *Indian* ∇ 18 | 10 | 16 | $16

University City | 60 S. 38th St. (bet. Chestnut & Market Sts.) | 215-662-0818

Even if you're not eligible for the "student discount", fans swear the "tasty", "wholesome" eats at this "basic" University City Indian offer "high bang for the buck" (buffet is $8.95 for lunch, $11.95 for dinner), and the "welcoming" staff is quick to "learn the habits of regulars"; some negativists describe it as a "run-of-the-mill" eatery in "shabby" digs, but most regard it as an "excellent value."

Sketch Café *Burgers* ∇ 24 | 18 | 19 | $14

Fishtown | 413 E. Girard Ave. (Columbia Ave.) | 215-634-3466 | www.sketchburger.com

The "juicy", "monster" hamburgers are "something to be reckoned with" at this "quirky" Fishtown burger shop offering a selection of patties ranging from "vegan to Kobe" beef, all served on "perfectly buttered" buns, and chances are you'll "need a doggy bag"; the ultracasual environs are "like an indoor BBQ with family and friends", where you "sketch while you wait" and sit in old church pews.

Sláinte ● *Pub Food* 16 | 17 | 19 | $24

University City | 3000 Market St. (30th St.) | 215-222-7400 | www.slaintephilly.com

"Everybody say 'SLAN-chee'", the "dazzlingly mispronounced" name of this "grown-up" Irish bar across from 30th Street Station that tends to attract "more commuters" than "frat buddies", thanks to its "convenient location", "standard" "tap/bottle list" and "decent" pub grub; still, regulars report a "loud, boisterous" scene during the week.

Slate ◑ *American* | 19 | 18 | 20 | $31 |

Rittenhouse | 102 S. 21st St. (Sansom St.) | 215-568-6886 |
www.slatephiladelphia.com

At this "charming", "welcoming" neighborhood gastropub in
Rittenhouse, some critics sniff that it "needs to do something to make
itself more memorable", and a pre-Survey chef change (which may
not be reflected in the Food score) just might do the trick; still,
many local loyalists "recommend" it as a "moderately priced option" when
you and your "friends" or "someone special" want to "catch up" over
small plates backed by an "interesting" "wine-by-the-glass list", and
protest "this place doesn't get as much credit as it deserves."

Slate Bleu *French* | ▽ 23 | 20 | 21 | $48 |

Doylestown | 100 S. Main St. (Green St.) | 215-348-0222 |
www.slatebleu.com

"Exceptional" "classic" French fare with "great wines to match" in a
"simple", "elegant" setting makes this Doylestown bistro a "reliable
choice" for a "special evening"; critics grouse that the service can be
"slow" and contend that, at such "high prices", the kitchen "could do
so much more" – though the prix fixe dinners ($27 for two courses,
$34 for three) may assuage wallet-watchers.

SLiCE *Pizza* | 22 | 10 | 19 | $17 |

NEW **Rittenhouse** | 1740 Sansom St. (18th St.) | 215-557-9299
South Philly | 1180 S. 10th St. (Federal St.) | 215-463-0868 ⊄
www.slicepa.com

"Outstanding" Neapolitan pies made with "über-fresh" ingredients
(plus "to-die-for" salads) are served by a "pleasant", "chipper" staff
at these "tiny storefront" pizzerias in South Philly (cash-only and –
go figure – no slices) and Rittenhouse; the "decor is nonexistent"
and there's no real "ambiance", either – just "addictive", "awesome"
"'za" that gives "pizza-making a whole new meaning."

Sly Fox Brewery *Pub Food* | 13 | 12 | 15 | $25 |

Phoenixville | 519 Kimberton Rd. (bet. Pothouse & Seven Stars Rds.) |
610-935-4540
Royersford | 312 N. Lewis Rd. (Royersford Rd.) | 610-948-8088
www.slyfoxbeer.com

The "large selection of craft-brewed beers" contains at least "one to
suit everyone's tastes" at these brewpubs in the western 'burbs,
which also offer a "masses-friendly menu" of "basic pub fare" that
many find "unexceptional"; most find the service "efficient, but not
outstanding", and report that it can get "loud at game time", particularly at Phoenixville, which added TVs in its move to new digs
across the road in May 2010.

Smith & Wollensky ◑ *Steak* | 22 | 21 | 22 | $62 |

Rittenhouse | Rittenhouse Hotel | 210 W. Rittenhouse Sq. (bet. Locust &
Walnut Sts.) | 215-545-1700 | www.smithandwollensky.com

"Reliably good" steaks come with a "nice view" of Rittenhouse
Square at this "impressive" but "low-key" meatery in the Rittenhouse
Hotel, where "neighbors", "celebs" and others "enjoy a slice of

	FOOD	DECOR	SERVICE	COST

Philly" and "classic steakhouse" service with "some humor thrown in", especially when "Irish Mike and Dublin Dave" are pouring downstairs; the budget-conscious say they'd go only with a "gift certificate or on expense account", while critics decry it as an "exercise in pretentious excess."

Smiths Restaurant *American*

	∇ 16	14	17	$26

Rittenhouse | 39-41 S. 19th St. (bet. Chestnut & Ludlow Sts.) | 267-546-2669 | www.smiths-restaurant.com

"Comfortable without being trendy", this "often overlooked" Rittenhouse Square gastropub has a rep as a "solid neighborhood" "bar scene" and a "great place for relatively cheap private parties", with "good", "standard" American grub; the service is "not rushed or over-the-top", and the digs are "nicely appointed", but detractors decry the "awful noise level" and "frat-party" vibe during "happy hour."

Smokin' Betty's *American/BBQ*

	20	19	17	$27

Washington Square West | 116 S. 11th St. (Sansom St.) | 215-922-6500 | www.smokinbettys.com

Fans of this New American–BBQ on a corner in Wash West call it a "great addition to the neighborhood", where a "young bar crowd" and lots of "off-duty doctors and nurses from Jefferson" head for a "good variety of menu items", including "delicious" "meats" and "ribs", served in a "modern" industrial setting with "big windows"; most feel the staff is "still learning" the ropes, but give it credit for "trying hard."

Snackbar ◐ *American*

	22	21	20	$39

Rittenhouse | 253 S. 20th St. (Rittenhouse Sq.) | 215-545-5655 | www.snackbarltd.com

"Comfort food" "perfect" for "sharing" and "sexy" "signature cocktails" make this "tiny", "hip" New American "hangout" a block off Rittenhouse Square a "real" "gem", complete with "romantic" "fireplace" and private "alcove" table; it's "not a place to count your calories", even with the "small-plate" portions, and unless you opt for sidewalk dining, you sit at "tables so close" together your neighbors "become your friends by the end of the evening."

Snockey's Oyster & Crab House *Seafood*

	21	13	17	$29

South Philly | 1020 S. Second St. (Washington Ave.) | 215-339-9578 | www.snockeys.com

You "travel back" in time at this "classic", "bare-bones" "old-time oyster house" (circa 1912) in South Philly, and while it's probably "not the place for a romantic" meal ("lack of ambiance"), fans insist "they do it right" with "fresh", "reasonably priced" seafood "with very few frills" and "reliable", "friendly" service; though "parking can be a problem", most agree it's "worth the effort."

⚡ Sola ⑤Ⓜ *American*

	27	19	24	$53

Bryn Mawr | 614 W. Lancaster Ave. (Penn St.) | 610-526-0123 | www.solabyob.com

"It can be hard to snag a seat" at Dave Clouser's New American BYO "treasure" in Bryn Mawr, thanks to his "excellent", "elegant" dishes "presented superbly" by an "attentive" staff (which, some fret, seems a "smidge overworked"), and $40 weekly prix fixes worthy of "that special bottle", served in Schott Zwiesel stemware ($2 corkage); the only downside is the "tight space", but if you "run out of conversation", "you'll be able to listen in on your neighbor."

Solaris Grille *American*   14 | 17 | 15 | $31
Chestnut Hill | 8201 Germantown Ave. (Hartwell St.) | 215-242-3400 | www.solarisgrille.com

As the name suggests, this Chestnut Hill New American "bistro" is a "sunny place" for "young moms" with "kids" to "gather" on the "porch" or "alfresco" "patio", but many insist "consistency is sorely needed", and tepid ratings reflect the perceptions of "mediocre" chow and "unpredictable" service; at least it "doesn't break the budget."

SoleFood *Seafood*   ▽ 20 | 22 | 21 | $45
Washington Square West | Loews Philadelphia Hotel | 1200 Market St. (12th St.) | 215-231-7300 | www.loewshotels.com

Af-fin-ity abounds for this seafooder in the Loews near City Hall, where fans heap praise on its "interesting menu" focused on local ingredients, "great service" and "nice happy-hour specials", all in a "lovely" "art deco" space (highlighted by a "hypnotic mosaic above the kitchen") where "couples" settle into "semicircle tables" for "privacy"; there's "live music" Wednesdays–Fridays, plus a late-night bar scene that is "not for romantics or staid older folks."

NEW Sonata M *American*   ▽ 23 | 17 | 20 | $46
Northern Liberties | Liberties Walk | 1030 N. American St. (Wildey St.) | 215-238-1240 | www.sonatarestaurant.com

While many fans of Mark Tropea's "lovely", "modern" New American BYO "destination" in Northern Liberties' Liberties Walk want to "keep" it a "secret", they can't help but rhapsodize about the "innovative menus" and "warm, knowledgeable" service; oenophiles advise "bring your best wine" for the $31 prix fixe dinners served on Wednesdays, Thursdays and Sundays.

South St. Souvlaki M *Greek*   22 | 14 | 21 | $21
South St. | 509 South St. (bet. 5th & 6th Sts.) | 215-925-3026

Finatics insist it's "no fish story" that Tom Vasiliades' "casual" Greek "mainstay" on South Street "keeps the crowds coming back" with "reliably excellent", "reasonably priced" taverna staples; though some say the room has all the "ambiance of a rushed crowded cafe", "fabulous and friendly" waitresses "who have been there since the place opened" maintain a "homey atmosphere."

Southwark M *American*   25 | 23 | 23 | $44
South St. | 701 S. Fourth St. (Bainbridge St.) | 215-238-1888 | www.southwarkrestaurant.com

Customers "feel right at home" at this "old-timey bar" off South Street, a "family affair" where it's "like watching a sitcom" listening to barkeep Kip Waide banter as he mixes "amazing" "throwback cocktails", while chef-wife Sheri Waide uses a "deft touch" to "create" "tasty" New American fare (and her own charcuterie) from "seasonal ingredients"; the "quiet", "dimly lit" interior is "inviting", as is the small outdoor garden.

☑ Sovana Bistro 🅼 *French/Mediterranean*   27 | 22 | 24 | $48

Kennett Square | 696 Unionville Rd. (Rte. 926) | 610-444-5600 | www.sovanabistro.com

"Competition for tables can be fierce" at Nicholas Farrell's French-Med bistro "gem" that's "worth the drive" to "horse country" outside Kennett Square, where he "knocks" the "socks off" "locavores" with "terrific" "presentations" of "amazing" dishes ("heavenly cheese plates", "gourmet pizzas") from his "100-mile menu"; the "warm" front-of-the-house provides "impeccable" service, while the servers are "knowledgeable", and even though it offers a "nice wine list", BYO is permitted with an $8 corkage.

Spasso *Italian*   23 | 18 | 23 | $38

Old City | 34 S. Front St. (bet. Chestnut & Market Sts.) | 215-592-7661 | www.spassoitaliangrill.com

Cronies claim "you can't go wrong" at this "family"-friendly Italian, housed in a "brick-walled" "former historic warehouse" in Old City, whether you opt for "melt-in-your-mouth" "calamari", "gnocchi" or any other "homey, rustic" "favorite" "like your grandmother would make" – and "if it's not on the menu, ask", for they "love a challenge"; yes, the "noise can be deafening", but the "accommodating" staff keeps a "steady" course; BYO is ok on Tuesdays.

NEW Sprig & Vine 🅂🅼 *Vegetarian*   – | – | – | M

New Hope | Union Sq. | 450 Union Square Dr. (York Rd.) | 215-693-1427 | www.sprigandvine.com

Vegetables in refined preparations are the centerpiece at this BYO vegan tucked into an upscale shopping strip near New Hope's main drag; the eco-friendly MO extends to the handsome, all-green setting – be assured, for example, that the sumptuous booths are not real leather.

Spring Mill Café 🅼 *French*   24 | 22 | 23 | $44

Conshohocken | 164 Barren Hill Rd. (bet. Ridge Pike & River Rd.) | 610-828-2550 | www.springmill.com

You'll "think you've arrived in Provence" after one bite of the "fabulous" "country French cuisine" at Michele Haines' "cozy" BYO "treasure" in Conshy, where "classic" dishes "made with attention to detail" are served in a "delightful" "home setting" with "lots of atmosphere", and midweek $25 prix fixe dinners (Tuesdays–Thursdays) help keep the price points "reasonable"; a few wish she'd "change the menu" now and then.

NEW Square 1682 *American*   21 | 24 | 22 | $54

Rittenhouse | The Palomar | 121 S. 17th St. (Sansom St.) | 215-563-5008 | www.square1682.com

Charlie Trotter's alum Guillermo Tellez offers "lots of options between large and small plates" on his "thoughtfully prepared", "local and organic"-focused menu at this "chic", "beautifully decorated" New American on the second floor of the Hotel Palomar near

Rittenhouse Square; the "street-level bar" lends itself to "flirty drinks and appetizers", and while a few grumble about "small portions" and "attitude" that's "thicker than the steaks", most see lots of "potential" overall.

Standard Tap ● American   22 | 15 | 17 | $27

Northern Liberties | 901 N. Second St. (Poplar St.) | 215-238-0630 | www.standardtap.com

There's "something for everyone" on Carolynn Angle's "daily blackboard menu" at Philly's "first official gastropub", sitting on a Northern Liberties corner, where a "deliberately small beer list" complements "foolproof" American grub; whether you settle into "Hogwarts-style wooden booths" or dine "alfresco" on the "rooftop deck", aficionados advise the "funky" setting is "not the place if you actually want to talk to your date" (especially if you are "over 30"), while descriptions of the service range from "friendly" to "nonexistent."

Stella Blu ⊠ American   21 | 20 | 20 | $44

West Conshohocken | 101 Ford St. (Front St.) | 610-825-7060 | www.stellablurestaurant.com

A "friendly", "lively crowd" gathers at this sleek, "middle-of-the-road pub" in West Conshy for "tasty" New American grub (don't miss the "lobster mac 'n' cheese") and "nice bar" action, thanks to 24 wines by the glass in a "trendy" setting; just "don't expect to be able to have a conversation" during "happy hour."

Steve's   23 | 6 | 17 | $11
Prince of Steaks ⊟ Cheesesteaks

Northeast Philly | 2711 Comly Rd. (Roosevelt Blvd.) | 215-677-8020 ●
Northeast Philly | 7200 Bustleton Ave. (St. Vincent St.) | 215-338-0985 ●
Langhorne | 1617 E. Lincoln Hwy. (Highland Pkwy.) | 215-943-4640
www.stevesprinceofsteaks.com

Loyalists forget about the "wars" between the big sandwich guns Downtown and head to these stands in Northeast Philly and Bucks for a "quick, yummy lunch" of "stuffed, glorious cheesesteak on a perfect roll"; Whizards warn "don't look for intriguing decor" and "be prepared to order before you hit the register" or else "be ready" for "attitude."

St. Stephens Green ● Irish   18 | 17 | 18 | $28

Fairmount | 1701 Green St. (17th St.) | 215-769-5000 | www.saintstephensgreen.com

There's plenty of "Irish flair" in the air at this "unassuming" Fairmount gastropub that delights an "in-town crowd" with its "warm wood tables and fireplace atmosphere" and "well-thought-out" beer list; offering "something for everyone", the menu "has more hits than misses", and if you're not up to lingering or "people-watching" from the "windows", regulars report that "bar service is much quicker."

Sullivan's Steakhouse *Steak*

23 | 21 | 21 | $54

King of Prussia | King of Prussia Mall | 700 W. DeKalb Pike (Mall Blvd.) | 610-878-9025 | www.sullivansteakhouse.com

Carnivores commend these "classy" meatery chain links in KoP and Wilmington as a "top-end steakhouse experience" – i.e. "perfect" beef and "generous" sides served in "dark", "noisy dining rooms" by an "accommodating" staff, with a thriving "pickup" "scene" full of "hot connections" at the bar "during happy hour"; "it's not cheap", but most agree "it's worth every penny."

Summer Kitchen Ⓜ *Eclectic*

∇ 21 | 13 | 18 | $35

Penns Park | Rte. 232 & Penns Park Rd. | 215-598-9210 | www.thesummerkitchen.net

Residents of Central Bucks savor the experience of brunch or "dinner with friends" on the "outside patio" at this "cozy" "village" BYO where Mario Korenstein's "creative and consistently, beautifully done" Eclectic cuisine, including the signature paella, reflects his "Cuban origins"; the "plain" dining room is brightened by "pleasant" service and "moderate" sums on the bill.

Supper *American*

23 | 22 | 22 | $50

South St. | 926 South St. (10th St.) | 215-592-8180 | www.supperphilly.com

Mitch Prensky's "open kitchen" runs like the "proverbial well-oiled machine" at his "creative" New American on South Street, where the "bold" "farmhouse" cuisine in "varying-size plates" is served by an "enthusiastic" staff in an "unpretentious, warmly decorated" space highlighted by a "chandelier made of pots and pans"; assorted specials, including $35 weeknight prix fixes and BYO option Sundays and Wednesdays, make it a "perfect date spot for foodies" on a budget.

Susanna Foo's Gourmet Kitchen *Asian*

24 | 23 | 22 | $52

Radnor | Radnor Financial Ctr. | 555 E. Lancaster Ave. (Iven Ave.) | 610-688-8808 | www.susannafoo.com

"Welcome home, Susanna" – now "far removed from the bustle of the city", the city's best-known Chinese chef has settled in to her "drop-dead beautiful" Main Line Pan-Asian, and it shows in a bump-up in scores since the last Survey; acolytes insist the "creative dishes" (and those "fabulous dumplings") are "worth every dime of the big bucks you will spend", while "attentive" service and "sublimely relaxing" environs make it a "good date place for suburban hipsters."

Sushikazu Ⓩ *Japanese*

- | - | - | M

Blue Bell | 920 DeKalb Pike (Skippack Pike) | 610-272-7767

This Japanese BYO, tucked away off a busy intersection in Blue Bell, offers a midpriced menu that includes sushi, tempura and teriyaki, plus one of the few omakase options in the suburbs, in cramped yet tranquil, Zen-like surroundings; the chef hails from the late Yama in Horsham.

Swanky Bubbles ❶ *Asian*　　　　19 | 19 | 19 | $40

Old City | 10 S. Front St. (Market St.) | 215-928-1200 |
www.swankybubbles.com

Finatics "love, love, love the sushi" at this Old City nightspot that
creates "a bit of a scene" "geared toward the younger crowd" that
digs the "decent" Pan-Asian fare and "late-night" buzz"; despite ob-
jections that it's "pricey" and "not so swanky", many say it's "great
for a bachelorette party" when "champagne drinks" are flowing and
the DJ is spinning on weekends.

Z Swann Lounge ❶ *American/French*　　26 | 26 | 27 | $59

Logan Square | Four Seasons Hotel | 1 Logan Sq.
(bet. Benjamin Franklin Pkwy. & 18th St.) | 215-963-1500 |
www.fourseasons.com

"The Four Seasons still is, well, the Four Seasons" on Logan Square,
and though some say this lounge plays "second fiddle" to the "famous Fountain", fans insist it more than "holds its own" "for an elegant but casual meal or drink", afternoon tea or Sunday brunch
buffet, with "impeccable" service, "outstanding" New American and
French fare, and a "civilized", "less formal" setting; many call it the
city's "best place for after-work drinks" in town – "particularly if you
have a trust account."

Sweet Basil Thai Cuisine Ⓜ *Thai*　　23 | 17 | 21 | $34

Chadds Ford | 275 Wilmington-W. Chester Pike (Smith Bridge) |
610-358-4015

"Don't let the strip-mall location" dissuade you from this "great little"
Thai BYO on Route 202 in Chadds Ford, according to fans who report
"competently prepared" fare in a "clean, contemporary" setting,
with a "pleasant" staff and a chef who "always checks" in on diners;
add $10.95 two-course lunches and no corkage – "now that's a find."

Sweet Lorraine's *Eclectic*　　　∇ 17 | 19 | 18 | $26
(fka Spotted Hog)

Lahaska | Peddler's Vill. | Rte. 263 & Street Rd. | 215-794-4040 |
www.peddlersvillage.com

This Eclectic "light dining option" at the Peddler's Village "shopping
mecca" in Lahaska (formerly the Spotted Hog) offers "casual"
"sandwiches, soups and salads" in a "country setting"; while it's
"convenient", most deem the fare merely "average" and insiders advise you "to avoid peak hours" "on heavy tourist days."

Sweet Lucy's Smokehouse *BBQ*　　24 | 13 | 17 | $21

Northeast Philly | 7500 State Rd. (bet. Bleigh Ave. & Rhawn St.) |
215-333-9663 | www.sweetlucys.com

For some of the "best" BBQ and "sides" in Philly, 'cuennoisseurs
head to this BYO in a "warehouse" near the Tacony-Palmyra Bridge
in the Northeast, which "puts the pig in pig-out" with "industrial-
strength" eats that provide "a taste of home without having to put
up with your relatives"; settle into a "roomy wood booth" and "keep
saying to yourself that you can diet tomorrow" – especially on
Mondays, when it offers a $19.95 all-you-can-eat "feast."

	FOOD	DECOR	SERVICE	COST

Swift Half, The ☾ *American*   ▽ 18 | 15 | 21 | $24

Northern Liberties | Piazza at Schmidt's | 1001 N. Second St. (Wildey St.) | 215-923-4600 | www.swifthalfpub.com

"Superb beer" "on tap" and "imaginative" New American grub is on offer at this "modern" gastropub "cousin" of the Good Dog in Northern Liberties' Piazza at Schmidt's complex; while cynics find "nothing really exciting" about it, most find it "certainly adequate" for "watching a game" or raising a glass late (until 1 AM, and folks in the business get a discount), and see a "ton of potential" for improvement.

Sycamore Ⓜ *American*   - | - | - | M

Lansdowne | 14 S. Lansdowne Ave. (Baltimore Ave.) | 484-461-2867 | www.sycamorebyo.com

"Creative combinations" of "first-class, imaginative ingredients" "work" together and "surprise" aficionados of this "sophisticated", yet "understated" candlelit New American in unlikely Lansdowne; the BYO policy is "amped up" by creative mixers for DIY cocktails, and insiders advise sticking around for chef Sam Jacobson's "consistently good" desserts.

Table 31 ⊠ *Italian*   21 | 21 | 19 | $58

Logan Square | Comcast Ctr. | 1701 JFK Blvd. (17th St.) | 215-567-7111 | www.table-31.com

Surveyors say Chris Scarduzio's "sleek" Italian at the Comcast Center is "finally settling into a niche" with "solid" cooking, a "bargain" bar menu augmented by a "delectable wine selection" and a "quiet", "urbane" "elegance" that "makes you feel special"; the "outdoor cafe" on the "plaza" "offers" an "unparalleled alfresco" experience for weekday lunch, and while many praise the "accommodating" staff, a few find service "hard to come by."

Tacconelli's Pizzeria Ⓜ⇄ *Pizza*   25 | 9 | 16 | $19

Port Richmond | 2604 E. Somerset St. (bet. Almond & Thompson Sts.) | 215-425-4983 | www.tacconellispizzeria.com

They share a family tree, but that's about it for these cash-only, "no-nonsense", brick-oven destinations in Port Richmond (the pizza-only original, where you call in advance on weekends to "reserve your dough", which some find an "annoyance") and Maple Shade (which also sells salads); though a few declare "they should get over themselves", most agree they put out the best "thin-crust" pies in the region, "hands-down."

Tai Lake ☾ *Chinese*   ▽ 27 | 9 | 14 | $29

Chinatown | 134 N. 10th St. (bet. Cherry & Race Sts.) | 215-922-0698

"Pick your meal from the tank" at this "noisy and frenetic" Chinatown Cantonese seafooder, and you're assured of a "fresh", "authentic" meal at a "reasonable price"; its late hours (until 3 AM) are "handy" when you "want something substantive to cure the munchies", and at that hour, "who cares" if the "waiters" are "indifferent"; it also allows BYO with no corkage, even though it has a liquor license.

	FOOD	DECOR	SERVICE	COST

☒ Talula's Table *European*   27 | 20 | 26 | $125

Kennett Square | 102 W. State St. (Union St.) | 610-444-8255 |
www.talulastable.com

"Sure, you gotta wait a year" for a reservation (and show up at 7 PM sharp) at this "foodie's paradise" in the back of a Kennett Square market-cum-takeaway, but fans insist it's "worth it" for the eight-course, $125-a-head Euro-style "farmhouse-table dinners" for groups of five to 14 people that are like "a wonderful homey dinner party" – except with "knowledgeable" servers; it's a "culinary adventure" that'll make even hardcore gourmands "cry uncle."

Tamarindo's ☒ *Mexican*   21 | 15 | 19 | $32

Broad Axe | Homemaker's Shopping Plaza | 36 W. Skippack Pike (Butler Pike) | 215-619-2390

"Creative", "authentic Mexican" cuisine and "margaritas on the house" – "what's not to like" about this "simple" BYO in a "cheery strip mall" in Broad Axe, where owner Fernando Sauri is "always there" to supervise his "knowledgeable" staff; the "low-tech" location easily accommodates "office lunch get-togethers" and other "large groups."

Tampopo ☒ *Japanese/Korean*   22 | 11 | 16 | $13

Rittenhouse | 104 S. 21st St. (bet. Chestnut & Walnut Sts.) |
215-557-9593
University City | 269 S. 44th St. (bet. Locust & Spruce Sts.) |
215-386-3866 ☒
Washington Square West | 719 Sansom St. (bet. 7th & 8th Sts.) |
215-238-9373
www.tampoporestaurant.com

It's "hard to go wrong with the variety of yummy bento box options", at these "utilitarian" Japanese-Korean BYO "holes-in-the-wall" in Rittenhouse, Wash West and University City that are the stuff of a "college student's/wannabe-hipster's dream"; though some are irked over "bus-your-own policy" and "staffers who seem aggrieved" when asked "to do anything that interrupts their gossiping", many swear you "can't beat" 'em for "quick", "cheap" and "delish" dining.

Tandoor India *Indian*   ▽ 18 | 9 | 15 | $21

University City | 106 S. 40th St. (bet. Chestnut & Walnut Sts.) |
215-222-7122

You can "fill your belly on a shoestring" at the "bargain" buffet ($7.95 lunch, $10.95 dinner) of this "reliable" University City Indian BYO near the Penn campus, and those who "choose to order from the menu" "won't be disappointed", either; regulars report that "recent renovations definitely improved the atmosphere."

Tango *American*   20 | 19 | 20 | $42

Bryn Mawr | 39 Morris Ave. (Lancaster Ave.) | 610-526-9500 |
www.tastetango.com

Fans say this "go-to" New American "favorite" set in a onetime "railroad car" in the Bryn Mawr SEPTA station is on the right track with an "adventurous, changeable menu" offering a "good variety" of "dependable" eats, "pleasant" service and a room furnished with

	FOOD	DECOR	SERVICE	COST

"cozy bench seats and plush window treatments", from which you can "watch the trains go by"; while a few sniff there's "nothing outstanding" about it, others contend "sometimes you (just) want reliable."

Taqueria La Michoacana *Mexican*   23 | 13 | 17 | $21

Norristown | 301 E. Main St. (Arch St.) | 610-292-1971

"Go where the Mexicans go" urge aficionados of this "authentic" taqueria "find" whose "wonderful guac and giant glasses of horchata" make it the "No. 1 reason to visit Norristown"; "no-nonsense" but "pleasant" environs belie the "downscale" neighborhood, and "good prices" and "gracious" service also make it "worth the drive."

Taqueria La Veracruzana ● *Mexican*   23 | 8 | 16 | $14

South Philly | 908 Washington Ave. (9th St.) | 215-465-1440

This "charming", no-frills BYO in the Italian Market is the "gold standard" for "super-cheap, super-delicious" Mex specialties and "fulfilling" takeout; you can "watch the matriarch prepare tortillas" in the "transporting" setting where the service is "friendly" and "efficient."

Tavern 17 ● *American*   16 | 16 | 13 | $33

Rittenhouse | Radisson Plaza-Warwick Hotel | 220 S. 17th St. (Chancellor St.) | 215-790-1799 | www.tavern17restaurant.com

"Happy-hour specials" (including "tasty gourmet sliders"), "people-watching" and Friday night music attract "hotel guests" and "yuppie types" to this "nonthreatening" New American in the Radisson Plaza-Warwick; cynics shrug "eh" and report "uneven" eats and a staff that "seems to be perpetually in training."

NEW Tavolo *Italian*   21 | 21 | 22 | $47

Huntingdon Valley | 2519 Huntingdon Pike (Welsh Rd.) | 215-938-8401 | www.augustocuisine.com

Augusto Jalon's Italian BYO in an old Victorian is a "welcome addition" to Huntingdon Valley, where locals proclaim he "has it right" with his "interesting" menu of "homemade" pastas, "exciting entrees" and more, and while it may be a "little pricey for a spontaneous dinner", the majority touts it as "a destination spot for sure"; some report "slow" pacing, so expect to be there for a "long evening."

Teca ●☒ *Italian*   23 | 22 | 19 | $38

West Chester | 38 E. Gay St. (Walnut St.) | 610-738-8244

"Value" abounds at this "chic" Italian in Downtown West Chester, whose "great tapas-style" dishes and "low-key" vibe remind devotees of "a little cafe in Italy", and sidewalk tables offer the "height of people-watching" as you "feast your eyes on the human parade"; the "bartenders" "do know their wines", but some oenophiles warn that their recommendations can get "expensive."

Ted's Montana Grill *Steak*   18 | 16 | 18 | $31

Avenue of the Arts | 260 S. Broad St. (Spruce St.) | 215-772-1230
Warrington | 1512 Main St. (bet. Hwy. 611 & Street Rd.) | 215-491-1170
tedsmontanagrill.com

Ted Turner's Montana-themed American steakhouse chain links across from the Kimmel Center and in Warrington described as decent "meat-and-meet" spots, where adherents appreciate the "lean and mean" "difference" of bison burgers, as well as "beef, chicken and fish options", which all come in "ample portions"; it's easy to get behind the "eco-friendly" "touches, like recycled paper straws and table covers" in the "roomy", Craftsman-style setting.

Teikoku *Japanese/Thai* 23 | 23 | 19 | $44

Newtown Square | 5492 West Chester Pike (bet. Delchester & Garrett Mill Rds.) | 610-644-8270 | www.teikokurestaurant.com

A "perfect marriage" of Japanese and Thai is the arrangement at this "serene" "escape" in Newtown Square, which "feels like a city restaurant" thanks to the "beautiful" space with a 15-ft. gabled bamboo ceiling and waterfall; they "manage to get it all right", from the "sushi to the curries" to "attentive" service, and it not only "works with the kids", it's also "nice enough for date night", especially on Sundays, when it's BYO with no corkage.

☑ 10 Arts *American* 22 | 23 | 23 | $60

Avenue of the Arts | Ritz-Carlton Hotel | 10 S. Broad St. (City Hall) | 215-523-8273 | www.10arts.com

You don't have to be "Tom and Padma" to enjoy *Top Chef* finalist Jennifer Carroll's "refined" New American cuisine at Eric Ripert's "upscale" establishment in the Ritz-Carlton on the Avenue of the Arts, where "pink lighting", a soaring "wine tower" and a "cavernous" Parthenon-like "rotunda" add a "wow factor" to the experience; while some critics say the fare is "overpriced" and "does not live up to expectations", it's generally deemed "solid" overall.

Ten Stone *American* 17 | 16 | 19 | $22

Graduate Hospital | 2063 South St. (21st St.) | 215-735-9939 | www.tenstone.com

The "amazing beer selection" and "solid" American grub "hit the spot" (the latter's also "great for hangovers") at this "old-world" G-Ho "neighborhood" watering hole where you "get your darts and pool games going" or just "watch a game" on one of the "numerous TVs"; insiders assert "good luck getting a seat at the bar on a weekend evening", especially when the "frat-house crowd" drops in.

Tequila's Restaurant *Mexican* 25 | 25 | 24 | $42

Rittenhouse | 1602 Locust St. (16th St.) | 215-546-0181 | www.tequilasphilly.com

"Fantastic", "authentic Mexican flavors" "served up" in a "high-energy", "fine-dining atmosphere" keep regulars "going back again and again" to this Rittenhouse mainstay; "friendly" servers impress with the "amazing feat of carrying drinks on their head" in an "haute" setting featuring attractive "murals", while the bar wows with 105 "selections of tequila", including the house brand Siembra Azul.

Teresa's Cafe of Wayne *Italian* 22 | 15 | 21 | $33

Wayne | 124 N. Wayne Ave. (Lancaster Ave.) | 610-293-9909 | www.teresas-cafe.com

At this contemporary "standby" in Wayne, even regulars are "surprised by how surprised they are by Italian fare that's "always better" than they "expect" – while it's "nothing cutting-edge", the owners clearly "care about quality" and put out "honest portions"; a "great" wine "selection" (36 by the glass) from Teresa's Next Door, augmented by a BYO policy with no corkage, and "attentive" service help make it an "easy, out-on-the-town" experience.

Teresa's Next Door ● *Belgian* | 22 | 18 | 21 | $30 |

Wayne | 124-126 N. Wayne Ave. (Lancaster Ave.) | 610-293-0119 | www.teresas-cafe.com

With 210 beers by the bottle and 26 on tap, this "popular" Belgian "destination" attached to Teresa's Cafe of Wayne garners vote after vote for "best" brew selection in the "western 'burbs" – not to overlook the "world-class" steak frites, "great" cheese plates, "meaty" mussels and other Euro pub selections; the quarters are "serviceable", and the staff is "knowledgeable", though critics chide some for being "über-beer snobs" – still, overall it's "well worth it."

Tex Mex Connection *Tex-Mex* | ∇ 17 | 16 | 19 | $30 |

North Wales | 201 E. Walnut St. (2nd St.) | 215-699-9552 | www.texmexconnection.com

Some swear the margaritas at this Central Montco Tex-Mex are so "strong and delicious" that "all you need is the salsa and chips" to "have yourself a great meal", which is more than critics can say about fare they describe as "tired and uninventive"; still, loyalists laud the management for its "community involvement", while assorted nightly entertainment makes it a "fun" option for many.

Thai Orchid *Thai* | 24 | 18 | 22 | $28 |

Blue Bell | Blue Bell Shopping Ctr. | 1748 DeKalb Pike (Township Line Rd.) | 610-277-9376 | www.thaiorchidofbluebell.com

The "consistent, authentic" Thai cuisine at this BYO "winner" (sibling of Conshy's Chiangmai) in a Blue Bell strip mall can put a "smile on your face" with its "reasonable" prices and "good lunch deals"; "pleasant" service and "comfortable" environs also make it a "winner" that "fills a suburban void."

Thai Singha House *Thai* | 22 | 13 | 19 | $23 |

University City | 3939 Chestnut St. (39th St.) | 215-382-8001

A "superb range" of "outstanding" Thai dishes at "low prices" (especially "good lunch deals") makes this University City spot on the "edge of the Penn campus" a "standby" for "students" and "neighborhood" residents; "prompt", "friendly" service helps make up for digs many find "cramped" and "tired."

333 Belrose ⊠ *American* | 22 | 20 | 21 | $44 |

Radnor | 333 Belrose Ln. (King of Prussia Rd.) | 610-293-1000 | www.333belrose.com

"Tucked off the main roads" in a Radnor "farmhouse", this New American "staple" caters to both "picky eaters" and those who favor "innovative" chow with a "tantalizing, eclectic" menu of "reliable" fare, served by a "welcoming" staff in a "snappy" setting featuring "ginormous semi-abstract paintings of flowers" and a "lovely" patio that's perfect for "ladies who lunch"; "swingles" pack the "cacopho-nous" "happy hour", when "friendly bartenders" sling drinks to "men with Joe Biden hair plugs" and "cougars" who look ready to "pounce."

Tierra Colombiana *Colombian/Cuban*   24 | 19 | 21 | $30

North Philly | 4535-39 N. Fifth St. (3 blocks south of Roosevelt Blvd.) | 215-324-6086

The kitchen "totally nails" the "dishes" at this Colombian-Cuban off the Boulevard in the "frontier" of North Philly, where a "fabulous mix of cultures" settles in for "yummy", "affordable" meals (breakfast through dinner) and walks away with "absolutely no complaints" about the "authentic" eats, "friendly" service or "small but charm-ing" digs; in sum – it's "worth the outing"; P.S. don't miss salsa danc-ing on Thursdays in the "nightclub."

Tiffin *Indian*   25 | 12 | 18 | $22

Northern Liberties | 710 W. Girard Ave. (Franklin St.) | 215-922-1297
Mount Airy | 7105 Emlen St. (W. Mt. Pleasant Ave.) | 215-242-3656
Wynnewood | 50 E. Wynnewood Rd. (Williams Rd.) | 610-642-3344
NEW **Elkins Park** | Elkins Park Sq. | 8080 Old York Rd. (Church Rd.) | 215-635-9205
www.tiffin.com

"Dependable", "affordable", "delicious" are just a few of the super-latives that flow over this fast-growing, "no-frills" Indian BYO mini-chain rooted in a Girard Avenue storefront; supporters have "fun" working their "way through the menu", whether it's delivery by "nat-tily" dressed drivers, eat-in or "beautifully packaged" takeout ("my stovetop may start collecting dust").

NEW Tiffin etc. *Indian*   23 | 11 | 17 | $22

Northern Liberties | 712 W. Girard Ave. (Franklin St.) | 215-925-0770 | www.tiffin.com

"Affordable" Indian street fare such as "naan-esque pizzas" may "sound weird at first", but this casual offshoot of Tiffin next to its flagship location on the fringe of Northern Liberties has turned many skeptics into "believers"; the look is "basic" and critics report "scat-tered" service – "unquestionably the food is the main attraction" here.

Time ● *Continental*   ▽ 20 | 19 | 20 | $37

Washington Square West | 1315 Sansom St. (bet. Juniper & 13th Sts.) | 215-985-4800 | www.timerestaurant.net

You may need to "read lips" at this otherwise "relaxing" Wash West "hangout" (and sibling of nearby Vintage), especially "after 10 PM" when things get "really hopping"; the "ambitious" Euro-Continental cuisine served by a "competent" staff is a "pleasant surprise" to many, and "those looking for something a little more than the bar scene" can head "upstairs" to the Bohemian "absinthe bar."

☑ Tinto ● *Spanish*   27 | 23 | 23 | $54

Rittenhouse | 114 S. 20th St. (Sansom St.) | 215-665-9150 | www.tintorestaurant.com

"Basque in the glow" of Jose Garces' *"Iron Chef-ness"* at his "sexy", "go-to" small-plates "standard" near Rittenhouse Square ("comple-

	FOOD	DECOR	SERVICE	COST

menting" Amada crosstown), where the pintxos' "unusual flavors and combinations" make for "exhilarating" meals, orchestrated by a "knowledgeable" staff that also helps you navigate an "awesome wine list"; insiders suggest the "tasting menu is the way to go", unless you're willing to "throw all caution of a budget to the wind."

Tír na nÓg *Pub Food* | 17 | 17 | 17 | $29 |

Logan Square | The Phoenix | 1600 Arch St. (16th St.) | 267-514-1700 | www.tirnanogphilly.com

"Who wouldn't" want to grab "happy hour" and a "Guinness" (or three) at this "convivial" "gastropub of the Irish variety" across from JFK Plaza, where the "traditional fare" matches well with "rugby and soccer" on TV; a few claim your "hair will grow an inch" as you "wait to be served", suggesting that some of the staff may be taking the name (which means "land of eternal youth") a bit too literally.

Tony Luke's Old Philly Style | 26 | 8 | 16 | $13 |
Sandwiches ● *Cheesesteaks*

South Philly | 39 E. Oregon Ave. (Front St.) | 215-551-5725 | www.tonylukes.com

Devotees of this "joint"near the stadiums in South Philly happily "fughettabout" the others as they "wait in line" to order at the window and dig into "authentic" cheesesteaks that were voted the city's best in this Survey, as well as "roast pork Italian" sandwiches "made in heaven"; it's "streetside dining at its best", complete with "quintessential Philly" service that comes "with a smile."

Toscana 52 *Italian* | 20 | 21 | 19 | $39 |

Feasterville | 4603 Street Rd. (Lincoln Hwy.) | 215-942-7770 | www.toscana52.com

"They make you feel at home" at this "updated" Tuscan off Route 1 in Feasterville where an "innovative" menu that changes "weekly" is served in a "very nice" setting featuring a communal table beneath a cupola and open kitchen (which some find a "bit kitschy"), while "flat-screen TVs abound" in the stone-walled "bar area" where you can choose from "dozens of wines by the glass"; in sum, an "enjoyable" choice for "date night" or an outing with friends.

Totaro's *Eclectic* | 24 | 13 | 22 | $46 |

Conshohocken | 729 E. Hector St. (bet. Righter & Walnut Sts.) | 610-828-9341 | www.totaros.com

"Hiding" on a "back street" in "working-class" Conshy, this Eclectic "seems like your typical neighborhood" "hole-in-the-wall" tavern, but beyond the "large bar filled with locals and a TV" in front there's "mouthwatering", "big-city cuisine" being served in "large" portions in the back and "upstairs"; insiders whisper if you "stick to the specials menu", "you can't go wrong."

Trattoria Giuseppe *Italian* | - | - | - | M |

Newtown Square | 4799 West Chester Pike (Rockridge Rd.) | 610-353-4871 | www.mussotra.com

"You're out of luck" if you fail to "make reservations" at this warm Newtown Square Italian that's set up to resemble a Sicilian piazza, where Main Liners in-the-know are raving about "food that's as close to being in Italy as you can get" (including "bruschetta to die for"), served by a "phenomenal" staff that appears unperturbed even "when super-busy."

Trattoria San Nicola *Italian*
22 | 19 | 22 | $37

Paoli | 4 Manor Rd. (Lancaster Ave.) | 610-695-8990 | www.tsannicola.com

This "pleasant" Main Line trattoria "sets the gold standard for noise control" while "beautiful murals" impart a "Tuscan villa feel"; add "reliable yet creative" fare and the fact that "no one rushes you through the evening", and the result is "what your neighborhood Italian place should be, and so few are."

Trax Café ⧄ Ⓜ *American*
22 | 18 | 21 | $40

Ambler | 27 W. Butler Pike (Maple St.) | 215-591-9777 | www.traxcafe.com

"You know the food is fresh when you can watch the chef walk to the vegetable garden and pick it" aver fans of this "dependable" Traditional American BYO set in a "converted train station" across from the train stop in Ambler; though some find it "a bit pricey for the neighborhood", while others rail at the "cramped", "loud" setting, it "continues to be a favorite" of most.

Tre Scalini Ⓜ *Italian*
24 | 17 | 20 | $43

South Philly | 1915 E. Passyunk Ave. (bet. McKean & Mifflin Sts.) | 215-551-3870

"Bravo!" exclaim boosters of this "venerable" BYO "gem" on the East Passyunk strip where the staff will treat you "like a member of the immediate family" and the kitchen will make you "feel like your Italian mother-in-law cooked to impress you"; despite some who find the current location "cold" compared to its pre-2007 address, the majority agrees "this one is a keeper."

Tria ● *Eclectic*
23 | 20 | 22 | $30

Rittenhouse | 123 S. 18th St. (Sansom St.) | 215-972-8742
Washington Square West | 1137 Spruce St. (12th St.) | 215-629-9200
www.triacafe.com

An "amazing" triad of "wine, beer and cheese" plus "tasty" "small-plates" "nosh" star at these "intimate" but "jeans-casual" "urban oases" in Rittenhouse and Wash West where "knowledgeable" staffers help turn the "Sunday school" discounts into "learning" "experiences" (so you can "plagiarize their pairings like mad"); the effect is "smart and sexy without being pretentious"; an offshoot called Biba is due to open at 3131 Walnut Street in the summer of 2010.

Trio *Asian*
24 | 18 | 23 | $30

Fairmount | 2624 Brown St. (Taney St.) | 215-232-8746 | www.triobyob.com

Set in a "converted" row house in the "far reaches" of Fairmount, this "comfortable" "neighborhood" BYO elicits a "wow" from boosters who aren't above "killing someone for a parking space" to dine on "terrific" Pan-Asian cuisine served by some of the "friendliest people around"; it's a perfect "date-night place", especially on the "cozy roof deck."

	FOOD	DECOR	SERVICE	COST

Triumph Brewing Co. ● *American/Eclectic* | 18 | 18 | 17 | $28

Old City | 117 Chestnut St. (2nd St.) | 215-625-0855
New Hope | 400 Union Square Dr. (Main St.) | 215-862-8300
www.triumphbrewing.com

There's "always something new brewing" – and it's usually "awesome" – at these homespun pubs in New Hope and Old City that project a "nice, hip vibe" even if they remind some of a "warehouse"; "tasty" Traditional American eats (notably "burgers") and a "super-friendly" staff also help attract the "happy-hour" and "late-night" crowds.

Trolley Car Café *Diner* | 16 | 15 | 16 | $18

East Falls | 3269 S. Ferry Rd. (bet. Kelly Dr. & Ridge Ave.) | 267-385-6703

Trolley Car Diner & Deli *Diner*

Mount Airy | 7619 Germantown Ave. (Cresheim Valley Dr.) | 215-753-1500
www.trolleycardiner.com

"Ok, it's a diner in a trolley car", but the "decent", down-home" grub "with a bit of an upscale twist" rings a bell for fans of this "fun" Mount Airy "hangout" where "you'll never leave hungry"; while it's a "kid-friendly" operation, the "snazzy spiked milkshakes" are strictly for the "mommies"; the East Falls sibling opened post-Survey.

NEW Tweed ☒Ⓜ *American* | - | - | - | M

Washington Square West | 114 S. 12th St. (Sansom St.) | 215-923-3300 | www.tweedrestaurant.com

Put a bull's-eye on Washington Square West and only source ingredients from within a concentric circle 100 miles out – that's the locavore M.O. at this finely tailored New American, where chef David Cunningham uses French technique on his midpriced menu; a street-level lounge with a zinc-topped bar gives way to a dramatic staircase leading to a contemporary, white-tablecloth dining room.

Twenty Manning Grill *American* | - | - | - | M

Rittenhouse | 261 S. 20th St. (bet. Locust & Spruce Sts.) | 215-731-0900 | www.twentymanning.com

Audrey Taichman has revamped her Audrey Claire sibling off of Rittenhouse Square as a neighborhood drop-in with an accessible, modest-priced New American menu from chef Kiong Banh and a bar stocked with herb- and fruit-filled drinks and local beers; the cheery setting features a white tin ceiling, lemon-colored banquettes, wide windows and corner sidewalk seating.

211 York ☒Ⓜ *American* | 22 | 18 | 22 | $43

Jenkintown | 211 Old York Rd. (bet. Greenwood & Summit Aves.) | 215-517-5117 | www.211york.com

While Timothy Papa's "consistently good" menu of New American fare is "aiming to be upscale", it's "very reasonably priced" and "never seems to change", which is just fine for devotees of this "intimate", "loungelike storefront" spot on Jenkintown's strip; its "lovely small bar", manned by a "great bartender", serves as a waiting area for the Hiway Theatre just across the street.

| | FOOD | DECOR | SERVICE | COST |

☑ **Umai Umai** ⓩ *Asian*   26 | 20 | 23 | $35

Fairmount | 533 N. 22nd St. (Brandywine St.) | 215-988-0707 |
www.umaiumai.com

"Regulars" keep "coming back" to Alexander McCoy's "hidden" Asian BYO in Fairmount; "top-grade" sushi and a "constantly changing menu" of entrees, plus a "sweet", "helpful" staff working in "one of the most romantic environments" (the volcanic rock notwithstanding), make it "great for a date."

Umbria ⓩⓜ *Eclectic*   24 | 16 | 24 | $42

Mount Airy | 7131 Germantown Ave. (bet. Mt. Airy & Mt. Pleasant Aves.) | 215-242-6470

"Fabulous" Eclectic fare and "service fit for royalty" in a "laid-back" setting attract an "arty crowd" to Alisa Consorto's "serene" BYO in a "storefront" on Mount Airy's Germantown Avenue; it's open for dinner only, Wednesdays–Saturdays, so "reservations are a must."

☑ **Union Trust** *Steak*   24 | 28 | 23 | $74

Washington Square West | 717 Chestnut St. (7th St.) | 215-925-6000 |
www.uniontruststeakhouse.com

A "beautiful steak" deserves a "dramatic" setting, so carnivores commend this "outstanding" meatery in a "vaulted-ceilinged" "old bank" in Wash West, where you can "gawk" from the "mezzanine bar" above or the "raw bar" below; fans put their "trust" in the "outstanding" beef and seafood and "snappy", "sophisticated" "service with a "smile" (nothing "stuffy"), though a few naysayers snipe that they "need to step it up a notch" at these prices.

Upstares & Sotto Varalli *Italian/Seafood*   23 | 22 | 23 | $48

Avenue of the Arts | 231 S. Broad St. (Locust St.) | 215-546-6800 |
www.varalliusa.com

For a lunch or dinner "before a show", "fashionable people" regard this two-story Avenue of the Arts Italian seafooder as a "top choice", thanks to "reliable" eats and "drinks", including a $45 tasting menu ($60 with wine), served by folks who are "pleasant and attentive, no matter how busy" they are; "live jazz" on Fridays and Saturdays is another plus, and while some sniff that it doesn't "rock your world", most agree it's "does not disappoint", either.

Urban Saloon ❶ *Pub Food*   18 | 18 | 18 | $22

Fairmount | 2120 Fairmount Ave. (21st St.) | 215-808-0348

"Peanut butter–bacon burger" with "tater tots" may be "weird" but it's "worth the calories" insist fans of this "brick-walled" "watering hole across from Eastern State Penitentiary" in Fairmount; while cynics dismiss it as "typical meat market", most insist it's fine for a "quick bite" over a "Phils game" or for quizzo - that is, "if you like being put down by the Comic Book Guy from *The Simpsons*."

Uzu Sushi *Japanese*   ▽ 23 | 12 | 21 | $37

Old City | 104 Market St. (Front St.) | 215-923-9290 | www.uzuphilly.com
This "tiny" Japanese in Old City boasts a "wide selection" of "creative" sushi and sashimi, but some grumbling is heard over "portions too

small for the prices" ("hey, are we in Manhattan or San Francisco?");
praise for the "friendly" service balances out complaints about the
dark (not in a romantic way)" storefront setting.

Valanni ● *Mediterranean*   24 | 21 | 21 | $44

Washington Square West | 1229 Spruce St. (bet. 12th & 13th Sts.) |
215-790-9494 | www.valanni.com

"Youth and hormones abound" in the "eclectic mix of Philadelphians"
that flocks to this "sleek" Wash West Med for some "elegantly
plated" "culinary magic" that "won't blow your budget", served in
surroundings, which include a "boisterous" bar, that are at the "top
end" of the scale since an expansion/renovation; "attentive" service
comes from "stylish and beautiful" servers who could be "wannabe
models" as they sling "buttery" "lobster mac 'n' cheese" and
other "interesting dishes."

Varga Bar ● *American*   20 | 19 | 20 | $29

Washington Square West | 941 Spruce St. (10th St.) | 215-627-5200 |
www.vargabar.com

Fans tout this "cute", "slightly upscale" gastropub on a corner in
Wash West as the "perfect spot" to "meet after work" – preferably "at
the bar" where those in-the-know go with what the "friendly bartenders" recommend, and the space adorned with "pinup girls" is
"reminiscent of dad's bar in the basement" ("may not be the place to
take a date"); a few cynics find the New American menu "too trendy",
and dismiss it as a "trying-to-be-different-but-not burger pub."

NEW Verdad *Spanish*   19 | 18 | 16 | $48

Bryn Mawr | 818 W. Lancaster Ave. (Bryn Mawr Ave.) | 610-520-9100 |
www.verdadrestaurant.com

The 'truth' about this Main Line Spanish–Nuevo Latino depends on the
beholder – fans tout it as a "unique" experience when you "don't
want to drive into the city", highlighted by "delicious" "tapas" and "creative" "tequila" "drinks" delivered by a "helpful" staff; detractors report "unacceptable waits", "chaotic" service and overall "'tude",
and declare any claims of a "memorable" experience *"no es verdad."*

Vesuvio ● *Italian*   ▽ 14 | 14 | 17 | $29

South Philly | 736-38 S. Eighth St. (Fitzwater St.) | 215-922-8380 |
www.vesuvio-online.com

The complement of TVs, "couches" and "fireplace" at this "fun" Italian
tap in South Philly makes sports fans feel like they're "watching the
game at a friend's house"; if you're "crunched" for "money", "drink
specials" and "values" on the "unique" menu can be appealing, but
a falling Food score reflects the perception of "less-than-amazing"
bar food that's "inconsistent", to boot.

ⓔ Vetri ⊠ *Italian*   28 | 23 | 27 | $97

Washington Square West | 1312 Spruce St. (bet. Broad & 13th Sts.) |
215-732-3478 | www.vetriristorante.com

A "religious experience" is how devotees describe Marc Vetri's
"splendid" Italian "splurge", rated No. 1 for Food in this Survey and
deemed a sure way to "impress your date" (or anyone) thanks to its

"quaint" Wash West brownstone setting, "polished" service, "wonderful" wine pairings and "sublime" tasting menus (a $115 six-course served Mondays–Fridays and $135 eight-course on Saturdays); though most agree it's "worth every penny", you may want "a stiff drink just before the check arrives."

Victor Café *Italian*
20 | 20 | 22 | $41

South Philly | 1303-05 Dickinson St. (bet. Dickinson & 13th Sts.) | 215-468-3040 | www.victorcafe.com

"Opera-singing waiters", "decent" food at "reasonable prices" and a room decorated with "music memorabilia" have made this "old" South Philly Italian "warhorse" one of the best "entertainment values" in the "aria" for decades; regulars recommend it when dining with "people who can't be quiet" – for they'll "have to button up" when the "young folks pour their hearts into their performances."

Victory Brewing Co. ● *Pub Food*
17 | 15 | 18 | $24

Downingtown | 420 Acorn Ln. (Chestnut St.) | 610-873-0881 | www.victorybeer.com

While this "busy", "well-oiled" brewpub in Downingtown may be "beer-first", fans insist it's "no slouch in the food business", either, citing "better-than-average" pub grub selections that are "good enough" to "complement" the nearly two dozen beers on tap; the "industrial-chic" space is "clean and spacious", but it can get "loud"; if you like wine, it's also BYO.

Vientiane Café 🖼⊄ *Laotian/Thai*
23 | 14 | 21 | $21

West Philly | 4728 Baltimore Ave. (bet. 47th & 48th Sts.) | 215-726-1095

"Simplicity can be delicious" assert aficionados who tout this "low-key" Laotian-Thai BYO on a "funky" West Philly block as a fine "date option" with "upscale but reasonably priced" grub and "efficient" service; given the tight space of the otherwise "pleasant storefront", the staffers "do the best they can" to "make you feel at home" – but "consider takeout" if the "line is too long."

Vietnam *Vietnamese*
25 | 18 | 21 | $26

Chinatown | 221 N. 11th St. (bet. Race & Vine Sts.) | 215-592-1163 | www.eatatvietnam.com

Such "superb eating experiences" "shouldn't cost this little" fret phonatics of the Lai family's "classy" Vietnamese on the east side of 11th Street in Chinatown, where you're likely to run into "chefs from other restaurants" indulging in the "superior", "super-addictive" fare; the "cozy" digs are "always crowded" and service can "seem a bit rushed", but the pace is a bit more relaxed at the "minuscule bar" on the "third floor."

Vietnam Café 🖼 *Vietnamese*
24 | 22 | 23 | $24

West Philly | 816 S. 47th St. (Baltimore Ave.) | 215-729-0260 | www.eatatvietnam.com

Because it's "spacious" and "off the beaten track", it's "much easier to get seated" at the Lai family's "modern" offshoot in West Philly, where "knowledgeable" folks "make you feel at home" over "first-rate" "rolls" and "noodle bowls"; in sum, it's the "same great food" as Chinatown, with "better parking."

Vietnam Palace *Vietnamese*   23 | 18 | 20 | $24

Chinatown | 222 N. 11th St. (bet. Race & Vine Sts.) | 215-592-9596 | www.vietnampalacephilly.com

Bring a "group" of "beginners" or veterans to Nhon T. Nguyen's "pleasant" "best-buy" in Chinatown (on the west side of 11th Street) for "top-notch" Vietnamese "treats" from the "extensive menu", and you'll "walk out full, satisfied and with money in your pockets"; service is "fast but never rushed", even during "lunch" rush during shows at the "Convention Center."

Villa di Roma ⊄ *Italian*   23 | 10 | 19 | $30

South Philly | Italian Mkt. | 936 S. Ninth St. (bet. Christian St. & Washington Ave.) | 215-592-1295

The "aroma" from the "gravy pot" will "pull you in" off the "street" to this cash-only, "old-school" Italian in the Italian Market, where you'll encounter "long waits" for the "luscious meatballs", "melt-in-your-mouth" "eggplant parmigiana" and other "classic" dishes; "don't expect to be coddled" by "waitresses" who come "from a lost era", but as long as you "don't take it personally", *paesani* promise you will "leave happy."

NEW Village Whiskey *American*   24 | 21 | 21 | $35

Rittenhouse | 118 S. 20th St. (Sansom St.) | 215-665-1088 | www.villagewhiskey.com

"Insanely moist" hamburgers, assorted "pickles" and 80-plus whiskies make for "yummy" combos at Jose Garces' "swanky cool", "Prohibition-style" American "gem" next to Tinto in Rittenhouse; there are no reservations, so it can "take up to an hour and a half" to snag a "tiny" table or score a stool in front of an "amazing bartender" in the "matchbox-sized" space – you can "consider the wait penance for all the bad burgers you've had before."

Vintage ●🖫 *French*   20 | 22 | 19 | $32

Washington Square West | 129 S. 13th St. (bet. Chestnut & Walnut Sts.) | 215-922-3095 | www.vintage-philadelphia.com

This "snug", "unpretentious" French bistro (read: "chick bar") in Wash West is a "happy-hour favorite", offering 60 wines by the glass that you can match with "multiple small plates", served by a "staff that knows its stuff"; reading the "wall made out of wine boxes" is as much a part of the "convivial" scene as "sitting in the window" and "watching the Sips crowd stroll by", but it can get "loud", so some counsel "bring cough drops, because you'll be hoarse the next day."

Warmdaddy's ●🅼 *Soul Food*   22 | 19 | 20 | $35

South Philly | RiverView Plaza | 1400 S. Columbus Blvd. (Reed St.) | 215-462-2000 | www.warmdaddys.com

"Excellent jazz-infused Southern food and Sunday gospel brunches" are the main selling points of this South Philly soul fooder; while patrons might be cool to its "strip-mall location" (though there's "park-

FOOD | DECOR | SERVICE | COST

ing available) and "loud" airs, most put away their complaints for love of the "cornbread" and "fried chicken", "bluesy" atmosphere" (thanks to frequent "live music") and "understated, charming" service.

Warsaw Cafe *E European*

20 | 17 | 20 | $36

Rittenhouse | 306 S. 16th St. (Spruce St.) | 215-546-0204 | www.warsawcafephilly.com

When you need a "pierogi and borscht fix", this "authentic" Eastern European on the edge of the Rittenhouse Square neighborhood dishes up "affordable", "non-trendy" "classics" "with a Polish accent" and "old-home flavor" in its "charming room out of old Vienna"; "convenient" to the "Kimmel Center", this "old favorite continues to please", as evidenced by an uptick in scores since the last Survey.

Washington Crossing Inn Ⓜ *American*

20 | 21 | 20 | $43

Washington Crossing | 1295 General Washington Memorial Blvd. (General Knox Rd.) | 215-493-3634 | www.washingtoncrossinginn.com

Though this "old-fashioned" Colonial inn near the "historic" site of that famous boat ride in Upper Bucks "takes you back in time", it also boasts "quite a following of locals", thanks to the "beautiful" environs, "formal, yet friendly" service and live music "on certain nights"; most agree the Traditional American fare "could be a bit more imaginative", and navigate toward the "lighter fare" on the bar menu – but either way, "visiting relatives will be impressed."

Washington House *American*

- | - | - | M

Sellersville | 136 N. Main St. (Temple Ave.) | 215-257-3000 | www.washingtonhouse.net

"George Washington did not sleep here" but there's still lots of 18th-century lore attached to this "historic but casual" New American set in a circa-1742 "country inn", where the environs may remind you of "your favorite grandmother's house"; devotees find the "inventive" fare "medium-pricey", but insist that "you definitely receive the quality you pay for", and with a "first-class music venue", the Sellersville Theater, next door, locals see "no need to go to the city."

Water Works Ⓜ *Mediterranean*

21 | 27 | 21 | $58

Fairmount | 640 Water Works Dr. (Kelly Dr.) | 215-236-9000 | www.thewaterworksrestaurant.com

The "fascinating architecture" of the city's historic water works and "spectacular" views of the Schuylkill River make you feel like you're in "a scene" from a "movie" at this Med small-plates "splurge" behind the Philadelphia Museum of Art, whether you're on the terrace for a "romantic dinner" or "inside" for a "long lunch"; while the "reasonably tasty" fare (washed down by 150 kinds of bottled water) and "smooth" service win praise, most agree the "gorgeous location" is the main "reason to be here."

Whip Tavern *Pub Food*

23 | 23 | 21 | $30

Coatesville | 1383 N. Chatham Rd. (Springdell Rd.) | 610-383-0600 | www.whiptavern.com

Tally ho, you "feel like you've been transported to England" at this "adorable" Albion-themed spot near Coatesville, where "traditional" pub "favorites plus upscale specialties" appeal to Chester County "horsey" types, who "gather" "by the fire" or "cool off with a pint on the patio overlooking the Brandywine"; there's beer and wine only, and a $2.50 corkage to bring spirits; a post-Survey chef change may outdate the Food score.

White Dog Cafe *Eclectic*   20 19 19 $37

University City | 3420 Sansom St. (bet. 34th & 36th Sts.) | 215-386-9224 | www.whitedog.com

"Like a warm trip home to hippie parents who love you", this "environmentally friendly" Eclectic "landmark" on the Penn campus has "freshened up" since founder Judy Wicks stepped back, but adherents still don their "tweed blazers" to "rub elbows" with "professors and students" and lap up "tail-waggin' good" dishes that "please vegetarians and meat lovers alike", served by a "super-friendly" staff; though a few bark that it's an "old dog that should be put to rest", a branch in Wayne is due to be whelped in late 2010.

White Elephant *Thai*   24 20 22 $34

Huntingdon Valley | 759 Huntingdon Pike (bet. Cottman & Filmont Aves.) | 215-663-1495 | www.whiteelephant.us

Huntingdon Valleyans "know a bargain is on their doorstep" when it comes to this "traditional" Thai BYO "surprise" "hidden" in a strip mall, offering "amazing" dishes with "subtle flavors", such as the "Evil Jungle Princess", and "smiling" service in "dark", "cozy" environs with an "elephant motif"; best of all, "your wallet doesn't complain" afterward.

William Penn Inn *American/Continental*   20 22 22 $44

Gwynedd | William Penn Inn | 1017 DeKalb Pike (Sumneytown Pike) | 215-699-9272 | www.williampenninn.com

A favorite of those who "like getting dressed up", this circa-1714 "inn" in Gwynedd wins many votes as Central Montgomery County's "classiest" choice for "special occasions" (e.g. "your grandmother's 80th birthday") and Sunday "brunch" ($23.95 all-you-can-eat); devotees "rarely" encounter any "surprises" in the "consistent" American-Continental "standards" served by "people who have been there" for so long, "they are part of the decor", and the $25 early-bird specials help make it "popular among the mature crowd."

Winberie's *American*   17 18 17 $29

Wayne | 1164 Valley Forge Rd. (bet. Anthony Wayne Dr. & Valley Ford Rd.) | 610-293-9333 | www.selectrestaurants.com

"Far from fine dining" it may be, this "friendly neighborhood tavern" in a "historic building" by Route 202 in Wayne nonetheless provides "good", "chain"-style Traditional American chow at "reasonable prices" and a "wonderful beer selection"; regulars recommend an "outside table during nice weather at lunchtime", but some who find the fare "hit-or-miss" prefer to "hang out at the bar" instead.

	FOOD	DECOR	SERVICE	COST

Wine Thief *American* | 20 | 16 | 20 | $33 |

Mount Airy | 7152 Germantown Ave. (Mount Airy Ave.) | 215-242-6700 | www.winethiefbistro.com

There's "great cooking" going on, complemented by a "nice", "unpretentious wine list" and "friendly", "knowledgeable" service at this "pleasant", "trying-to-please" American in Mount Airy; many keep it in mind when they want to "steal" away for a "fun" "evening" without being "robbed" when the check comes.

Winnie's Le Bus *American* | 21 | 18 | 20 | $24 |

Manayunk | 4266 Main St. (bet. Green & Shurs Lns.) | 215-487-2663 | www.lebusmanayunk.com

"Terrific vegetarian" eats and plenty of "old-fashioned food, like your grandmother's", plus a "good beer selection" keep this casual "kid"-friendly New American cafe in Manayunk "always full" of "happy campers" "any time of day" (notably at "brunch"); boosters liken it to a foodie's "Tommy Hilfiger" – "sporty, good quality, not fancy", with the "friendliest" service and "super choices" of "fantastic" "baked goods and breads."

World Café Live *Eclectic* | 16 | 17 | 17 | $28 |

University City | 3025 Walnut St. (bet. 30th & 31st Sts.) | 215-222-1400 | www.worldcafelive.com

"Pull up a chair, a guitar and some soup" – that's the lyrical refrain heard at this University City Eclectic housed in a "concert venue", whose culinary "repertoire" revolves around live performances in an "intimate" setting ("you're so close, the act might eat some" of your meal); though most concede it's "certainly not haute cuisine" ("think TGI Friday's meets Jones"), "where else can you listen to XPN while eating cheap (besides your office)?"

Xochitl ● *Mexican* | 23 | 20 | 21 | $42 |

Society Hill | 408 S. Second St. (Pine St.) | 215-238-7280 | www.xochitlphilly.com

Lucio Palazzo took over the kitchen mid-Survey (which may not be reflected in the Food score) at this "comfortable", "upscale" Mexican in Society Hill, lowering prices while still eliciting cries of "yum" for his "memorable" "small plates" that pair well with the "many specialty drink options"; despite "irregular" service, most deem it worth a spot on the "foodie radar screen"; P.S. try pronouncing the name before you start imbibing – it's "so-CHEET."

Yakitori Boy ● *Japanese* | 19 | 19 | 19 | $30 |

Chinatown | 211 N. 11th St. (Race St.) | 215-923-8088 | www.yakitoriboy-japas.com

"Gather up your friends" and "get your karaoke on" at this "bustling", bi-level Chinatown "izakaya" whose assorted "Japanese tapas" (aka 'japas') range from "sushi" to traditional "yakitori" dishes such as "gizzards" ("not for the fainthearted"), while service varies from "quick" to "iffy"; you can "rent a room" upstairs and "keep eating and singing all evening", until the "bartender jumps onto the bar and outperforms you all."

	FOOD	DECOR	SERVICE	COST

Yalda Grill *Mideastern*
▽ 22 | 12 | 18 | $21

Horsham | 222 Horsham Rd. (Easton Rd.) | 215-444-9502 |
www.yaldagrill.com

You'll forget you're in a "strip center" in Horsham after entering this
Afghan BYO where it's "like being on a very foreign vacation",
thanks to "genial", "larger-than-life" owner "Mo" Rahpo, who dishes
out "fabulous" "grilled meats" and "wonderful" "pizza with yogurt
and eggplant" in a dinerlike room bedecked with pictures and memorabilia from Afghanistan; fans tout it as a "must-try, at least once."

☑ Yangming *Chinese/Continental*
25 | 21 | 23 | $38

Bryn Mawr | 1051 Conestoga Rd. (Haverford Rd.) | 610-527-3200 |
www.yangmingrestaurant.com

Michael Wei's Bryn Mawr Mandarin-Continental "hasn't lost a
step" in its 20 years attest Main Liners who rave about the "beautiful
setting", "knowledgeable servers" and "tasty", "progressive" dining
options, such as "shrimp and honey walnuts" and Peking duck
"carved tableside", all of which keep it "packed", "even midweek";
whether you're "dressed up or casual", partisans promise "you cannot go wrong" here.

Yardley Inn *American*
22 | 22 | 22 | $40

Yardley | 82 E. Afton Ave. (Delaware Ave.) | 215-493-3800 |
www.yardleyinn.com

A "picturesque" view of the Delaware River and "quaint", "romantic" "porch" seating highlight this "top-notch" Bucks New American
where the kitchen "puts a playful spin" on "comfort food", the "wonderful bar" dispenses a "mean martini" and the "gracious" staff
"makes you feel at home"; the "early-bird special" ($19.95, until
6:15 PM, and all night on Tuesdays) is a "very good value."

Zacharias Creek
Side Cafe ⊠Ⓜ *American*
▽ 24 | 20 | 23 | $35

Worcester | Center Point Shopping Ctr. | 2960 Skippack Pike
(Valley Forge Rd.) | 610-584-5650 | www.zachariascreeksidecafe.com

"The "comfortable" creek-side "patio" at this "relaxed" Worcester
New American BYO is "a wonderful place to spend a summer
evening" for "Mr. and Mrs. Suburbia", but insiders advise the "arty"
interior can get "noisy" – so "BYO earplugs"; it offers "creative"
"downtown food without the trip" at prices that "won't break the
wallet", served by staffers who "really go out of their way to
accommodate" patrons.

☑ Zahav *Israeli*
25 | 23 | 24 | $48

Society Hill | 237 St. James Pl. (2nd St.) | 215-625-8800 |
www.zahavrestaurant.com

A "revelation" to many, Michael Solomonov's "upper-crust" nouveau Israeli "fires on all 18 cylinders" in "spare", "modern" digs in
Society Hill Towers, where the *mazel tovs* flow for its "addictive"
hummus, "homemade breads", "coal-grilled meats and fish" and
"enough adventurous things" to "scare your entire family" ("duck
hearts, anyone?"); "let the staff guide you" as you "drop your pay-

check" (a few wonder if the name is "Hebrew for 'overpriced'"), and don't skip the "creative" "specialty drinks."

Zakes Cafe *American*　　　　　　　23 | 13 | 19 | $29

Fort Washington | 444 S. Bethlehem Pike (Lafayette Ave Connector) | 215-654-7600

They can sure "pack" those "ladies who lunch" into the "tight space" of this "charming" little "stone" "house" in Fort Washington, where "consistently excellent", "reasonably priced" New American "sandwiches", "quiche" and "light" fare (with the occasional Vietnamese touch) are followed by "killer desserts" from the counter; dinner (Wednesdays–Saturdays) is a "bargain" and keep in mind it's BYO.

NEW Zama *Japanese*　　　　　∇ 26 | 24 | 25 | $44

Rittenhouse | 128 S. 19th St. (Sansom St.) | 215-568-1027 | www.zamarestaurant.com

Watch Pod alum Hiroyuki 'Zama' Tanaka "do his magic" at the "top-grade" sushi bar of his upscale Japanese off Rittenhouse Square, while "impeccable" service ensures a "pleasant", peaceful experience amid the wooden slats and rice-paper sculpture; thanks to "excellent" fin fare and "delicious" specialty cocktails, "you don't leave with an empty stomach – maybe just an empty wallet."

NEW Zavino *Italian*　　　　　∇ 22 | 21 | 22 | $28

Washington Square West | 112 S. 13th St. (Sansom St.) | 215-732-2400 | www.zavino.com

Wash West scenesters "love the combination of wine and pizza", hence the name ('za + vino – get it?) of Steve Gonzalez's snug, "upscale" corner lounge; "cozy up to the bar for a great first date" with "small", "tasty" pies and similarly mini-portioned appetizers that don't carry a "hefty price tag" (though the plates can add up), served by "knowledgeable" folks.

Z Zento *Japanese*　　　　　　　26 | 10 | 19 | $35

Old City | 138 Chestnut St. (2nd St.) | 215-925-9998 | www.zentocontemporary.com

"Outstanding" "nouvelle" sushi (both round and "square") and "inexpensive" "noodle soups" pack 'em into a "minuscule" room that "could not be more basic" at this Japanese BYO run by a Morimoto alum in Old City; loyalists find "special touches that raise it above the competition" but really wish they'd install a "vestibule" to cut down on the "cold in the winter."

Zinc Ⓜ *French/Seafood*　　　　　23 | 20 | 23 | $43

Washington Square West | 246 S. 11th St. (bet. Locust & Spruce Sts.) | 215-351-9901 | www.zincbarphilly.com

Caribou Cafe's "smart", "intimate" bistro sibling in Washington Square West is at once "adorable and sophisticated", and admirers laud the "simple" contemporary French cuisine as something to "remember", complemented by a "nice selection of apéritifs" at the zinc bar and "solid" service; in sum, it's a "little bit of France for a little bit of money."

	FOOD	DECOR	SERVICE	COST

Zocalo *Mexican*

20 | 18 | 19 | $34

University City | 3600 Lancaster Ave. (36th St.) | 215-895-0139 |
www.zocalophilly.com

For "solid Mexican" cuisine "just west of Drexel's campus", all "roads" seem to "converge" on this long-running, oft-"overlooked" University City cantina; a "warm", south-of-the-border atmosphere pervades the "fenced-in patio" during "nice weather", abetted by "terrific" margaritas, and while a few find the fare "unadventurous", most regard it as "reliable and authentic."

Zorba's Taverna Ⓜ *Greek*

20 | 10 | 19 | $26

Fairmount | 2230 Fairmount Ave. (bet. 22nd & 23rd Sts.) | 215-978-5990

It "ain't fancy", but this Greek BYO tavern run by a father and son in a Fairmount storefront turns out "hearty", "straight-ahead" "favorites" that taste "straight out" of a "kitchen in the countryside", at prices that make it a "good value for your dollar" (though pita costs "extra"); the service might not be "professional or fast" enough for some, but it is "good-humored and unfussy."

Lancaster/Berks Counties

	FOOD	DECOR	SERVICE	COST

TOP FOOD

24 Lily's on Main | *Amer.*
23 Gibraltar | *Med./Seafood*
22 Five Guys | *Burgers*
21 Gusto | *Italian*
20 Bird-in-Hand | *PA Dutch*

TOP DECOR

21 Gibraltar
19 Lily's on Main
  Iron Hill
18 Plain & Fancy Farm
17 J.B. Dawson's/Austin's

TOP SERVICE

22 Gibraltar
  Gusto
20 Lily's on Main
  Plain & Fancy Farm
  Good 'N Plenty

BEST BUYS

1. Five Guys
2. Qdoba
3. Isaac's
4. Plain & Fancy Farm
5. Bird-in-Hand

Bensí *Italian* · 17 | 16 | 17 | $29

Wyomissing | Shoppes at Wyomissing | 700 Woodland Rd.
(Crossing Dr.) | 610-375-3222 | www.bensirestaurants.com
See review in the Philadelphia Directory.

Bird-in-Hand Family Restaurant ⊠ *PA Dutch* · 20 | 15 | 20 | $22

Bird-in-Hand | 2760 Old Philadelphia Pike (Ronks Rd.) | 717-768-1500 |
www.bird-in-hand.com

"Go hungry" to this "family-style" all-you-can-eat Pennsylvania
Dutch in Lancaster County, where you'll get "more food than any human should eat"; "fresh" selections of breakfast, lunch and dinner
fare make it "one of the best in Amish land" in the eyes of many, but for
some, it's more about the "group-outing fun" than the just "ok" eats.

Checkers Bistro ⊠ Ⓜ *Eclectic* · - | - | - | M

Lancaster | 300 W. James St. (N. Mulberry St.) | 717-509-1069 |
www.checkersbistro.com

"One of the hidden gems of Lancaster", this contemporary Eclectic
offers "consistently great" "small plates" in an updated 100-year-old
building graced with works by area artists; those who've tried it report
owners who are "always on-site" overseeing "well-informed" staffers
who serve "good pours" of wine (and you can BYO for no corkage).

El Serrano *Nuevo Latino* · ▽ 22 | 20 | 18 | $36

Lancaster | 2151 Columbia Ave. (Rte. 741 S.) | 717-397-6191 |
www.elserrano.com

"Killer blue margaritas" complement the Nuevo Latin and Peruvian
fare at this Lancaster establishment, where the "breathtaking"
South American setting features a courtyard, as well as marble columns and mahogany tables imported from Peru; the "large portions" offer "good value for the money", while live music on
weekends and wine tastings help make it a destination.

Five Guys *Burgers* · 22 | 9 | 16 | $11

Lancaster | 1962 Fruitville Pike (Rte. 30) | 717-569-7730
Lancaster | 2090 E. Lincoln Hwy. (Rte. 30) | 717-299-4470
www.fiveguys.com
See review in the Philadelphia Directory.

Menus, photos, voting and more – free at ZAGAT.com

	FOOD	DECOR	SERVICE	COST

⌷ Gibraltar *Mediterranean/Seafood*   23 | 21 | 22 | $60

Lancaster | 931 Harrisburg Pike (Race Ave.) | 717-397-2790 |
www.gibraltargrille.com

Though the "food is always good" at this Med near Franklin &
Marshall, it "can surprise to the upside" with "creative presentations" of seafood that make it "perfect for the fish lover", while
appealing to oenophiles with a "great wine" list of some 300 labels; "from the outside" "you'd never guess it had any atmosphere", but the "elegant" interior makes "you almost forget you're
in Lancaster" – except during "parents weekend", when it
can get "overcrowded."

Good 'N Plenty ⌷ *PA Dutch*   18 | 15 | 20 | $27

Smoketown | 150 Eastbrook Rd. (Rte. 30) | 717-394-7111 |
www.goodnplenty.com

"Prepare to eat lots" at this "basic", "family-style" Pennsylvania
Dutch in Lancaster County where "sweet Mennonite servers" keep
piling on "great fried chicken and buttered noodles" and other home
cooking for tables full of "tourists" and "big family groups" in a two-
story farmhouse; some quip the name "refers to how much room
you need in the waistband of your pants."

Gracie's 21st
Century Cafe ⌷Ⓜ *Eclectic*   - | - | - | E

Pine Forge | 1534 Manatawny Rd. (King St.) | 610-323-4004 |
www.gracies21stcentury.com

"Vibrant" chef-owner Gracie Skiadas' "elegantly whimsical" Eclectic
is "worth the ride" to the Pottstown area for "delicious", "creative"
fare that reflects "her interest in organic, Greek and Southwest
foods"; the atmosphere is "inviting" in the "white adobe rooms"
warmed by three fireplaces or outside on the recently refurbished
patio; it's open Wednesdays–Saturdays.

Green Hills Inn ⌷ *American/French*   - | - | - | E

Reading | 2444 Morgantown Rd. (Love Rd.) | 610-777-9611 |
www.greenhillsinn.com

While the jury's hung on the new ownership team – between those
who feel they're "doing a good job" and others who think it's in
"decline" – stalwarts still regard this "cozy" upmarket country inn
near Reading as a "safe bet" for formal French-American fare (duck
breast, lobster cakes) and "good-to-very-good" service in three "elegant" dining rooms; the $29.95 three-course dinner prix fixe is a
"cap to a pleasant day" exploring Berks County outlets.

Gusto ⌷ *Italian*   21 | 14 | 22 | $26

Lancaster | 335 N. Queen St. (Walnut St.) | 717-945-6906 |
www.gusto335.com

"Imaginative" entrees, "delicious" pizzas and "amazing sandwiches"
are backed by a "well-thought-out" wine list at this "classy" Italian,
a "real find" for "reasonably priced" dining in Downtown Lancaster;
"solid" service helps many overlook the "dull" digs and makes it a
"great place to go with a group – as long as you get there early."

Haydn Zug's *American* ▽ 23 | 19 | 22 | $54

East Petersburg | 1987 State St. (Rte. 72) | 717-569-5746 |
www.haydnzugs.com

Seems like this "reliable" Traditional American in East Petersburg
"has been here forever", delivering "magnificent" meals and an "excellent wine list" in an "old-fashioned steakhouse" setting; "if you're looking for innovation, look elsewhere", but most "can't wait to go back."

Iron Hill Brewery & Restaurant *American* 19 | 19 | 20 | $28

Lancaster | 781 Harrisburg Pike (Race Ave.) | 717-291-9800 |
www.ironhillbrewery.com

See review in the Philadelphia Directory.

Isaac's Restaurant & Deli *Deli* 17 | 12 | 16 | $17

Ephrata | Cloister Shopping Ctr. | 120 N. Reading Rd. (Rte. 272) |
717-733-7777

Lancaster | Granite Run Sq. | 1559 Manheim Pike (Rte. 283) |
717-560-7774

Lancaster | Sycamore Ct. | 245 Centerville Rd. (Rte. 30) | 717-393-1199

Lancaster | 25 N. Queen St. (King St.) | 717-394-5544

Lancaster | The Shoppes at Greenfield | 565 Greenfield Rd. (Rte. 30) |
717-393-6067

Lititz | 4 Trolley Run Rd. (Rte. 501) | 717-625-1181

Strasburg | Shops at Traintown | 226 Gap Rd. (Rte. 896) | 717-687-7699

Wyomissing | Village Sq. | 94 Commerce Dr. (bet. Papermill &
State Hill Rds.) | 610-376-1717

www.isaacsdeli.com

See review in the Philadelphia Directory.

J.B. Dawson's *American* 18 | 17 | 20 | $29

Lancaster | Park City Ctr. | 491 Park City Ctr. (Rte. 30) | 717-399-3996

Austin's *American*

Reading | 1101 Snyder Rd. (Van Reed Rd.) | 610-678-5500 |
www.jbdawsons.com

See review in the Philadelphia Directory.

Lancaster Dispensing - | - | - | I
Company ❷ *Pub Food*

Lancaster | 33 N. Market St. (Queen St.) | 717-299-4602 |
www.dispensingco.com

The "basic pub fare" and "decent craft beer selection" "always seem
to please" at this taproom in Downtown Lancaster, where "great
bands" play on weekends; while some find the "Victorian" setting
"comfortable", others grouse that they "pack you in like sardines."

Lemon Grass Thai *Thai* 20 | 15 | 17 | $24

Lancaster | 2481 Lincoln Hwy. E. (Eastbrook Rd.) | 717-295-1621

See review in the Philadelphia Directory.

Z Lily's on Main *American* 24 | 19 | 20 | $34

Ephrata | Brossman Business Complex | 124 E. Main St. (Lake St.) |
717-738-2711 | www.lilysonmain.com

"More than you'd expect from a small rural town", this "appealing"
Lancaster County New American offers "wonderful" dishes featur-

ing "interesting combinations" of "fresh, quality ingredients" (the "lobster mac 'n' cheese is to die for"), "creative cocktails" and a "very nice wine list" in an "inviting", art deco "adaptation of a business space"; though some say it can get "crowded and noisy", most report "no disappointments" here.

Miller's Smorgasbord *PA Dutch* | 18 | 14 | 18 | $27 |

Ronks | 2811 Lincoln Hwy. E. (Ronks Rd.) | 717-687-6621 | www.millerssmorgasbord.com

With a buffet table "groaning" under "more good comfort food than you can possibly consume", this Pennsylvania Dutch in Lancaster County is a "longtime favorite" of those "who appreciate plenty", so wear "loose pants" and be assured the staff will "keep your glass or cup full"; sure, it's "kitschy" and there's a "gift shop", but what else do you expect from a "tourist destination"?

Plain & Fancy Farm *PA Dutch* | 19 | 18 | 20 | $22 |

Bird-in-Hand | 3121 Old Philadelphia Pike (bet. N. Harvest & Old Leacock Rds.) | 717-767-8436 | www.plainandfancyfarm.com

"Real Amish home cooking and atmosphere" are the draw at this Regional American set in a Lancaster County farmhouse, where country cognoscenti with "big appetites" can't get enough of the $18.95 all-you-can-eat (though à la carte dishes are available too) and neighborhood "buggy rides"; insiders insist the "fried chicken" will cure "what ails you", and as "kitschy" as it may be, most agree it's a "tourist attraction that you can't get annoyed at."

Qdoba Mexican Grill *Mexican* | 18 | 11 | 15 | $12 |

Lancaster | Park City Ctr. | 387 Park City Ctr. (Ring Rd.) | 717-299-4766 | www.qdoba.com

See review in the Philadelphia Directory.

Shady Maple Smorgasbord ⊠ *PA Dutch* | 20 | 14 | 18 | $21 |

East Earl | 129 Toddy Dr. (28th Division Hwy.) | 717-354-8222 | www.shady-maple.com

While it offers a discount to folks who've had gastric-bypass surgery (must present a card), it's "too bad they don't have tableside treadmills" as well at this "unbeatable" Pennsylvania Dutch all-you-can-eat "cultural experience", part of a "gigantic" farmer's market in Lancaster County; "gourmands" from "miles around" gather for "delicious" "breakfast binges", as well as daily lunch and dinner menus brimming with "cholesterol-laden goodies", so expect "all the ambiance of a high school cafeteria" and "horrendous" waits on Saturdays.

Stoudt's Black Angus *American* | 19 | 17 | 20 | $40 |

Adamstown | 2800 N. Reading Rd. (Pennsylvania Tpke., exit 286) | 717-484-4386 | www.stoudtsbeer.com

Going on a half-century off the Pennsylvania Turnpike in Adamstown, the pub and dining room attached to this pioneering microbrewery roll out "very good" German-influenced Traditional American chow (steaks, seafood), but it's the "handcrafted ale" that is the real "hit"; "don't miss the beer festivals" and assorted nightly entertainment in the Victorian setting full of old-time political memorabilia.

New Jersey Suburbs

Anthony's 🅼 *Italian*   22 | 19 | 21 | $35

Haddon Heights | 512 Station Ave. (White Horse Pike) | 856-310-7766 | www.anthonyscuisine.com

Whether for "celebrations or a romantic night out", "you're in for a treat" at this "solid" BYO "hideaway" in a Haddon Heights storefront; thanks to chef John Pilarz's "traditional" Italian fare ("stick to the basics" advise insiders), "fair prices" and "dependable" service from "friendly" owner Anthony Iannone and his staff; there's "usually not a wait" and regulars recommend taking an après-meal "walk around town."

Anton's at the Swan 🅼 *American*   22 | 22 | 21 | $50

Lambertville | Swan Hotel | 43 S. Main St. (Swan St.) | 609-397-1960 | www.antons-at-the-swan.com

Cognoscenti call this "candlelit" "Victorian" "retreat" in Lambertville's Swan Hotel a "must-stop" for a "special occasion" or "intimate dinner with that special someone", thanks to "well-prepared" New American fare from "a menu that wows", a setting that "oozes charm" and "graceful" service befitting the venue's name; insiders enjoy sitting outside or cozying by the "fireplace" in the bar, where you can order the "same food at a lesser price."

Ariana *Afghan*   22 | 16 | 21 | $28

Voorhees | Eagle Plaza Shopping Ctr. | 700 Haddonfield-Berlin Rd. (White Horse Rd.) | 856-784-1100 | www.restaurantariana.com
See review in the Philadelphia Directory.

Bahama Breeze *Caribbean*   17 | 18 | 18 | $27

Cherry Hill | Cherry Hill Mall | 2000 Rte. 38 (Haddonfield Rd.) | 856-317-8317 | www.bahamabreeze.com
See review in the Philadelphia Directory.

Baja Fresh Mexican Grill *Mexican*   17 | 10 | 14 | $12

Mount Laurel | 10A Centerton Rd. (Hartford Rd.) | 856-802-0892
NEW **Voorhees** | 1120 White Horse Rd. (bet. Echelon & Haddonfield Berlin Rds.) | 856-784-5955
www.bajafresh.com
See review in the Philadelphia Directory.

Barnsboro Inn *American*

22 | 20 | 20 | $37

Sewell | 699 Main St. (Center St.) | 856-468-3557 |
www.barnsboroinn.com

For a "real" "inn" experience with lots of "old-school charm", "locals"
and others head to this New American in Sewell offering "first-rate"
fare and "friendly" service in a circa-1720 "rustic" building that
most find as "cozy as grandma's parlor"; a few find the space too
"cramped" for comfort, however, and opt for the "fun, easy" six-seat
bar, especially in "winter", when you can "sit by the fireplace."

Barone's Tuscan Grille *Italian*

22 | 19 | 21 | $32

Moorestown | 280 Young Ave. (Main St.) | 856-234-7900 |
www.baronerestaurants.com

Villa Barone *Italian*

Collingswood | 753 Haddon Ave. (bet. Frazer & Washington Aves.) |
856-858-2999 | www.villabaronesite.com

"Old-fashioned" Italian favorites "cooked to your taste" and "pleasant"
service are the signatures of these South Jersey BYOs that ooze
"rustic charm"; they're "go-to" destinations for a large "party", "locals'
night out" or "lunch" outside – in Moorestown's "outdoor garden
area" or on the sidewalk patio in Collingswood.

Benihana *Japanese*

19 | 18 | 20 | $35

Pennsauken | 5255 Marlton Pike (Lexington Ave.) | 856-665-6320 |
www.benihana.com

See review in the Philadelphia Directory.

Bistro di Marino Ⓜ *Italian*

23 | 18 | 20 | $32

Collingswood | 492 Haddon Ave. (Crestmont Terrace) | 856-858-1700 |
www.bistrodimarino.com

"Authentic" Italian cuisine is served by a staff that "bends over back-
wards to make you happy" at this Collingswood "bistro", which
many tout as a "bargain" for its $9.95 lunch buffet and BYO, which
"helps keep costs down"; though some find the "exposed-brick" interior too "cramped" for comfort, others insist it "doesn't detract"
from the experience, and a planned outdoor courtyard, slated to
open in 2010, should alleviate the crunch.

Blackbird Dining Establishment Ⓜ *American*

25 | 19 | 22 | $40

Collingswood | 619 Collings Ave. (White Horse Pike) | 856-854-3444 |
www.blackbirdnj.com

"Impress a date or a business prospect" at Alex Capasso's "little, little" New American BYO "off the main drag" in Collingswood, where
his "fresh, well-executed" fare, including the "lightest and tastiest
gnocchi on the planet", is served by an "attentive" staff; though a
few complain that the "noise level" can be "too much", most would
agree that "this blackbird can sing to me anytime."

Bobby Chez Ⓜ *Seafood*

22 | 11 | 18 | $23

Cherry Hill | Village Walk Shopping Ctr. | 1990 Rte. 70 E.
(Old Orchard Rd.) | 856-751-7575

(continued)

(continued)

Bobby Chez

Collingswood | 33 W. Collings Ave. (Haddon Ave.) | 856-869-8000 Ⓢ
Mount Laurel | Centerton Sq. | Marter Ave. & Rte. 38 (Centeron Rd.) |
856-234-4146
Sewell | 100 Hurffville Cross Keys Rd. (Glassboro Cross Keys Rd.) |
856-262-1001
www.bobbychezcrabcakes.com

Aficionados assert "you can't go wrong" with the "melt-in-your-mouth" "crab cakes", "rotisserie chicken" and "lobster mashed potatoes" ("decadence on a fork") at this affordable seafood chain popular mainly for "high-quality" takeout, though it sports a few tables for those who just can't wait to "take them home"; there's "not much atmosphere", but "friendly counter service" compensates; P.S. the "daily specials are an excellent value."

Bonefish Grill *Seafood*   21 | 19 | 20 | $35

Deptford | 1709 Deptford Center Rd. (Almonessen Rd.) |
856-848-6261
Marlton | 500 Rte. 73 N. (Marlton Pike) | 856-396-3122
www.bonefishgrill.com
See review in the Philadelphia Directory.

Braddock's Ⓜ *American*   20 | 20 | 22 | $46

Medford | 39 S. Main St. (Coates St.) | 609-654-1604 |
www.braddocks.com

Fans say this "quaint", "atmospheric" Traditional America in historic Medford is somewhat "expensive, but worth it" for a "special date", "family occasion" or entertaining "out-of-towners", serving "excellent" brunches and other "consistent good" fare in a 19th-century clapboard house with a porch where you can "watch small-village traffic go by"; cynics, though, sniff that it "needs to enter the 21st century" or "lower its prices."

Brio Tuscan Grille *Italian*   19 | 22 | 20 | $33

Cherry Hill | Town Place at Garden State | 901 Haddonfield Rd. (Rte. 70) |
856-910-8166 | www.brioitalian.com

"Comfortable", "family-friendly" "surroundings" and "humongous portions" of "nicely presented" "traditional" Italian fare win fans for this "surprisingly non-kitschy" Cherry Hill link; a few purists dismiss it as "corporate" and "bland", and others warn it "can be very noisy" ("especially on weekends"), but most agree it's on the "nicer side of chains" and the prices are "reasonable."

Café Gallery *Continental*   20 | 22 | 20 | $43

Burlington | 219 High St. (Pearl St.) | 609-386-6150 |
www.cafegalleryburlington.com

"Beautiful views" from the "riverbanks" of the Delaware and "charming art-gallery decor" set the stage for an "affordable" Sunday brunch ($21.75) or "elegant" dinner ("especially around sunset") at this "reliable" Burlington Continental; the service is "friendly" and the "traditional" fare, which comes in "large" portions, is "well worth having."

	FOOD	DECOR	SERVICE	COST

Caffe Aldo Lamberti *Italian* | 24 | 23 | 24 | $47 |

Cherry Hill | 2011 Marlton Pike W. (Haddonfield Rd.) | 856-663-1747 | www.caffelamberti.com

It's "hard to beat" the "ultrafresh seafood" and other "top-notch" *mangiare*, "outstanding" wine list and "professional" service at the Lamberti family's "sprawling" flagship Italian in Cherry Hill, where a "swank" redo, including the addition of a new wine room, has enhanced the "upscale" vibe; most are "willing to overlook the prices" and declare it "one of the best in South Jersey" for a "date night", "special occasion" or entertaining "clients" and "out-of-town guests."

Ⓩ Capital Grille, The *Steak* | 26 | 24 | 25 | $66 |

Cherry Hill | Cherry Hill Mall | 2000 Rte. 38 (Haddonfield Rd.) | 856-665-5252 | www.thecapitalgrille.com

See review in the Philadelphia Directory.

Casona Ⓜ *Cuban* | 20 | 20 | 20 | $36 |

Collingswood | 563 Haddon Ave. (Knight Ave.) | 856-854-5555 | www.mycasona.com

"Cuba meets Victoriana" at this Collingswood BYO housed in a 100-year-old mansion complete with wraparound porch, a "wonderful setting" for a "ropa vieja fix" and other "delicious", "modern" island eats that offer a "delightful change from the predictable selections of the neighborhood"; the fare is "served with passion and care", and if you BYO "tequila" or "rum", "they will mix (drinks) for you."

Ⓩ Catelli *Italian* | 25 | 23 | 24 | $47 |

Voorhees | The Plaza | 1000 Main St. (Evesham Rd.) | 856-751-6069 | www.catellirestaurant.com

"They know what they're doing" at this "upscale" Italian in Voorhees, a "solid choice" for a "special event" or entertaining "guests or clients", thanks to chef Louis Imbesi's "sophisticated" cuisine, "top-notch" service and "lovely" surroundings, including a "romantic" "sun room"; "generous" "wine pairings" and nightly prix fixes offer "excellent value" and help make this "fine-dining experience" "worth the visit."

Cheesecake Factory *American* | 20 | 19 | 19 | $29 |

Cherry Hill | Marketplace at Garden State Park | 931 Haddonfield Rd. (bet. Graham & Severn Aves.) | 856-665-7550 | www.thecheesecakefactory.com

See review in the Philadelphia Directory.

Chez Elena Wu *Chinese/Japanese* | 22 | 19 | 21 | $33 |

Voorhees | Ritz Shopping Ctr. | 910 Haddonfield-Berlin Rd. (Laurel Oak Blvd.) | 856-566-3222 | www.chezelenawu.com

Even without "Elena", supporters say this Chinese-Japanese BYO "inside a nondescript strip mall" in Voorhees delivers "tasty" cooking in a "surprisingly romantic" setting, and is a "convenient" (if somewhat "pricey") option "before or after a movie" at the Showcase at the Ritz; a few insist it's "not the same" "since being sold", but most agree it's "worth the visit" as long as you "stick to the simple stuff."

	FOOD	DECOR	SERVICE	COST

Chickie's & Pete's Cafe ● *Pub Food* 18 16 17 $25
Bordentown | 183 Rte. 130 (Elizabeth St.) | 609-298-9182 |
www.chickiesandpetes.com
See review in the Philadelphia Directory.

Chophouse, The *Seafood/Steak* 24 22 23 $56
Gibbsboro | 4 S. Lakeview Dr. (Clementon Rd.) | 856-566-7300 |
www.thechophouse.us
For a "big-city" steakhouse experience, carnivores head to
"Gibbsboro?" – but seriously, "top-notch" steaks and a "terrific" wine
list served by a "polished" staff in a "gorgeous" space with an "outstanding view" of the lake make this meatery in the "sticks" "simply a
must" for most; "come with an expense account" and don't miss the
"lively" "downstairs" bar "for a nightcap" (though some demur at
the spectacle of "cougars" "sipping wine and batting their lashes").

Coconut Bay Fusion Cuisine *Asian* ▽ 23 21 22 $26
(fka Coconut Bay Asian Cuisine)
Voorhees | Echelon Vlg. Plaza | 1120 White Horse Rd. (bet. Echelon Rd. &
Executive Dr.) | 856-783-8878
Fans tout this "inexpensive" Asian BYO in Voorhees as a "perfect midweek 'I-don't-want-to-cook'" solution for its "tasty", "well-prepared"
"Chinese, Japanese and Vietnamese" fare with a European accent;
"competent" service and a "lovely", low-lit setting seal the deal.

Cork *American* 22 18 20 $40
Westmont | 90 Haddon Ave. (Cooper St.) | 856-833-9800 |
www.corknj.com
The wide "selection" of "small plates", "flatbreads" and "full-size
meals" at this "intimate" New American "does not disappoint"
Westmonters, who also laud the "well-thought-out" wine list and
"above-average" "craft beer" selection; though a few feel the "cozy"
digs could "use some upscaling", most regard it as a good "bang for the
buck" and a solid choice when they don't "want to go over to the city."

DeAnna's 🈂🅜 *Italian* ▽ 24 19 21 $41
Lambertville | 54 N. Franklin St. (Coryell St.) | 609-397-8957 |
www.deannasrestaurant.com
Aficionados attest there's "culinary mastery" on display in the
"wonderful homemade pastas" and "divine" specials at this
Lambertville Italian "tucked awkwardly into a small row house",
where the staff's always "busy" and musical acts perform on
Thursdays and Fridays (which are "ok if you don't mind them almost
sitting at your table"); for those who find the "tight" digs "annoy-
ing", regulars recommend "sitting at the bar" and "soaking up the atmosphere"; there's a $20 dinner prix fixe Tuesdays and Wednesdays.

Dream Cuisine Café 🈂🅜 *French* - - - M
Cherry Hill | Tuscany Mktpl. | 1990 Marlton Pike E. (Old Orchard Rd.) |
856-751-2800 | www.dreamcuisinecafe.net
Those in-the-know tout this simple New French BYO, reminiscent of
a European cafe, as a "laid-back" "island of excellence" amid Cherry

Hill's usual New American or Italian bent; chef Vincent Fanari (ex Philly's The Plough & the Stars) creates an affordable menu, based on dishes from his native Nice, so "be prepared to spend some time" over "housemade pastas" "presented" without "pretense."

El Azteca *Mexican*

| 19 | 11 | 18 | $22 |

Mount Laurel | Ramblewood Shopping Ctr. | 1155 Rte. 73 N. (Church Rd.) | 856-914-9302

The Mexican specialties are "fresh", "mouthwatering" and "cheap" at this BYO cantina in Mount Laurel's Ramblewood Shopping Center; the service is "familylike" and the vibe "relaxed" in the "no-frills" environs, making it a *"mi casa* kind of a place" – "don't forget to bring your own tequila."

Elements Café Ⓜ *American*

| ∇ 22 | 18 | 21 | $37 |

Haddon Heights | 517 Station Ave. (White Horse Pike) | 856-546-8840 | www.elementscafe.com

"You can really have it your way" at Fred Kellermann's "charming" New American in Haddon Heights, where you "mix and match" "creative" "tapas-style" "choices that frequently change" and "always surprise"; "attentive" service helps you "ignore" the space that some find "drab", and while BYO is a "bonus" for the budget conscious, a few warn that a "big eater can spend a lot" here.

Filomena Cucina Italiana *Italian*

| 22 | 21 | 21 | $40 |

Clementon | 1380 Blackwood-Clementon Rd. (Millbridge Rd.) | 856-784-6166 | www.filomenascucina.com

Filomena Lakeview *Italian*

Deptford | 1738 Cooper St. (Almonesson Rd.) | 856-228-4235 | www.filomenalakeview.com

Italian food "prepared with love and art" wins praise for these South Jersey twins; Deptford is the "place to be seen" with a menu with "something nearly everyone will order" and "bartenders who are a delight", while the more casual, "festive" (some say "loud") Clementon location specializes in $19.95 prix fixes from 3:30–6:30 PM weekdays.

Five Guys *Burgers*

| 22 | 9 | 16 | $11 |

Cherry Hill | 1650 Kings Hwy. N. (Rte. 70) | 856-795-1455
NEW **Cinnaminson** | 127G Rte. 130 (bet. Bridgeboro Rd. & Front St.) | 856-829-5200
Deptford | 2000 Clements Bridge Rd. (Hurffville Rd.) | 856-845-5489
Moorestown | East Gate Square Shopping Ctr. | 1650 Nixon Dr. (Rte. 38) | 856-866-0200
Mount Ephraim | Audubon Shopping Ctr. | 130 Black Horse Pike (bet. Kennedy Dr. & Pershing Ave.) | 856-672-0442
Sicklerville | 493 Berlin Cross Keys Rd. (Williamstown Erial Rd.) | 856-875-5558
Voorhees | Eagle Plaza Shopping Ctr. | 700 Haddonfield-Berlin Rd. (White Horse Rd.) | 856-783-5588
www.fiveguys.com

See review in the Philadelphia Directory.

	FOOD	DECOR	SERVICE	COST

Fleming's Prime Steakhouse *Steak* | 24 | 23 | 24 | $62 |

Marlton | 500 Rte. 73 N. (bet. Baker Blvd. & Lincoln Dr.) | 856-988-1351 | www.flemingssteakhouse.com
See review in the Philadelphia Directory.

❷ Fuji Ⓜ *Japanese* | 27 | 20 | 23 | $44 |

Haddonfield | Shops at 116 | 116 Kings Hwy. E. (Tanner St.) | 856-354-8200 | www.fujirestaurant.com
Matt Ito is the "real deal" and while there's "nothing glamorous" about his "superior" Japanese BYO "off the main drag" in Haddonfield, his "amazing", "innovative" tasting menus of "melt-in-your-mouth" sushi are miles "beyond the California roll mentality" and "put 'celebrity chefs' to shame"; its "odd location" notwithstanding, most think it "should be better known."

Full Moon Café *Eclectic* | 18 | 10 | 18 | $26 |

Lambertville | 23 Bridge St. (Union St.) | 609-397-1096 | www.cafefullmoon.com
Fans howl with happiness at this "friendly" Eclectic breakfast-lunch "hangout" on Lambertville's main drag, extolling its "diverse menu" of "tasty" "omelets" and sandwiches and "efficient, friendly" service in a "designed-for-tourists" setting, which a few feel is "in need of an update"; it's "especially busy on weekends", while dinner, which is served only on the "night of the full moon", is a "real event."

GG's Ⓢ *American*   ∇ | 26 | 24 | 25 | $47 |

Mount Laurel | DoubleTree Guest Suites Mount Laurel | 515 Fellowship Rd. (Rte. 73) | 856-222-0335 | www.ggsrestaurant.com
Those in-the-know call this Mount Laurel New American a "diamond in the rough", providing "enjoyable business lunches" and other "phenomenal" fare in a "sophisticated", "special occasion"-worthy setting that belies the "not very eye-appealing" DoubleTree Guest Suites where it's housed; a "friendly bar scene" and live piano nightly (except Mondays) add to its allure.

❷ Giumarello's Ⓜ *Italian* | 26 | 22 | 23 | $52 |

Westmont | 329 Haddon Ave. (bet. Coulter Ave. & Kings Hwy.) | 856-858-9400 | www.giumarellos.com
"You will feel at home" at this "old-school", "classic" Italian in Westmont (and you'll feel "even better when someone else is footing the bill"), thanks to "consistently delicious", "no-fuss" dishes that "can't be beat" and servers who "make you think they're your best friend"; the "cozy, intimate" setting is ideal for a "celebration", and "happy hour" in the "fabulous bar" helps make it "better than most in the area."

Hamilton's Grill Room *Mediterranean* | 24 | 19 | 21 | $52 |

Lambertville | 8 Coryell St. (Union St.) | 609-397-4343 | www.hamiltonsgrillroom.com
Touted as one of the "all-time favorites" in Lambertville, this "romantic" BYO is a "little tricky to find", but those who do are wowed by "creative", "wood-fired" Mediterranean "grill food", which can be

even more "pleasant" "if you can sit on the landing portion on the canal"; it's "deservedly popular" and "tables are tight", so book a table and look forward to "strolling around" town "after dinner" or a "nightcap" at the Boat House "across the alley."

High Street Grill *American*

▽ 21 | 19 | 21 | $35

Mount Holly | 64 High St. (bet. Brainerd & Garden Sts.) | 609-265-9199 | www.highstreetgrill.net

An "eclectic" "mix" of "blue-collar locals", "prominent lawyers, judges and politicians" frequents this "casual" New American near the courthouse in Mount Holly, and most extol John McDevitt's "ambitious" cooking, the "solid craft-beer selection" and "good prices"; whether it's "super-crowded or practically empty", the staff is always "attentive" in the space outfitted with "wood all over the place", and an upstairs piano bar.

ⓩ Il Fiore *Italian*

26 | 16 | 23 | $32

Collingswood | 693-695 Haddon Ave. (Collings Ave.) | 856-833-0808

"Be prepared to wait, even with reservations" at this "modest" Italian BYO regarded by many as "one of Collingswood's best" and a "must-stop" for "satisfying" portions of "fantastic" food "cooked just right" and "professional" service; though the "cozy" digs are "always crowded", many "bring friends and family" here, for "the price is right."

Inn of the Hawke *American*

20 | 18 | 20 | $32

Lambertville | 74 S. Union St. (Mt. Hope St.) | 609-397-9555

"Great burgers" and "awesome house-fried potato chips" highlight the American pub fare menu at this watering hole "a few blocks off the beaten path" in Lambertville, which also boasts an "above-average" draft and bottled beer list, and everything is "priced right"; the mood is "relaxed" in the "cozy" environs, where you can "sit around the fire" or take in the night "outside on the patio" with "friendly locals."

Joe Pesce *Italian/Seafood*

21 | 16 | 19 | $42

Collingswood | 833 Haddon Ave. (bet. Collings Ave. & Cuthbert Blvd.) | 856-833-9888 | www.joepescerestaurant.com

See review in the Philadelphia Directory.

Joe's Peking Duck House Ⓜ⇗ *Chinese*

22 | 11 | 20 | $23

Marlton | Marlton Crossing Shopping Ctr. | 145 Rte. 73 S. (Rte. 70) | 856-985-1551 | www.joespekingduckhouse.com

Sinophiles swear "it doesn't get any better" than this modest Chinese BYO "tucked" in a Marlton strip mall, known for its signature "duck", "salt-based squid" and other "comfort-food" offerings "made from scratch"; "quick, efficient" service makes up for the nondescript digs, and partisans promise you'll "never leave hungry" – as long as you bring cash ("no credit cards").

Kibitz Room *Deli*

21 | 9 | 15 | $18

Cherry Hill | Shoppes at Holly Ravine | 100 Springdale Rd. (Evesham Rd.) | 856-428-7878 | www.thekibitzroom.com

Noshers who don't feel like making the "trek back home to Brooklyn" head to these delis in Cherry Hill and Rittenhouse Square for "mile-high" "sandwiches", "gigundo" "salads" and service with a "what-taya want?"; "save room for the pickle bar", which is "worth the visit and the swollen ankles", and remember there's "no kibitzing here, just eating."

Kuzina by Sofia *Greek*   22 | 14 | 20 | $27

Cherry Hill | Sawmill Village | 404 Rte. 70 W. (Sawmill Rd.) |
856-429-1061 | www.kuzinabysofia.com
"Authentic, filling" meze "made from scratch" "transports" you to the "Greek isles" at this "family-run" BYO "find" in a "Cherry Hill strip mall" where "careful and friendly" folks "keep it together" even when it's "packed"; there's a live band on Saturday nights, but perhaps more important, a meal here "won't break the bank."

La Campagne Ⓜ *French*   22 | 21 | 22 | $52

Cherry Hill | 312 Kresson Rd. (Brace Rd.) | 856-429-7647 |
www.lacampagne.com
A working fireplace helps create a "comfortable and romantic mood" at this "rustic" French BYO set in a "beautiful" circa-1841 house in Cherry Hill, where you may need to "let out your belt when you're done" after a meal of "delicious", "traditional" fare and "eye-popping desserts"; "great cooking lessons" are offered Thursdays.

La Esperanza *Mexican*   25 | 17 | 23 | $27

Lindenwold | 40 E. Gibbsboro Rd. (White Horse Pike) | 856-782-7114 |
www.mexicanhope.com
"No fusion or confusion" – just "authentic", "lovingly prepared" Mex specialties are served at this "mom-and-pop" cantina tucked "out of the way" in Lindenwold; it's "not fancy by any means", but "that's ok" with admirers who are "never disappointed" and "never leave hungry", thanks to "generous portions" of "guacamole" "made fresh to order", "belly-busting" burritos and more, backed by a "great selection of tequilas."

La Locanda *Italian*   ▽ 25 | 18 | 19 | $40

Voorhees | Echelon Village Plaza | 1120 White Horse Rd.
(Haddonfield-Berlin Rd.) | 856-627-3700 | www.lalocandaonline.com
"Don't be fooled by its shopping-center location" in Voorhees – this white-tablecloth BYO "gem" doesn't offer "make-believe American Italian", but "amazing *mangiare*, served by an "experienced" staff that "pampers" you; sure, "it's a little pricey", but most "consistently enjoy" the experience and liken it to "dining in the old country."

Lambertville Station *American*   18 | 19 | 19 | $39

Lambertville | 11 Bridge St. (Delaware River) | 609-397-8300 |
www.lambertvillestation.com
Housed in a "beautiful" restored Victorian-era rail station with "lovely" views of the canal and Delaware River, this "vintage" American is a "pleasant" stop for "tourists" and others "after wandering the shops in Lambertville"; a few find the fare merely "service-able" and think "the menu could use an update", but for most it's "worth the hike" for "quality wines by the glass", tasty "tapas" and winter "game" specials served by a "friendly" staff.

	FOOD	DECOR	SERVICE	COST

Lilly's on the Canal M *Eclectic*   21 | 21 | 20 | $39

Lambertville | 2 Canal St. (Bridge St.) | 609-397-6242 |
www.lillysgourmet.com

Groupies gush "they get it right every time" at this "terrific"
Lambertville Eclectic where you "cannot go wrong" for a "casual"
lunch or dinner break on a "day of shopping", thanks to "flavorful,
fresh" cooking and an "unbelievable selection" of "scrumptious desserts"; the atmosphere is "relaxed", and while some caution that the
first floor can be "too loud", the "waterside patio" is "delightful" in
the "warm months"; it's BYO-friendly with no corkage.

Little Café, A S M *Eclectic*   ∇ 24 | 17 | 22 | $40

Voorhees | Plaza Shoppes | 118 White Horse Rd. E. (Burnt Mill Rd.) |
856-784-3344 | www.alittlecafenj.com

Marianne Cuneo Powell takes you to a "world of gastronomic delight"
with "imaginative" Eclectic "dishes" at her "hidden gem" of a BYO in
a Voorhees strip mall; the "quiet", "dark" space is either "intimate"
or "cramped", depending on who you ask, but "bargain" $30 prix
fixe dinners enable many to overlook the "small size."

Little Tuna, The *Seafood*   19 | 16 | 19 | $35

Haddonfield | 141 Kings Hwy. E. (Haddon Ave.) | 856-795-0888 |
www.thelittletuna.com

"Fresh", "simple" seafood and steaks at "reasonable prices" "star"
at this "quaint", "neighborhood" BYO in "high-rent" Haddonfield, a
"convenient" option for "business lunches"; the vibe is "friendly" in
the "cute" space, where the chef-owner can be seen visiting tables,
and for a quieter experience, regulars recommend the second floor.

Maggiano's Little Italy *Italian*   20 | 18 | 19 | $34

Cherry Hill | Cherry Hill Mall | 2000 Rte. 38 (bet. Cherry Hill Mall Dr. &
Haddonfield Rd.) | 856-792-4470 | www.maggianos.com
See review in the Philadelphia Directory.

Manon M ⊅ *French*   24 | 18 | 22 | $50

Lambertville | 19 N. Union St. (Bridge St.) | 609-397-2596
"Outstanding" "country French cooking" served in a "tiny" room
with a rendition of van Gogh's 'Starry, Starry Night' on the ceiling
makes for a "wonderful" experience at this cash-only BYO run by a
"delightful" couple in "quaint" Lambertville; "close your eyes" and
you "could be in Provence" – which may be advisable when the
"cramped" space gets "crowded."

Mastoris ● *Diner*   20 | 11 | 17 | $25

Bordentown | 144 Rte. 130 (Rte. 206) | 609-298-4650 |
www.mastoris.com
"Everything is huge" at this 50-year-old "old-fashioned" "Jersey
diner" on Route 130 in Bordentown, from the "never-ending" menu
to the "absurd portions" to many of the "people", making it a "perfect place for Michelle Obama to never visit"; still, "wonderful"
"cheese bread" and "cinnamon bread", "why-fight-it prices" and
"professional service" garner it a "big following."

McCormick & Schmick's *Seafood*   21 | 21 | 21 | $47

Cherry Hill | Garden State Park | 941 Haddonfield Rd. (Rte. 70) |
856-317-1711 | www.mccormickandschmicks.com
See review in the Philadelphia Directory.

Megu Sushi *Japanese*   26 | 17 | 21 | $39

Cherry Hill | Village Walk Shopping Ctr. | 1990 Rte. 70 E. (Old Orchard Rd.) |
856-489-6228 | www.megusushi.com
Cherry Hillers who've discovered this funky-bright Japanese BYO
"hidden" in Village Walk report a "big variety" of "imaginative, super
sushi" and some of the "best hibachi" (teppanyaki) on the Jersey
"side of the river"; "cheerful and welcoming" service also make it a
keeper for many.

Mélange @ Haddonfield Ⓜ *Creole/Southern*   25 | 19 | 23 | $40

Haddonfield | 18 Tanner St. (Kings Hwy.) | 856-354-1333 |
www.melangerestaurants.com
"If you can't get to the Big Easy", Joe Brown's "tried-and-true" Creole-
Southern BYO in Downtown Haddonfield offers a "touch of New
Orleans" with "enormous portions" of "creatively prepared" eats,
and it's clear he "cares about his customers" as he's packing up
"leftovers"; while a few knock the "bland" digs, most are already
"planning the next visit" over their "after-dinner coffee."

Mexican Food Factory *Mexican*   19 | 18 | 19 | $29

Marlton | 601 Rte. 70 W. (Cropwell Rd.) | 856-983-9222
The "lines out the door" at this thirtysomething Marlton Mex cantina "say it all" about the "authentic", "adventurous" eats and margaritas made "from scratch" ("no sticky pre-made mix"), even if a
few grumble that it's "a bit expensive for what you get"; the dark
room is graced by "Frida Kahlo" prints, while the back "deck" offers
refuge from "all the hustle and bustle of Route 70."

Mikado *Japanese*   23 | 15 | 21 | $31

Cherry Hill | 2320 Rte. 70 W. (Union Ave.) | 856-665-4411
Maple Shade | 468 S. Lenola Rd. (Kings Hwy.) | 856-638-1801
Marlton | Elmwood Shopping Ctr. | 793 Rte. 70 E. (Troth Rd.) |
856-797-8581
www.mikado-us.com
"Consistency is the true mark" of this Japanese trio, which offers an
array of "fresh" sushi that'll "leave your head reeling" as well as
"tried-and-true" teppanyaki from "dynamic", "entertaining" chefs
(at Marlton and Maple Shade only); while the Cherry Hill location
underwent a post-Survey "renovation", proponents posit "who
needs decor" with such "reasonable prices for the quality"?; keep in
mind that Marlton has a liquor license, while the other two are BYO.

Mirabella Cafe *Italian*   23 | 17 | 21 | $33

Cherry Hill | Barclay Farms Shopping Ctr. | 210 Rte. 70 E. (Kings Hwy.) |
856-354-1888 | www.mirabellacafe.com
"Big portions" and "big tastes" are the draw at "gnocchi genius" Joe
Palombo's "romantic", Tuscan-style BYO "treasure" in Cherry Hill's
Barclay Farms, where "delicious homemade pastas" and other "tra-

ditional" treats are pushed by "perfectly attentive" staffers who are "not in your face, but around when you need them"; on Sundays, it offers all-you-can-eat fusilli with gravy at $15.99.

Nifty Fifty's *Diner* | 19 | 19 | 19 | $14 |

Clementon | 1310 Blackwood-Clementon Rd. (Millbridge Rd.) | 856-346-1950

Turnersville | 4670 Black Horse Pike (Fries Mill Rd.) | 856-875-1950
www.niftyfiftys.com

See review in the Philadelphia Directory.

No. 9 Ⓜ *American* | 24 | 14 | 22 | $47 |

Lambertville | 9 Klines Ct. (Bridge St.) | 609-397-6380

There's a reason it's "not easy" to get into Matthew Kane's "tiny box" of a New American BYO "without a reservation", namely, superb "seasonal food" and service in a "homey" if sometimes "noisy" setting; its fans regard it as an "extraordinary value" for the "best food in the New Hope/Lambertville area."

Norma's Eastern Mediterranean Restaurant *Mideastern* | 22 | 15 | 22 | $25 |

Cherry Hill | Barclay Farms Shopping Ctr. | 132-145 Rte. 70 E. (Kings Hwy.) | 856-795-1373 | www.normasrestaurant.com

"Basic Middle Eastern" fare is "done perfectly" at this "no-frills", "family-owned" strip-center BYO in Cherry Hill, where management "wants to ensure you are happy" and even provides a "belly dancer" Friday and Saturday nights if you don't want to "concentrate on the food" exclusively; even with a "Wegmans" "down the street", the attached grocery store is "worth a visit."

Nunzio Ristorante Rustico *Italian* | 24 | 22 | 22 | $42 |

Collingswood | 706 Haddon Ave. (Collings Ave.) | 856-858-9840 | www.nunzios.net

At his "festive" BYO in Downtown Collingswood, Nunzio Patruno's "imaginative" Italian cooking is showcased in a "breathtaking" room with transporting "murals", where the "attentive" staff provides "top-notch" service, "even on the most crowded nights" (when "noise levels" soar); "if you can't afford to go" to the old country, you might "splurge" for a seat at the chef's table instead.

Ota-Ya Ⓜ *Japanese* | 23 | 13 | 20 | $34 |

Lambertville | 21 Ferry St. (Union St.) | 609-397-9228 | www.ota-ya.com

See review in the Philadelphia Directory.

Penang *Malaysian/Thai* | 21 | 16 | 18 | $26 |

Maple Shade | 480 Rte. 38 E. (Cutler Ave.) | 856-755-0188 | www.penangnj.com

See review in the Philadelphia Directory.

P.F. Chang's China Bistro *Chinese* | 20 | 20 | 20 | $31 |

Marlton | Promenade at Sagemore | 500 Rte. 73 S. (Rte. 70) | 856-396-0818 | www.pfchangs.com

See review in the Philadelphia Directory.

FOOD DECOR SERVICE COST

Pietro's Coal Oven Pizzeria *Pizza* | 21 | 15 | 17 | $24 |

Marlton | 140 Rte. 70 W. (Rte. 73) | 856-596-5500 |
www.pietrospizza.com
See review in the Philadelphia Directory.

Pizzicato *Italian* | 19 | 17 | 19 | $31 |

Marlton | Promenade at Sagemore | 500 Rte. 73 S. (Rte. 70) |
856-396-0880 | www.pizzicatoristorante.com
See review in the Philadelphia Directory.

P.J. Whelihan's ● *Pub Food* | 16 | 15 | 16 | $23 |

Cherry Hill | 1854 E. Marlton Pike (Greentree Rd.) | 856-424-8844
Haddonfield | 700 Haddon Ave. (Ardmore Ave.) | 856-427-7888
Maple Shade | 396 S. Lenola Rd. (Kings Hwy.) | 856-234-2345
Medford Lakes | 61 Stokes Rd. (Hampshire Rd.) | 609-714-7900
Sewell | 425 Hurffville-Cross Keys Rd. (Regulus Dr.) | 856-582-7774
www.pjspub.com
"Every sporting event you could ever want to watch" is on view at
this "unpretentious", "local" American pub chain popular for
"wings" and "good solid pub grub"; while it's a "good family place"
(read: "noisy children"), the scene starts "kickin'" at "happy hour"
with the "office crowd" and takes off around 11 with "all the twenty-
somethings", when the decibels approach a "loud roar."

Ponzio's *Diner* | 20 | 13 | 19 | $24 |

Cherry Hill | 7 Rte. 70 W. (Kings Hwy.) | 856-428-4808 | www.ponzios.com
A "huge menu" of "yummy food" at "reasonable prices" and waitresses who "treat you like regulars" make "loving" this "upper-class"
"Jersey diner" "institution" in Cherry Hill a "requirement" for fans;
the "wait's not too long" in the space that seems "bigger than Madison
Square Garden", and many insist they "could eat here every day" –
and "plenty of people do."

Pop Shop *American* | 21 | 17 | 18 | $19 |

Collingswood | 729 Haddon Ave. (Collings Ave.) | 856-869-0111 |
www.thepopshopusa.com
At this "kid-tastic" "'50s" "throwback" in Collingswood, the "interesting, varied menu" of "gourmet comfort food" features a "bazillion
types of grilled cheese" and milkshakes that "take you to heaven",
while the booths are frequently "overflowing" with "shouting children" ("get me an aspirin"); many describe the service as "young
and inexperienced", so "be prepared to wait", but most agree it's
"fun" for "families and singles" alike.

Pub, The *Steak* | 19 | 14 | 19 | $35 |

Pennsauken | Airport Circle | 7600 Kaighns Ave. (Crescent Blvd.) |
856-665-6440 | www.thepubnj.com
It's "Ozzie and Harriet in Pennsauken" all the way at this "classic"
steakhouse whose "no-fuss steaks" and "terrific" "salad bar" are a
constant in this "ever-changing, overdesigned world"; "you have to
see it to believe" the "big, boisterous" dining room replete with
"suits of armor", "heraldic flags" and "old-school waitresses", so
"bring your appetite, your sense of irony and your grandmother."

	FOOD	DECOR	SERVICE	COST

Red Hot & Blue *BBQ*
16 | 11 | 16 | $26

Cherry Hill | Holiday Inn | 2175 Old Marlton Pike (bet. Rte. 70 & Sayer Ave.) | 856-665-7427 | www.redhotanblue.com

Even many who "don't like chains" head to this BBQ link in Cherry Hill for "hearty" ribs "with tons of sides", and "bring the family" for the $15.95 all-you-can-eat deal on Thursdays, while "sometimes excellent" live music Thursdays–Saturdays helps make up for the "Holiday Inn setting"; a few critics, though, dismiss the 'cue as just "ok – no more, no less."

Redstone American Grill *American*
20 | 21 | 20 | $38

Marlton | Promenade at Sagemore | 500 Rte. 73 S. (Brick Rd.) | 856-396-0332 | www.redstonegrill.com

See review in the Philadelphia Directory.

Rick's Ⓜ *Italian*
∇ 20 | 13 | 21 | $32

Lambertville | 19 S. Main St. (Ferry St.) | 609-397-0051 | www.ricksitalian.com

You'll "wait in line for a seat" at Alex Cormier's "reliably good, home-style" Italian BYO in a Lambertville row house serving "unbelievable" seafood medley linguine and other "reliably good" dishes that earn it an "avid following"; the retro-1950s "knotty-pine" dining room has a "homey" vibe, though some find it a bit "cramped."

Ritz Seafood Ⓜ *Asian/Seafood*
25 | 15 | 21 | $36

Voorhees | Ritz Shopping Ctr. | 910 Haddonfield-Berlin Rd. (Laurel Oak Blvd.) | 856-566-6650 | www.ritzseafood.com

Dan Hover's "fin-tastic" seafood "presentations" make this Pan-Asian "diamond in the rough" in a "little strip mall" by the movie theater in Voorhees a good stop "before or after" a show, but keep in mind it's "small" and "gets crowded easily"; Gloria Cho leads a staff of "friendly waiters" amid a romantic setting complete with four waterfalls; P.S. regulars suggest you save room for the "amazing desserts."

Robin's Nest *American*
∇ 22 | 17 | 18 | $34

Mount Holly | 2 Washington St. (White St.) | 609-261-6149 | www.robinsnestmountholly.com

It's like "stepping back in time" and into "grandmom's house" at this "quaint" Mount Holly Traditional American bistro where "imagination guides the menu" and "good home cooking" results; it's set in a 19th-century building with "quaint, soothing country decor", and feathering the nest is a "stone patio" by the Rancocas Creek, a "picturesque" setting for lunch on a "beautiful day."

⛉ Sagami Ⓜ *Japanese*
27 | 15 | 21 | $36

Collingswood | 37 Crescent Blvd. (bet. Collingswood Circle & Haddon Ave.) | 856-854-9773

"Don't judge a book by its cover" admonish fans undeterred by the "'70s decor" and "tight parking" at this Collingswood Japanese BYO where there are "lines out the door" for some of the "best sushi this side of Tokyo" and "high-quality" cooked items, including "hot sukiyaki" that's just the thing on a "cold winter evening"; the staff is "nice" and the atmosphere "interesting", but "claustrophobics" caution that the low ceilings make it "best for the 5-foot-8-and-under crowd."

Sakura Spring *Chinese/Japanese* ∇ 22 | 21 | 23 | $31

Cherry Hill | 1871 Marlton Pike E. (Greentree Rd.) | 856-489-8018 | www.sakuraspring.com

"Hidden in a small mall", this contemporary, white-tablecloth Cherry Hill Pan-Asian BYO is a "step way above typical", with its "large menu" of "authentic", "fresh" Japanese and Chinese dishes, both done "extremely well", making it a winner no matter "which nationality" you want to "hit that night"; some find it "a little pricey", but "lovely presentations" and "friendly" service help make the affair "well worth it."

Sapori *Italian* ∇ 25 | 18 | 24 | $40

Collingswood | 601 Haddon Ave. (Harvard Ave.) | 856-858-2288 | www.sapori.info

Franco Lombardo "will take care of you" at his rustic, "cozy" BYO in Collingswood, offering "authentic", "home-cooked" Italian fare ("good fish dishes", "heavenly tiramisu") that "elicits a wow" (or at least an "mmm") from fans; it's a fine spot to "celebrate", and for those who find it "a little more expensive" than the norm, the $40 prix fixe dinner Sundays–Thursdays is an option.

Seasons 52 *American* - | - | - | M

NEW **Cherry Hill** | Plaza of Cherry Hill Shopping Ctr. | 2000 Rte. 38 (Haddonfield Rd.) | 856-665-1052 | www.seasons52.com
See review in the Philadelphia Directory.

☑ Siri's Thai French Cuisine *French/Thai* 26 | 21 | 25 | $40

Cherry Hill | 2117 Rte. 70 W. (bet. Haddonfield Rd. & Penn Ave.) | 856-663-6781 | www.siris-nj.com

The "ideal marriage" of French and Thai is still going strong at this "elegant", white-linen BYO in an "unassuming" Cherry Hill strip mall; as a "pioneer" of this "fusion", the "solid" kitchen is still one of the "best in South Jersey, *pas de question*", "maintaining its high standards" and turning out "great homemade desserts", and while a few feel the decor "could use a little updating", nearly all agree the experience is "always superlative."

Tacconelli's Pizzeria Ⓜ✦ *Pizza* 25 | 9 | 16 | $19

Maple Shade | 450 S. Lenola Rd. (Rte. 38) | 856-638-0338 | www.tacconellispizzerianj.com
See review in the Philadelphia Directory.

Ted's on Main ⊠Ⓜ *American* ∇ 26 | 16 | 24 | $38

Medford | 20 S. Main St. (Bank St.) | 609-654-7011 | www.tedsonmain.net

Ted Iwachiw's "intimate" New American BYO "jewel" is a "real find" in "charming" Downtown Medford according to locals who have come to "expect excellence" here – i.e. "well-conceived, interesting" dishes served by a "friendly", "unobtrusive" staff in a "cozy setting";

"reasonable prices", including $30 prix fixe dinners Tuesday–Thursdays, are another reason "reservations are a must."

Tortilla Press *Mexican*   23 | 19 | 21 | $28

Collingswood | 703 Haddon Ave. (Collings Ave.) | 856-869-3345 | www.thetortillapress.com

Tortilla Press Cantina Ⓜ *Mexican*

Pennsauken | 7716 Maple Ave. (Haddonfield Rd.) | 856-356-2050 | www.tortillapresscantina.com

Groupies gush over the "creative Mexican cooking" going on at Mark Smith's "innovative" BYO in Collingswood, which "doesn't disappoint" "soccer moms" and other locals who come for "addictive" "guacamole" and "cutting-edge" *comida* at "reasonable" prices; when "windows to the street are open", and if you "remembered to bring tequila" for margaritas, the decor doesn't seem so "average", after all; the Pennsauken cantina spin-off, which reopened in December 2009, serves liquor, including a modest wine list.

NEW Très Elena Wu ⓈⓂ *Asian*   – | – | – | M

Mount Laurel | 3131 Route 38 (Larchmont Blvd.) | 856-608-8888 | www.treselenawu.com

The founders of Voorhees' Chez Elena Wu have resurfaced in a Mount Laurel strip center with this bistro that should be attractive to couples, families and business-lunchers (plus bargain-hunters – it's BYO); the French-influenced Asian menu hits all the usual points from China to Thailand, while the lushly decorated digs include a sushi bar.

William Douglas Steakhouse *Steak*   ▽ 24 | 22 | 24 | $63

Cherry Hill | Garden State Park | 941 Haddonfield Rd. (Rte. 70) | 856-665-6100 | www.williamdouglassteakhouse.com

"Romantics" enjoy the "snuggie" booths while "expense-account" types "impress clients" at this "clubby" steakhouse next to corporate twin McCormick & Schmick's in Cherry Hill, where the "horse"-theme decor pays homage to the former racetrack site where it's located; expect "awesome" steaks and lots of specials (half-priced bar menu before 6:30 and after 9 PM), augmented by "amazing" live piano music Thursdays–Sundays.

Wilmington/Nearby Delaware

TOP FOOD

26 Moro | *Mediterranean*
25 Mikimotos | *Asian/Japanese*
    Krazy Kat's | *French*
    Harry's Seafood | *Seafood*
24 Green Room | *French*

TOP DECOR

27 Green Room
23 Krazy Kat's
    Harry's Seafood
21 Domaine Hudson
    Moro

TOP SERVICE

25 Green Room
24 Domaine Hudson
    Toscana Kitchen
23 Harry's Savoy
    Krazy Kat's

BEST BUYS

1. Jake's Hamburgers
2. Brew HaHa!
3. Five Guys
4. Charcoal Pit
5. 2 Fat Guys

Back Burner ☒ *American*   22 | 19 | 19 | $43

Hockessin | 425 Hockessin Corner (Old Lancaster Pike) | 302-239-2314 | www.backburner.com

The "pumpkin mushroom soup" and other "well-prepared" eats keep 'em coming back to this "comfortable", "laid-back" New American "tucked away" in a Hockessin strip mall; the "country" hospitality means if you "go more than once, the staff will remember how you like your drink."

Blue Parrot Bar & Grille ●Ⓜ *Cajun*   17 | 17 | 17 | $28

Wilmington | 1934 W. Sixth St. (Union St.) | 302-655-8990 | www.blueparrotgrille.com

It's "Mardi Gras every day" at "one of Wilmington's best-kept secrets", this "funky", "low-key" Cajun that gets "three cheers" from fans for "divine" nachos, "outstanding" drinks and servers with "a sense of humor", plus "live music" that "never disappoints"; in summer, "aim for a table on the terrace" advise insiders.

Brew HaHa! *Coffeehouse*   17 | 15 | 20 | $11

Greenville | Powder Mill Sq. | 3842 Kennett Pike (Buck Rd.) | 302-658-6336
Wilmington | Rockford Shops | 1420 N. du Pont St. (Delaware Ave.) | 302-778-2656
Wilmington | Branmar Plaza | 1812 Marsh Rd. (Silverside Rd.) | 302-529-1125
Wilmington | Concord Gallery | 3636 Concord Pike (Silverside Rd.) | 302-478-7227
Wilmington | Shops of Limestone Hills | 5329 Limestone Rd. (bet. Ocheltree Ln. & Stoney Batter Rd.) | 302-234-9600
Wilmington | 835 N. Market St. (bet. 8th & 9th Sts.) | 302-777-4499 ☒
www.brew-haha.com

"Friendly" baristas, "people-watching" and "laptop coolness" are the selling points of this "cost-efficient" java chain in Wash West and Delaware, a "great local coffee option" for those who "don't want to support the big corporate giants"; "tasty sandwiches", "comfortable sofas" and a "handsome" clientele make it tempting for many to "spend the afternoon" here.

Buckley's Tavern *American*
FOOD	DECOR	SERVICE	COST
18	17	19	$33

Centerville | 5812 Kennett Pike (Twaddell Mill Rd.) | 302-656-9776 | www.buckleystavern.org

"Blue jeans, old money and modern American comfort food" mix well at this "always crowded" "horse-country standard" in northern Delaware, a "casual, anything-goes" "break from the suburban franchises", where the "accommodating" staff goes "above and beyond"; most agree the "decent" grub is best enjoyed on the "nice patio in back" and the rooftop, and insiders know you get 50% off by wearing "jammies" to Sunday "brunch."

Capers & Lemons *Italian*
22	21	22	$43

Wilmington | The Commons at Little Falls | 301 Little Falls Dr. (Lancaster Pike) | 302-256-0524 | www.capersandlemons.com

Devotees declare the "best of Italy comes to Wilmington" at this "bustling", "trendy" bistro, which offers "something for everyone" ("outstanding" pastas, veal and beef and "wood-fired pizzas") at "reasonable" prices; the "comfortable" space has an "open" feel, and there's a covered outdoor patio, and service comes "with a snap."

Charcoal Pit *Burgers*
20	14	18	$15

Wilmington | 2600 Concord Pike (Woodrow Ave.) | 302-478-2165 ◗
Wilmington | 5200 Pike Creek Center Blvd. (bet. New Linden Hill Rd. & Skyline Dr.) | 302-999-7483
Wilmington | 714 Greenbank Rd. (Kirkwood Hwy.) | 302-998-8853
www.charcoalpit.net

"Generations" of Delawareans wax "nostalgic" about this "'50s" "malt-shop" mini-chain, where "there's nothing better" than a "black-and-white" shake, burger, fries and maybe a "mammoth sundae", served by waitresses who "treat you like family and have been there forever"; there's "nothing nouveau" about the "kitschy" digs – complete with jukeboxes – and most "love it like that"; the Greenbank Road location has a sports-bar theme and a liquor license.

China Royal 🅼 *Chinese*
▽ 17	11	17	$25

Wilmington | 1845 Marsh Rd. (Silverside Rd.) | 302-475-3686

Despite its "bare-bones" environs, "patrons" keep "coming back" to this long-running Chinese in a North Wilmington "strip mall" for a "plethora" of choices (including a "few tasty Thai entrees"), served "so fast" that you "feel they are trying to evict you"; a declining Food score reflects the sentiment that it "used to be better", leading some to surmise that it "suffers from having too much on the menu."

NEW Columbus Inn *American*
-	-	-	M

Wilmington | 2216 Pennsylvania Ave. (Woodlawn Ave.) | 302-571-1492 | www.columbusinn.com

Spiffed up and updated after a long rehab, this Wilmington landmark serves the business community, ladies-who-lunch and dining couples with a variety of settings, including a wood-appointed lounge with Prohibition-inspired cocktails, contemporary dining room with glassed-in wine case and scenic patio; Philly transplant Chris D'Ambro's menu includes refined twists on New American staples.

	FOOD	DECOR	SERVICE	COST

Corner Bistro *Eclectic* — 19 | 16 | 21 | $27

Wilmington | Talleyville Towne Shoppes | 3604 Silverside Rd.
(Concord Pike) | 302-477-1778 | www.mybistro.com

An "oasis in an otherwise depressing vista of strip malls", this "trendy" North Wilmington Eclectic "keeps running smoothly" with an "imaginative" menu with "amusing" item names that "changes with the seasons" and "great wine list on the blackboard"; a "solicitous" staff "gets you in and out in a jiffy", and the "easygoing" environment makes it the "sort of comfortable local place you just drop into again and again."

Culinaria ⬛Ⓜ *American* — 23 | 19 | 22 | $38

Wilmington | Branmar Plaza | 1812 Marsh Rd. (Silverside Rd.) |
302-475-4860 | www.culinariarestaurant.com

The "shopping-center" "exterior belies the greatness inside" this "tiny", "funky" New American in northern Wilmington that's "always crowded for a reason" – i.e. "eclectic", well-executed" dishes featuring "fresh ingredients, plated well", as well as staples such as "mashed potatoes almost as good as my mother makes", in "very nice" portions; the service is "adequate", but "be prepared to wait for a table", because space is "limited" and there are "no reservations."

Deep Blue ⬛ *Seafood* — 22 | 21 | 21 | $48

Wilmington | 111 W. 11th St. (bet. Orange & Tatnall Sts.) |
302-777-2040 | www.deepbluebarandgrill.com

Afishionados attest "they do know how to cook fish" at this seafooder in "the heart of Wilmington", where "young and beautiful" "attorneys and bankers" "meet and greet" in the "rockin' bar scene", while foodies linger in the "smart, urban" dining room, which a few critics say "looks too much like a cafeteria" and "needs better lighting"; a "fine wine list" and "knowledgeable" service help make this place a "winner."

Domaine Hudson *American* — 24 | 21 | 24 | $49

Wilmington | 1314 N. Washington St. (bet. 13th & 14th Sts.) |
302-655-9463 | www.domainehudson.com

"Wonderful pairings" of "outstanding wines" and "sophisticated" New American small plates, an "expanded craft beer menu" and "fantastic" service from an "informed" staff make this "opulent", yet "cozy" "wine bar" in Downtown Wilmington a "standout with legs"; "reasonable" pours (and "samples" from the cellar) and "tasting portions" enable you to enjoy the experience "without breaking your credit rating."

Eclipse Bistro *American* — ∇ 23 | 19 | 24 | $50

Wilmington | 1020 N. Union St. (bet. 10th & 11th Sts.) |
302-658-1588 | www.eclipsebistro.com

The "dishes are always changing" on the seasonal menu at this "hip" American "bistro" in Downtown Wilmington, where the "reliable" cuisine is more "home cooking than fine dining", and the service is "friendly" and "attentive"; "thrifty wine prices" and an "intimate" dining room also help make this a "nice standby" for many.

Feby's Fishery *Seafood*

21 | 14 | 19 | $32

Wilmington | 3701 Lancaster Pike (bet. Centre & du Pont Rds.) | 302-998-9501 | www.febysfishery.com

"Steady fresh" fin fare and $29.95 all-you-can-eat crab nights Tuesdays and Thursdays make this Wilmington seafooder-cum-"takeout market" a "habit" for many afishionados who keep coming back for "one delicious meal after another"; the waitresses make you "feel like family" in the maritime-themed digs (which some find "cheesy"), and nearly all agree "you won't be disappointed" here.

NEW FireStone *American*

- | - | - | I

Wilmington | 110 S. West St. (Water St.) | 302-658-6626 | www.firestoneriverfront.com

Set in an office building on the Christina River, this Wilmington New American offers items such as grilled and BBQ beef, handmade pizzas and seafood in a fieldstone-walled dining room; happy-hour and late-night scenesters gravitate to the enormous, multiple-TVed bar, and in good weather pack the patio overlooking the water.

Five Guys *Burgers*

22 | 9 | 16 | $11

Wilmington | 2217 Concord Pike (Murphy Rd.) | 302-654-5489
Wilmington | 3234B Kirkwood Hwy. | 302-998-2955
www.fiveguys.com

See review in the Philadelphia Directory.

Green Room *French*

24 | 27 | 25 | $64

Wilmington | Hotel du Pont | 11th & Market Sts. | 302-594-3154 | www.hoteldupont.com

"Ah, fine dining still exists" sigh supporters of the Hotel du Pont's "formal" French "grande dame" in Wilmington, citing its "baronial" space beneath "high coffered ceilings" that makes women feel like "Cinderella arriving at the ball", "knowledgeable" service and "creative" cuisine (including an "incomparable" Sunday brunch buffet); "piano music coming from the balcony" makes a meal feel like a "mini-vacation", and adds to an ambiance "you just don't find anymore" (jackets required on Friday and Saturday evenings).

Harry's Savoy Grill *American*

24 | 21 | 23 | $46

Wilmington | 2020 Naamans Rd. (Foulk Rd.) | 302-475-3000 | www.harrysseafoodgrill.com

"Two words: prime rib!" are on everyone's lips at Xavier Teixido's Wilmington New American, where an "older crowd" raves over the "well-executed" grub and service that "matches", as well as an "extensive" wine list; the prices are "reasonable", and for those few who find the room a bit "cavelike", the outdoor covered patio full of flora may offer some relief.

Harry's Seafood Grill *Seafood*

25 | 23 | 22 | $47

Wilmington | 101 S. Market St. (Shipley St.) | 302-777-1500 | www.harrysseafoodgrill.com

"Impress your date" with "freshly shucked oysters" and "imaginative" fish preparations, served by a staff that's "eager to please", at this "stunning" seafood sibling of Harry's Savoy Grill on the Christina River in Wilmington, where the "lovely outdoor deck" overlooking the water offers an escape from the "kinda noisy", "active bar scene" with a mostly "mature" crowd; it's "pricey", but most concur it's "worth it."

Hibachi *Japanese* | 18 | 17 | 20 | $29 |

Wilmington | 5607 Concord Pike (Naamans Rd.) | 302-477-0194
See review in the Philadelphia Directory.

Iron Hill Brewery & Restaurant *American* | 19 | 19 | 20 | $28 |

Newark | Traders Alley | 147 E. Main St. (bet. Chapel & Haines Sts.) | 302-266-9000
Wilmington | 710 S. Justison St. (Beech St.) | 302-658-8200
www.ironhillbrewery.com
See review in the Philadelphia Directory.

Jake's Hamburgers *Burgers* | 20 | 7 | 16 | $9 |

Bear | 1643 Pulaski Hwy. (Porter Rd.) | 302-832-2230
New Castle | 150 S. du Pont Hwy./Rte. 113 (Rte. 273) | 302-322-0200
Wilmington | Roselle Ctr. | 2401 Kirkwood Hwy. (Rte. 141) | 302-994-6800
www.jakeshamburgers.com
While they may be "under the radar" outside of the 302 (though a franchise plan is expanding the brand), many look no further than these "neighborhood joints" for "amazingly fresh" burgers and "creamy milkshakes", as well as hot dogs, sandwiches and even salads with "varied ingredients"; there's "no decor", just "good prices", and you can always "go buy peanuts somewhere else."

Jasmine *Asian* | 23 | 20 | 20 | $31 |

Wilmington | Concord Gallery | 3618 Concord Pike (Mt. Lebanon Rd.) | 302-479-5618
"Not your father's Chinese restaurant", this "lovely" Pan-Asian in a Wilmington shopping center doles out a "nice mixture of cuisines", including "wonderful sushi", in a "hip" setting, where many can be seen "hanging at the bar"; while a few gripe about "indifferent" service, most report that it's usually "crowded, with good reason."

☒ Krazy Kat's *French* | 25 | 23 | 23 | $58 |

Montchanin | Inn at Montchanin Vill. | 504 Montchanin Rd. (Kirk Rd.) | 302-888-4200 | www.montchanin.com
The "Kat's out of the bag" about this "fun" French in northern Delaware, despite the name a "sane choice" for a "purrfect" meal of "expertly prepared" fare (including "elegant" breakfasts and "fantastic" Sunday brunches), served by a "friendly", "competent" staff in a "whimsical" space decorated with felines "everywhere"; it's "perfect for small weddings" and other "special occasions."

Lamberti's Cucina *Italian* | 18 | 14 | 18 | $34 |

Wilmington | Prices Corner Shopping Ctr. | 1300 Centerville Rd. (Kirkwood Hwy.) | 302-995-6955
Wilmington | 514 Philadelphia Pike (Marsh Rd.) | 302-762-9094
www.lambertis.com
The portions at this Wilmington Italian duo "make a Hungry Man meal look like an appetizer" according to adherents, who "love

every bite" of the "traditional favorites and modern interpretations", which are brought to table by "gracious" servers; "good value for the money" is another reason so many designate it a "dining destination."

La Tolteca *Mexican* 20 | 14 | 21 | $20

Wilmington | Fairfax Shopping Ctr. | 2209 Concord Pike (Rte. 141) | 302-778-4646
Wilmington | Talleyville Shopping Ctr. | 4015 Concord Pike (bet. Brandywine Blvd. & Silverside Rd.) | 302-478-9477
www.lastoltecas.com

"Great simple Mexican food" at "reasonable prices" is the main draw of these Wilmington twins; your order comes "quick" amid "clean", "cheery" surroundings (a "little cheesy" to some), and cognoscenti caution just "watch that bar tab"; P.S. the Friday night "mariachi band" at the Talleyville location adds to the fun.

Lucky's Coffee Shop *American* ▽ 15 | 15 | 16 | $18

Wilmington | 4003 Concord Pike (Silverside Rd.) | 302-477-0240 | www.luckyscoffeeshop.com

"Don't let the name fool you" – this is a "full-service" eatery in Wilmington's Talleyville mall dishing out "funky" and "consistently good" New American breakfast, lunch and dinner fare anytime you "want a quick meal" with minimal fuss, in a '60s retro setting; detractors claim it's "nothing special" and warn that the kitchen can "seem challenged" if you "deviate from the suggested menu preparations."

Mexican Post *Mexican* 16 | 14 | 16 | $24

Wilmington | 3100 Naamans Rd. (Shipley Rd.) | 302-478-3939 | www.mexicanpost.com
See review in the Philadelphia Directory.

⨯ Mikimotos 25 | 18 | 19 | $37
Asian Grill & Sushi Bar *Asian/Japanese*

Wilmington | 1212 N. Washington St. (12th St.) | 302-656-8638 | www.mikimotos.com

While there's lots of "hype" surrounding this slick Japanese-Pan-Asian in Downtown Wilmington, aficionados aver that "reasonably priced", "fresh", "inventive sushi" is the way it "grabs business"; whether you go for a "quick lunch" or for happy hour, "be prepared" for a "busy", "loud" scene, as well as lighting that can be "problematic for older eyes" according to critics.

⨯ Moro Ⓢ Ⓜ *Mediterranean* 26 | 21 | 23 | $63

Wilmington | 1307 N. Scott St. (bet. 13th & 14th Sts.) | 302-777-1800 | www.mororestaurant.net

Boasting what many call the "best wine list in Delaware", this "trendy", "elegant" Med in an "offbeat" spot in Downtown Wilmington sets the standard for "high-end dining" with "fabulous" small plates and "telepathic" servers who "know their stuff"; sure, it's "expensive", but when you want to "treat yourself to a wonderful experience", it "saves the drive to Philadelphia."

	FOOD	DECOR	SERVICE	COST

Mrs. Robino's *Italian* ▽ 14 | 12 | 17 | $20

Wilmington | 520 N. Union St. (bet. 5th & 6th Sts.) | 302-652-9223
www.mrsrobinos.com

Surveyors are split over this Wilmington Little Italy "red-gravy"
"staple" – fans insist the late founder's "spirit" must be "proud" o
the "excellent homemade pastas" at "very reasonable prices"
served in a retro scene straight out of "*The Godfather*"; foes fail "t
understand the allure" and insists it "has seen better days."

Orillas Tapas *Spanish* ▽ 23 | 21 | 22 | $37

Wilmington | 413 N. Market St. (5th St.) | 302-427-9700 |
www.orillastapasbar.com

Julio Lazzarini does a "beautiful job" "bringing Spanish flair t
Wilmington" with his tapas bar located "within walking distance o
Rodney Square", where his "delicious little plates", "prepared wit
love and pride", and "ample" "wine list" are "lots of fun to share wit
friends" or a "date" , and "you can tailor" your evening to "your pal
ate and wallet"; though some grouse that it gets "cramped" an
"noisy" when it's "busy", most agree it's "worth a try."

Pomodoro Ⓜ *Italian* - | - | - | M

Wilmington | 729 N. Union St. (8th St.) | 302-574-9800 |
www.pomodorowilmington.com

"This place is love" exclaim surveyors smitten with this Wilmingto
trattoria where the "real Italian chef's" "inventive, memorable" spe
cials (including "fabulous seafood") go beyond the usual "red
gravy" standards and are "worth every calorie"; add "great" servic
and you can see why it's "worth the trip."

Rasa Sayang *Malaysian* ▽ 25 | 17 | 22 | $28

Wilmington | Independence Mall | 1601 Concord Pike (Foulk Rd.) |
302-543-5286 | www.rasasayangusa.com

Malaysian cuisine is "hard to come by" in Wilmington, so locals ap
preciate the "wonderful array" of "exotic" "choices" at this bright
roomy eatery in Independence Mall; though the servers provid
"fast-paced service", they'll take time out to "offer" "excellent rec
ommendations if you simply ask."

Sullivan's Steakhouse *Steak* 23 | 21 | 21 | $54

Wilmington | Brandywine Town Ctr. | 5525 Concord Pike (Naamans Rd.)
302-479-7970 | www.sullivanssteakhouse.com
See review in the Philadelphia Directory.

Toscana Kitchen & Bar *Italian* 24 | 20 | 24 | $40

Wilmington | Rockford Shops | 1412 N. du Pont St. (Delaware Ave.) |
302-654-8001 | www.toscanakitchen.com

"Fantastic" "nouveau Italian" cooking from a "well-designed menu" i
"worth the trip" to Dan (Deep Blue) Butler's trattoria in a Wilmingto
shopping center; patrons in "jeans and fur coats seem equally a
home", and "you'll run into everyone here from Joe Biden to the gu
next door" "seeking" "reliably mouthwatering pastas" and more
served by a "competent" staff.

2 Fat Guys *American*

22 | 15 | 18 | $19

Hockessin | 701 Ace Memorial Dr. (Rte. 41) | 302-235-0333 |
www.2fatguys.net

Caterers-cum-restaurateurs Jeff Cook and Tom Craft put the *essen*
in Hockessin at their homey, family-friendly American sports pub
off Route 41, dishing out the "best burgers" and "interesting twists
on the standard grill fare" in huge quantities, including the 'Burger
Challenge', a four-hamburger, five-grilled-cheese-sandwich combo
that must be eaten in 20 minutes.

Union City Grille *Steak*

22 | 19 | 23 | $42

Wilmington | 805 N. Union St. (8th St.) | 302-654-9780 |
www.unioncitygrill.com

This "reliable" "neighborhood institution" in Wilmington has taken
on a "hip" "new twist" as it tries to "reach new audiences" with a
contemporary American steakhouse concept that offers a $2-an-
ounce filet special on Sundays and $30 prix fixes on Mondays and
Tuesdays; if you seek a "romantic" evening, "sit by the fire on a
couch in the bar."

Walter's Steakhouse *Steak*

▽ 22 | 15 | 22 | $43

Wilmington | 802 N. Union St. (8th St.) | 302-652-6780 |
www.waltersteakhouse.com

It's like "stepping back in time" at this "family"-run, leather-bound
chophouse in Wilmington that caters to "regulars" and others with
"reliable" steaks and prime ribs and "warm, friendly" service in a
"mid-1950s" setting; whether in a booth in the bar area, most agree
it's "good for a solo dinner" or perhaps an "intimate" evening, and
it's open most nights until 11 – which is "late" for locals.

Washington St. Ale House ◐ *Pub Food*

15 | 16 | 16 | $28

Wilmington | 1206 Washington St. (12th St.) | 302-658-2537 |
www.wsalehouse.com

Though it can get "ridiculously loud", this local bar "within easy
reach of Downtown offices" in Wilmington is a "good option" for a
"business lunch" or "watching a sporting event"; while the "typical
pub" offerings may "not be for foodies", it offers some "interesting
specials", served by a "quick" staff, and the "cozy dining room with
fireplace" is "great for thawing out on a cold winter day."

Menus, photos, voting and more – free at ZAGAT.com

INDEXES

Cuisines 196
Locations 209
Special Features 227

LOCATION MAPS

Center City & Environs 222
Society Hill | South Street | Queen Village 224
Northern Liberties | Old City 226

All restaurants are in the Philadelphia area unless otherwise noted (LB=Lancaster/Berks Counties; NJ=New Jersey Suburbs; DE=Wilmington/Nearby Delaware).

Cuisines

Includes names, locations and Food ratings.

AFGHAN

Ariana	**multi.**	22
Kabul	**Old City**	21
Yalda Grill	**Horsham**	22

AMERICAN

NEW Adsum	**South St**	–
Alfa	**Rittenhouse**	17
America B&G	**multi.**	18
NEW American Pub	**Ave of Arts**	15
Anton's/Swan	**Lambertville/NJ**	22
Back Burner	**Hockessin/DE**	22
Barnsboro Inn	**Sewell/NJ**	22
Bay Pony Inn	**Lederach**	21
Bistro 7	**Old City**	24
Black Bass	**Lumberville**	21
Blackbird	**Collingswood/NJ**	25
Bliss	**Ave of Arts**	21
Blue Bell Inn	**Blue Bell**	20
Blue Pear	**W Chester**	23
Braddock's	**Medford/NJ**	20
Brick Hotel	**Newtown**	16
NEW Brick House	**Willow Grove**	17
Bridget Foy's	**South St**	19
Bridgetown Mill	**Langhorne**	24
Bridget's Steak	**Ambler**	23
Broad Axe Tav.	**Ambler**	16
Buckley's	**Centerville/DE**	18
Café Estelle	**N Liberties**	23
Cafette	**Ches Hill**	20
Z Capogiro	**multi.**	27
Catherine's	**Unionville**	28
Cedar Hollow	**Malvern**	17
Centre Bridge	**New Hope**	22
Cheesecake	**multi.**	20
Chestnut Grill	**Ches Hill**	17
Chlöe	**Old City**	26
Christopher's	**Wayne**	16
NEW City Tap House	**Univ City**	–
City Tavern	**Old City**	19
Cock 'n Bull	**Lahaska**	18
NEW Columbus Inn	**Wilming/DE**	–
NEW Cooperage	**Washington Sq W**	–
Cooper's	**Manayunk**	22
Copabanana	**multi.**	17

Cork	**Westmont/NJ**	22
Culinaria	**Wilming/DE**	23
Darling's	**multi.**	17
Dave & Buster's	**multi.**	12
Day by Day	**Rittenhouse**	23
Derek's	**Manayunk**	22
NEW Dettera	**Ambler**	21
Devil's Alley	**Rittenhouse**	19
Devil's Den	**S Philly**	19
Dilworth. Inn	**W Chester**	25
Dining Car	**NE Philly**	19
NEW Doghouse	**Downingtown**	–
Dom. Hudson	**Wilming/DE**	24
Drafting Rm.	**Exton**	16
Du Jour	**multi.**	18
Earth Bread	**Mt Airy**	21
Eclipse Bistro	**Wilming/DE**	23
Elements Café	**Haddon Hts/NJ**	22
Epicurean	**Phoenixville**	20
Fayette St.	**Consho**	23
Field House	**Chinatown**	12
NEW Firecreek	**Downingtown**	20
NEW FireStone	**Wilming/DE**	–
Z NEW Fond	**S Philly**	27
Z Fork	**Old City**	24
Fountain Side	**Horsham**	20
Four Dogs	**W Chester**	20
Freight House	**Doylestown**	16
Friday Sat. Sun.	**Rittenhouse**	24
Funky Lil' Kitchen	**Pottstown**	25
Gables	**Chadds Ford**	23
NEW Garces Trading	**Washington Sq W**	–
Gen. Lafayette	**Lafayette Hill**	18
Gen. Warren	**Malvern**	25
GG's	**Mt Laurel/NJ**	26
Gold Standard	**W Philly**	17
Good Dog	**Rittenhouse**	22
Grace Tav.	**Graduate Hospital**	21
NEW Green Eggs	**S Philly**	26
Green Hills Inn	**Reading/LB**	–
Gullifty's	**Rosemont**	15
Gypsy Saloon	**W Consho**	22
Half Moon	**Kennett Sq**	20
Hank's Place	**Chadds Ford**	21
Happy Rooster	**Rittenhouse**	18
Hard Rock	**Chinatown**	13

Menus, photos, voting and more - free at ZAGAT.com

Harry's Savoy | **Wilming/DE**	24	Memphis Tap | **Port Richmond**	23
NEW Harvest | **Glen Mills**	-	Mendenhall Inn | **Mendenhall**	19
Havana | **New Hope**	18	Mercato | **Washington Sq W**	25
NEW Hawthornes | **S Philly**	22	Meridith's | **Berwyn**	20
Haydn Zug's | **E Petersburg/LB**	23	Meritage | **Graduate Hospital**	25
NEW HeadHouse | **Society Hill**	-	**NEW** MidAtlantic | **Univ City**	20
NEW Healthy Bites | **S Philly**	-	Misconduct Tav. | **Rittenhouse**	19
High St. | **Mt Holly/NJ**	21	**NEW** MIXX | **Villanova**	17
Honey | **Doylestown**	26	More Than Ice Crm. |	20
Inn/Hawke | **Lambertville/NJ**	20	**Washington Sq W**	
Iron Hill | **multi.**	19	Moshulu | **DE River**	22
Isaac Newton's | **Newtown**	17	New Tavern | **Bala Cynwyd**	21
Jake's | **Manayunk**	25	New Wave | **Queen Vill**	17
Z James | **S Philly**	27	Nicholas | **S Philly**	22
J.B. Dawson's/Austin's | **multi.**	18	**Z** Nineteen | **Ave of Arts**	23
Johnny Brenda | **Fishtown**	21	Noble Cookery | **Rittenhouse**	20
Jones | **Washington Sq W**	20	Nodding Head | **Rittenhouse**	19
Joseph Ambler | **N Wales**	21	No. 9 | **Lambertville/NJ**	24
Kaya's | **Havertown**	19	N. 3rd | **N Liberties**	23
K.C.'s Alley | **Ambler**	16	Old Guard Hse. | **Gladwyne**	22
Keating's | **DE River**	18	Orchard | **Kennett Sq**	27
Kimberton Inn | **Kimberton**	25	Pace One | **Thornton**	21
Kite & Key | **Fairmount**	16	Paddock/Devon | **Wayne**	15
Knight House | **Doylestown**	23	Paradigm | **Old City**	20
Knock | **Washington Sq W**	16	Parc Bistro | **Skippack**	23
NEW Kraftwork | **Fishtown**	-	**NEW** Paul | **Washington Sq W**	22
Lambertville Station |	18	Phil's Tav. | **Blue Bell**	18
Lambertville/NJ		Pistachio Grille | **Maple Glen**	20
Lancaster Dispensing |	-	P.J. Whelihan's | **multi.**	16
Lancaster/LB		Plate | **Ardmore**	14
Landing | **New Hope**	18	Pop Shop | **Collingswood/NJ**	21
La Terrasse | **Univ City**	19	Prohibition | **N Philly**	22
Z Lily's on Main | **Ephrata/LB**	24	Pub/Kitchen | **Graduate Hospital**	22
Local 44 | **W Philly**	16	Public Hse./Logan | **Logan Sq**	14
London Grill | **Fairmount**	17	Pumpkin | **Graduate Hospital**	26
L2 | **Graduate Hospital**	19	Redstone | **multi.**	20
Lucky's Coffee | **Wilming/DE**	15	Rembrandt's | **Fairmount**	19
NEW Lucky 7 | **Fairmount**	17	**Z** Rest. Alba | **Malvern**	27
NEW Mac's Tavern | **Old City**	-	**NEW** Resurrection Ale | **S Philly**	24
NEW MaGerks | **Ft Wash**	15	Riverstone Café | **Exton**	18
Majolica | **Phoenixville**	24	Robin's Nest | **Mt Holly/NJ**	22
Manayunk Brew. | **Manayunk**	17	Rose Tattoo | **Fairmount**	22
Marathon Grill | **multi.**	18	Rouge | **Rittenhouse**	22
Marathon/Sq. | **Rittenhouse**	18	Rouget | **Newtown**	24
Marigold Kitchen | **Univ City**	24	Royal Tavern | **S Philly**	24
Mastoris | **Bordentown/NJ**	20	**Z NEW** R2L | **Rittenhouse**	21
Z Matyson | **Rittenhouse**	27	Salt & Pepper | **S Philly**	25
Max Brenner | **Rittenhouse**	19	Seasons 52 | **multi.**	-
McFadden's | **multi.**	15	Silk City | **N Liberties**	21
Mémé | **Rittenhouse**	23	Simon Pearce | **W Chester**	22

Slate | **Rittenhouse**	19
Smiths | **Rittenhouse**	16
Smokin' Betty | **Washington Sq W**	20
Snackbar | **Rittenhouse**	22
Z Sola | **Bryn Mawr**	27
Solaris Grille | **Ches Hill**	14
NEW Sonata | **N Liberties**	23
Southwark | **South St**	25
NEW Square 1682 | **Rittenhouse**	21
Standard Tap | **N Liberties**	22
Stella Blu | **W Consho**	21
Stoudt's | **Adamstown/LB**	19
Supper | **South St**	23
Z Swann Lounge | **Logan Sq**	26
Swift Half | **N Liberties**	18
Sycamore | **Lansdowne**	-
Tango | **Bryn Mawr**	20
Tavern 17 | **Rittenhouse**	16
Ted's Montana | **multi.**	18
Ted's/Main | **Medford/NJ**	26
Z 10 Arts | **Ave of Arts**	22
Ten Stone | **Graduate Hospital**	17
333 Belrose | **Radnor**	22
Trax Café | **Ambler**	22
Triumph Brewing | **multi.**	18
Trolley Car | **multi.**	16
NEW Tweed | **Washington Sq W**	-
Twenty Manning | **Rittenhouse**	-
211 York | **Jenkintown**	22
2 Fat Guys | **Hockessin/DE**	22
Union City Grille | **Wilming/DE**	22
Urban Saloon | **Fairmount**	18
Varga Bar | **Washington Sq W**	20
NEW Village Whiskey | **Rittenhouse**	24
Wash. Cross. | **Wash Cross**	20
Washington Hse. | **Sellersville**	-
William Penn | **Gwynedd**	20
Winberie's | **Wayne**	17
Wine Thief | **Mt Airy**	20
Winnie's Le Bus | **Manayunk**	21
Yardley Inn | **Yardley**	22
Zacharias | **Worcester**	24
Zakes Cafe | **Ft Wash**	23

ARGENTINEAN

NEW Hoof + Fin | **Queen Vill**	-

ASIAN

Azie | **Media**	23
Z Buddakan | **Old City**	26
Bunha Faun | **Malvern**	24
Coconut Bay | **Voorhees/NJ**	23
FuziOn | **Worcester**	21
NEW Kumo Asian | **N Wales**	-
Masamoto | **Glen Mills**	26
Nectar | **Berwyn**	24
Pod | **Univ City**	23
Ritz Seafood | **Voorhees/NJ**	25
NEW Sampan | **Washington Sq W**	21
Shangrila | **Devon**	21
Susanna Foo's | **Radnor**	24
NEW Très Elena | **Mt Laurel/NJ**	-
Trio | **Fairmount**	24
Z Umai Umai | **Fairmount**	26

BAKERIES

Cake | **Ches Hill**	20
Mastoris | **Bordentown/NJ**	20
More Than Ice Crm. | **Washington Sq W**	20
Ponzio's | **Cherry Hill/NJ**	20

BARBECUE

Bomb Bomb BBQ | **S Philly**	23
NEW Bull Durham | **W Chester**	-
Devil's Alley | **Rittenhouse**	19
El Camino Real | **N Liberties**	21
NEW Percy St. BBQ | **South St**	20
Q BBQ | **Old City**	16
Red Hot/Blue | **Cherry Hill/NJ**	16
Rib Crib | **Germantown**	24
Smokin' Betty | **Washington Sq W**	20
Sweet Lucy's | **NE Philly**	24

BELGIAN

Abbaye | **N Liberties**	20
Belgian Café | **Fairmount**	19
Beneluxx | **Old City**	20
Eulogy Belgian | **Old City**	19
Monk's Cafe | **Rittenhouse**	22
Teresa's Next Dr. | **Wayne**	22

BRAZILIAN

Chima | **Logan Sq**	21
Fogo de Chão | **Ave of Arts**	24

BRITISH

Whip Tavern | **Coatesville**	23

BURGERS

NEW Bobby's Burger | **Univ City**	-
Charcoal Pit | **Wilming/DE**	20

Charlie's Hamburg. | **Folsom** 23
Cheeseburger/Paradise | 14
  Langhorne
NEW Doghouse | —
  Downingtown
Five Guys | **multi.** 22
NEW 500º | **Rittenhouse** —
Jake's Hamburg. | **multi.** 20
Manayunk Brew. | **Manayunk** 17
McFadden's | **multi.** 15
Nifty Fifty's | **multi.** 19
Pop Shop | **Collingswood/NJ** 21
Rembrandt's | **Fairmount** 19
Rouge | **Rittenhouse** 22
Ruby's | **multi.** 16
Sketch Café | **Fishtown** 24

BURMESE

Rangoon | **Chinatown** 23

CAJUN

Blue Parrot | **Wilming/DE** 17
Bourbon Blue | **Manayunk** 18
Z High St. Caffé | **W Chester** 26

CALIFORNIAN

California Cafe | **King of Prussia** 20
El Fuego | **multi.** 19

CARIBBEAN

Bahama Breeze | **multi.** 17

CHEESESTEAKS

Campo's Deli | **Old City** 23
Dalessandro's | **Roxborough** 23
Geno's Steaks | **S Philly** 18
Jim's Steaks | **multi.** 23
Z Pat's Steaks | **S Philly** 21
Steve's Steaks | **multi.** 23
Tony Luke's | **S Philly** 26

CHINESE

(* dim sum specialist)
Abacus | **Lansdale** 24
Auspicious | **Ardmore** 19
Beijing | **Univ City** 17
Charles Plaza | **Chinatown** 24
Chez Elena Wu | **Voorhees/NJ** 22
Z Chifa | **Washington Sq W** 25
China Royal | **Wilming/DE** 17
Chun Hing | **Wynnefield** 22

CinCin | **Ches Hill** 23
Duck Sauce | **Newtown** 24
East Cuisine | **Ambler** 21
Four Rivers | **Chinatown** 26
Han Dynasty | **multi.** 24
H.K. Golden* | **Chinatown** 20
Hunan | **Ardmore** —
Imperial Inn* | **Chinatown** 20
Joe's Peking* | **Marlton/NJ** 22
Joy Tsin Lau* | **Chinatown** 20
Kingdom of Veg.* | **Chinatown** 25
Lee How Fook | **Chinatown** 25
Mandarin Gdn. | **Willow Grove** 22
Marg. Kuo | **Wayne** 23
Marg. Kuo Mandarin | **Frazer** 22
Marg. Kuo Media | **Media** 24
Marg. Kuo Peking | **Media** 27
Mustard Greens | **Queen Vill** 22
New Harmony* | **Chinatown** 22
Ocean Harbor* | **Chinatown** 21
P.F. Chang's | **multi.** 20
Ray's Cafe | **Chinatown** 23
Sakura Spring | **Cherry Hill/NJ** 22
Sang Kee | **multi.** 23
Shiao Lan Kung | **Chinatown** 23
Singapore Kosher | **Chinatown** 20
Tai Lake | **Chinatown** 27
Z Yangming | **Bryn Mawr** 25

COFFEEHOUSES

Almaz Café | **Rittenhouse** 21
Bonté Wafflerie | **multi.** 21
Brew HaHa! | **multi.** 17
Café L'Aube | **Graduate Hospital** 25
Z La Colombe | **Rittenhouse** 24

COFFEE SHOPS/
DINERS

Ardmore Station | **Ardmore** 18
Hank's Place | **Chadds Ford** 21
Little Pete's | **multi.** 18
Mastoris | **Bordentown/NJ** 20
Mayfair Diner | **NE Philly** 15
Melrose Diner | **S Philly** 15
Morning Glory | **S Philly** 22
Nifty Fifty's | **multi.** 19
Ponzio's | **Cherry Hill/NJ** 20
Ruby's | **multi.** 16
Silk City | **N Liberties** 21
Trolley Car | **multi.** 16

COLOMBIAN

Tierra Colombiana | **N Philly**	24

CONTINENTAL

Café Gallery | **Burlington/NJ**	20
Cascade Lodge | **Kintnersville**	20
Duling-Kurtz | **Exton**	25
Farmicia | **Old City**	22
🔒 Fountain | **Logan Sq**	28
Seven Stars Inn | **Phoenixville**	20
Time | **Washington Sq W**	20
William Penn | **Gwynedd**	20
🔒 Yangming | **Bryn Mawr**	25

CREOLE

Bourbon Blue | **Manayunk**	18
Daddy Mims | **Phoenixville**	23
🔒 High St. Caffé | **W Chester**	26
Marsha Brown | **New Hope**	21
Mélange | **Haddonfield/NJ**	25

CUBAN

Casona | **Collingswood/NJ**	20
¡Cuba! | **Ches Hill**	16
🔒 Cuba Libre | **Old City**	22
Tierra Colombiana | **N Philly**	24

DELIS

Ben & Irv Deli | **Hunt Vly**	19
Campo's Deli | **Old City**	23
Famous 4th St. Deli | **multi.**	24
Hymie's Deli | **Merion Sta**	19
Isaac's | **multi.**	17
Kibitz Room | **multi.**	21
Murray's Deli | **Bala Cynwyd**	18

DESSERT

🔒 Capogiro | **multi.**	27
Cheesecake | **multi.**	20
Darling's | **multi.**	17
Golosa | **S Philly**	26
More Than Ice Crm. | **Washington Sq W**	20
Naked Choco. | **Ave of Arts**	24

EASTERN EUROPEAN

Max & David's | **Elkins Pk**	21

ECLECTIC

AllWays Café | **Hunt Vly**	23
Augusto's | **Warminster**	-
Beige & Beige | **Hunt Vly**	17

Bridgid's | **Fairmount**	20
Cafe Preeya | **Hunt Vly**	21
Cafette | **Ches Hill**	20
Carman's Country | **S Philly**	26
Checkers Bistro | **Lancaster/LB**	-
Chick's | **South St**	21
🆕 Con Murphy's | **Logan Sq**	17
Continental | **Old City**	22
Continental Mid-town | **Rittenhouse**	22
Corner Bistro | **Wilming/DE**	19
Day by Day | **Rittenhouse**	23
Full Moon | **Lambertville/NJ**	18
Full Plate | **N Liberties**	19
Georges' | **Wayne**	22
Gracie's | **Pine Forge/LB**	-
Havana | **New Hope**	18
Johnny Brenda | **Fishtown**	21
🔒 Lacroix | **Rittenhouse**	27
Lancaster Dispensing | **Lancaster/LB**	-
Lilly's/Canal | **Lambertville/NJ**	21
Little Café | **Voorhees/NJ**	24
Meridith's | **Berwyn**	20
Mirna's Café | **multi.**	22
Pub/Penn Valley | **Narberth**	19
Reading Terminal Mkt. | **Chinatown**	24
Roller's/Flying Fish | **Ches Hill**	19
Rx | **Univ City**	24
Sabrina's Café | **multi.**	24
Serrano | **Old City**	21
Sidecar | **Graduate Hospital**	23
Spence's Remedy | **W Chester**	21
Summer Kitchen | **Penns Park**	21
Sweet Lorraine's | **Lahaska**	17
Totaro's | **Consho**	24
Tria | **multi.**	23
Triumph Brewing | **multi.**	18
Umbria | **Mt Airy**	24
White Dog | **Univ City**	20
World Café | **Univ City**	16

EGYPTIAN

Aya's Café | **Logan Sq**	19

ERITREAN

Dahlak | **multi.**	22

ETHIOPIAN

Abyssinia | **Univ City**	23
Almaz Café | **Rittenhouse**	21

EUROPEAN

Bonté Wafflerie | multi.	21
Pub/Kitchen | Graduate Hospital	22
Z Talula's Table | Kennett Sq	27

FONDUE

Beneluxx | Old City	20
Melting Pot | multi.	19

FRENCH

NEW Amuse | Ave of Arts	-
Beau Monde | Queen Vill	23
Z Birchrunville Store | Birchrunville	28
Bunha Faun | Malvern	24
Café L'Aube | Graduate Hospital	25
Chez Colette | Rittenhouse	20
Cochon | Queen Vill	26
Dream Café | Cherry Hill/NJ	-
Z Fountain | Logan Sq	28
FuziOn | Worcester	21
NEW Gemelli | Narberth	23
Z Gilmore's | W Chester	28
Golden Pheasant | Erwinna	23
Green Hills Inn | Reading/LB	-
Green Room | Wilming/DE	24
Happy Rooster | Rittenhouse	18
Hotel du Village | New Hope	23
Inn/Phillips Mill | New Hope	25
Z Krazy Kat's | Montchanin/DE	25
La Campagne | Cherry Hill/NJ	22
La Na | Media	18
Z Le Bec-Fin | Rittenhouse	27
Majolica | Phoenixville	24
Manon | Lambertville/NJ	24
Nan | Univ City	26
Z Parc | Rittenhouse	22
Z Siri's | Cherry Hill/NJ	26
Z Swann Lounge | Logan Sq	26
Zinc | Washington Sq W	23

FRENCH (BISTRO)

NEW A La Maison | Ardmore	-
NEW Avril | Bala Cynwyd	14
Z Bibou | S Philly	27
Bistro St. Tropez | Rittenhouse	19
Bistrot/Minette | Queen Vill	25
Brasserie 73 | Skippack	22
Caribou Cafe | Washington Sq W	21
La Belle Epoque | Media	21
Z Le Bar Lyonnais | Rittenhouse	27

Z Parc | Rittenhouse	22
Slate Bleu | Doylestown	23
Z Sovana Bistro | Kennett Sq	27
Spring Mill | Consho	24
Supper | South St	23
Vintage | Washington Sq W	20

GASTROPUB

Abbaye | Belgian | N Liberties	20
Devil's Den | Amer. | S Philly	19
Kildare's | Irish | multi.	16
Kite & Key | Amer. | Fairmount	16
NEW Kraftwork | Amer. | Fishtown	-
Local 44 | Amer. | W Philly	16
Memphis Tap | Amer. | Port Richmond	23
Pub/Kitchen | Euro. | Graduate Hospital	22
Royal Tavern | Amer. | S Philly	24
Sidecar | Eclectic | Graduate Hospital	23
Slate | Amer. | Rittenhouse	19
Smiths | Amer. | Rittenhouse	16
Smokin' Betty | Amer./BBQ | Washington Sq W	20
St. Stephens Green | Amer./Irish | Fairmount	18
Swift Half | Amer. | N Liberties	18
Urban Saloon | Pub | Fairmount	18

GERMAN

Brauhaus Schmitz | South St	19
Otto's Brauhaus | Horsham	19

GREEK

Athena | Glenside	22
Z Dmitri's | multi.	24
Effie's | Washington Sq W	21
Z Estia | Ave of Arts	25
Kanella | Washington Sq W	25
Kuzina | Cherry Hill/NJ	22
Lourdas Greek | Bryn Mawr	21
Olive Tree | Downingtown	23
South St. Souvlaki | South St	22
Zorba's Taverna | Fairmount	20

INDIAN

Bindi | Washington Sq W	24
Chinnar Indian | Berwyn	23
Ekta | multi.	-
Karma | Old City	21

CUISINES

Khajuraho | **Ardmore**	20	Caffe Casta Diva | **Rittenhouse**	26
King of Tandoor | **Fairmount**	23	Caffe Valentino | **S Philly**	22
Minar Palace | **Washington Sq W**	18	Capers/Lemons | **Wilming/DE**	22
New Delhi | **Univ City**	23	**NEW** Carluccio's | **S Philly**	25
New Samosa | **Washington Sq W**	-	**Z** Catelli | **Voorhees/NJ**	25
Palace of Asia | **Ft Wash**	22	Chiarella's | **S Philly**	22
NEW Saffron | **multi.**	-	Core De Roma | S | **South St**	25
Sitar India | **Univ City**	18	Criniti | S | **S Philly**	18
Tandoor India | **Univ City**	18	Cucina Forte | N | **S Philly**	26
Tiffin | **multi.**	25	D'Angelo's | **Rittenhouse**	24
NEW Tiffin etc. | **N Liberties**	23	Dante & Luigi | **S Philly**	23

IRISH

		Davio's | N | **Rittenhouse**	25
Fergie's Pub | **Washington Sq W**	16	DeAnna's | **Lambertville/NJ**	24
Kildare's | **multi.**	16	Dolce | **Old City**	17
Molly Maguire's | **Phoenixville**	16	Ernesto's 1521 | **Rittenhouse**	19
Plough & Stars | **Old City**	20	Fellini Cafe | **Ardmore**	19
Shanachie | **Ambler**	13	Fellini Cafe | **Newtown Sq**	22
St. Stephens Green | **Fairmount**	18	Filomena | S | **multi.**	22
Tír na nÓg | **Logan Sq**	17	Fiorello's Café | **W Chester**	17

ISRAELI

		Fountain Side | **Horsham**	20
Z Zahav | **Society Hill**	25	**NEW** Franco's Osteria | **Wynnefield**	-

ITALIAN

(N=Northern; S=Southern)

		Franco's Tratt. | **East Falls**	22
NEW Amis | **Washington Sq W**	24	From the Boot | **multi.**	21
Anthony's | **Haddon Hts/NJ**	22	**NEW** Gemelli | **Narberth**	23
NEW Apollinare | **N Liberties**	-	Girasole | **Ave of Arts**	21
August | **S Philly**	25	**Z** Giumarello's | N | **Westmont/NJ**	26
Avalon | N | **W Chester**	25		
NEW Avril | **Bala Cynwyd**	14	Gnocchi | **South St**	19
Barone's/Villa Barone | **multi.**	22	Gusto | **Lancaster/LB**	21
Bella Cena | **Rittenhouse**	20	Gypsy Saloon | **W Consho**	22
Bella Tori | N | **Langhorne**	18	HighNote Cafe | S | **S Philly**	23
Bella Tratt. | **Manayunk**	23	Hostaria Da Elio | **South St**	23
Bellini Grill | **Rittenhouse**	21	Il Cantuccio | N | **N Liberties**	21
Bensí | **multi.**	17	**Z** Il Fiore | **Collingswood/NJ**	26
Z Birchrunville Store | **Birchrunville**	28	Illuminare | **Fairmount**	15
		Il Portico | N | **Rittenhouse**	21
Bistro di Marino | **Collingswood/NJ**	23	Il Tartufo | N | **Manayunk**	21
		Italian Bistro | **multi.**	17
Bistro La Baia | **Graduate Hospital**	19	Joe Pesce | **multi.**	21
Bistro La Viola | **Rittenhouse**	24	La Collina | N | **Bala Cynwyd**	22
Bistro Romano | **Society Hill**	22	La Famiglia | **Old City**	23
Bocelli | **multi.**	20	La Fontana | **Rittenhouse**	21
Bomb Bomb BBQ | **S Philly**	23	La Locanda | **Voorhees/NJ**	25
Bona Cucina | N | **Upper Darby**	23	La Locanda/Ghiottone | **Old City**	24
Branzino | **Rittenhouse**	23	Lamberti's | **Wilming/DE**	18
Brio | **Cherry Hill/NJ**	19	L'Angolo | S | **S Philly**	26
Buca di Beppo | **multi.**	16	Langostini | **S Philly**	-
Caffe Aldo | **Cherry Hill/NJ**	24	LaScala's | **Washington Sq W**	19
		La Veranda | **DE River**	22

Menus, photos, voting and more – free at ZAGAT.com

La Viola Ovest | **Rittenhouse**	23	
Le Castagne | N | **Rittenhouse**	25	
🄩 Le Virtù | S | **S Philly**	26	
Limoncello | N | **W Chester**	23	
L'Oca | N | **Fairmount**	23	
Maggiano's | **multi.**	20	
Maggio's | **Southampton**	18	
Mama Palma's | S | **Rittenhouse**	23	
Mamma Maria | **S Philly**	22	
Marco Polo | **Elkins Pk**	20	
Maria's/Summit | **Roxborough**	21	
Marra's | S | **S Philly**	21	
Melograno | N | **Rittenhouse**	24	
Mercato | N | **Washington Sq W**	25	
Mirabella | **Cherry Hill/NJ**	23	
Mix | **Rittenhouse**	17	
Modo Mio | **N Liberties**	26	
Moonstruck | **NE Philly**	21	
🄩 Mr. Martino's | **S Philly**	24	
Mrs. Robino's | **Wilming/DE**	14	
Newtown Grill | N | **Newtown Sq**	19	
Nunzio | **Collingswood/NJ**	24	
🄩 Osteria | N | **N Philly**	27	
Paradiso | **S Philly**	25	
Penne | **Univ City**	18	
Piccolo Tratt. | **multi.**	22	
Pietro's Pizza | **multi.**	21	
Pizzicato | **multi.**	19	
Pomodoro | **Wilming/DE**	-	
Porcini | **Rittenhouse**	23	
Portofino | **Washington Sq W**	20	
Positano Coast | **Society Hill**	21	
Primavera Pizza | **Ardmore**	19	
PTG | **Roxborough**	23	
Radicchio | N | **Old City**	25	
Ralph's | **S Philly**	23	
Rick's | **Lambertville/NJ**	20	
Ristorante Castello | **N Wales**	17	
Rist. La Buca | **Washington Sq W**	22	
Rist. Panorama | N | **Old City**	23	
Riverstone | **S Philly**	25	
Rist. Positano | S | **Ardmore**	20	
Rist. Primavera | **Wayne**	20	
Rist. San Marco | **Ambler**	26	
Roberto's Tratt. | S | **Erdenheim**	19	
Salento | S | **Rittenhouse**	23	
Saloon | **S Philly**	24	
Sapori | **Collingswood/NJ**	25	
🄩 Savona | **Gulph Mills**	27	
Scannicchio's | **S Philly**	23	

Scoogi's | **Flourtown**	19	
🄽🄴🅆 Shank's Original | **multi.**	23	
Spasso | **Old City**	23	
Table 31 | **Logan Sq**	21	
🄽🄴🅆 Tavolo | **Hunt Vly**	21	
Teca | **W Chester**	23	
Teresa's Cafe | **Wayne**	22	
Toscana 52 | N | **Feasterville**	20	
Toscana Kit. | N | **Wilming/DE**	24	
Trattoria Giuseppe | S | **Newtown Sq**	-	
Tratt. San Nicola | **Paoli**	22	
Tre Scalini | **S Philly**	24	
Upstares/Sotto | N | **Ave of Arts**	23	
Vesuvio | **S Philly**	14	
🄩 Vetri | **Washington Sq W**	28	
Victor Café | N | **S Philly**	20	
Villa di Roma | **S Philly**	23	
🄽🄴🅆 Zavino | **Washington Sq W**	22	

JAMAICAN

Jamaican Jerk | **Ave of Arts**	19

JAPANESE

(* sushi specialist)

Aki | **Washington Sq W**	21
August Moon* | **Norristown**	20
Azie* | **Villanova**	23
Benihana | **multi.**	19
🄩 Bluefin* | **Plymouth Meeting**	28
Bonjung Japanese* | **Collegeville**	26
Café Con Chocolate | **S Philly**	-
Chez Elena Wu* | **Voorhees/NJ**	22
🄽🄴🅆 Doma* | **Logan Sq**	-
East Cuisine | **Ambler**	21
🄽🄴🅆 Fat Salmon* | **Washington Sq W**	-
🄩 Fuji | **Haddonfield/NJ**	27
Fuji Mtn.* | **Rittenhouse**	20
Haru* | **Old City**	20
Harusame | **Ardmore**	22
Hibachi* | **multi.**	18
Hikaru* | **multi.**	20
Hokka Hokka* | **Ches Hill**	23
Izumi | **S Philly**	25
Jasmine* | **Wilming/DE**	23
Kingyo* | **Rittenhouse**	-
Kisso Sushi* | **Old City**	25
Kotatsu | **Ardmore**	24
Lai Lai Garden* | **Blue Bell**	19
Manayunk Brew.* | **Manayunk**	17
Marg. Kuo* | **Wayne**	23

Marg. Kuo Mandarin* | **Frazer**	22
Marg. Kuo Media* | **Media**	24
Marg. Kuo Peking* | **Media**	27
Megu* | **Cherry Hill/NJ**	26
Mikado* | **Ardmore**	20
Mikado* | **multi.**	23
NEW Mikimotos* | **Wilming/DE**	25
Miraku | **Spring House**	–
Mizu* | **multi.**	20
NEW Momiji | **Society Hill**	–
Z Morimoto | **Washington Sq W**	28
Oishi* | **Newtown**	25
Ooka* | **multi.**	24
Osaka* | **multi.**	23
Ota-Ya* | **multi.**	23
Raw Sushi* | **Washington Sq W**	25
NEW Ro-Zu* | **S Philly**	–
Z Sagami* | **Collingswood/NJ**	27
Sakura Spring | **Cherry Hill/NJ**	22
Shiroi Hana* | **Rittenhouse**	24
Sushikazu* | **Blue Bell**	–
Swanky Bubbles* | **Old City**	19
Tampopo | **multi.**	22
Teikoku | **Newtown Sq**	23
Uzu Sushi* | **Old City**	23
Yakitori Boy | **Chinatown**	19
NEW Zama* | **Rittenhouse**	26
Z Zento* | **Old City**	26

JEWISH

Ben & Irv Deli | **Hunt Vly**	19
Famous 4th St. Deli | **multi.**	24
Honey's Sit | **N Liberties**	25
Hymie's Deli | **Merion Sta**	19
Kibitz Room | **Cherry Hill/NJ**	21

KOREAN

(* barbecue specialist)

August Moon* | **Norristown**	20
NEW Doma | **Logan Sq**	–
Gaya* | **Blue Bell**	–
Giwa | **Rittenhouse**	23
Jong Ka Jib | **E Oak Ln**	25
NEW Miga | **Rittenhouse**	–
Tampopo | **multi.**	22

KOSHER/
KOSHER-STYLE

Max & David's | **Elkins Pk**	21
New Harmony | **Chinatown**	22
Singapore Kosher | **Chinatown**	20

LAOTIAN

Cafe de Laos | **S Philly**	24
Vientiane Café | **W Philly**	23

LEBANESE

Cedars | **South St**	22
NEW Leila Cafe | **Washington Sq W**	–

MALAYSIAN

Aqua | **Washington Sq W**	21
Banana Leaf | **Chinatown**	21
Penang | **multi.**	21
Rasa Sayang | **Wilming/DE**	25

MEDITERRANEAN

Al Dar Bistro | **Bala Cynwyd**	19
Arpeggio | **Spring House**	23
Audrey Claire | **Rittenhouse**	23
Byblos | **Rittenhouse**	18
Figs | **Fairmount**	23
Z Gibraltar | **Lancaster/LB**	23
Hamilton's | **Lambertville/NJ**	24
La Pergola | **Jenkintown**	19
Little Marakesh | **Dresher**	–
Max & David's | **Elkins Pk**	21
Mirna's Café | **multi.**	22
Z Moro | **Wilming/DE**	26
NEW Munk/Nunn | **Manayunk**	–
Novità Bistro | **Graduate Hospital**	18
Pistachio Grille | **Maple Glen**	20
Privé | **Old City**	21
Z Sovana Bistro | **Kennett Sq**	27
Valanni | **Washington Sq W**	24
Water Works | **Fairmount**	21
Zacharias | **Worcester**	24

MEXICAN

Baja Fresh | **multi.**	17
Café Con Chocolate | **S Philly**	–
Cantina Caballitos/Segundos | **multi.**	21
Copabanana | **multi.**	17
Coyote Cross. | **Consho**	21
Z Distrito | **Univ City**	25
El Azteca | **Mt Laurel/NJ**	19
El Azteca I | **Washington Sq W**	20
El Camino Real | **N Liberties**	21
El Fuego | **multi.**	19
NEW El Rey | **Rittenhouse**	–
El Sarape | **multi.**	23

El Vez	Washington Sq W	23
José Pistola's	Rittenhouse	15
La Esperanza	Lindenwold/NJ	25
La Lupe	S Philly	21
Las Bugambilias	South St	24
Las Cazuelas	N Liberties	24
La Tolteca	Wilming/DE	20
Lolita	Washington Sq W	26
NEW Más Mexicali	W Chester	-
Mexican Food	Marlton/NJ	19
Mexican Post	multi.	16
Qdoba	multi.	18
Tamarindo's	Broad Axe	21
Taq. La Michoacana	Norristown	23
Taq. La Veracruz.	S Philly	23
Tequila's	Rittenhouse	25
Tortilla Press	multi.	23
Xochitl	Society Hill	23
Zocalo	Univ City	20

MIDDLE EASTERN

Alyan's	South St	24
Bitar's	S Philly	25
Maoz Veg.	multi.	23
Norma's	Cherry Hill/NJ	22

MOROCCAN

Fez Moroccan	South St	19
Little Marakesh	Dresher	-
Marrakesh	South St	25

NOODLE SHOPS

Nan Zhou	Chinatown	23
Pho 75	multi.	22
Sang Kee	multi.	23

NUEVO LATINO

Alma de Cuba	Rittenhouse	25
El Serrano	Lancaster/LB	22
NEW Verdad	Bryn Mawr	19

PAKISTANI

| Kabobeesh | Univ City | 26 |

PAN-LATIN

NEW Avenida	Mt Airy	22
Mixto	Washington Sq W	20
Pura Vida	N Liberties	-

PARAGUAYAN

| Arbol Café | N Liberties | 17 |

CUISINES

PENNSYLVANIA DUTCH

Bird-in-Hand	Bird-in-Hand/LB	20
Good/Plenty	Smoketown/LB	18
Miller's Smorgas.	Ronks/LB	18
Plain/Fancy Farm	Bird-in-Hand/LB	19
Shady Maple	East Earl/LB	20

PERSIAN

| Persian Grill | Lafayette Hill | 21 |

PERUVIAN

| Chifa | Washington Sq W | 25 |
| El Serrano | Lancaster/LB | 22 |

PIZZA

California Pizza	multi.	19
Celebre's	S Philly	24
Cooper's	Manayunk	22
Du Jour	Haverford	18
Gullifty's	Rosemont	15
Illuminare	Fairmount	15
Maggio's	Southampton	18
Mama Palma's	Rittenhouse	23
Manayunk Brew.	Manayunk	17
Marra's	S Philly	21
Osteria	N Philly	27
Pietro's Pizza	multi.	21
NEW Pizzeria Stella	Society Hill	22
Pizzicato	Marlton/NJ	19
Primavera Pizza	Ardmore	19
SLiCE	multi.	22
Tacconelli's	multi.	25

POLISH

| Warsaw Cafe | Rittenhouse | 20 |

POLYNESIAN

| Moshulu | DE River | 22 |

PORTUGUESE

| NEW Koo Zee Doo | N Liberties | 25 |

PUB FOOD

America B&G	multi.	18
Black Sheep	Rittenhouse	17
Chickie's/Pete's	multi.	18
Dark Horse	Society Hill	19
Dock Street	Univ City	21
Elephant/Castle	Rittenhouse	11
Fadó Irish	Rittenhouse	17

Fergie's Pub | **Washington Sq W**	16
Field House | **Chinatown**	12
Fox & Hound | **multi.**	11
Good Dog | **Rittenhouse**	22
Grey Lodge | **NE Philly**	19
Gullifty's | **Rosemont**	15
Happy Rooster | **Rittenhouse**	18
Inn/Hawke | **Lambertville/NJ**	20
K.C.'s Alley | **Ambler**	16
NEW Lucky 7 | **Fairmount**	17
Manayunk Brew. | **Manayunk**	17
McFadden's | **multi.**	15
McGillin's | **Washington Sq W**	16
Misconduct Tav. | **Rittenhouse**	19
Molly Maguire's | **Phoenixville**	16
Monk's Cafe | **Rittenhouse**	22
Moriarty's | **Washington Sq W**	20
National Mech. | **Old City**	18
Nodding Head | **Rittenhouse**	19
N. 3rd | **N Liberties**	23
P.J. Whelihan's | **multi.**	16
Plough & Stars | **Old City**	20
Pub/Penn Valley | **Narberth**	19
Rock Bottom | **King of Prussia**	14
Sláinte | **Univ City**	16
Sly Fox | **multi.**	13
Standard Tap | **N Liberties**	22
Teresa's Next Dr. | **Wayne**	22
Victory Brewing | **Downingtown**	17
Wash. St. Ale | **Wilming/DE**	15

SANDWICHES

Ben & Irv Deli | **Hunt Vly**	19
Campo's Deli | **Old City**	23
Geno's Steaks | **S Philly**	18
Hymie's Deli | **Merion Sta**	19
Isaac's | **multi.**	17
Jim's Steaks | **multi.**	23
Z John's Roast Pork | **S Philly**	27
Z Pat's Steaks | **S Philly**	21
Tony Luke's | **S Philly**	26

SEAFOOD

Anastasi | **S Philly**	23
Athena | **Glenside**	22
Blackfish | **Consho**	25
Bobby Chez | **multi.**	22
Bonefish Grill | **multi.**	21
Branzino | **Rittenhouse**	23
Bridget's Steak | **Ambler**	23
Chart House | **DE River**	20

Chophouse | **Gibbsboro/NJ**	24
Clam Tavern | **Clifton Hts**	22
Creed's | **King of Prussia**	24
Deep Blue | **Wilming/DE**	22
Devon Seafood | **Rittenhouse**	23
DiNardo's | **Old City**	19
Z Dmitri's | **multi.**	24
Doc Magrogan | **W Chester**	17
Feby's Fish. | **Wilming/DE**	21
NEW fish | **Graduate Hospital**	25
Gables | **Chadds Ford**	23
Z Gibraltar | **Lancaster/LB**	23
Hamilton's | **Lambertville/NJ**	24
Harry's Seafood | **Wilming/DE**	25
Joe Pesce | **multi.**	21
Legal Sea | **multi.**	19
Little Tuna | **Haddonfield/NJ**	19
Manny's | **multi.**	20
Marco Polo | **Elkins Pk**	20
McCormick/Schmick | **multi.**	21
Z Nineteen | **Ave of Arts**	23
Oyster House | **Rittenhouse**	23
Palm | **Ave of Arts**	24
Phillips Sea. | **Logan Sq**	16
Radicchio | **Old City**	25
Rist. La Buca | **Washington Sq W**	22
Ritz Seafood | **Voorhees/NJ**	25
Seafood Unltd. | **Rittenhouse**	21
Snockey's Oyster | **S Philly**	21
SoleFood | **Washington Sq W**	20
Tai Lake | **Chinatown**	27
Upstares/Sotto | **Ave of Arts**	23
Zinc | **Washington Sq W**	23

SMALL PLATES

(See also Spanish tapas specialist)

Chick's | **Eclectic** | **South St**	21
Continental | **Eclectic** | **Old City**	22
Continental Mid-town | **Eclectic** | **Rittenhouse**	22
Derek's | **Amer.** | **Manayunk**	22
Z Distrito | **Mex.** | **Univ City**	25
Dom. Hudson | **Amer.** | **Wilming/DE**	24
Elements Café | **Amer.** | **Haddon Hts/NJ**	22
Epicurean | **Amer.** | **Phoenixville**	20
Friday Sat. Sun. | **Amer.** | **Rittenhouse**	24
Havana | **Eclectic** | **New Hope**	18
Honey | **Amer.** | **Doylestown**	26

Menus, photos, voting and more – free at ZAGAT.com

Z Lacroix | Eclectic | **Rittenhouse** 27

MangoMoon | Asian | **Manayunk** 17

Modo Mio | Italian | **N Liberties** 26

NEW M Rest. | Pan-Latin | 21
Washington Sq W

Riverstone Café | Amer. | **Exton** 18

NEW Sampan | Asian | 21
Washington Sq W

Snackbar | Amer. | **Rittenhouse** 22

Stella Blu | Amer. | **W Consho** 21

Teca | Italian | **W Chester** 23

Tria | Eclectic | **multi.** 23

Valanni | Med. | **Washington Sq W** 24

Water Works | Med. | **Fairmount** 21

Yakitori Boy | Japanese | 19
Chinatown

SOUL FOOD

Geechee Girl | **Germantown** 21

Ms. Tootsie's | **South St** 25

Warmdaddy's | **S Philly** 22

SOUTHERN

Carversville Inn | **Carversville** 25

NEW Cooperage | -
Washington Sq W

Down Home | **Chinatown** 17

Geechee Girl | **Germantown** 21

Honey's Sit | **N Liberties** 25

Jack's Firehse. | **Fairmount** 19

Marsha Brown | **New Hope** 21

Ms. Tootsie's | **South St** 25

Warmdaddy's | **S Philly** 22

SOUTHWESTERN

Adobe Cafe | **multi.** 20

Cactus | **Manayunk** 17

Mission Grill | **Logan Sq** 18

SPANISH

(* tapas specialist)

Z Amada* | **Old City** 28

Bar Ferdinand* | **N Liberties** 23

Orillas Tapas* | **Wilming/DE** 23

Z Tinto* | **Rittenhouse** 27

NEW Verdad | **Bryn Mawr** 19

STEAKHOUSES

Z Barclay Prime | **Rittenhouse** 27

Bonefish Grill | **multi.** 21

Brandywine Prime | **Chadds Ford** 22

Bridget's Steak | **Ambler** 23

Butcher/Singer | **Rittenhouse** 24

Z Capital Grille | **multi.** 26

Chima | **Logan Sq** 21

Chophouse | **Gibbsboro/NJ** 24

Chops | **multi.** 21

Creed's | **King of Prussia** 24

Davio's | **Rittenhouse** 25

Del Frisco's | **Ave of Arts** 20

Delmonico's | **Wynnefield** 25

Fleming's | **multi.** 24

Fogo de Chão | **Ave of Arts** 24

Hibachi | **multi.** 18

Morton's | **multi.** 26

Newtown Grill | **Newtown Sq** 19

Palm | **Ave of Arts** 24

NEW Parker's Prime | 21
Newtown Sq

Pietro's Prime | **W Chester** 23

Z Prime Rib | **Rittenhouse** 27

Pub | **Pennsauken/NJ** 19

Ruth's Chris | **multi.** 23

Saloon | **S Philly** 24

Seven Stars Inn | **Phoenixville** 20

Smith/Wollensky | **Rittenhouse** 22

Sullivan's Steak | **multi.** 23

Ted's Montana | **multi.** 18

Union City Grille | **Wilming/DE** 22

Z Union Trust | 24
Washington Sq W

Walter's Steak. | **Wilming/DE** 22

William Douglas | **Cherry** 24
Hill/NJ

TAIWANESE

Han Dynasty | **multi.** 24

Ray's Cafe | **Chinatown** 23

TEAROOMS

Mary Cassatt | **Rittenhouse** -

Ray's Cafe | **Chinatown** 23

TEX-MEX

Tex Mex Connect. | **N Wales** 17

THAI

Aqua | **Washington Sq W** 21

Cafe de Laos | **S Philly** 24

Chabaa Thai | **Manayunk** 25

Chiangmai | **Consho** 25

Flavor | **Wayne** 19

La Na | **Media** 18

Lemon Grass | **multi.** 20

MangoMoon	**Manayunk**	17
Mikado	**Ardmore**	20
My Thai	**Graduate Hospital**	22
Nan	**Univ City**	26
Pattaya	**Univ City**	20
Penang	**multi.**	21
Pho Thai Nam	**Blue Bell**	23
Sakura Spring	**Cherry Hill/NJ**	22
Siam Cuisine	**multi.**	22
Silk Cuisine	**Bryn Mawr**	21
☑ Siri's	**Cherry Hill/NJ**	26
Sweet Basil	**Chadds Ford**	23
Teikoku	**Newtown Sq**	23
Thai Orchid	**Blue Bell**	24
Thai Singha	**Univ City**	22
Vientiane Café	**W Philly**	23
White Elephant	**Hunt Vly**	24

TURKISH

| Divan | **Graduate Hospital** | 20 |
| Konak | **Old City** | 23 |

VEGETARIAN

(* vegan)

AllWays Café	**Hunt Vly**	23
Ariana	**Voorhees/NJ**	22
☑ Blue Sage	**Southampton**	26
Full Plate*	**N Liberties**	19
☑ Horizons*	**South St**	27
Kingdom of Veg.*	**Chinatown**	25
Maoz Veg.	**multi.**	23
Mi Lah Veg.*	**Rittenhouse**	21
New Harmony*	**Chinatown**	22
New Samosa	**Washington Sq W**	–
Singapore Kosher	**Chinatown**	20
NEW Sprig & Vine*	**New Hope**	–
Winnie's Le Bus	**Manayunk**	21

VENEZUELAN

| Sazon | **N Liberties** | 22 |

VIETNAMESE

Ha Long Bay	**Bryn Mawr**	21
NEW Le Viet	**S Philly**	–
☑ Nam Phuong	**S Philly**	26
Pho 75	**multi.**	22
Pho Thai Nam	**Blue Bell**	23
Pho Xe Lua	**Chinatown**	24
Vietnam	**Chinatown**	25
Vietnam Café	**W Philly**	24
Vietnam Palace	**Chinatown**	23

Locations

Includes names, cuisines, Food ratings and, for locations that are mapped, top list with map coordinates.

Philadelphia

AVENUE OF THE ARTS
(See map on page 222)

TOP FOOD

Capital Grille	Steak	**E7**	26
Morton's	Steak	**F7**	26
Estia	Greek	**F7**	25
Palm	Steak	**F7**	24
Fogo de Chão	Brazilian/Steak	**E7**	24
Naked Choco.	Dessert	**F7**	24
Ruth's Chris	Steak	**G7**	23
Upstares/Sotto	Italian/Seafood	**F7**	23
Nineteen	Amer./Seafood	**F7**	23
Bobby Chez	Seafood	**I7**	22

LISTING

NEW American Pub	Amer.	15
NEW Amuse	French	-
Bliss	Amer.	21
Bobby Chez	Seafood	22
Ⓩ Capital Grille	Steak	26
Del Frisco's	Steak	20
Ⓩ Estia	Greek	25
Fogo de Chão	Brazilian/Steak	24
Girasole	Italian	21
Italian Bistro	Italian	17
Jamaican Jerk	Jamaican	19
Marathon Grill	Amer.	18
McCormick/Schmick	Seafood	21
Morton's	Steak	26
Naked Choco.	Dessert	24
Ⓩ Nineteen	Amer./Seafood	23
Palm	Steak	24
Ruth's Chris	Steak	23
Ted's Montana	Steak	18
Ⓩ 10 Arts	Amer.	22
Upstares/Sotto	Italian/Seafood	23

CHINATOWN
(See map on page 222)

TOP FOOD

Vietnam	Viet.	**B9**	25
Lee How Fook	Chinese	**B9**	25
Reading Terminal Mkt.	Eclectic	**D8**	24
Charles Plaza	Chinese	**B9**	24
Rangoon	Burmese	**C10**	23
Shiao Lan Kung	Chinese	**C9**	23
Sang Kee	Chinese	**B10, D10**	23
Vietnam Palace	Viet.	**B9**	23
Siam Cuisine	Thai	**D9**	22
New Harmony	Chinese/Veg.	**C10**	22

LISTING

Banana Leaf	Malaysian	21
Charles Plaza	Chinese	24
Down Home	Southern	17
Field House	Amer.	12
Four Rivers	Chinese	26
Hard Rock	Amer.	13
H.K. Golden	Chinese	20
Imperial Inn	Chinese	20
Joy Tsin Lau	Chinese	20
Kingdom of Veg.	Chinese/Veg.	25
Lee How Fook	Chinese	25
Maggiano's	Italian	20
Melting Pot	Fondue	19
Nan Zhou	Noodles	23
New Harmony	Chinese/Veg.	22
Ocean Harbor	Chinese	21
Penang	Malaysian	21
Pho 75	Viet.	22
Pho Xe Lua	Viet.	24
Rangoon	Burmese	23
Ray's Cafe	Taiwanese	23
Reading Terminal Mkt.	Eclectic	24
Sang Kee	Chinese	23
Shiao Lan Kung	Chinese	23
Siam Cuisine	Thai	22
Singapore Kosher	Chinese/Veg.	20
Tai Lake	Chinese	27
Vietnam	Viet.	25
Vietnam Palace	Viet.	23
Yakitori Boy	Japanese	19

DELAWARE RIVERFRONT

Chart House	Seafood	20
Dave & Buster's	Amer.	12

L
O
C
A
T
I
O
N
S

Hibachi	Japanese	18
Keating's	Amer.	18
La Veranda	Italian	22
Moshulu	Amer.	22

EAST FALLS/ MANAYUNK/ ROXBOROUGH

Adobe Cafe	SW	20
Bella Tratt.	Italian	23
Bourbon Blue	Cajun/Creole	18
Cactus	SW	17
Chabaa Thai	Thai	25
Cooper's	Amer.	22
Dalessandro's	Cheesestks.	23
Derek's	Amer.	22
Franco's Tratt.	Italian	22
Hikaru	Japanese	20
Il Tartufo	Italian	21
Jake's	Amer.	25
Kildare's	Pub	16
Manayunk Brew.	Pub	17
MangoMoon	Asian	17
Maria's/Summit	Italian	21
NEW Munk/Nunn	Med.	-
PTG	Italian	23
Trolley Car	Diner	16
Winnie's Le Bus	Amer.	21

FAIRMOUNT

Belgian Café	Belgian	19
Bridgid's	Eclectic	20
Figs	Med.	23
Illuminare	Italian	15
Jack's Firehse.	Southern	19
King of Tandoor	Indian	23
Kite & Key	Amer.	16
Little Pete's	Diner	18
L'Oca	Italian	23
London Grill	Amer.	17
NEW Lucky 7	Amer.	17
Rembrandt's	Amer.	19
Rose Tattoo	Amer.	22
Sabrina's Café	Eclectic	24
St. Stephens Green	Irish	18
Trio	Asian	24
Z Umai Umai	Asian	26
Urban Saloon	Pub	18
Water Works	Med.	21
Zorba's Taverna	Greek	20

FISHTOWN

Ekta	Indian	-
Johnny Brenda	Amer./Eclectic	21
NEW Kraftwork	Amer.	-
Sketch Café	Burgers	24

GRADUATE HOSPITAL

Bistro La Baia	Italian	19
Café L'Aube	Coffee	25
Divan	Turkish	20
NEW fish	Seafood	25
Grace Tav.	Amer.	21
L2	Amer.	19
Meritage	Amer.	25
My Thai	Thai	22
Novità Bistro	Med.	18
Pub/Kitchen	Euro.	22
Pumpkin	Amer.	26
Sidecar	Eclectic	23
Ten Stone	Amer.	17

LOGAN SQUARE

(See map on page 222)

TOP FOOD

Fountain	Continental/French	C4	28
Swann Lounge	Amer./French	C4	26
Chima	Brazilian/Steak	D4	21

LISTING

Aya's Café	Egyptian	19
Chima	Brazilian/Steak	21
NEW Con Murphy's	Eclectic	17
Darling's	Amer.	17
NEW Doma	Japanese/Korean	-
Du Jour	Amer.	18
Z Fountain	Continental/French	28
Mexican Post	Mex.	16
Mission Grill	SW	18
Phillips Sea.	Seafood	16
Public Hse./Logan	Amer.	14
Z Swann Lounge	Amer./French	26
Table 31	Italian	21
Tír na nÓg	Pub	17

NORTHEAST PHILLY

Chickie's/Pete's	Pub	18
Copabanana	Amer./Mex.	17
Dave & Buster's	Amer.	12
Dining Car	Amer.	19
Grey Lodge	Pub	19
Italian Bistro	Italian	17

Jim's Steaks | *Cheesestks.* 23
Mayfair Diner | *Diner* 15
Moonstruck | *Italian* 21
Nifty Fifty's | *Diner* 19
Pho 75 | *Viet.* 22
Steve's Steaks | *Cheesestks.* 23
Sweet Lucy's | *BBQ* 24

NORTHERN LIBERTIES

(See map on page 226)

TOP FOOD

Modo Mio | *Italian* | **A3** 26
Koo Zee Doo | *Portug.* | **E2** 25
Honey's Sit | *Jewish/Southern* | **D1** 25
Tiffin | *Indian* | **A1** 25
Dmitri's | *Greek* | **C2** 24
Las Cazuelas | *Mex.* | **A1** 24
Café Estelle | *Amer.* | **F1** 23
Tiffin etc. | *Indian* | **A1** 23
Bar Ferdinand | *Spanish* | **B2** 23
N. 3rd | *Amer.* | **D2** 23

LISTING

Abbaye | *Belgian* 20
🆕 Apollinare | *Italian* -
Arbol Café | *Paraguayan* 17
Bar Ferdinand | *Spanish* 23
Café Estelle | *Amer.* 23
Cantina Caballitos/Segundos | *Mex.* 21
Darling's | *Amer.* 17
🅉 Dmitri's | *Greek* 24
El Camino Real | *BBQ/Mexican* 21
Full Plate | *Eclectic* 19
Honey's Sit | *Jewish/Southern* 25
Il Cantuccio | *Italian* 21
🆕 Koo Zee Doo | *Portug.* 25
Las Cazuelas | *Mex.* 24
McFadden's | *Pub* 15
Modo Mio | *Italian* 26
N. 3rd | *Amer.* 23
Pura Vida | *Pan-Latin* -
Sazon | *Venez.* 22
Silk City | *Amer.* 21
🆕 Sonata | *Amer.* 23
Standard Tap | *Amer.* 22
Swift Half | *Amer.* 18
Tiffin | *Indian* 25
🆕 Tiffin etc. | *Indian* 23

NORTH PHILLY

Jong Ka Jib | *Korean* 25
🅉 Osteria | *Italian* 27
Prohibition | *Amer.* 22
Qdoba | *Mex.* 18
Tierra Colombiana | *Colombian/Cuban* 24

NORTHWEST PHILLY

(Chestnut Hill/Germantown/Mt. Airy)
🆕 Avenida | *Pan-Latin* 22
Bocelli | *Italian* 20
Cafette | *Eclectic* 20
Cake | *Bakery* 20
Chestnut Grill | *Amer.* 17
CinCin | *Chinese* 23
¡Cuba! | *Cuban* 16
Dahlak | *Eritrean* 22
Earth Bread | *Amer.* 21
Geechee Girl | *Southern* 21
Hokka Hokka | *Japanese* 23
Manny's | *Seafood* 20
Osaka | *Japanese* 23
Rib Crib | *BBQ* 24
Roller's/Flying Fish | *Eclectic* 19
Solaris Grille | *Amer.* 14
Tiffin | *Indian* 25
Trolley Car | *Diner* 16
Umbria | *Eclectic* 24
Wine Thief | *Amer.* 20

OLD CITY

(See map on page 226)

TOP FOOD

Amada | *Spanish* | **J2** 28
Buddakan | *Asian* | **J1** 26
Zento | *Japanese* | **J2** 26
Chlöe | *Amer.* | **I2** 26
Radicchio | *Italian* | **G1** 25
Han Dynasty | *Chinese* | **J3** 24
Fork | *Amer.* | **J2** 24
La Locanda/Ghiottone | *Italian* | **H2** 24
Bistro 7 | *Amer.* | **J2** 24
Spasso | *Italian* | **J3** 23

LISTING

🅉 Amada | *Spanish* 28
Ariana | *Afghan* 22
Beneluxx | *Belgian* 20
Bistro 7 | *Amer.* 24
🅉 Buddakan | *Asian* 26

LOCATIONS

Salento	*Italian*	23
Seafood Unltd.	*Seafood*	21
NEW Shank's Original	*Italian*	23
Shiroi Hana	*Japanese*	24
Slate	*Amer.*	19
SLiCE	*Pizza*	22
Smith/Wollensky	*Steak*	22
Smiths	*Amer.*	16
Snackbar	*Amer.*	22
NEW Square 1682	*Amer.*	21
Tampopo	*Japanese/Korean*	22
Tavern 17	*Amer.*	16
Tequila's	*Mex.*	25
Z Tinto	*Spanish*	27
Tria	*Eclectic*	23
Twenty Manning	*Amer.*	-
NEW Village Whiskey	*Amer.*	24
Warsaw Cafe	*E Euro*	20
NEW Zama	*Japanese*	26

SOUTH PHILLY

Adobe Cafe	*SW*	20
Anastasi	*Seafood*	23
August	*Italian*	25
Z Bibou	*French*	27
Bitar's	*Mideast.*	25
Bomb Bomb BBQ	*BBQ/Italian*	23
Café Con Chocolate	*Japanese/Mexican*	-
Cafe de Laos	*Laotian/Thai*	24
Caffe Valentino	*Italian*	22
Cantina Caballitos/Segundos	*Mex.*	21
Z Capogiro	*Amer./Dessert*	27
NEW Carluccio's	*Italian*	25
Carman's Country	*Eclectic*	26
Celebre's	*Pizza*	24
Chiarella's	*Italian*	22
Chickie's/Pete's	*Pub*	18
Criniti	*Italian*	18
Cucina Forte	*Italian*	26
Dante & Luigi	*Italian*	23
Devil's Den	*Amer.*	19
Z NEW Fond	*Amer.*	27
Geno's Steaks	*Cheesestks.*	18
Golosa	*Dessert*	26
NEW Green Eggs	*Amer.*	26
NEW Hawthornes	*Amer.*	22
NEW Healthy Bites	*Amer.*	-
HighNote Cafe	*Italian*	23
Izumi	*Japanese*	25

Z James	*Amer.*	27
Z John's Roast Pork	*Sandwiches*	27
La Lupe	*Mex.*	21
L'Angolo	*Italian*	26
Langostini	*Italian*	-
Legal Sea	*Seafood*	19
NEW Le Viet	*Viet.*	-
Z Le Virtù	*Italian*	26
Mamma Maria	*Italian*	22
Marra's	*Italian*	21
McFadden's	*Pub*	15
Melrose Diner	*Diner*	15
Morning Glory	*Diner*	22
Z Mr. Martino's	*Italian*	24
Z Nam Phuong	*Viet.*	26
Nicholas	*Amer.*	22
Paradiso	*Italian*	25
Z Pat's Steaks	*Cheesestks.*	21
Pho 75	*Viet.*	22
Ralph's	*Italian*	23
NEW Resurrection Ale	*Amer.*	24
Riverstone	*Italian*	25
Royal Tavern	*Amer.*	24
NEW Ro-Zu	*Japanese*	-
Sabrina's Café	*Eclectic*	24
Saloon	*Italian/Steak*	24
Salt & Pepper	*Amer.*	25
Scannicchio's	*Italian*	23
NEW Shank's Original	*Italian*	23
SLiCE	*Pizza*	22
Snockey's Oyster	*Seafood*	21
Taq. La Veracruz.	*Mex.*	23
Tony Luke's	*Cheesestks.*	26
Tre Scalini	*Italian*	24
Vesuvio	*Italian*	14
Victor Café	*Italian*	20
Villa di Roma	*Italian*	23
Warmdaddy's	*Soul Food*	22

UNIVERSITY CITY

Abyssinia	*Ethiopian*	23
Beijing	*Chinese*	17
NEW Bobby's Burger	*Burgers*	-
Z Capogiro	*Amer./Dessert*	27
NEW City Tap House	*Amer.*	-
Copabanana	*Amer./Mex.*	17
Z Distrito	*Mex.*	25
Dock Street	*Pub*	21
Kabobeesh	*Pakistani*	26
La Terrasse	*Amer./French*	19

Lemon Grass | *Thai*	20
Marathon Grill | *Amer.*	18
Marigold Kitchen | *Amer.*	24
NEW MidAtlantic | *Amer.*	20
Mizu | *Japanese*	20
Nan | *French/Thai*	26
New Delhi | *Indian*	23
Pattaya | *Thai*	20
Penne | *Italian*	18
Pod | *Asian*	23
Qdoba | *Mex.*	18
Rx | *Eclectic*	24
Sang Kee | *Chinese*	23
Sitar India | *Indian*	18
Sláinte | *Pub*	16
Tampopo | *Japanese/Korean*	22
Tandoor India | *Indian*	18
Thai Singha | *Thai*	22
White Dog | *Eclectic*	20
World Café | *Eclectic*	16
Zocalo | *Mex.*	20

WASHINGTON SQUARE WEST

(See map on page 222)

TOP FOOD

Vetri | *Italian* | **G7**	28
Morimoto | *Japanese* | **E11**	28
Capogiro | *Amer./Dessert* | **F8**	27
Lolita | *Mex.* | **F7**	26
Mercato | *Amer./Italian* | **G8**	25
Kanella | *Greek* | **G9**	25
Chifa | *Chinese/Peruvian* | **E11**	25
Raw Sushi | *Japanese* | **F8**	25
Amis | *Italian* | **H7**	24
Bindi | *Indian* | **F8**	24

LISTING

Aki | *Japanese*	21
NEW Amis | *Italian*	24
Aqua | *Malaysian/Thai*	21
Bindi | *Indian*	24
Bonté Wafflerie | *Coffee*	21
Brew HaHa! | *Coffee*	17
☒ Capogiro | *Amer./Dessert*	27
Caribou Cafe | *French*	21
☒ Chifa | *Chinese/Peruvian*	25
Chops | *Steak*	21
NEW Cooperage | *Southern*	-
Effie's | *Greek*	21

El Azteca I | *Mex.*	20
El Fuego | *Cal./Mex.*	19
☒ El Vez | *Mex.*	23
NEW Fat Salmon | *Japanese*	-
Fergie's Pub | *Pub*	16
NEW Garces Trading | *Amer.*	-
Joe Pesce | *Italian/Seafood*	21
Jones | *Amer.*	20
Kanella | *Greek*	25
Knock | *Amer.*	16
LaScala's | *Italian*	19
NEW Leila Cafe | *Lebanese*	-
Lolita | *Mex.*	26
Maoz Veg. | *Mideast./Veg.*	23
Marathon Grill | *Amer.*	18
McGillin's | *Pub*	16
Mercato | *Amer./Italian*	25
Minar Palace | *Indian*	18
Mixto | *Pan-Latin*	20
More Than Ice Crm. | *Dessert*	20
Moriarty's | *Pub*	20
☒ Morimoto | *Japanese*	28
NEW M Rest. | *Pan-Latin*	21
New Samosa | *Indian/Veg.*	-
NEW Paul | *Amer.*	22
Portofino | *Italian*	20
Raw Sushi | *Japanese*	25
Rist. La Buca | *Italian*	22
NEW Sampan | *Asian*	21
Smokin' Betty | *Amer./BBQ*	20
SoleFood | *Seafood*	20
Tampopo | *Japanese/Korean*	22
Time | *Continental*	20
Tria | *Eclectic*	23
NEW Tweed | *Amer.*	-
☒ Union Trust | *Steak*	24
Valanni | *Med.*	24
Varga Bar | *Amer.*	20
☒ Vetri | *Italian*	28
Vintage | *French*	20
NEW Zavino | *Italian*	22
Zinc | *French/Seafood*	23

WEST PHILLY

Dahlak | *Eritrean*	22
Gold Standard | *Amer.*	17
Jim's Steaks | *Cheesestks.*	23
Local 44 | *Amer.*	16
Vientiane Café | *Laotian/Thai*	23
Vietnam Café | *Viet.*	24

WYNNEFIELD

California Pizza	*Pizza*	19
Chun Hing	*Chinese*	22
Delmonico's	*Steak*	25
NEW Franco's Osteria	*Italian*	–

Philadelphia Suburbs

BUCKS COUNTY

Augusto's	*Eclectic*	–
Bella Tori	*Italian*	18
Black Bass	*Amer.*	21
Z Blue Sage	*Veg.*	26
Brick Hotel	*Amer.*	16
Bridgetown Mill	*Amer.*	24
Carversville Inn	*Southern*	25
Cascade Lodge	*Continental*	20
Centre Bridge	*Amer.*	22
Cheeseburger/Paradise	*Burgers*	14
Cock 'n Bull	*Amer.*	18
Duck Sauce	*Chinese*	24
El Sarape	*Mex.*	23
Five Guys	*Burgers*	22
Freight House	*Amer.*	16
Golden Pheasant	*French*	23
Havana	*Amer./Eclectic*	18
Honey	*Amer.*	26
Hotel du Village	*French*	23
Inn/Phillips Mill	*French*	25
Isaac Newton's	*Amer.*	17
J.B. Dawson's/Austin's	*Amer.*	18
Knight House	*Amer.*	23
Landing	*Amer.*	18
Maggio's	*Italian/Pizza*	18
Marsha Brown	*Creole/Southern*	21
Nifty Fifty's	*Diner*	19
Oishi	*Asian*	25
Ooka	*Japanese*	24
Ota-Ya	*Japanese*	23
P.F. Chang's	*Chinese*	20
Piccolo Tratt.	*Italian*	22
Rouget	*Amer.*	24
Siam Cuisine	*Thai*	22
Slate Bleu	*French*	23
NEW Sprig & Vine	*Veg.*	–
Steve's Steaks	*Cheesestks.*	23
Summer Kitchen	*Eclectic*	21
Sweet Lorraine's	*Eclectic*	17
Ted's Montana	*Steak*	18

Toscana 52	*Italian*	20
Triumph Brewing	*Amer./Eclectic*	18
Wash. Cross.	*Amer.*	20
Washington Hse.	*Amer.*	–
Yardley Inn	*Amer.*	22

CHESTER COUNTY

America B&G	*Amer.*	18
Avalon	*Italian*	25
Z Birchrunville Store	*French/Italian*	28
Blue Pear	*Amer.*	23
Bonefish Grill	*Seafood*	21
Buca di Beppo	*Italian*	16
NEW Bull Durham	*BBQ*	–
Catherine's	*Amer.*	28
Daddy Mims	*Creole*	23
Dilworth. Inn	*Amer.*	25
Doc Magrogan	*Seafood*	17
Drafting Rm.	*Amer.*	16
Duling-Kurtz	*Continental*	25
Epicurean	*Amer.*	20
Fiorello's Café	*Italian*	17
Four Dogs	*Amer.*	20
Z Gilmore's	*French*	28
Half Moon	*Amer.*	20
Han Dynasty	*Chinese*	24
Z High St. Caffé	*Cajun/Creole*	26
Iron Hill	*Amer.*	19
Isaac's	*Deli*	17
Kildare's	*Pub*	16
Kimberton Inn	*Amer.*	25
Limoncello	*Italian*	23
Majolica	*Amer./French*	24
Marg. Kuo Mandarin	*Chinese/Japanese*	22
NEW Más Mexicali	*Mex.*	–
Mendenhall Inn	*Amer.*	19
Molly Maguire's	*Pub*	16
Orchard	*Amer.*	27
Pietro's Prime	*Steak*	23
Riverstone Café	*Amer.*	18
Seven Stars Inn	*Continental*	20
Simon Pearce	*Amer.*	22
Sly Fox	*Pub*	13
Z Sovana Bistro	*French/Med.*	27
Spence's Remedy	*Eclectic*	21
Z Talula's Table	*Euro.*	27
Teca	*Italian*	23
Whip Tavern	*Pub*	23

DELAWARE COUNTY

America B&G	*Amer.*	18
Azie	*Asian*	23
Bona Cucina	*Italian*	23
Bonefish Grill	*Seafood*	21
Brandywine Prime	*Steak*	22
Charlie's Hamburg.	*Burgers*	23
Clam Tavern	*Seafood*	22
Fellini Cafe	*Italian*	22
Five Guys	*Burgers*	22
Gables	*Amer.*	23
Hank's Place	*Diner*	21
NEW Harvest	*Amer.*	-
Hibachi	*Japanese*	18
Iron Hill	*Amer.*	19
J.B. Dawson's/Austin's	*Amer.*	18
Jim's Steaks	*Cheesestks.*	23
Kaya's	*Amer.*	19
La Belle Epoque	*French*	21
La Na	*French/Thai*	18
Marg. Kuo Media	*Chinese/Japanese*	24
Marg. Kuo Peking	*Chinese/Japanese*	27
Masamoto	*Asian*	26
Newtown Grill	*Italian/Steak*	19
Nifty Fifty's	*Diner*	19
Pace One	*Amer.*	21
NEW Parker's Prime	*Steak*	21
P.F. Chang's	*Chinese*	20
Qdoba	*Mex.*	18
Ruby's	*Diner*	16
Sweet Basil	*Thai*	23
Sycamore	*Amer.*	-
Teikoku	*Japanese/Thai*	23
Trattoria Giuseppe	*Italian*	-

KING OF PRUSSIA

Bahama Breeze	*Carib.*	17
Baja Fresh	*Mex.*	17
California Cafe	*Cal.*	20
California Pizza	*Pizza*	19
Cheesecake	*Amer.*	20
Creed's	*Seafood/Steak*	24
Fox & Hound	*Pub*	11
Kildare's	*Pub*	16
Legal Sea	*Seafood*	19
Lemon Grass	*Thai*	20
Maggiano's	*Italian*	20
Melting Pot	*Fondue*	19
Morton's	*Steak*	26

Rock Bottom	*Pub*	14
Ruby's	*Diner*	16
Ruth's Chris	*Steak*	23
Seasons 52	*Amer.*	-
Sullivan's Steak	*Steak*	23

MAIN LINE

NEW A La Maison	*French*	-
Al Dar Bistro	*Med.*	19
Ardmore Station	*Diner*	18
August Moon	*Japanese/Korean*	20
Auspicious	*Chinese*	19
NEW Avril	*Italian/French*	14
Azie	*Asian*	23
Bunha Faun	*Asian/French*	24
Cedar Hollow	*Amer.*	17
Chinnar Indian	*Indian*	23
Chops	*Steak*	21
Christopher's	*Amer.*	16
NEW Doghouse	*Amer.*	-
Du Jour	*Amer.*	18
Ekta	*Indian*	-
Fellini Cafe	*Italian*	19
NEW Firecreek	*Amer.*	20
Five Guys	*Burgers*	22
Flavor	*Thai*	19
Fleming's	*Steak*	24
NEW Gemelli	*Italian*	23
Gen. Warren	*Amer.*	25
Georges'	*Eclectic*	22
Gullifty's	*Amer.*	15
Ha Long Bay	*Viet.*	21
Harusame	*Japanese*	22
Hibachi	*Japanese*	18
Hunan	*Chinese*	-
Hymie's Deli	*Deli*	19
Khajuraho	*Indian*	20
Kotatsu	*Japanese*	24
La Collina	*Italian*	22
Lourdas Greek	*Greek*	21
Manny's	*Seafood*	20
Marg. Kuo	*Chinese/Japanese*	23
Meridith's	*Amer.*	20
Mikado	*Japanese/Thai*	20
NEW MIXX	*Amer.*	17
Murray's Deli	*Deli*	18
Nectar	*Asian*	24
New Tavern	*Amer.*	21
Old Guard Hse.	*Amer.*	22
Olive Tree	*Greek*	23

Osaka | *Japanese*	23
Paddock/Devon | *Amer.*	15
Plate | *Amer.*	14
Primavera Pizza | *Pizza*	19
Pub/Penn Valley | *Eclectic*	19
Qdoba | *Mex.*	18
Z Rest. Alba | *Amer.*	27
Rist. Positano | *Italian*	20
Rist. Primavera | *Italian*	20
Ruby's | *Diner*	16
NEW Saffron | *Indian*	-
Sang Kee | *Chinese*	23
Z Savona | *Italian*	27
Shangrila | *Asian*	21
Silk Cuisine | *Thai*	21
Z Sola | *Amer.*	27
Susanna Foo's | *Asian*	24
Tango | *Amer.*	20
Taq. La Michoacana | *Mex.*	23
Teresa's Cafe | *Italian*	22
Teresa's Next Dr. | *Belgian*	22
333 Belrose | *Amer.*	22
Tiffin | *Indian*	25
Tratt. San Nicola | *Italian*	22
NEW Verdad | *Spanish*	19
Victory Brewing | *Pub*	17
Winberie's | *Amer.*	17
Z Yangming | *Chinese/Continental*	25

MONTGOMERY COUNTY

Abacus | *Chinese*	24
AllWays Café | *Eclectic*	23
Arpeggio | *Med.*	23
Athena | *Greek/Seafood*	22
Baja Fresh | *Mex.*	17
Bay Pony Inn | *Amer.*	21
Beige & Beige | *Eclectic*	17
Ben & Irv Deli | *Deli*	19
Benihana | *Japanese*	19
Bensí | *Italian*	17
Blackfish | *Amer./Seafood*	25
Blue Bell Inn | *Amer.*	20
Z Bluefin | *Japanese*	28
Bocelli | *Italian*	20
Bonefish Grill | *Seafood*	21
Bonjung Japanese | *Japanese*	26
Brasserie 73 | *French*	22
NEW Brick House | *Amer.*	17
Bridget's Steak | *Amer./Steak*	23

Broad Axe Tav. | *Amer.*	16
Cafe Preeya | *Eclectic*	21
California Pizza | *Pizza*	19
Cheesecake | *Amer.*	20
Chiangmai | *Thai*	25
Coyote Cross. | *Mex.*	21
Dave & Buster's | *Amer.*	12
NEW Dettera | *Amer.*	21
East Cuisine | *Chinese/Japanese*	21
El Sarape | *Mex.*	23
Fayette St. | *Amer.*	23
Fountain Side | *Amer./Italian*	20
From the Boot | *Italian*	21
Funky Lil' Kitchen | *Amer.*	25
FuziOn | *Asian*	21
Gaya | *Korean*	-
Gen. Lafayette | *Amer.*	18
Gypsy Saloon | *Amer./Italian*	22
Han Dynasty | *Chinese*	24
Hibachi | *Japanese*	18
Iron Hill | *Amer.*	19
J.B. Dawson's/Austin's | *Amer.*	18
Joseph Ambler | *Amer.*	21
K.C.'s Alley | *Pub*	16
NEW Kumo Asian | *Asian*	-
Lai Lai Garden | *Asian*	19
La Pergola | *East Euro./Mideast.*	19
Little Marakesh | *Moroccan*	-
NEW MaGerks | *Amer.*	15
Mandarin Gdn. | *Chinese*	22
Marco Polo | *Italian*	20
Max & David's | *Med.*	21
Miraku | *Japanese*	-
Mirna's Café | *Eclectic/Med.*	22
Ooka | *Japanese*	24
Otto's Brauhaus | *German*	19
Palace of Asia | *Indian*	22
Parc Bistro | *Amer.*	23
Persian Grill | *Persian*	21
P.F. Chang's | *Chinese*	20
Phil's Tav. | *Amer.*	18
Pho Thai Nam | *Thai/Viet.*	23
Pistachio Grille | *Amer./Med.*	20
P.J. Whelihan's | *Pub*	16
Redstone | *Amer.*	20
Ristorante Castello | *Italian*	17
Rist. San Marco | *Italian*	26
Roberto's Tratt. | *Italian*	19
NEW Saffron | *Indian*	-
Scoogi's | *Italian*	19

Restaurant	Cuisine	Rating
Shanachie	Indian	13
Sly Fox	Pub	13
Spring Mill	French	24
Stella Blu	Amer.	21
Sushikazu	Japanese	-
Tamarindo's	Mex.	21
NEW Tavolo	Italian	21
Tex Mex Connect.	Tex-Mex	17
Thai Orchid	Thai	24
Tiffin	Indian	25
Totaro's	Eclectic	24
Trax Café	Amer.	22
211 York	Amer.	22
White Elephant	Thai	24
William Penn	Amer./Continental	20
Yalda Grill	Mideast.	22
Zacharias	Amer.	24
Zakes Cafe	Amer.	23

Lancaster/ Berks Counties

ADAMSTOWN

Stoudt's	Amer.	19

BIRD-IN-HAND

Bird-in-Hand	PA Dutch	20
Plain/Fancy Farm	PA Dutch	19

EAST EARL

Shady Maple	PA Dutch	20

EAST PETERSBURG

Haydn Zug's	Amer.	23

EPHRATA

Isaac's	Deli	17
Z Lily's on Main	Amer.	24

LANCASTER

Checkers Bistro	Eclectic	-
El Serrano	Nuevo Latino	22
Five Guys	Burgers	22
Z Gibraltar	Med./Seafood	23
Gusto	Italian	21
Iron Hill	Amer.	19
Isaac's	Deli	17
J.B. Dawson's/Austin's	Amer.	18
Lancaster Dispensing	Pub	-
Lemon Grass	Thai	20
Qdoba	Mex.	18

LITITZ

Isaac's	Deli	17

PINE FORGE

Gracie's	Eclectic	-

READING

Green Hills Inn	Amer./French	-
J.B. Dawson's/Austin's	Amer.	18

RONKS

Miller's Smorgas.	PA Dutch	18

SMOKETOWN

Good/Plenty	PA Dutch	18

STRASBURG

Isaac's	Deli	17

WYOMISSING

Bensí	Italian	17
Isaac's	Deli	17

New Jersey

BORDENTOWN

Chickie's/Pete's	Pub	18
Mastoris	Diner	20

BURLINGTON

Café Gallery	Continental	20

CHERRY HILL

Bahama Breeze	Carib.	17
Bobby Chez	Seafood	22
Brio	Italian	19
Caffe Aldo	Italian	24
Z Capital Grille	Steak	26
Cheesecake	Amer.	20
Dream Café	French	-
Five Guys	Burgers	22
Kibitz Room	Deli	21
Kuzina	Greek	22
La Campagne	French	22
Maggiano's	Italian	20
McCormick/Schmick	Seafood	21
Megu	Japanese	26
Mikado	Japanese	23
Mirabella	Italian	23
Norma's	Mideast.	22
P.J. Whelihan's	Pub	16
Ponzio's	Diner	20

LOCATIONS

Red Hot/Blue	*BBQ*	16
Sakura Spring	*Chinese/Japanese*	22
Seasons 52	*Amer.*	-
🄩 Siri's	*French/Thai*	26
William Douglas	*Steak*	24

CINNAMINSON

Five Guys	*Burgers*	22

CLEMENTON

Filomena	*Italian*	22
Nifty Fifty's	*Diner*	19

COLLINGSWOOD

Barone's/Villa Barone	*Italian*	22
Bistro di Marino	*Italian*	23
Blackbird	*Amer.*	25
Bobby Chez	*Seafood*	22
Casona	*Cuban*	20
🄩 Il Fiore	*Italian*	26
Joe Pesce	*Italian/Seafood*	21
Nunzio	*Italian*	24
Pop Shop	*Amer.*	21
🄩 Sagami	*Japanese*	27
Sapori	*Italian*	25
Tortilla Press	*Mex.*	23

DEPTFORD

Bonefish Grill	*Seafood*	21
Filomena	*Italian*	22
Five Guys	*Burgers*	22

GIBBSBORO

Chophouse	*Seafood/Steak*	24

HADDONFIELD

🄩 Fuji	*Japanese*	27
Little Tuna	*Seafood*	19
Mélange	*Creole/Southern*	25
P.J. Whelihan's	*Pub*	16

HADDON HEIGHTS

Anthony's	*Italian*	22
Elements Café	*Amer.*	22

LAMBERTVILLE

Anton's/Swan	*Amer.*	22
DeAnna's	*Italian*	24
Full Moon	*Eclectic*	18
Hamilton's	*Med.*	24
Inn/Hawke	*Amer.*	20
Lambertville Station	*Amer.*	18
Lilly's/Canal	*Eclectic*	21
Manon	*French*	24

No. 9	*Amer.*	24
Ota-Ya	*Japanese*	23
Rick's	*Italian*	20

LINDENWOLD

La Esperanza	*Mex.*	25

MAPLE SHADE

Mikado	*Japanese*	23
Penang	*Malaysian/Thai*	21
P.J. Whelihan's	*Pub*	16
Tacconelli's	*Pizza*	25

MARLTON

Bonefish Grill	*Seafood*	21
Fleming's	*Steak*	24
Joe's Peking	*Chinese*	22
Mexican Food	*Mex.*	19
Mikado	*Japanese*	23
P.F. Chang's	*Chinese*	20
Pietro's Pizza	*Pizza*	21
Pizzicato	*Italian*	19
Redstone	*Amer.*	20

MEDFORD

Braddock's	*Amer.*	20
Ted's/Main	*Amer.*	26

MEDFORD LAKES

P.J. Whelihan's	*Pub*	16

MOORESTOWN

Barone's/Villa Barone	*Italian*	22
Five Guys	*Burgers*	22

MOUNT EPHRAIM

Five Guys	*Burgers*	22

MOUNT HOLLY

High St.	*Amer.*	21
Robin's Nest	*Amer.*	22

MOUNT LAUREL

Baja Fresh	*Mex.*	17
Bobby Chez	*Seafood*	22
El Azteca	*Mex.*	19
GG's	*Amer.*	26
NEW Très Elena	*Asian*	-

PENNSAUKEN

Benihana	*Japanese*	19
Pub	*Steak*	19
Tortilla Press	*Mex.*	23

Menus, photos, voting and more – free at ZAGAT.com

SEWELL

Barnsboro Inn	*Amer.*	22
Bobby Chez	*Seafood*	22
P.J. Whelihan's	*Pub*	16

SICKLERVILLE

Five Guys	*Burgers*	22

TURNERSVILLE

Nifty Fifty's	*Diner*	19

VOORHEES

Ariana	*Afghan*	22
Baja Fresh	*Mex.*	17
Ø Catelli	*Italian*	25
Chez Elena Wu	*Chinese/Japanese*	22
Coconut Bay	*Asian*	23
Five Guys	*Burgers*	22
La Locanda	*Italian*	25
Little Café	*Eclectic*	24
Ritz Seafood	*Asian/Seafood*	25

WESTMONT

Cork	*Amer.*	22
Ø Giumarello's	*Italian*	26

Delaware

BEAR

Jake's Hamburg.	*Burgers*	20

CENTERVILLE

Buckley's	*Amer.*	18

GREENVILLE

Brew HaHa!	*Coffee*	17

HOCKESSIN

Back Burner	*Amer.*	22
2 Fat Guys	*Amer.*	22

MONTCHANIN

Ø Krazy Kat's	*French*	25

NEWARK

Iron Hill	*Amer.*	19

NEW CASTLE

Jake's Hamburg.	*Burgers*	20

WILMINGTON

Blue Parrot	*Cajun*	17
Brew HaHa!	*Coffee*	17
Capers/Lemons	*Italian*	22
Charcoal Pit	*Burgers*	20
China Royal	*Chinese*	17
NEW Columbus Inn	*Amer.*	-
Corner Bistro	*Eclectic*	19
Culinaria	*Amer.*	23
Deep Blue	*Seafood*	22
Dom. Hudson	*Amer.*	24
Eclipse Bistro	*Amer.*	23
Feby's Fish.	*Seafood*	21
NEW FireStone	*Amer.*	-
Five Guys	*Burgers*	22
Green Room	*French*	24
Harry's Savoy	*Amer.*	24
Harry's Seafood	*Seafood*	25
Hibachi	*Japanese*	18
Iron Hill	*Amer.*	19
Jake's Hamburg.	*Burgers*	20
Jasmine	*Asian*	23
Lamberti's	*Italian*	18
La Tolteca	*Mex.*	20
Lucky's Coffee	*Amer.*	15
Mexican Post	*Mex.*	16
Ø Mikimotos	*Asian/Japanese*	25
Ø Moro	*Med.*	26
Mrs. Robino's	*Italian*	14
Orillas Tapas	*Spanish*	23
Pomodoro	*Italian*	-
Rasa Sayang	*Malaysian*	25
Sullivan's Steak	*Steak*	23
Toscana Kit.	*Italian*	24
Union City Grille	*Steak*	22
Walter's Steak.	*Steak*	22
Wash. St. Ale	*Pub*	15

LOCATIONS

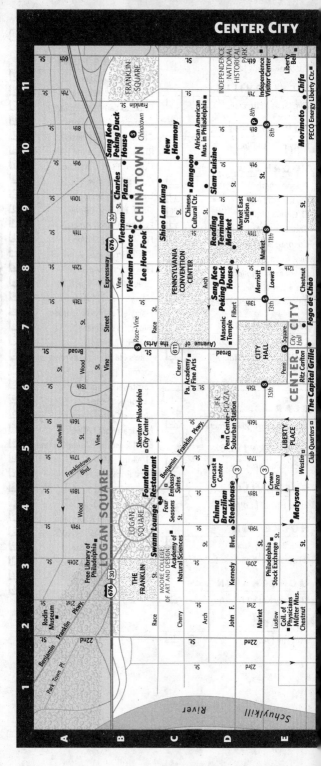

Menus, photos, voting and more – free at ZAGAT.com

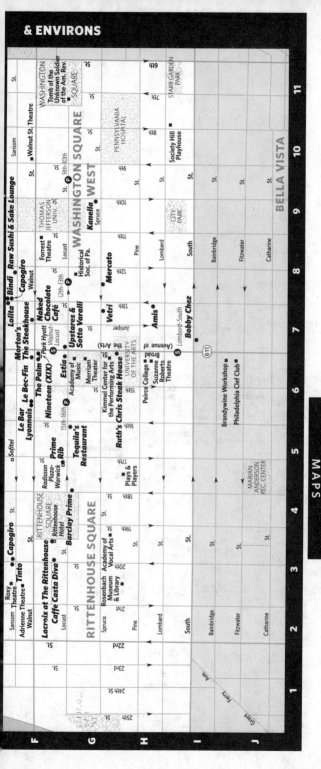

& ENVIRONS

RITTENHOUSE SQUARE

WASHINGTON SQUARE

WASHINGTON WEST

BELLA VISTA

WASHINGTON SQUARE — Tomb of the Unknown Soldier of the Am. Rev.

Walnut St. Theatre

Sansom

Raw Sushi & Sake Lounge

Bindi · Capogiro · Lolita

Morton's · The Steakhouse

Le Bec-Fin · Le Bar Lyonnais

Naked Chocolate Café

The Palm · Capogiro

Nineteen (XIX) · Prime Rib

Upstares & Sotto Varalli

Vetri · Mercato

Estia · Amis

Bobby Chez

Kanella

Vetri

Tequila's Restaurant

Ruth's Chris Steak House

Kimmel Center for the Performing Arts

Academy of Music

Merriam Theater

UNIVERSITY OF THE ARTS

Peirce College

Suzanne Roberts Theatre

Brandywine Workshop

Philadelphia Clef Club

Park Hyatt

Forrest Theatre

Historical Soc. of Pa.

THOMAS JEFFERSON UNIV.

PENNSYLVANIA HOSPITAL

Society Hill Playhouse

STARR GARDEN PARK

CITY PARK

Lacroix at The Rittenhouse

Caffe Casta Diva

Barclay Prime

Radisson Plaza-Warwick

Sofitel

Roxy Theatre · Capogiro

Adrienne Theatre · Tinto

Sansom

RITTENHOUSE SQUARE

Rittenhouse Hotel

Academy of Vocal Arts

Rosenbach Museum & Library

Plays & Players

MARIAN ANDERSON REC. CENTER

Walnut

Locust

Spruce

Pine

Lombard

South

Bainbridge

Fitzwater

Catharine

Lombard-South

Walnut-Locust

9th-10th

15th-16th

25th · 24th St. · 23rd · 22nd · 21st · 20th · 19th · 18th · 17th

Broad (Avenue of the Arts)

15th · 12th-13th · Juniper · 13th · 12th · 11th · 10th · 9th · 8th · 7th · 6th

611

Grays Ferry Ave

MAPS

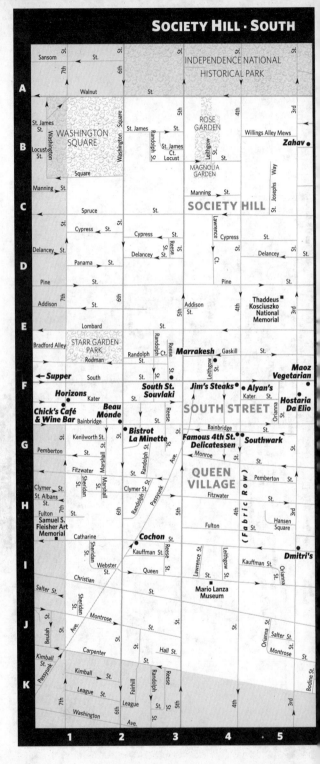

SOCIETY HILL · SOUTH

Menus, photos, voting and more – free at ZAGAT.com

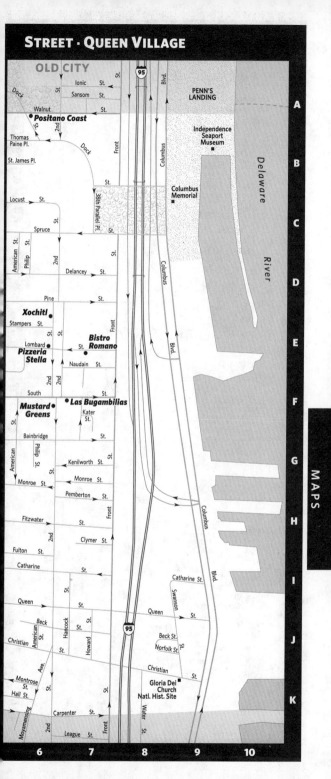

STREET · QUEEN VILLAGE

OLD CITY

Ionic St.
Sansom St.
Dock St.
95
Blvd.

PENN'S
LANDING

Walnut St.
● Positano Coast
2nd St.

Thomas
Paine Pl.
Dock

St. James Pl.

Front

Independence
Seaport
Museum

Columbus

Delaware

St.

Columbus
Memorial ■

Locust St.

38th Parallel Pl.

Spruce St.

American St.
Philip
2nd St.

St.

Columbus

River

Delancey St.

Pine St.

Front

Xochitl ●

Stampers St.

2nd St.

St.

Lombard ● St.
Pizzeria
Stella

Bistro
Romano

Blvd.

Naudain St.

2nd St.

South St.

Mustard ● ● Las Bugambilias
Greens

Kater
St.

St.

Bainbridge St.

American

Philip St.

Kenilworth St.

Monroe St.
Monroe St.

Pemberton St.

Front

Columbus

Fitzwater St.

2nd

Clymer St.

Fulton St.

Catharine St.

St.

Catharine St.

Blvd.

Queen St.

Queen St.

Swanson St.

Beck St.

American St.

Hancock St.

St.

95

Beck St.

Norfolk St.

St.

Christian St.

St.

Howard

Christian St.

Montrose St.

Ave.

St.

St.

Gloria Dei
Church
Natl. Hist. Site ■

Hall St.

Moyamensing

2nd

Carpenter St.

Front

Water St.

League St.

6   7   8   9   10

A B C D E F G H I J K

MAPS

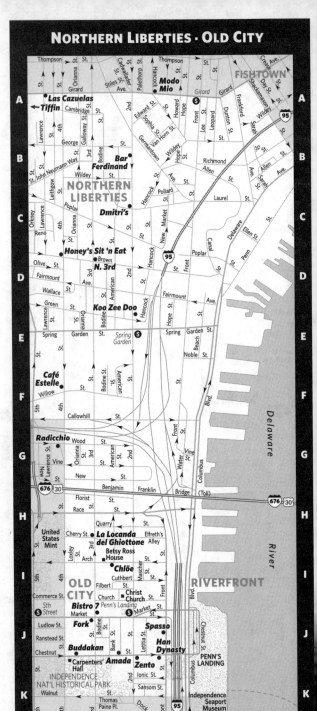

NORTHERN LIBERTIES · OLD CITY

Menus, photos, voting and more - free at ZAGAT.com

Special Features

Listings cover the best in each category and include names, locations and Food ratings. Multi-location restaurants' features may vary by branch.

BREAKFAST

(See also Hotel Dining)

Ardmore Station | **Ardmore**	18
Ben & Irv Deli | **Hunt Vly**	19
Bird-in-Hand | **Bird-in-Hand/LB**	20
Carman's Country | **S Philly**	26
Darling's | **multi.**	17
Down Home | **Chinatown**	17
Famous 4th St. Deli | **South St**	24
Full Moon | **Lambertville/NJ**	18
Hank's Place | **Chadds Ford**	21
Honey's Sit | **N Liberties**	25
Hymie's Deli | **Merion Sta**	19
🔣 La Colombe | **Rittenhouse**	24
La Lupe | **S Philly**	21
Little Pete's | **Rittenhouse**	18
Marathon Grill | **multi.**	18
Mastoris | **Bordentown/NJ**	20
Max Brenner | **Rittenhouse**	19
Mayfair Diner | **NE Philly**	15
Melrose Diner | **S Philly**	15
Morning Glory | **S Philly**	22
Murray's Deli | **Bala Cynwyd**	18
Nifty Fifty's | **multi.**	19
Ponzio's | **Cherry Hill/NJ**	20
Reading Terminal Mkt. | **Chinatown**	24
Ruby's | **multi.**	16
Sabrina's Café | **S Philly**	24
Sweet Lorraine's | **Lahaska**	17
Tierra Colombiana | **N Philly**	24
Trolley Car | **Mt Airy**	16

BRUNCH

Bay Pony Inn | **Lederach**	21
Beau Monde | **Queen Vill**	23
Black Bass | **Lumberville**	21
Black Sheep | **Rittenhouse**	17
Brick Hotel | **Newtown**	16
Buckley's | **Centerville/DE**	18
Café Gallery | **Burlington/NJ**	20
Cafette | **Ches Hill**	20
Caribou Cafe | **Washington Sq W**	21
Carman's Country | **S Philly**	26
Chart House | **DE River**	20
Cock 'n Bull | **Lahaska**	18

🆕 Columbus Inn | **Wilming/DE**	-
Continental | **Old City**	22
🔣 Cuba Libre | **Old City**	22
Dark Horse | **Society Hill**	19
Darling's | **multi.**	17
Epicurean | **Phoenixville**	20
Fadó Irish | **Rittenhouse**	17
Figs | **Fairmount**	23
🔣 Fork | **Old City**	24
🔣 Fountain | **Logan Sq**	28
Four Dogs | **W Chester**	20
Golden Pheasant | **Erwinna**	23
Green Room | **Wilming/DE**	24
Gullifty's | **Rosemont**	15
Hibachi | **DE River**	18
Iron Hill | **multi.**	19
Jack's Firehse. | **Fairmount**	19
Jake's | **Manayunk**	25
Jones | **Washington Sq W**	20
Khajuraho | **Ardmore**	20
Kildare's | **multi.**	16
Kimberton Inn | **Kimberton**	25
La Campagne | **Cherry Hill/NJ**	22
🔣 Lacroix | **Rittenhouse**	27
Lambertville Station | **Lambertville/NJ**	18
Las Cazuelas | **N Liberties**	24
Little Pete's | **Fairmount**	18
Marathon Grill | **multi.**	18
Marathon/Sq. | **Rittenhouse**	18
Max Brenner | **Rittenhouse**	19
Mixto | **Washington Sq W**	20
Monk's Cafe | **Rittenhouse**	22
More Than Ice Crm. | **Washington Sq W**	20
Morning Glory | **S Philly**	22
Moshulu | **DE River**	22
Newtown Grill | **Newtown Sq**	19
New Wave | **Queen Vill**	17
Nodding Head | **Rittenhouse**	19
Pace One | **Thornton**	21
Palace of Asia | **Ft Wash**	22
Plough & Stars | **Old City**	20
Rembrandt's | **Fairmount**	19
Robin's Nest | **Mt Holly/NJ**	22

Rx | **Univ City**	24
Solaris Grille | **Ches Hill**	14
Spring Mill | **Consho**	24
Standard Tap | **N Liberties**	22
Summer Kitchen | **Penns Park**	21
⚡ Swann Lounge | **Logan Sq**	26
Tango | **Bryn Mawr**	20
Tortilla Press | **Collingswood/NJ**	23
Valanni | **Washington Sq W**	24
Wash. Cross. | **Wash Cross**	20
White Dog | **Univ City**	20
William Penn | **Gwynedd**	20
Yardley Inn | **Yardley**	22

BUFFET

(Check availability)

America B&G | **Chester Springs**	18
Bay Pony Inn | **Lederach**	21
Bella Tori | **Langhorne**	18
Bird-in-Hand | **Bird-in-Hand/LB**	20
Bistro di Marino | **Collingswood/NJ**	23
Brandywine Prime | **Chadds Ford**	22
Brick Hotel | **Newtown**	16
Café Gallery | **Burlington/NJ**	20
Chinnar Indian | **Berwyn**	23
Cock 'n Bull | **Lahaska**	18
Dahlak | **Germantown**	22
Drafting Rm. | **Exton**	16
Ekta | **Bryn Mawr**	-
Fiorello's Café | **W Chester**	17
Georges' | **Wayne**	22
Green Room | **Wilming/DE**	24
Hibachi | **multi.**	18
Karma | **Old City**	21
Keating's | **DE River**	18
Khajuraho | **Ardmore**	20
Kingdom of Veg. | **Chinatown**	25
⚡ Lacroix | **Rittenhouse**	27
Limoncello | **W Chester**	23
Manayunk Brew. | **Manayunk**	17
Marg. Kuo Mandarin | **Frazer**	22
Miller's Smorgas. | **Ronks/LB**	18
New Delhi | **Univ City**	23
New Samosa | **Washington Sq W**	-
⚡ Nineteen | **Ave of Arts**	23
Otto's Brauhaus | **Horsham**	19
Paddock/Devon | **Wayne**	15
Palace of Asia | **Ft Wash**	22
Riverstone Café | **Exton**	18
NEW Saffron | **Bala Cynwyd**	-

Shady Maple | **East Earl/LB**	20
Sitar India | **Univ City**	18
⚡ Swann Lounge | **Logan Sq**	26
Sweet Lucy's | **NE Philly**	24
Tandoor India | **Univ City**	18
Wash. Cross. | **Wash Cross**	20
William Penn | **Gwynedd**	20
Winberie's | **Wayne**	17

BUSINESS DINING

⚡ Amada | **Old City**	28
NEW Amuse | **Ave of Arts**	-
NEW Apollinare | **N Liberties**	-
Azie | **multi.**	23
⚡ Barclay Prime | **Rittenhouse**	27
Bella Tori | **Langhorne**	18
Benihana | **Pennsauken/NJ**	19
Black Bass | **Lumberville**	21
Blackfish | **Consho**	25
Blue Bell Inn | **Blue Bell**	20
Blue Pear | **W Chester**	23
Bonefish Grill | **multi.**	21
Brandywine Prime | **Chadds Ford**	22
Broad Axe Tav. | **Ambler**	16
Butcher/Singer | **Rittenhouse**	24
⚡ Capital Grille | **Ave of Arts**	26
NEW Carluccio's | **S Philly**	25
⚡ Chifa | **Washington Sq W**	25
Chima | **Logan Sq**	21
Chops | **Bala Cynwyd**	21
NEW Columbus Inn | **Wilming/DE**	-
Del Frisco's | **Ave of Arts**	20
NEW Dettera | **Ambler**	21
Dilworth. Inn | **W Chester**	25
Doc Magrogan | **W Chester**	17
Dom. Hudson | **Wilming/DE**	24
NEW El Rey | **Rittenhouse**	-
⚡ Estia | **Ave of Arts**	25
NEW Firecreek | **Downingtown**	20
Fleming's | **Radnor**	24
Fogo de Chão | **Ave of Arts**	24
NEW Franco's Osteria | **Wynnefield**	-
⚡ Fuji | **Haddonfield/NJ**	27
Gen. Warren | **Malvern**	25
Georges' | **Wayne**	22
Girasole | **Ave of Arts**	21
Green Room | **Wilming/DE**	24
NEW Harvest | **Glen Mills**	-
⚡ Il Fiore | **Collingswood/NJ**	26

Menus, photos, voting and more – free at ZAGAT.com

Il Portico	**Rittenhouse**	21
J.B. Dawson's/Austin's	**multi.**	18
Joe Pesce	**Washington Sq W**	21
La Veranda	**DE River**	22
Ø Le Bec-Fin	**Rittenhouse**	27
Le Castagne	**Rittenhouse**	25
Legal Sea	**King of Prussia**	19
Marg. Kuo	**Wayne**	23
McCormick/Schmick	**multi.**	21
Morton's	**Ave of Arts**	26
Newtown Grill	**Newtown Sq**	19
Ø Nineteen	**Ave of Arts**	23
Noble Cookery	**Rittenhouse**	20
Ø Osteria	**N Philly**	27
Oyster House	**Rittenhouse**	23
Palm	**Ave of Arts**	24
Parc Bistro	**Skippack**	23
NEW Parker's Prime	**Newtown Sq**	21
NEW Paul	**Washington Sq W**	22
P.F. Chang's	**multi.**	20
Phillips Sea.	**Logan Sq**	16
Pietro's Prime	**W Chester**	23
Ø Prime Rib	**Rittenhouse**	27
Privé	**Old City**	21
Rist. Panorama	**Old City**	23
Rouget	**Newtown**	24
Ø NEW R2L	**Rittenhouse**	21
Ruth's Chris	**multi.**	23
Saloon	**S Philly**	24
NEW Sampan	**Washington Sq W**	21
Ø Savona	**Gulph Mills**	27
Smith/Wollensky	**Rittenhouse**	22
NEW Sprig & Vine	**New Hope**	–
NEW Square 1682	**Rittenhouse**	21
Sullivan's Steak	**multi.**	23
Susanna Foo's	**Radnor**	24
Table 31	**Logan Sq**	21
Tavern 17	**Rittenhouse**	16
Ted's Montana	**Warrington**	18
Ø 10 Arts	**Ave of Arts**	22
Time	**Washington Sq W**	20
Toscana 52	**Feasterville**	20
NEW Très Elena	**Mt Laurel/NJ**	–
NEW Tweed	**Washington Sq W**	–
Ø Union Trust	**Washington Sq W**	24
NEW Verdad	**Bryn Mawr**	19
Washington Hse.	**Sellersville**	–
Water Works	**Fairmount**	21

| William Douglas | **Cherry Hill/NJ** | 24 |
| **Ø** Zahav | **Society Hill** | 25 |

BYO

Abacus	**Lansdale**	24
NEW A La Maison	**Ardmore**	–
Alyan's	**South St**	24
Anthony's	**Haddon Hts/NJ**	22
Aqua	**Washington Sq W**	21
Arbol Café	**N Liberties**	17
Ariana	**multi.**	22
Arpeggio	**Spring House**	23
Athena	**Glenside**	22
Audrey Claire	**Rittenhouse**	23
August	**S Philly**	25
Augusto's	**Warminster**	–
Auspicious	**Ardmore**	19
Avalon	**W Chester**	25
NEW Avril	**Bala Cynwyd**	14
Aya's Café	**Logan Sq**	19
Banana Leaf	**Chinatown**	21
Barone's/Villa Barone	**multi.**	22
Beige & Beige	**Hunt Vly**	17
Beijing	**Univ City**	17
Bellini Grill	**Rittenhouse**	21
Ø Bibou	**S Philly**	27
Bindi	**Washington Sq W**	24
Ø Birchrunville Store	**Birchrunville**	28
Bistro di Marino	**Collingswood/NJ**	23
Bistro La Baia	**Graduate Hospital**	19
Bistro La Viola	**Rittenhouse**	24
Bistro 7	**Old City**	24
Blackbird	**Collingswood/NJ**	25
Blackfish	**Consho**	25
Ø Bluefin	**Plymouth Meeting**	28
Ø Blue Sage	**Southampton**	26
Bobby Chez	**multi.**	22
Bocelli	**multi.**	20
Bona Cucina	**Upper Darby**	23
Bonjung Japanese	**Collegeville**	26
Branzino	**Rittenhouse**	23
Bunha Faun	**Malvern**	24
Café Con Chocolate	**S Philly**	–
Cafe de Laos	**S Philly**	24
Café Estelle	**N Liberties**	23
Cafe Preeya	**Hunt Vly**	21
Cafette	**Ches Hill**	20
Caffe Casta Diva	**Rittenhouse**	26
Caffe Valentino	**S Philly**	22

Cake	**Ches Hill**	20	**NEW** Gemelli	**Narberth**	23
NEW Carluccio's	**S Philly**	25	**Z** Gilmore's	**W Chester**	28
Carman's Country	**S Philly**	26	Giwa	**Rittenhouse**	23
Casona	**Collingswood/NJ**	20	Gnocchi	**South St**	19
Catherine's	**Unionville**	28	Gold Standard	**W Philly**	17
Chabaa Thai	**Manayunk**	25	Golosa	**S Philly**	26
Charles Plaza	**Chinatown**	24	**NEW** Green Eggs	**S Philly**	26
Chez Elena Wu	**Voorhees/NJ**	22	Green Hills Inn	**Reading/LB**	-
Chiangmai	**Consho**	25	Ha Long Bay	**Bryn Mawr**	21
Chiarella's	**S Philly**	22	Hamilton's	**Lambertville/NJ**	24
Chinnar Indian	**Berwyn**	23	Han Dynasty	**multi.**	24
Chlöe	**Old City**	26	Hank's Place	**Chadds Ford**	21
Chun Hing	**Wynnefield**	22	Honey's Sit	**N Liberties**	25
Cochon	**Queen Vill**	26	**NEW** Hoof + Fin	**Queen Vill**	-
Coconut Bay	**Voorhees/NJ**	23	Hostaria Da Elio	**South St**	23
Copabanana	**Univ City**	17	Hunan	**Ardmore**	-
Cucina Forte	**S Philly**	26	Il Cantuccio	**N Liberties**	21
Daddy Mims	**Phoenixville**	23	**Z** Il Fiore	**Collingswood/NJ**	26
Darling's	**N Liberties**	17	Inn/Phillips Mill	**New Hope**	25
Day by Day	**Rittenhouse**	23	Isaac's	**multi.**	17
Z Dmitri's	**multi.**	24	Izumi	**S Philly**	25
NEW Doma	**Logan Sq**	-	Jamaican Jerk	**Ave of Arts**	19
Dream Café	**Cherry Hill/NJ**	-	Joe Pesce	**Collingswood/NJ**	21
Duck Sauce	**Newtown**	24	Joe's Peking	**Marlton/NJ**	22
Du Jour	**Haverford**	18	Jong Ka Jib	**E Oak Ln**	25
East Cuisine	**Ambler**	21	Kabobeesh	**Univ City**	26
Effie's	**Washington Sq W**	21	Kabul	**Old City**	21
Ekta	**Bryn Mawr**	-	Kanella	**Washington Sq W**	25
El Azteca	**Mt Laurel/NJ**	19	Kaya's	**Havertown**	19
Elements Café	**Haddon Hts/NJ**	22	Khajuraho	**Ardmore**	20
Famous 4th St. Deli	**multi.**	24	Kibitz Room	**multi.**	21
NEW Fat Salmon	**Washington Sq W**	-	Kingdom of Veg.	**Chinatown**	25
Fayette St.	**Consho**	23	King of Tandoor	**Fairmount**	23
Fellini Cafe	**Ardmore**	19	Kisso Sushi	**Old City**	25
Fellini Cafe	**Newtown Sq**	22	Kotatsu	**Ardmore**	24
Figs	**Fairmount**	23	**NEW** Kumo Asian	**N Wales**	-
Flavor	**Wayne**	19	Kuzina	**Cherry Hill/NJ**	22
Z NEW Fond	**S Philly**	27	La Campagne	**Cherry Hill/NJ**	22
Fountain Side	**Horsham**	20	La Fontana	**Rittenhouse**	21
Four Rivers	**Chinatown**	26	La Locanda	**Voorhees/NJ**	25
From the Boot	**Lafayette Hill**	21	La Locanda/Ghiottone	**Old City**	24
Z Fuji	**Haddonfield/NJ**	27	La Lupe	**S Philly**	21
Full Moon	**Lambertville/NJ**	18	La Na	**Media**	18
Full Plate	**N Liberties**	19	L'Angolo	**S Philly**	26
Funky Lil' Kitchen	**Pottstown**	25	Langostini	**S Philly**	-
FuziOn	**Worcester**	21	La Pergola	**Jenkintown**	19
NEW Garces Trading	**Washington Sq W**	-	Las Cazuelas	**N Liberties**	24
Geechee Girl	**Germantown**	21	La Viola Ovest	**Rittenhouse**	23
			Lee How Fook	**Chinatown**	25

Restaurant	Location	Rating
Lemon Grass	multi.	20
NEW Le Viet	S Philly	–
Little Café	Voorhees/NJ	24
Little Marakesh	Dresher	–
Little Tuna	Haddonfield/NJ	19
L'Oca	Fairmount	23
Lolita	Washington Sq W	26
Lourdas Greek	Bryn Mawr	21
Majolica	Phoenixville	24
Mama Palma's	Rittenhouse	23
Mamma Maria	S Philly	22
Manny's	multi.	20
Manon	Lambertville/NJ	24
Marathon Grill	Ave of Arts	18
Marg. Kuo Mandarin	Frazer	22
Marigold Kitchen	Univ City	24
Masamoto	Glen Mills	26
Z Matyson	Rittenhouse	27
Max & David's	Elkins Pk	21
Megu	Cherry Hill/NJ	26
Mélange	Haddonfield/NJ	25
Melograno	Rittenhouse	24
Mercato	Washington Sq W	25
Meridith's	Berwyn	20
Mikado	multi.	23
Mi Lah Veg.	Rittenhouse	21
Minar Palace	Washington Sq W	18
Mirabella	Cherry Hill/NJ	23
Miraku	Spring House	–
Mirna's Café	multi.	22
Mizu	multi.	20
Modo Mio	N Liberties	26
NEW Momiji	Society Hill	–
More Than Ice Crm.	Washington Sq W	20
Z Mr. Martino's	S Philly	24
Ms. Tootsie's	South St	25
Nan	Univ City	26
Nan Zhou	Chinatown	23
New Harmony	Chinatown	22
New Samosa	Washington Sq W	–
Nicholas	S Philly	22
No. 9	Lambertville/NJ	24
Norma's	Cherry Hill/NJ	22
Novità Bistro	Graduate Hospital	18
Nunzio	Collingswood/NJ	24
Oishi	Newtown	25
Olive Tree	Downingtown	23
Ooka	Willow Grove	24
Orchard	Kennett Sq	27
Ota-Ya	multi.	23
NEW Paul	Washington Sq W	22
Penang	Maple Shade/NJ	21
Pho Thai Nam	Blue Bell	23
Piccolo Tratt.	multi.	22
Pistachio Grille	Maple Glen	20
Pop Shop	Collingswood/NJ	21
Porcini	Rittenhouse	23
PTG	Roxborough	23
Pumpkin	Graduate Hospital	26
Pura Vida	N Liberties	–
Radicchio	Old City	25
Ray's Cafe	Chinatown	23
Rick's	Lambertville/NJ	20
Ristorante Castello	N Wales	17
Riverstone	S Philly	25
Ritz Seafood	Voorhees/NJ	25
Rouget	Newtown	24
NEW Ro-Zu	S Philly	–
Rx	Univ City	24
Sabrina's Café	S Philly	24
NEW Saffron	multi.	–
Z Sagami	Collingswood/NJ	27
Sakura Spring	Cherry Hill/NJ	22
Salento	Rittenhouse	23
Salt & Pepper	S Philly	25
Sang Kee	Univ City	23
Sapori	Collingswood/NJ	25
Sazon	N Liberties	22
Scannicchio's	S Philly	23
Shiao Lan Kung	Chinatown	23
Siam Cuisine	Newtown	22
Silk Cuisine	Bryn Mawr	21
Singapore Kosher	Chinatown	20
Z Siri's	Cherry Hill/NJ	26
SLiCE	multi.	22
Z Sola	Bryn Mawr	27
NEW Sonata	N Liberties	23
NEW Sprig & Vine	New Hope	–
Spring Mill	Consho	24
Summer Kitchen	Penns Park	21
Sushikazu	Blue Bell	–
Sweet Basil	Chadds Ford	23
Sweet Lucy's	NE Philly	24
Sycamore	Lansdowne	–
Tacconelli's	multi.	25
Z Talula's Table	Kennett Sq	27
Tamarindo's	Broad Axe	21
Tampopo	multi.	22
Tandoor India	Univ City	18

Taq. La Veracruz. | **S Philly**	23	Dahlak | **W Philly**	22
NEW Tavolo | **Hunt Vly**	21	Day by Day | **Rittenhouse**	23
Ted's/Main | **Medford/NJ**	26	El Azteca I | **Washington Sq W**	20
Thai Orchid | **Blue Bell**	24	Famous 4th St. Deli | **South St**	24
Tiffin | **multi.**	25	Fayette St. | **Consho**	23
NEW Tiffin etc. | **N Liberties**	23	Feby's Fish. | **Wilming/DE**	21
Tortilla Press | **Collingswood/NJ**	23	Figs | **Fairmount**	23
Trattoria Giuseppe | **Newtown Sq**	–	FuziOn | **Worcester**	21
Trax Café | **Ambler**	22	Havana | **New Hope**	18
Tre Scalini | **S Philly**	24	Hibachi | **Jenkintown**	18
Trio | **Fairmount**	24	Hunan | **Ardmore**	–
Trolley Car | **East Falls**	16	Hymie's Deli | **Merion Sta**	19
Z Umai Umai | **Fairmount**	26	Isaac's | **Lititz/LB**	17
Umbria | **Mt Airy**	24	Jack's Firehse. | **Fairmount**	19
Uzu Sushi | **Old City**	23	Jamaican Jerk | **Ave of Arts**	19
Vientiane Café | **W Philly**	23	Joe's Peking | **Marlton/NJ**	22
White Elephant | **Hunt Vly**	24	Joy Tsin Lau | **Chinatown**	20
Yalda Grill | **Horsham**	22	Kabul | **Old City**	21
Zacharias | **Worcester**	24	Karma | **Old City**	21
Zakes Cafe | **Ft Wash**	23	Khajuraho | **Ardmore**	20
Z Zento | **Old City**	26	Kibitz Room | **Cherry Hill/NJ**	21
Zorba's Taverna | **Fairmount**	20	Kildare's | **King of Prussia**	16
		Kisso Sushi | **Old City**	25
CATERING		Knight House | **Doylestown**	23
		Konak | **Old City**	23
Abacus | **Lansdale**	24	La Campagne | **Cherry Hill/NJ**	22
Abbaye | **N Liberties**	20	La Lupe | **S Philly**	21
Adobe Cafe | **Roxborough**	20	Lamberti's | **Wilming/DE**	18
Al Dar Bistro | **Bala Cynwyd**	19	La Pergola | **Jenkintown**	19
Alyan's | **South St**	24	Las Cazuelas | **N Liberties**	24
Ardmore Station | **Ardmore**	18	**Z** Le Bar Lyonnais | **Rittenhouse**	27
Athena | **Glenside**	22	**Z** Le Bec-Fin | **Rittenhouse**	27
August Moon | **Norristown**	20	Lemon Grass | **Lancaster/LB**	20
Augusto's | **Warminster**	–	Little Café | **Voorhees/NJ**	24
Barone's/Villa Barone | **multi.**	22	Little Marakesh | **Dresher**	–
Beijing | **Univ City**	17	Little Tuna | **Haddonfield/NJ**	19
Bellini Grill | **Rittenhouse**	21	Lourdas Greek | **Bryn Mawr**	21
Ben & Irv Deli | **Hunt Vly**	19	Mamma Maria | **S Philly**	22
Bistro St. Tropez | **Rittenhouse**	19	Marathon Grill | **multi.**	18
Bitar's | **S Philly**	25	Marathon/Sq. | **Rittenhouse**	18
Z Blue Sage | **Southampton**	26	Marg. Kuo Mandarin | **Frazer**	22
Bomb Bomb BBQ | **S Philly**	23	Maria's/Summit | **Roxborough**	21
Brick Hotel | **Newtown**	16	Mendenhall Inn | **Mendenhall**	19
Buca di Beppo | **Exton**	16	Moonstruck | **NE Philly**	21
Caffe Aldo | **Cherry Hill/NJ**	24	Moriarty's | **Washington Sq W**	20
Campo's Deli | **Old City**	23	**Z** Moro | **Wilming/DE**	26
Caribou Cafe | **Washington Sq W**	21	Mrs. Robino's | **Wilming/DE**	14
Z Catelli | **Voorhees/NJ**	25	Murray's Deli | **Bala Cynwyd**	18
Cedars | **South St**	22	No. 9 | **Lambertville/NJ**	24
Copabanana | **Univ City**	17		
Z Cuba Libre | **Old City**	22		

Norma's	**Cherry Hill/NJ**	22
Old Guard Hse.	**Gladwyne**	22
Otto's Brauhaus	**Horsham**	19
Pace One	**Thornton**	21
☑ Pat's Steaks	**S Philly**	21
Persian Grill	**Lafayette Hill**	21
Pho Xe Lua	**Chinatown**	24
Pizzicato	**Old City**	19
Red Hot/Blue	**Cherry Hill/NJ**	16
Rx	**Univ City**	24
Sabrina's Café	**S Philly**	24
Sang Kee	**Chinatown**	23
Seafood Unltd.	**Rittenhouse**	21
Shiroi Hana	**Rittenhouse**	24
Silk Cuisine	**Bryn Mawr**	21
☑ Siri's	**Cherry Hill/NJ**	26
Sitar India	**Univ City**	18
Tandoor India	**Univ City**	18
Tango	**Bryn Mawr**	20
Tex Mex Connect.	**N Wales**	17
Thai Singha	**Univ City**	22
333 Belrose	**Radnor**	22
Tierra Colombiana	**N Philly**	24
Trax Café	**Ambler**	22
Vesuvio	**S Philly**	14
Victor Café	**S Philly**	20
Vientiane Café	**W Philly**	23
White Elephant	**Hunt Vly**	24
Yardley Inn	**Yardley**	22

CELEBRITY CHEFS

Kiong Banh
Twenty Manning | **Rittenhouse** —

Jim Burke
☑ James | **S Philly** 27

Ralph Fernandez
Moshulu | **DE River** 22

Patrick Feury
Nectar | **Berwyn** 24

Bobby Flay
NEW Bobby's Burger | **Univ City** —

Susanna Foo
Susanna Foo's | **Radnor** 24

Jose Garces
☑ Amada | **Old City** 28
☑ Chifa | **Washington Sq W** 25
☑ Distrito | **Univ City** 25
NEW Garces Trading | **Washington Sq W** —

☑ Tinto | **Rittenhouse** 27
NEW Village Whiskey | **Rittenhouse** 24

Peter Gilmore
☑ Gilmore's | **W Chester** 28

Matt Ito
☑ Fuji | **Haddonfield/NJ** 27

Dionicio Jimenez
NEW El Rey | **Rittenhouse** —

Rich Landau
☑ Horizons | **South St** 27

Matthew Levin
☑ Lacroix | **Rittenhouse** 27

Michael McNally
London Grill | **Fairmount** 17

Masaharu Morimoto
☑ Morimoto | **Washington Sq W** 28

Nunzio Patruno
Nunzio | **Collingswood/NJ** 24

Guillermo Pernot
☑ Cuba Libre | **Old City** 22

Georges Perrier
Georges' | **Wayne** 22
☑ Le Bec-Fin | **Rittenhouse** 27

Georges Perrier/Chris Scarduzio
Table 31 | **Logan Sq** 21

Eric Ripert/Jennifer Carroll
☑ 10 Arts | **Ave of Arts** 22

Douglas Rodriguez
☑ Alma de Cuba | **Rittenhouse** 25

Michael Schulson
NEW Sampan | **Washington Sq W** 21

Gino Sena
La Famiglia | **Old City** 23

Bryan Sikora
☑ Talula's Table | **Kennett Sq** 27

Daniel Stern
NEW MidAtlantic | **Univ City** 20
☑NEW R2L | **Rittenhouse** 21

Scott Swiderski
☑ Buddakan | **Old City** 26

Francis Trzeciak
☑ Birchrunville Store | **Birchrunville** 28

Marc Vetri
NEW Amis | **Washington Sq W** 24
☑ Vetri | **Washington Sq W** 28

Marc Vetri/Jeff Michaud
☑ Osteria | **N Philly** 27

SPECIAL FEATURES

CHILD-FRIENDLY

(Alternatives to the usual fast-food places; * children's menu available)

Adobe Cafe* | **Roxborough**	20
Ardmore Station* | **Ardmore**	18
Ariana | **Old City**	22
Arpeggio* | **Spring House**	23
Athena | **Glenside**	22
Bahama Breeze* | **multi.**	17
Barone's/Villa Barone* | **multi.**	22
Bella Tratt.* | **Manayunk**	23
Ben & Irv Deli* | **Hunt Vly**	19
Bird-in-Hand* | **Bird-in-Hand/LB**	20
Bistro Romano* | **Society Hill**	22
Bitar's | **S Philly**	25
Blue Bell Inn* | **Blue Bell**	20
Bobby Chez | **multi.**	22
Bomb Bomb BBQ* | **S Philly**	23
Braddock's* | **Medford/NJ**	20
Brick Hotel* | **Newtown**	16
Bridget Foy's* | **South St**	19
Broad Axe Tav.* | **Ambler**	16
Buckley's* | **Centerville/DE**	18
Cafette* | **Ches Hill**	20
California Cafe* | **King of Prussia**	20
California Pizza* | **King of Prussia**	19
Campo's Deli* | **Old City**	23
☎ Capogiro | **multi.**	27
Charcoal Pit* | **Wilming/DE**	20
Chart House* | **DE River**	20
Cheesecake* | **King of Prussia**	20
Chestnut Grill* | **Ches Hill**	17
Chickie's/Pete's | **multi.**	18
Christopher's* | **Wayne**	16
City Tavern* | **Old City**	19
Cock 'n Bull* | **Lahaska**	–
NEW Columbus Inn* | **Wilming/DE**	–
Corner Bistro | **Wilming/DE**	19
Darling's* | **multi.**	17
Dave & Buster's* | **DE River**	12
Day by Day* | **Rittenhouse**	23
Delmonico's | **Wynnefield**	25
Devon Seafood* | **Rittenhouse**	23
DiNardo's* | **Old City**	19
Down Home* | **Chinatown**	17
Drafting Rm.* | **Exton**	16
Duling-Kurtz* | **Exton**	25
El Azteca* | **Mt Laurel/NJ**	19
El Azteca I* | **Washington Sq W**	20
Elephant/Castle* | **Rittenhouse**	11

Famous 4th St. Deli | **South St**	24
Feby's Fish.* | **Wilming/DE**	21
Fellini Cafe | **Ardmore**	19
Fellini Cafe | **Newtown Sq**	22
Filomena* | **multi.**	22
Four Dogs* | **W Chester**	20
Fuji Mtn. | **Rittenhouse**	20
FuziOn | **Worcester**	21
Geechee Girl | **Germantown**	21
Gen. Lafayette* | **Lafayette Hill**	18
Geno's Steaks | **S Philly**	18
☎ Gibraltar* | **Lancaster/LB**	23
Good/Plenty | **Smoketown/LB**	18
Gracie's* | **Pine Forge/LB**	–
Green Room* | **Wilming/DE**	24
Gullifty's* | **Rosemont**	15
Hank's Place* | **Chadds Ford**	21
Hard Rock* | **Chinatown**	13
Harry's Savoy* | **Wilming/DE**	24
Harry's Seafood* | **Wilming/DE**	25
Havana* | **New Hope**	18
Haydn Zug's* | **E Petersburg/LB**	23
Hibachi* | **multi.**	18
Honey's Sit* | **N Liberties**	25
Hymie's Deli* | **Merion Sta**	19
Il Portico | **Rittenhouse**	21
Inn/Hawke* | **Lambertville/NJ**	20
Iron Hill* | **multi.**	19
Isaac Newton's* | **Newtown**	17
Isaac's* | **multi.**	17
Italian Bistro* | **multi.**	17
Jack's Firehse.* | **Fairmount**	19
Jake's Hamburg. | **Wilming/DE**	20
J.B. Dawson's/Austin's* | **multi.**	18
Jim's Steaks* | **multi.**	23
Jones | **Washington Sq W**	20
Kabobeesh* | **Univ City**	26
Keating's* | **DE River**	18
Kibitz Room* | **Cherry Hill/NJ**	21
Kildare's* | **multi.**	16
Kimberton Inn | **Kimberton**	25
Konak* | **Old City**	23
La Campagne | **Cherry Hill/NJ**	22
La Esperanza* | **Lindenwold/NJ**	25
La Lupe | **S Philly**	21
Landing* | **New Hope**	18
La Pergola* | **Jenkintown**	19
Las Cazuelas | **N Liberties**	24
La Tolteca* | **Wilming/DE**	20
Little Pete's* | **multi.**	18

Little Tuna* | **Haddonfield/NJ**	19	
Maggiano's* | **multi.**	20	
Mama Palma's | **Rittenhouse**	23	
Mamma Maria | **S Philly**	22	
Manayunk Brew.* | **Manayunk**	17	
Mandarin Gdn. | **Willow Grove**	22	
Marathon Grill* | **multi.**	18	
Marathon/Sq.* | **Rittenhouse**	18	
Maria's/Summit* | **Roxborough**	21	
Marra's | **S Philly**	21	
Max Brenner* | **Rittenhouse**	19	
Mayfair Diner* | **NE Philly**	15	
McGillin's* | **Washington Sq W**	16	
Melrose Diner* | **S Philly**	15	
Mexican Food* | **Marlton/NJ**	19	
Mexican Post* | **Wilming/DE**	16	
Mikado | **Ardmore**	20	
Mikado | **Cherry Hill/NJ**	23	
Miller's Smorgas.* | **Ronks/LB**	18	
Mirna's Café* | **multi.**	22	
Moonstruck* | **NE Philly**	21	
Moriarty's* | **Washington Sq W**	20	
Moshulu* | **DE River**	22	
Mrs. Robino's* | **Wilming/DE**	14	
New Tavern* | **Bala Cynwyd**	21	
Nifty Fifty's* | **multi.**	19	
No. 9 | **Lambertville/NJ**	24	
Norma's* | **Cherry Hill/NJ**	22	
Old Guard Hse.* | **Gladwyne**	22	
Ooka* | **multi.**	24	
Ota-Ya | **Lambertville/NJ**	23	
Otto's Brauhaus* | **Horsham**	19	
Pace One* | **Thornton**	21	
Penne* | **Univ City**	18	
Persian Grill* | **Lafayette Hill**	21	
P.F. Chang's | **multi.**	20	
Pietro's Pizza* | **multi.**	21	
Pizzicato* | **multi.**	19	
Plate* | **Ardmore**	14	
Plough & Stars* | **Old City**	20	
Ponzio's* | **Cherry Hill/NJ**	20	
Pop Shop* | **Collingswood/NJ**	21	
Primavera Pizza* | **Ardmore**	19	
Pub* | **Pennsauken/NJ**	19	
Qdoba* | **multi.**	18	
Ralph's | **S Philly**	23	
Rangoon | **Chinatown**	23	
Red Hot/Blue* | **Cherry Hill/NJ**	16	
Rist. Positano | **Ardmore**	20	
Rist. Primavera* | **Wayne**	20	

Rock Bottom* | **King of Prussia**	14
Rose Tattoo | **Fairmount**	22
Ruby's* | **multi.**	16
Sabrina's Café | **S Philly**	24
🅉 Sagami | **Collingswood/NJ**	27
Scannicchio's | **S Philly**	23
Serrano | **Old City**	21
Seven Stars Inn* | **Phoenixville**	20
Shiao Lan Kung | **Chinatown**	23
Shiroi Hana | **Rittenhouse**	24
Siam Cuisine | **multi.**	22
Silk City | **N Liberties**	21
🅉 Siri's* | **Cherry Hill/NJ**	26
Sitar India | **Univ City**	18
Sketch Café* | **Fishtown**	24
Snockey's Oyster* | **S Philly**	21
Solaris Grille* | **Ches Hill**	14
South St. Souvlaki | **South St**	22
Spasso | **Old City**	23
Stoudt's* | **Adamstown/LB**	19
Sweet Lorraine's* | **Lahaska**	17
Sweet Lucy's* | **NE Philly**	24
Tamarindo's | **Broad Axe**	21
Tango* | **Bryn Mawr**	20
Teca | **W Chester**	23
Tex Mex Connect.* | **N Wales**	17
Tierra Colombiana* | **N Philly**	24
Tortilla Press* | **Collingswood/NJ**	23
Toscana Kit. | **Wilming/DE**	24
Totaro's* | **Consho**	24
Tre Scalini | **S Philly**	24
Trolley Car* | **Mt Airy**	16
Vesuvio* | **S Philly**	14
Victory Brewing* | **Downingtown**	17
Vietnam | **Chinatown**	25
Vietnam Palace | **Chinatown**	23
Villa di Roma | **S Philly**	23
Wash. Cross.* | **Wash Cross**	20
Wash. St. Ale* | **Wilming/DE**	15
White Dog* | **Univ City**	20
White Elephant | **Hunt Vly**	24
William Penn* | **Gwynedd**	20
Winberie's* | **Wayne**	17
Winnie's Le Bus* | **Manayunk**	21
🅉 Yangming | **Bryn Mawr**	25

DELIVERY/TAKEOUT

(D=delivery, T=takeout)

Abacus | D | **Lansdale**	24	
America B&G | D |	18	
Chester Springs		

Ardmore Station | D | **Ardmore** 18

August Moon | D | **Norristown** 20

Bahama Breeze | T | **Cherry Hill/NJ** 17

Beijing | D | **Univ City** 17

Ben & Irv Deli | D | **Hunt Vly** 19

Bobby Chez | T | **multi.** 22

Byblos | D | **Rittenhouse** 18

Campo's Deli | D | **Old City** 23

Cedars | D | **South St** 22

Celebre's | D | **S Philly** 24

Charcoal Pit | D | **Wilming/DE** 20

Charles Plaza | D | **Chinatown** 24

CinCin | D | **Ches Hill** 23

Copabanana | D | **Univ City** 17

Davio's | D | **Rittenhouse** 25

Day by Day | D | **Rittenhouse** 23

Effie's | D | **Washington Sq W** 21

Fez Moroccan | D | **South St** 19

Filomena | T | **multi.** 22

Fuji Mtn. | D | **Rittenhouse** 20

Full Moon | T | **Lambertville/NJ** 18

HighNote Cafe | D | **S Philly** 23

Hymie's Deli | D | **Merion Sta** 19

Italian Bistro | D | **Ave of Arts** 17

Joe's Peking | T | **Marlton/NJ** 22

Kingdom of Veg. | D | **Chinatown** 25

La Lupe | D | **S Philly** 21

Little Pete's | D | **multi.** 18

Marathon Grill | D | **multi.** 18

Marathon/Sq. | D | **Rittenhouse** 18

Marra's | D | **S Philly** 21

Mastoris | T | **Bordentown/NJ** 20

Mikado | D | **Ardmore** 20

Mikado | T | **Cherry Hill/NJ** 23

Mix | T | **Rittenhouse** 17

Murray's Deli | D | **Bala Cynwyd** 18

New Delhi | D | **Univ City** 23

New Harmony | D | **Chinatown** 22

Norma's | T | **Cherry Hill/NJ** 22

Ota-Ya | T | **Lambertville/NJ** 23

P.F. Chang's | T | **Marlton/NJ** 20

Seafood Unltd. | D | **Rittenhouse** 21

Shiroi Hana | D | **Rittenhouse** 24

Singapore Kosher | D | **Chinatown** 20

Sitar India | D | **Univ City** 18

Stella Blu | D | **W Consho** 21

Tandoor India | D | **Univ City** 18

Taq. La Veracruz. | D | **S Philly** 23

DINING ALONE

(Other than hotels and places with counter service)

AllWays Café | **Hunt Vly** 23

Ardmore Station | **Ardmore** 18

Beau Monde | **Queen Vill** 23

Ben & Irv Deli | **Hunt Vly** 19

Bitar's | **S Philly** 25

Black Sheep | **Rittenhouse** 17

Bobby Chez | **multi.** 22

Bonté Wafflerie | **multi.** 21

Brew HaHa! | **multi.** 17

Cafette | **Ches Hill** 20

Caribou Cafe | **Washington Sq W** 21

Charlie's Hamburg. | **Folsom** 23

Cheeseburger/Paradise | **Langhorne** 14

Chickie's/Pete's | **Bordentown/NJ** 18

Copabanana | **South St** 17

Criniti | **S Philly** 18

Dalessandro's | **Roxborough** 23

Devon Seafood | **Rittenhouse** 23

Down Home | **Chinatown** 17

Effie's | **Washington Sq W** 21

Famous 4th St. Deli | **South St** 24

Farmicia | **Old City** 22

Five Guys | **multi.** 22

Honey's Sit | **N Liberties** 25

🇿 Horizons | **South St** 27

Iron Hill | **Lancaster/LB** 19

Jake's Hamburg. | **New Castle/DE** 20

Jim's Steaks | **multi.** 23

🇿 John's Roast Pork | **S Philly** 27

K.C.'s Alley | **Ambler** 16

Kibitz Room | **Cherry Hill/NJ** 21

La Pergola | **Jenkintown** 19

Marathon Grill | **multi.** 18

Mayfair Diner | **NE Philly** 15

Mexican Post | **Old City** 16

Mizu | **Old City** 20

Monk's Cafe | **Rittenhouse** 22

Morning Glory | **S Philly** 22

New Samosa | **Washington Sq W** –

Nifty Fifty's | **multi.** 19

🇿 Pat's Steaks | **S Philly** 21

Pho 75 | **Chinatown** 22

P.J. Whelihan's | **Blue Bell** 16

Pop Shop | **Collingswood/NJ** 21

Positano Coast | **Society Hill** 21

Raw Sushi | **Washington Sq W** 25

Reading Terminal Mkt. | **Chinatown** | 24

Sang Kee | **Chinatown** | 23

Seafood Unltd. | **Rittenhouse** | 21

Sláinte | **Univ City** | 16

Steve's Steaks | **NE Philly** | 23

Tango | **Bryn Mawr** | 20

Ted's Montana | **Ave of Arts** | 18

Tony Luke's | **S Philly** | 26

Trolley Car | **Mt Airy** | 16

Zorba's Taverna | **Fairmount** | 20

ENTERTAINMENT

(Call for days and times of performances)

America B&G | bands | **Glen Mills** | 18

Bahama Breeze | Caribbean | **multi.** | 17

Bay Pony Inn | varies | **Lederach** | 21

Beau Monde | cabaret/DJ | **Queen Vill** | 23

Bella Cena | live music | **Rittenhouse** | 20

Bistro Romano | piano | **Society Hill** | 22

Blue Bell Inn | bands | **Blue Bell** | 20

Bourbon Blue | bands/DJ | **Manayunk** | 18

Buckley's | vocals | **Centerville/DE** | 18

Chickie's/Pete's | varies | **multi.** | 18

City Tavern | live music | **Old City** | 19

Cock 'n Bull | dinner theater | **Lahaska** | 18

Creed's | varies | **King of Prussia** | 24

☑ Cuba Libre | varies | **Old City** | 22

D'Angelo's | DJ | **Rittenhouse** | 24

Deep Blue | jazz/rock bands | **Wilming/DE** | 22

Epicurean | varies | **Phoenixville** | 20

Eulogy Belgian | bands | **Old City** | 19

Fadó Irish | DJ | **Rittenhouse** | 17

Fergie's Pub | bands | **Washington Sq W** | 16

Fez Moroccan | belly dancing | **South St** | 19

Filomena | live music | **multi.** | 22

☑ Fountain | bands | **Logan Sq** | 28

Four Dogs | acoustic | **W Chester** | 20

Freight House | DJ | **Doylestown** | 16

Gen. Lafayette | folk/rock | **Lafaye0tte Hill** | 18

Green Room | jazz/varies | **Wilming/DE** | 24

Gullifty's | varies | **Rosemont** | 15

Half Moon | varies | **Kennett Sq** | 20

Happy Rooster | karaoke | **Rittenhouse** | 18

Harry's Savoy | varies | **Wilming/DE** | 24

Havana | varies | **New Hope** | 18

HighNote Cafe | live music | **S Philly** | 23

☑ High St. Caffé | jazz | **W Chester** | 26

Jamaican Jerk | varies | **Ave of Arts** | 19

Joseph Ambler | pianist | **N Wales** | 21

Kildare's | bands/DJ | **multi.** | 16

Kimberton Inn | jazz | **Kimberton** | 25

Konak | Turkish | **Old City** | 23

La Collina | live music | **Bala Cynwyd** | 22

La Tolteca | mariachi | **Wilming/DE** | 20

Little Marakesh | belly dancing | **Dresher** | —

L2 | jazz | **Graduate Hospital** | 19

Maggiano's | jazz/piano | **King of Prussia** | 20

Mamma Maria | accordion | **S Philly** | 22

Manayunk Brew. | varies | **Manayunk** | 17

Marrakesh | belly dancing | **South St** | 25

McFadden's | bands/DJ | **N Liberties** | 15

Mendenhall Inn | varies | **Mendenhall** | 19

Norma's | belly dancing | **Cherry Hill/NJ** | 22

Plough & Stars | Irish bands | **Old City** | 20

☑ Prime Rib | bass/piano | **Rittenhouse** | 27

Reading Terminal Mkt. | jazz | **Chinatown** | 24

Red Hot/Blue | blues | **Cherry Hill/NJ** | 16

Rembrandt's | jazz | **Fairmount** | 19

Rist. San Marco | piano | **Ambler** | 26

Serrano | acoustic | **Old City** | 21

Silk City | live music | **N Liberties** | 21

Singapore Kosher | karaoke | **Chinatown** | 20

Spence's Remedy | jazz/rock Wed - Sat. | **W Chester** | 21

Sullivan's Steak | jazz | **multi.** | 23

Swanky Bubbles | DJ | **Old City**	19
Z Swann Lounge | jazz | **Logan Sq**	26
Tai Lake | karaoke | **Chinatown**	27
Taq. La Veracruz. | varies | **S Philly**	23
Tex Mex Connect. | varies | **N Wales**	17
Tierra Colombiana | salsa | **N Philly**	24
Tír na nÓg | live music/DJ | **Logan Sq**	17
Upstares/Sotto | jazz | **Ave of Arts**	23
Victor Café | opera/musical theater | **S Philly**	20
White Dog | live music | **Univ City**	20
William Penn | jazz | **Gwynedd**	20
World Café | varies | **Univ City**	16

FAMILY-STYLE

Beige & Beige | **Hunt Vly**	17
Bellini Grill | **Rittenhouse**	21
Bird-in-Hand | **Bird-in-Hand/LB**	20
Brio | **Cherry Hill/NJ**	19
Buca di Beppo | **Rittenhouse**	16
Fez Moroccan | **South St**	19
Gnocchi | **South St**	19
Good/Plenty | **Smoketown/LB**	18
Il Tartufo | **Manayunk**	21
Joy Tsin Lau | **Chinatown**	20
La Veranda | **DE River**	22
Maggiano's | **multi.**	20
Mandarin Gdn. | **Willow Grove**	22
Marg. Kuo | **Wayne**	23
Miller's Smorgas. | **Ronks/LB**	18
Pho Xe Lua | **Chinatown**	24
Plain/Fancy Farm | **Bird-in-Hand/LB**	19
Sang Kee | **Chinatown**	23
Scoogi's | **Flourtown**	19
Swanky Bubbles | **Old City**	19

FIREPLACES

America B&G | **Glen Mills**	18
Anton's/Swan | **Lambertville/NJ**	22
Arpeggio | **Spring House**	23
Avalon | **W Chester**	25
Back Burner | **Hockessin/DE**	22
Bay Pony Inn | **Lederach**	21
Beau Monde | **Queen Vill**	23
Bella Tori | **Langhorne**	18
Black Bass | **Lumberville**	21

Black Sheep | **Rittenhouse**	17
Blue Bell Inn | **Blue Bell**	20
Braddock's | **Medford/NJ**	20
Bridgetown Mill | **Langhorne**	24
Bridgid's | **Fairmount**	20
Buckley's | **Centerville/DE**	18
Carversville Inn | **Carversville**	25
Cascade Lodge | **Kintnersville**	20
Casona | **Collingswood/NJ**	20
Centre Bridge | **New Hope**	22
Chophouse | **Gibbsboro/NJ**	24
Cock 'n Bull | **Lahaska**	18
NEW Columbus Inn | **Wilming/DE**	-
Cork | **Westmont/NJ**	22
Coyote Cross. | **Consho**	21
Creed's | **King of Prussia**	24
NEW Dettera | **Ambler**	21
Devil's Alley | **Rittenhouse**	19
Devil's Den | **S Philly**	19
Dilworth. Inn | **W Chester**	25
Duling-Kurtz | **Exton**	25
Elephant/Castle | **Rittenhouse**	11
Epicurean | **Phoenixville**	20
Fadó Irish | **Rittenhouse**	17
Filomena | **multi.**	22
NEW Firecreek | **Downingtown**	20
Fogo de Chão | **Ave of Arts**	24
Four Dogs | **W Chester**	20
Gables | **Chadds Ford**	23
Gen. Lafayette | **Lafayette Hill**	18
Gen. Warren | **Malvern**	25
Georges' | **Wayne**	22
Z Giumarello's | **Westmont/NJ**	26
Golden Pheasant | **Erwinna**	23
Gold Standard | **W Philly**	17
Gracie's | **Pine Forge/LB**	-
NEW Green Eggs | **S Philly**	26
Green Hills Inn | **Reading/LB**	-
Harry's Savoy | **Wilming/DE**	24
Harry's Seafood | **Wilming/DE**	25
Havana | **New Hope**	18
NEW Hawthornes | **S Philly**	22
Hibachi | **Berwyn**	18
High St. | **Mt Holly/NJ**	21
Hokka Hokka | **Ches Hill**	23
Z Horizons | **South St**	27
Hotel du Village | **New Hope**	23
Illuminare | **Fairmount**	15
Inn/Phillips Mill | **New Hope**	25

Inn/Hawke	Lambertville/NJ	20	1726	La Famiglia*	Old City	23
** Z** James	S Philly	27	1732	Gen. Lafayette*	Lafayette Hill	18
Jones	Washington Sq W	20	1734	Joseph Ambler*	N Wales	21
Kildare's	multi.	16	1736	Seven Stars Inn	Phoenixville	20
Kimberton Inn	Kimberton	25	1740	Pace One*	Thornton	21
Z Krazy Kat's	Montchanin/DE	25	1742	Washington Hse.*	Sellersville	-
La Campagne	Cherry Hill/NJ	22	1743	Blue Bell Inn*	Blue Bell	20
Landing	New Hope	18	1745	Black Bass*	Lumberville	21
Las Cazuelas	N Liberties	24	1745	Gen. Warren*	Malvern	25
Marathon Grill	Washington Sq W	18	1750	Avenida*	Mt Airy	22
Marigold Kitchen	Univ City	24	1750	Brandywine Prime*	Chadds Ford	22
Mastoris	Bordentown/NJ	20	1756	Inn/Phillips Mill*	New Hope	25
McGillin's	Washington Sq W	16	1758	Dilworth. Inn*	W Chester	25
Mendenhall Inn	Mendenhall	19	1764	Brick Hotel*	Newtown	16
Mexican Post	Wilming/DE	16	1765	Yangming*	Bryn Mawr	25
Molly Maguire's	Phoenixville	16	1773	City Tavern*	Old City	19
Moriarty's	Washington Sq W	20	1776	DiNardo's*	Old City	19
Naked Choco.	Ave of Arts	24	1791	Bridgetown Mill*	Langhorne	24
Newtown Grill	Newtown Sq	19	1796	Kimberton Inn*	Kimberton	25
Old Guard Hse.	Gladwyne	22	1800	Bistro Romano*	Society Hill	22
P.J. Whelihan's	Medford Lakes/NJ	16	1800	Bourbon Blue*	Manayunk	18
Plough & Stars	Old City	20	1800	Limoncello*	W Chester	23
Pub	Pennsauken/NJ	19	1800	Old Guard Hse.*	Gladwyne	22
Redstone	Plymouth Meeting	20	1800	Robin's Nest*	Mt Holly/NJ	22
Ristorante Castello	N Wales	17	1801	London Grill*	Fairmount	17
Saloon	S Philly	24	1806	Snockey's Oyster*	S Philly	21
Scoogi's	Flourtown	19	1813	Carversville Inn*	Carversville	25
Seasons 52	King of Prussia	-	1817	Wash. Cross.*	Wash Cross	20
Serrano	Old City	21	1823	Braddock's*	Medford/NJ	20
Shanachie	Ambler	13	1830	Bay Pony Inn*	Lederach	21
Sly Fox	Royersford	13	1830	Duling-Kurtz*	Exton	25
Snackbar	Rittenhouse	22	1830	Rist. San Marco*	Ambler	26
Standard Tap	N Liberties	22	1832	Yardley Inn*	Yardley	22
St. Stephens Green	Fairmount	18	1833	New Tavern*	Bala Cynwyd	21
Z Swann Lounge	Logan Sq	26	1837	National Mech.*	Old City	18
Union City Grille	Wilming/DE	22	1840	Inn/Hawke*	Lambertville/NJ	20
Vesuvio	S Philly	14	1841	La Campagne*	Cherry Hill/NJ	22
Wash. Cross.	Wash Cross	20		
Wash. St. Ale	Wilming/DE	15		
Whip Tavern	Coatesville	23		
William Penn	Gwynedd	20		
Yardley Inn	Yardley	22		
Zacharias	Worcester	24		

HISTORIC PLACES

(Year opened; * building)

1681	Broad Axe Tav.*	Ambler	16
1714	William Penn*	Gwynedd	20
1720	Barnsboro Inn*	Sewell/NJ	22

SPECIAL FEATURES

1846 | Knight House* | **Doylestown** — 23

1849 | Dante & Luigi* | **S Philly** — 23

1851 | Catherine's* | **Unionville** — 28

1852 | Haydn Zug's* | **E Petersburg/LB** — 23

1854 | Tequila's* | **Rittenhouse** — 25

1855 | Mendenhall Inn* | **Mendenhall** — 19

1856 | High St.* | **Mt Holly/NJ** — 21

1857 | Golden Pheasant* | **Erwinna** — 23

1859 | Tavolo* | **Hunt Vly** — 21

1860 | McGillin's | **Washington Sq W** — 16

1863 | Lambertville Station* | **Lambertville/NJ** — 18

1864 | Slate Bleu* | **Doylestown** — 23

1868 | Rick's* | **Lambertville/NJ** — 20

1870 | Ernesto's 1521* | **Rittenhouse** — 19

1870 | Marsha Brown* | **New Hope** — 21

1886 | Cooperage* | **Washington Sq W** — -

1890 | Jack's Firehse.* | **Fairmount** — 19

1892 | Birchrunville Store* | **Birchrunville** — 28

1892 | Gilmore's* | **W Chester** — 28

1892 | Reading Terminal Mkt.* | **Chinatown** — 24

1893 | Lancaster Dispensing* | **Lancaster/LB** — -

1896 | Bella Tori* | **Langhorne** — 18

1896 | Rx* | **Univ City** — 24

1897 | Gables* | **Chadds Ford** — 23

1900 | Cactus* | **Manayunk** — 17

1900 | Checkers Bistro* | **Lancaster/LB** — -

1900 | Cucina Forte* | **S Philly** — 26

1900 | Elements Café* | **Haddon Hts/NJ** — 22

1900 | Ralph's | **S Philly** — 23

1900 | Rose Tattoo* | **Fairmount** — 22

1900 | Winnie's Le Bus* | **Manayunk** — 21

1903 | Dock Street* | **Univ City** — 21

1904 | Moshulu* | **DE River** — 22

1905 | Casona* | **Collingswood/NJ** — 20

1907 | Hotel du Village* | **New Hope** — 23

1907 | Marigold Kitchen* | **Univ City** — 24

1908 | Anastasi | **S Philly** — 23

1913 | Green Room | **Wilming/DE** — 24

1915 | Wine Thief* | **Mt Airy** — 20

1918 | Victor Café | **S Philly** — 20

1922 | Del Frisco's* | **Ave of Arts** — 20

1923 | Famous 4th St. Deli | **South St** — 24

1927 | Marra's | **S Philly** — 21

1929 | Miller's Smorgas. | **Ronks/LB** — 18

1930 | Anthony's* | **Haddon Hts/NJ** — 22

1930 | John's Roast Pork | **S Philly** — 27

1930 | Otto's Brauhaus | **Horsham** — 19

1930 | Pat's Steaks | **S Philly** — 21

1932 | Mayfair Diner | **NE Philly** — 15

1935 | Charlie's Hamburg. | **Folsom** — 23

1935 | Melrose Diner | **S Philly** — 15

1936 | Buckley's | **Centerville/DE** — 18

1939 | Cascade Lodge | **Kintnersville** — 20

1939 | Jim's Steaks | **W Philly** — 23

1940 | Mrs. Robino's | **Wilming/DE** — 14

1940 | Pub/Penn Valley* | **Narberth** — 19

1945 | Murray's Deli | **Bala Cynwyd** — 18

1948 | Tacconelli's | **Port Richmond** — 25

1950 | Ben & Irv Deli | **Hunt Vly** — 19

1951 | Pub | **Pennsauken/NJ** — 19

1953 | Columbus Inn | **Wilming/DE** — -

1955 | Hank's Place | **Chadds Ford** — 21

1955 | Hymie's Deli | **Merion Sta** — 19

1956 | Charcoal Pit | **Wilming/DE** — 20

1959 | Plain/Fancy Farm | **Bird-in-Hand/LB** — 19

1960 | Bomb Bomb BBQ | **S Philly** — 23

1960 | Dalessandro's | **Roxborough** — 23

1960 | Four Dogs | **W Chester** — 20

HOTEL DINING

Best Western Inn
    Palace of Asia | **Ft Wash** — 22

Black Bass Hotel
    Black Bass | **Lumberville** — 21

JACKET REQUIRED

LATE DINING

(Weekday closing hour)

SPECIAL FEATURES

Brauhaus Schmitz | 2 AM | **South St** — 19

Bridget Foy's | 12 AM | **South St** — 19

Bridget's Steak | 1 AM | **Ambler** — 23

Broad Axe Tav. | 12 AM | **Ambler** — 16

Byblos | 2 AM | **Rittenhouse** — 18

Cactus | 12 AM | **Manayunk** — 17

Cantina Caballitos/Segundos | varies | **multi.** — 21

Z Capogiro | 11:30 PM | **Univ City** — 27

Charcoal Pit | varies | **Wilming/DE** — 20

Cheeseburger/Paradise | 1 AM | **Langhorne** — 14

Chickie's/Pete's | varies | **multi.** — 18

Christopher's | 1 AM | **Wayne** — 16

NEW City Tap House | 1 AM | **Univ City** — —

Copabanana | varies | **multi.** — 17

Dalessandro's | 12 AM | **Roxborough** — 23

D'Angelo's | 12 AM | **Rittenhouse** — 24

Dark Horse | 12 AM | **Society Hill** — 19

Darling's | 12 AM | **N Liberties** — 17

Dave & Buster's | varies | **DE River** — 12

Dining Car | 24 hrs. | **NE Philly** — 19

El Camino Real | 1 AM | **N Liberties** — 21

Elephant/Castle | varies | **Rittenhouse** — 11

Eulogy Belgian | 1:30 AM | **Old City** — 19

Fadó Irish | 12 AM | **Rittenhouse** — 17

Fergie's Pub | 12 AM | **Washington Sq W** — 16

Fox & Hound | varies | **multi.** — 11

Fuji Mtn. | 1:30 AM | **Rittenhouse** — 20

Geno's Steaks | 24 hrs. | **S Philly** — 18

Good Dog | 1 AM | **Rittenhouse** — 22

Grace Tav. | 2 AM | **Graduate Hospital** — 21

Grey Lodge | 2 AM | **NE Philly** — 19

Gullifty's | 12 AM | **Rosemont** — 15

Harusame | 12 AM | **Ardmore** — 22

Imperial Inn | 12 AM | **Chinatown** — 20

Iron Hill | varies | **W Chester** — 19

Jim's Steaks | varies | **multi.** — 23

Johnny Brenda | 1 AM | **Fishtown** — 21

Jones | 12 AM | **Washington Sq W** — 20

José Pistola's | 1 AM | **Rittenhouse** — 15

Joy Tsin Lau | 11:30 PM | **Chinatown** — 20

K.C.'s Alley | 2 AM | **Ambler** — 16

Kildare's | 12 AM | **multi.** — 16

Kite & Key | 2 AM | **Fairmount** — 16

La Lupe | 12 AM | **S Philly** — 21

Lancaster Dispensing | 12 AM | **Lancaster/LB** — —

NEW Leila Cafe | 2 AM | **Washington Sq W** — —

Little Pete's | varies | **Rittenhouse** — 18

Local 44 | 12 AM | **W Philly** — 16

NEW Lucky 7 | 1 AM | **Fairmount** — 17

NEW Mac's Tavern | 1 AM | **Old City** — —

NEW MaGerks | 2 AM | **Ft Wash** — 15

Manayunk Brew. | 1 AM | **Manayunk** — 17

Maoz Veg. | 1 AM | **South St** — 23

Marathon Grill | 12 AM | **Washington Sq W** — 18

NEW Más Mexicali | 12 AM | **W Chester** — —

Mastoris | 1 AM | **Bordentown/NJ** — 20

Max Brenner | varies | **Rittenhouse** — 19

Mayfair Diner | 24 hrs. | **NE Philly** — 15

McFadden's | 2 AM | **multi.** — 15

McGillin's | 1 AM | **Washington Sq W** — 16

Melrose Diner | 24 hrs. | **S Philly** — 15

Memphis Tap | 12 AM | **Port Richmond** — 23

Mexican Post | varies | **Old City** — 16

Misconduct Tav. | 1:30 AM | **Rittenhouse** — 19

Molly Maguire's | 2 AM | **Phoenixville** — 16

Monk's Cafe | 1 AM | **Rittenhouse** — 22

Moriarty's | 1 AM | **Washington Sq W** — 20

Ms. Tootsie's | 12 AM | **South St** — 25

National Mech. | 1 AM | **Old City** — 18

New Wave | 1 AM | **Queen Vill** — 17

Nodding Head | 12 AM | **Rittenhouse** — 19

Z Pat's Steaks | 24 hrs. | **S Philly** — 21

Penang | 1 AM | **Chinatown** — 21

Phil's Tav. | 12 AM | **Blue Bell** — 18

P.J. Whelihan's | varies | **multi.** — 16

Prohibition | varies | **N Philly** — 22

Pub/Kitchen | 1 AM | **Graduate Hospital** — 22

Redstone | varies | **Plymouth Meeting** — 20

NEW Resurrection Ale | 12 AM | **S Philly** — 24

Royal Tavern | 1 AM | **S Philly** — 24

Shiao Lan Kung | 12:30 AM | **Chinatown** — 23

Silk City | 12 AM | **N Liberties** — 21

Sláinte | 1 AM | **Univ City** — 16

Slate | 1 AM | **Rittenhouse** — 19

Smith/Wollensky | 1:30 AM | **Rittenhouse** — 22

Snackbar | 1 AM | **Rittenhouse** — 22

Standard Tap | 1 AM | **N Liberties** — 22

Steve's Steaks | 12 AM | **NE Philly** — 23

St. Stephens Green | 12 AM | **Fairmount** — 18

Swanky Bubbles | 1 AM | **Old City** — 19

Z Swann Lounge | 12 AM | **Logan Sq** — 26

Swift Half | 1 AM | **N Liberties** — 18

Tai Lake | 3 AM | **Chinatown** — 27

Taq. La Veracruz. | 12 AM | **S Philly** — 23

Tavern 17 | 1 AM | **Rittenhouse** — 16

Teresa's Next Dr. | 1 AM | **Wayne** — 22

Time | 1 AM | **Washington Sq W** — 20

Tony Luke's | varies | **S Philly** — 26

Tria | varies | **multi.** — 23

Triumph Brewing | varies | **multi.** — 18

Varga Bar | 2 AM | **Washington Sq W** — 20

Vesuvio | 12 AM | **S Philly** — 14

Vintage | 2 AM | **Washington Sq W** — 20

Warmdaddy's | 2 AM | **S Philly** — 22

Wash. St. Ale | 1 AM | **Wilming/DE** — 15

Xochitl | 12 AM | **Society Hill** — 23

Yakitori Boy | 2 AM | **Chinatown** — 19

MEET FOR A DRINK

Abbaye | **N Liberties** — 20

Aki | **Washington Sq W** — 21

Al Dar Bistro | **Bala Cynwyd** — 19

Alfa | **Rittenhouse** — 17

Z Alma de Cuba | **Rittenhouse** — 25

NEW American Pub | **Ave of Arts** — 15

NEW Amis | **Washington Sq W** — 24

NEW Amuse | **Ave of Arts** — -

NEW Apollinare | **N Liberties** — -

Azie | **multi.** — 23

Bar Ferdinand | **N Liberties** — 23

Beau Monde | **Queen Vill** — 23

Belgian Café | **Fairmount** — 19

Beneluxx | **Old City** — 20

Bensí | **N Wales** — 17

Bistrot/Minette | **Queen Vill** — 25

Black Sheep | **Rittenhouse** — 17

Z Bluefin | **Plymouth Meeting** — 28

Blue Pear | **W Chester** — 23

NEW Bobby's Burger | **Univ City** — -

Bonefish Grill | **multi.** — 21

Brandywine Prime | **Chadds Ford** — 22

Brauhaus Schmitz | **South St** — 19

Broad Axe Tav. | **Ambler** — 16

NEW Bull Durham | **W Chester** — -

Butcher/Singer | **Rittenhouse** — 24

Cactus | **Manayunk** — 17

California Pizza | **Plymouth Meeting** — 19

Cantina Caballitos/Segundos | **S Philly** — 21

Capers/Lemons | **Wilming/DE** — 22

Z Capital Grille | **Ave of Arts** — 26

Caribou Cafe | **Washington Sq W** — 21

Cheeseburger/Paradise | **Langhorne** — 14

Chickie's/Pete's | **Bordentown/NJ** — 18

Chick's | **South St** — 21

Z Chifa | **Washington Sq W** — 25

Chops | **Bala Cynwyd** — 21

NEW City Tap House | **Univ City** — -

NEW Con Murphy's | **Logan Sq** — 17

Continental | **Old City** — 22

Continental Mid-town | **Rittenhouse** — 22

NEW Cooperage | **Washington Sq W** — -

Cooper's | **Manayunk** — 22

Coyote Cross. | **Consho** — 21

Z Cuba Libre | **Old City** — 22

Dark Horse | **Society Hill** — 19

Davio's | **Rittenhouse** — 25

Del Frisco's | **Ave of Arts** — 20

Delmonico's | **Wynnefield** — 25

Derek's | **Manayunk** — 22

SPECIAL FEATURES

Name	Location	Rating
NEW Dettera	Ambler	21
Devil's Alley	Rittenhouse	19
Devil's Den	S Philly	19
Doc Magrogan	W Chester	17
NEW Doghouse	Downingtown	-
Earth Bread	Mt Airy	21
El Camino Real	N Liberties	21
El Fuego	Rittenhouse	19
NEW El Rey	Rittenhouse	-
Eulogy Belgian	Old City	19
Fadó Irish	Rittenhouse	17
Fergie's Pub	Washington Sq W	16
Field House	Chinatown	12
NEW Firecreek	Downingtown	20
NEW FireStone	Wilming/DE	-
NEW Franco's Osteria	Wynnefield	-
Georges'	Wayne	22
Girasole	Ave of Arts	21
Good Dog	Rittenhouse	22
Grey Lodge	NE Philly	19
Happy Rooster	Rittenhouse	18
NEW Harvest	Glen Mills	-
NEW HeadHouse	Society Hill	-
Z Horizons	South St	27
Inn/Hawke	Lambertville/NJ	20
Iron Hill	multi.	19
J.B. Dawson's/Austin's	multi.	18
Jones	Washington Sq W	20
José Pistola's	Rittenhouse	15
Kite & Key	Fairmount	16
Knock	Washington Sq W	16
NEW Kraftwork	Fishtown	-
Local 44	W Philly	16
London Grill	Fairmount	17
L2	Graduate Hospital	19
NEW Lucky 7	Fairmount	17
NEW Mac's Tavern	Old City	-
NEW MaGerks	Ft Wash	15
Maggio's	Southampton	18
Manayunk Brew.	Manayunk	17
MangoMoon	Manayunk	17
NEW Más Mexicali	W Chester	-
Max Brenner	Rittenhouse	19
McCormick/Schmick	multi.	21
McFadden's	multi.	15
Memphis Tap	Port Richmond	23
Mexican Post	Logan Sq	16
NEW MidAtlantic	Univ City	20
Misconduct Tav.	Rittenhouse	19
Mission Grill	Logan Sq	18
Mix	Rittenhouse	17
Mixto	Washington Sq W	20
NEW MIXX	Villanova	17
Molly Maguire's	Phoenixville	16
Monk's Cafe	Rittenhouse	22
Moriarty's	Washington Sq W	20
NEW M Rest.	Washington Sq W	21
NEW Munk/Nunn	Manayunk	-
National Mech.	Old City	18
Newtown Grill	Newtown Sq	19
New Wave	Queen Vill	17
Z Nineteen	Ave of Arts	23
Noble Cookery	Rittenhouse	20
Z Osteria	N Philly	27
Paddock/Devon	Wayne	15
NEW Parker's Prime	Newtown Sq	21
Penne	Univ City	18
NEW Percy St. BBQ	South St	20
P.F. Chang's	multi.	20
Pietro's Prime	W Chester	23
P.J. Whelihan's	multi.	16
Plough & Stars	Old City	20
Z Prime Rib	Rittenhouse	27
Privé	Old City	21
Prohibition	N Philly	22
Pub/Kitchen	Graduate Hospital	22
Q BBQ	Old City	16
Redstone	Marlton/NJ	20
NEW Resurrection Ale	S Philly	24
Rist. Panorama	Old City	23
Roberto's Tratt.	Erdenheim	19
Royal Tavern	S Philly	24
Z NEW R2L	Rittenhouse	21
NEW Sampan	Washington Sq W	21
Shanachie	Ambler	13
Sidecar	Graduate Hospital	23
Silk City	N Liberties	21
Sláinte	Univ City	16
Slate	Rittenhouse	19
Sly Fox	multi.	13
Smiths	Rittenhouse	16
Smokin' Betty	Washington Sq W	20
Snackbar	Rittenhouse	22
NEW Square 1682	Rittenhouse	21
Standard Tap	N Liberties	22
St. Stephens Green	Fairmount	18
Supper	South St	23

2 Swann Lounge | **Logan Sq**	26	
Swift Half | **N Liberties**	18	
Table 31 | **Logan Sq**	21	
Tango | **Bryn Mawr**	20	
Tavern 17 | **Rittenhouse**	16	
Ted's Montana | **multi.**	18	
2 10 Arts | **Ave of Arts**	22	
Tequila's | **Rittenhouse**	25	
Teresa's Next Dr. | **Wayne**	22	
Time | **Washington Sq W**	20	
2 Tinto | **Rittenhouse**	27	
Tír na nÓg | **Logan Sq**	17	
Tortilla Press | **Pennsauken/NJ**	23	
Toscana 52 | **Feasterville**	20	
Tria | **Washington Sq W**	23	
Triumph Brewing | **multi.**	18	
NEW Tweed | **Washington Sq W**	-	
Twenty Manning | **Rittenhouse**	-	
2 Union Trust | **Washington Sq W**	24	
Urban Saloon | **Fairmount**	18	
Valanni | **Washington Sq W**	24	
Varga Bar | **Washington Sq W**	20	
NEW Verdad | **Bryn Mawr**	19	
NEW Village Whiskey | **Rittenhouse**	24	
Vintage | **Washington Sq W**	20	
Warmdaddy's | **S Philly**	22	
Water Works | **Fairmount**	21	
Xochitl | **Society Hill**	23	
Yakitori Boy | **Chinatown**	19	
NEW Zama | **Rittenhouse**	26	
NEW Zavino | **Washington Sq W**	22	

MICROBREWERIES

Dock Street | **Univ City**	21	
Earth Bread | **Mt Airy**	21	
Freight House | **Doylestown**	16	
Gen. Lafayette | **Lafayette Hill**	18	
Iron Hill | **multi.**	19	
Manayunk Brew. | **Manayunk**	17	
Nodding Head | **Rittenhouse**	19	
Rock Bottom | **King of Prussia**	14	
Sly Fox | **multi.**	13	
Stoudt's | **Adamstown/LB**	19	
Triumph Brewing | **multi.**	18	
Victory Brewing | **Downingtown**	17	

NATURAL/ORGANIC

AllWays Café | **Hunt Vly**	23	
Auspicious | **Ardmore**	19	

NEW Avril | **Bala Cynwyd**	14	
Bellini Grill | **Rittenhouse**	21	
Bensí | **N Wales**	17	
Bistro di Marino | **Collingswood/NJ**	23	
Bistro La Baia | **Graduate Hospital**	19	
Bistro La Viola | **Rittenhouse**	24	
Bistro 7 | **Old City**	24	
Bliss | **Ave of Arts**	21	
Brick Hotel | **Newtown**	16	
California Cafe | **King of Prussia**	20	
2 Catelli | **Voorhees/NJ**	25	
Charles Plaza | **Chinatown**	24	
Checkers Bistro | **Lancaster/LB**	-	
Chiangmai | **Consho**	25	
Chlöe | **Old City**	26	
Continental | **Old City**	22	
NEW Cooperage | **Washington Sq W**	-	
Corner Bistro | **Wilming/DE**	19	
D'Angelo's | **Rittenhouse**	24	
DeAnna's | **Lambertville/NJ**	24	
Derek's | **Manayunk**	22	
Dream Café | **Cherry Hill/NJ**	-	
Du Jour | **Haverford**	18	
Farmicia | **Old City**	22	
Funky Lil' Kitchen | **Pottstown**	25	
Half Moon | **Kennett Sq**	20	
Harry's Savoy | **Wilming/DE**	24	
NEW Healthy Bites | **S Philly**	-	
Il Tartufo | **Manayunk**	21	
Jack's Firehse. | **Fairmount**	19	
Jake's | **Manayunk**	25	
2 James | **S Philly**	27	
Kimberton Inn | **Kimberton**	25	
Knock | **Washington Sq W**	16	
2 Lacroix | **Rittenhouse**	27	
La Locanda/Ghiottone | **Old City**	24	
2 Le Bec-Fin | **Rittenhouse**	27	
Le Castagne | **Rittenhouse**	25	
Majolica | **Phoenixville**	24	
Marathon Grill | **Rittenhouse**	18	
Marco Polo | **Elkins Pk**	20	
Marigold Kitchen | **Univ City**	24	
Meritage | **Graduate Hospital**	25	
Mission Grill | **Logan Sq**	18	
NEW M Rest. | **Washington Sq W**	21	
Naked Choco. | **Ave of Arts**	24	
Nicholas | **S Philly**	22	
Noble Cookery | **Rittenhouse**	20	

Portofino | **Washington Sq W** 20
PTG | **Roxborough** 23
Pumpkin | **Graduate Hospital** 26
Z Rest. Alba | **Malvern** 27
Robin's Nest | **Mt Holly/NJ** 22
Roller's/Flying Fish | **Ches Hill** 19
Rouge | **Rittenhouse** 22
Royal Tavern | **S Philly** 24
Rx | **Univ City** 24
Salt & Pepper | **S Philly** 25
Sapori | **Collingswood/NJ** 25
Sazon | **N Liberties** 22
Simon Pearce | **W Chester** 22
Southwark | **South St** 25
NEW Square 1682 | **Rittenhouse** 21
Supper | **South St** 23
Swift Half | **N Liberties** 18
Z Talula's Table | **Kennett Sq** 27
Tavern 17 | **Rittenhouse** 16
Ted's Montana | **multi.** 18
Z 10 Arts | **Ave of Arts** 22
333 Belrose | **Radnor** 22
Vesuvio | **S Philly** 14
NEW Village Whiskey | **Rittenhouse** 24
Wash. Cross. | **Wash Cross** 20
Water Works | **Fairmount** 21
Whip Tavern | **Coatesville** 23
White Dog | **Univ City** 20
Winberie's | **Wayne** 17
Yardley Inn | **Yardley** 22

NOTEWORTHY NEWCOMERS

Adsum | **South St** –
A La Maison | **Ardmore** –
American Pub | **Ave of Arts** 15
Amis | **Washington Sq W** 24
Amuse | **Ave of Arts** –
Apollinare | **N Liberties** –
Avenida | **Mt Airy** 22
Avril | **Bala Cynwyd** 14
Bobby's Burger | **Univ City** –
Brick House | **Willow Grove** 17
Bull Durham | **W Chester** –
Carluccio's | **S Philly** 25
City Tap House | **Univ City** –
Columbus Inn | **Wilming/DE** –
Con Murphy's | **Logan Sq** 17
Cooperage | **Washington Sq W** –
Dettera | **Ambler** 21

Doghouse | **Downingtown** –
Doma | **Logan Sq** –
El Rey | **Rittenhouse** –
Fat Salmon | **Washington Sq W** –
Firecreek | **Downingtown** 20
FireStone | **Wilming/DE** –
fish | **Graduate Hospital** 25
500º | **Rittenhouse** –
Z Fond | **S Philly** 27
Franco's Osteria | **Wynnefield** –
Garces Trading | **Washington Sq W** –
Gemelli | **Narberth** 23
Green Eggs | **S Philly** 26
Harvest | **Glen Mills** –
Hawthornes | **S Philly** 22
HeadHouse | **Society Hill** –
Healthy Bites | **S Philly** –
Hoof + Fin | **Queen Vill** –
Koo Zee Doo | **N Liberties** 25
Kraftwork | **Fishtown** –
Kumo Asian | **N Wales** –
Leila Cafe | **Washington Sq W** –
Le Viet | **S Philly** –
Lucky 7 | **Fairmount** 17
Mac's Tavern | **Old City** –
MaGerks | **Ft Wash** 15
Más Mexicali | **W Chester** –
MidAtlantic | **Univ City** 20
Miga | **Rittenhouse** –
MIXX | **Villanova** 17
Momiji | **Society Hill** –
M Rest. | **Washington Sq W** 21
Munk/Nunn | **Manayunk** –
Parker's Prime | **Newtown Sq** 21
Paul | **Washington Sq W** 22
Percy St. BBQ | **South St** 20
Pizzeria Stella | **Society Hill** 22
Resurrection Ale | **S Philly** 24
Ro-Zu | **S Philly** –
Z R2L | **Rittenhouse** 21
Saffron | **multi.** –
Sampan | **Washington Sq W** 21
Shank's Original | **multi.** 23
Sonata | **N Liberties** 23
Sprig & Vine | **New Hope** –
Square 1682 | **Rittenhouse** 21
Tavolo | **Hunt Vly** 21
Tiffin etc. | **N Liberties** 23
Très Elena | **Mt Laurel/NJ** –

Tweed | **Washington Sq W** $\underline{-}$
Verdad | **Bryn Mawr** $\underline{19}$
Village Whiskey | **Rittenhouse** $\underline{24}$
Zama | **Rittenhouse** $\underline{26}$
Zavino | **Washington Sq W** $\underline{22}$

OFFBEAT

AllWays Café | **Hunt Vly** $\underline{23}$
Bitar's | **S Philly** $\underline{25}$
Bonté Wafflerie | **multi.** $\underline{21}$
Buca di Beppo | **multi.** $\underline{16}$
Carman's Country | **S Philly** $\underline{26}$
Charlie's Hamburg. | **Folsom** $\underline{23}$
Continental Mid-town | $\underline{22}$
  Rittenhouse
🄩 El Vez | **Washington Sq W** $\underline{23}$
Farmicia | **Old City** $\underline{22}$
Gracie's | **Pine Forge/LB** $\underline{-}$
Honey's Sit | **N Liberties** $\underline{25}$
Jake's Hamburg. | **New Castle/DE** $\underline{20}$
Jones | **Washington Sq W** $\underline{20}$
La Esperanza | **Lindenwold/NJ** $\underline{25}$
La Lupe | **S Philly** $\underline{21}$
Little Café | **Voorhees/NJ** $\underline{24}$
Little Pete's | **Rittenhouse** $\underline{18}$
Maggiano's | **Chinatown** $\underline{20}$
Manon | **Lambertville/NJ** $\underline{24}$
Melrose Diner | **S Philly** $\underline{15}$
🄩 Morimoto | **Washington Sq W** $\underline{28}$
Morning Glory | **S Philly** $\underline{22}$
Moshulu | **DE River** $\underline{22}$
Nifty Fifty's | **Turnersville/NJ** $\underline{19}$
Norma's | **Cherry Hill/NJ** $\underline{22}$
Ota-Ya | **multi.** $\underline{23}$
Penang | **Chinatown** $\underline{21}$
Pod | **Univ City** $\underline{23}$
Pop Shop | **Collingswood/NJ** $\underline{21}$
Pub | **Pennsauken/NJ** $\underline{19}$
Shanachie | **Ambler** $\underline{13}$
Silk City | **N Liberties** $\underline{21}$
Simon Pearce | **W Chester** $\underline{22}$
🄩 Siri's | **Cherry Hill/NJ** $\underline{26}$
Tacconelli's | **Port Richmond** $\underline{25}$
Trolley Car | **Mt Airy** $\underline{16}$

OPEN KITCHEN

🄩 Amada | **Old City** $\underline{28}$
NEW Amis | **Washington Sq W** $\underline{24}$
Audrey Claire | **Rittenhouse** $\underline{23}$
Avalon | **W Chester** $\underline{25}$
Bahama Breeze | **Cherry Hill/NJ** $\underline{17}$

Baja Fresh | **multi.** $\underline{17}$
Barone's/Villa Barone | $\underline{22}$
  Moorestown/NJ
Beijing | **Univ City** $\underline{17}$
Bella Cena | **Rittenhouse** $\underline{20}$
Beneluxx | **Old City** $\underline{20}$
Bistro 7 | **Old City** $\underline{24}$
Bistrot/Minette | **Queen Vill** $\underline{25}$
Bocelli | **Gwynedd** $\underline{20}$
Bonefish Grill | **multi.** $\underline{21}$
Café Estelle | **N Liberties** $\underline{23}$
California Cafe | **King of Prussia** $\underline{20}$
NEW Carluccio's | **S Philly** $\underline{25}$
Chophouse | **Gibbsboro/NJ** $\underline{24}$
Christopher's | **Wayne** $\underline{16}$
Darling's | **Logan Sq** $\underline{17}$
Delmonico's | **Wynnefield** $\underline{25}$
Devil's Alley | **Rittenhouse** $\underline{19}$
Devon Seafood | **Rittenhouse** $\underline{23}$
Dilworth. Inn | **W Chester** $\underline{25}$
🄩 Distrito | **Univ City** $\underline{25}$
🄩 Dmitri's | **multi.** $\underline{24}$
Dock Street | **Univ City** $\underline{21}$
NEW Doghouse | **Downingtown** $\underline{-}$
Dream Café | **Cherry Hill/NJ** $\underline{-}$
Du Jour | **Haverford** $\underline{18}$
Eclipse Bistro | **Wilming/DE** $\underline{23}$
El Fuego | **Rittenhouse** $\underline{19}$
🄩 Estia | **Ave of Arts** $\underline{25}$
Fayette St. | **Consho** $\underline{23}$
Fellini Cafe | **Ardmore** $\underline{19}$
Figs | **Fairmount** $\underline{23}$
Fiorello's Café | **W Chester** $\underline{17}$
NEW Firecreek | **Downingtown** $\underline{20}$
NEW fish | **Graduate Hospital** $\underline{25}$
Five Guys | **Mt Ephraim/NJ** $\underline{22}$
Fleming's | **multi.** $\underline{24}$
🄩 Fork | **Old City** $\underline{24}$
Funky Lil' Kitchen | **Pottstown** $\underline{25}$
Gables | **Chadds Ford** $\underline{23}$
NEW Gemelli | **Narberth** $\underline{23}$
GG's | **Mt Laurel/NJ** $\underline{26}$
🄩 Gibraltar | **Lancaster/LB** $\underline{23}$
Gnocchi | **South St** $\underline{19}$
Good Dog | **Rittenhouse** $\underline{22}$
NEW Green Eggs | **S Philly** $\underline{26}$
Harry's Seafood | $\underline{25}$
  Wilming/DE
High St. | **Mt Holly/NJ** $\underline{21}$
Il Cantuccio | **N Liberties** $\underline{21}$

SPECIAL FEATURES

Illuminare | **Fairmount**	15
Joe Pesce | **Collingswood/NJ**	21
Joe's Peking | **Marlton/NJ**	22
Jones | **Washington Sq W**	20
Kabobeesh | **Univ City**	26
Karma | **Old City**	21
Keating's | **DE River**	18
Kibitz Room | **Cherry Hill/NJ**	21
La Locanda/Ghiottone | **Old City**	24
La Lupe | **S Philly**	21
Lancaster Dispensing | **Lancaster/LB**	–
L'Angolo | **S Philly**	26
Las Cazuelas | **N Liberties**	24
NEW Le Viet | **S Philly**	–
Z Le Virtù | **S Philly**	26
Lilly's/Canal | **Lambertville/NJ**	21
L'Oca | **Fairmount**	23
Lolita | **Washington Sq W**	26
Maggio's | **Southampton**	18
Majolica | **Phoenixville**	24
Masamoto | **Glen Mills**	26
Max & David's | **Elkins Pk**	21
Melograno | **Rittenhouse**	24
Mémé | **Rittenhouse**	23
Mercato | **Washington Sq W**	25
Mikado | **Ardmore**	20
Mi Lah Veg. | **Rittenhouse**	21
Mirabella | **Cherry Hill/NJ**	23
More Than Ice Crm. | **Washington Sq W**	20
Morning Glory | **S Philly**	22
Z Moro | **Wilming/DE**	26
Morton's | **multi.**	26
Ms. Tootsie's | **South St**	25
Murray's Deli | **Bala Cynwyd**	18
Z Osteria | **N Philly**	27
Paradiso | **S Philly**	25
Pho Thai Nam | **Blue Bell**	23
Pizzicato | **Marlton/NJ**	19
Pomodoro | **Wilming/DE**	–
Privé | **Old City**	21
Pumpkin | **Graduate Hospital**	26
Pura Vida | **N Liberties**	–
Radicchio | **Old City**	25
Z Rest. Alba | **Malvern**	27
Z NEW R2L | **Rittenhouse**	21
Sabrina's Café | **Fairmount**	24
Salt & Pepper | **S Philly**	25
Seasons 52 | **King of Prussia**	–

Sidecar | **Graduate Hospital**	23
SLiCE | **S Philly**	22
NEW Square 1682 | **Rittenhouse**	21
Sullivan's Steak | **multi.**	23
Supper | **South St**	23
Susanna Foo's | **Radnor**	24
Z Talula's Table | **Kennett Sq**	27
Ted's Montana | **Warrington**	18
Teresa's Next Dr. | **Wayne**	22
Z Tinto | **Rittenhouse**	27
Toscana Kit. | **Wilming/DE**	24
Urban Saloon | **Fairmount**	18
Zacharias | **Worcester**	24
Z Zahav | **Society Hill**	25
NEW Zavino | **Washington Sq W**	22

OUTDOOR DINING

(G=garden; P=patio; S=sidewalk; T=terrace)

Abbaye | S | **N Liberties**	20
Adobe Cafe | P | **Roxborough**	20
Z Alma de Cuba | S | **Rittenhouse**	25
Anton's/Swan | P | **Lambertville/NJ**	22
Arpeggio | S | **Spring House**	23
Athena | P | **Glenside**	22
Audrey Claire | S | **Rittenhouse**	23
Bay Pony Inn | T | **Lederach**	21
Beau Monde | T | **Queen Vill**	23
Bella Cena | S | **Rittenhouse**	20
Bistro La Baia | S | **Graduate Hospital**	19
Bistro La Viola | S | **Rittenhouse**	24
Bistrot/Minette | G, S | **Queen Vill**	25
Bliss | S | **Ave of Arts**	21
Blue Parrot | P | **Wilming/DE**	17
Branzino | G, P | **Rittenhouse**	23
Brasserie 73 | P | **Skippack**	22
Brick Hotel | G | **Newtown**	16
Bridget Foy's | S | **South St**	19
Bridgetown Mill | P | **Langhorne**	24
Buckley's | G, T | **Centerville/DE**	18
Café Gallery | T | **Burlington/NJ**	20
Cafette | G | **Ches Hill**	20
Caffe Aldo | P | **Cherry Hill/NJ**	24
Caribou Cafe | T | **Washington Sq W**	21
Catherine's | P | **Unionville**	28
Centre Bridge | T | **New Hope**	22
Chart House | T | **DE River**	20

Chestnut Grill | P, S | **Ches Hill** 17
Ζ Chifa | S | **Washington Sq W** 25
City Tavern | G | **Old City** 19
NEW Columbus Inn | P | –
  Wilming/DE
Continental | S | **Old City** 22
Continental Mid-town | P, S | 22
  Rittenhouse
Coyote Cross. | P | **Consho** 21
Ζ Cuba Libre | S | **Old City** 22
Derek's | P, S | **Manayunk** 22
Devon Seafood | P | **Rittenhouse** 23
Dilworth. Inn | P | **W Chester** 25
El Serrano | G | **Lancaster/LB** 22
Figs | S | **Fairmount** 23
Ζ Fork | S | **Old City** 24
Four Dogs | P | **W Chester** 20
Freight House | P, T | **Doylestown** 16
FuziOn | P | **Worcester** 21
Gables | P | **Chadds Ford** 23
Gen. Warren | P | **Malvern** 25
Ζ Giumarello's | P | 26
  Westmont/NJ
Golden Pheasant | G, T | 23
  Erwinna
Gracie's | G, P | **Pine Forge/LB** –
Hamilton's | P | **Lambertville/NJ** 24
Harry's Savoy | P, T | **Wilming/DE** 24
Havana | P | **New Hope** 18
Hostaria Da Elio | P | **South St** 23
Illuminare | G, T | **Fairmount** 15
Inn/Phillips Mill | G | **New Hope** 25
Inn/Hawke | P | **Lambertville/NJ** 20
Isaac Newton's | G | **Newtown** 17
Izumi | S | **S Philly** 25
Jack's Firehse. | P, S | **Fairmount** 19
Jamaican Jerk | G | **Ave of Arts** 19
Joseph Ambler | P | **N Wales** 21
Keating's | T | **DE River** 18
La Campagne | P | **Cherry Hill/NJ** 22
Landing | G, T | **New Hope** 18
La Veranda | T | **DE River** 22
Lilly's/Canal | P | **Lambertville/NJ** 21
Lolita | S | **Washington Sq W** 26
Maggiano's | P | **multi.** 20
Manayunk Brew. | T | **Manayunk** 17
Mémé | S | **Rittenhouse** 23
Mexican Food | P | **Marlton/NJ** 19
Morning Glory | G, P | **S Philly** 22
Moshulu | T | **DE River** 22
Newtown Grill | P | **Newtown Sq** 19

New Wave | S | **Queen Vill** 17
Ζ Nineteen | T | **Ave of Arts** 23
Otto's Brauhaus | G | **Horsham** 19
Pace One | G | **Thornton** 21
Ζ Parc | S | **Rittenhouse** 22
Pattaya | P, S | **Univ City** 20
Pietro's Pizza | P, S, T | **multi.** 21
Pizzicato | S | **Old City** 19
Plate | P | **Ardmore** 14
Plough & Stars | S | **Old City** 20
Positano Coast | P | **Society Hill** 21
Privé | S | **Old City** 21
Rembrandt's | S | **Fairmount** 19
Robin's Nest | T | **Mt Holly/NJ** 22
Rouge | P | **Rittenhouse** 22
Rx | S | **Univ City** 24
Ζ Savona | T | **Gulph Mills** 27
Serrano | S | **Old City** 21
Solaris Grille | G, P | **Ches Hill** 14
Spasso | P | **Old City** 23
Spring Mill | P | **Consho** 24
Summer Kitchen | P | **Penns Park** 21
Swift Half | P | **N Liberties** 18
Tango | P | **Bryn Mawr** 20
Taq. La Veracruz. | S | **S Philly** 23
Teca | P, S | **W Chester** 23
333 Belrose | P | **Radnor** 22
Tír na nÓg | P | **Logan Sq** 17
Toscana Kit. | P | **Wilming/DE** 24
Tria | S | **Rittenhouse** 23
Twenty Manning | S | **Rittenhouse** –
Varga Bar | S | **Washington Sq W** 20
Vesuvio | S | **S Philly** 14
Wash. Cross. | G, P | **Wash Cross** 20
Wash. St. Ale | P | **Wilming/DE** 15
Water Works | T | **Fairmount** 21
Winberie's | P | **Wayne** 17
Zocalo | P | **Univ City** 20

PARKING
(V=valet, *=validated)
Ζ Alma de Cuba | V | 25
  Rittenhouse
Ζ Amada | V | **Old City** 28
Ariana | V | **Old City** 22
Ζ Barclay Prime | V | **Rittenhouse** 27
Bella Cena* | **Rittenhouse** 20
Black Bass | V | **Lumberville** 21
Bliss* | **Ave of Arts** 21
Bourbon Blue | V | **Manayunk** 18
Branzino* | **Rittenhouse** 23

Bridget's Steak | V | **Ambler**	23	
Broad Axe Tav. | V | **Ambler**	16	
Buca di Beppo* | V | **Rittenhouse**	16	
Z Buddakan | V | **Old City**	26	
Butcher/Singer | V | **Rittenhouse**	24	
Caffe Aldo | V | **Cherry Hill/NJ**	24	
Z Capital Grille | V | **multi.**	26	
Centre Bridge | V | **New Hope**	22	
Chart House | V | **DE River**	20	
Chez Colette | V | **Rittenhouse**	20	
Chiarella's | V | **S Philly**	22	
Chima | V* | **Logan Sq**	21	
Chophouse | V | **Gibbsboro/NJ**	24	
Chops | V | **multi.**	21	
NEW Columbus Inn | V | **Wilming/DE**	-	
NEW Con Murphy's* | **Logan Sq**	17	
NEW Cooperage | V | **Washington Sq W**	-	
Cooper's | V* | **Manayunk**	22	
Z Cuba Libre | V | **Old City**	22	
D'Angelo's* | **Rittenhouse**	24	
Dave & Buster's* | **DE River**	12	
Davio's | V | **Rittenhouse**	25	
Del Frisco's | V | **Ave of Arts**	20	
Delmonico's | V | **Wynnefield**	25	
NEW Dettera | V | **Ambler**	21	
Devil's Alley* | V | **Rittenhouse**	19	
DiNardo's* | V | **Old City**	19	
Dolce | V | **Old City**	17	
Elephant/Castle* | V | **Rittenhouse**	11	
NEW El Rey* | V | **Rittenhouse**	-	
El Serrano | V | **Lancaster/LB**	22	
Z El Vez* | V | **Washington Sq W**	23	
Z Estia | V* | **Ave of Arts**	25	
Filomena | V | **Deptford/NJ**	22	
NEW FireStone | V | **Wilming/DE**	-	
Fleming's | V | **multi.**	24	
Fogo de Chão | V | **Ave of Arts**	24	
Z NEW Fond | V | **S Philly**	27	
Z Fountain | V | **Logan Sq**	28	
Fox & Hound* | V | **Rittenhouse**	11	
NEW Franco's Osteria | V | **Wynnefield**	-	
Freight House | V | **Doylestown**	16	
Fuji Mtn.* | V | **Rittenhouse**	20	
Z Giumarello's | V | **Westmont/NJ**	26	
Green Room | V | **Wilming/DE**	24	
H.K. Golden* | V | **Chinatown**	20	
Il Portico | V | **Rittenhouse**	21	
Il Tartufo | V | **Manayunk**	21	
Iron Hill* | **W Chester**	19	
Jake's | V* | **Manayunk**	25	
Joe Pesce* | V | **Washington Sq W**	21	
Jones | V | **Washington Sq W**	20	
Joy Tsin Lau* | V | **Chinatown**	20	
Keating's | V | **DE River**	18	
Kildare's | V | **King of Prussia**	16	
La Collina | V | **Bala Cynwyd**	22	
Z Lacroix | V | **Rittenhouse**	27	
La Famiglia | V | **Old City**	23	
LaScala's* | V | **Washington Sq W**	19	
La Veranda | V | **DE River**	22	
Z Le Bar Lyonnais | V | **Rittenhouse**	27	
Z Le Bec-Fin | V | **Rittenhouse**	27	
Z Lily's on Main* | V | **Ephrata/LB**	24	
NEW Mac's Tavern | V | **Old City**	-	
Maggiano's | V* | **multi.**	20	
Manayunk Brew. | V | **Manayunk**	17	
Marsha Brown | V | **New Hope**	21	
Mary Cassatt | V | **Rittenhouse**	-	
Z Matyson* | V | **Rittenhouse**	27	
McCormick/Schmick | V | **Ave of Arts**	21	
Melting Pot* | V | **Chinatown**	19	
Meritage* | V | **Graduate Hospital**	25	
NEW Miga* | V | **Rittenhouse**	-	
Z Morimoto | V | **Washington Sq W**	28	
Morton's | V | **multi.**	26	
Moshulu | V | **DE River**	22	
Ms. Tootsie's | V | **South St**	25	
NEW Munk/Nunn | V | **Manayunk**	-	
Nectar | V | **Berwyn**	24	
Newtown Grill | V | **Newtown Sq**	19	
Z Nineteen | V* | **Ave of Arts**	23	
Paddock/Devon | V | **Wayne**	15	
Palm | V | **Ave of Arts**	24	
Paradigm | V | **Old City**	20	
Penne | V | **Univ City**	18	
NEW Percy St. BBQ* | V | **South St**	20	
Pho Xe Lua* | V | **Chinatown**	24	
NEW Pizzeria Stella* | V | **Society Hill**	22	
Pod | V | **Univ City**	23	
Pomodoro | V | **Wilming/DE**	-	
Portofino* | V | **Washington Sq W**	20	
Positano Coast | V | **Society Hill**	21	
Z Prime Rib | V | **Rittenhouse**	27	

Pumpkin*	**Graduate Hospital**	26
Rist. La Buca*	**Wash Sq**	22
Rist. Panorama	V*	**Old City**	23
Rist. Primavera	V	**Wayne**	20
🖪 NEW R2L	V	**Rittenhouse**	21
Ruth's Chris	V	**Ave of Arts**	23
🖪 Savona	V	**Gulph Mills**	27
Seasons 52	V	**King of Prussia**	-
Shiroi Hana*	**Rittenhouse**	24
Smith/Wollensky	V	**Rittenhouse**	22
Solaris Grille*	**Ches Hill**	14
SoleFood	V	**Washington Sq W**	20
NEW Square 1682	V	**Rittenhouse**	21
Sullivan's Steak	V	**King of Prussia**	23
Susanna Foo's	V	**Radnor**	24
Swanky Bubbles	V	**Old City**	19
🖪 Swann Lounge	V	**Logan Sq**	26
Table 31	V	**Logan Sq**	21
Tavern 17*	**Rittenhouse**	16
Tír na nÓg	V	**Logan Sq**	17
Triumph Brewing	V	**Old City**	18
🖪 Union Trust	V	**Washington Sq W**	24
Victor Café	V	**S Philly**	20
Water Works	V	**Fairmount**	21
William Penn	V	**Gwynedd**	20
Winnie's Le Bus*	**Manayunk**	21

PEOPLE-WATCHING

Alfa	**Rittenhouse**	17
🖪 Alma de Cuba	**Rittenhouse**	25
Almaz Café	**Rittenhouse**	21
🖪 Amada	**Old City**	28
NEW Amis	**Washington Sq W**	24
NEW Amuse	**Ave of Arts**	-
Audrey Claire	**Rittenhouse**	23
NEW Avril	**Bala Cynwyd**	14
Azie	**multi.**	23
🖪 Barclay Prime	**Rittenhouse**	27
Bar Ferdinand	**N Liberties**	23
Belgian Café	**Fairmount**	19
Bindi	**Washington Sq W**	24
Bistro di Marino	**Collingswood/NJ**	23
Bistrot/Minette	**Queen Vill**	25
Black Bass	**Lumberville**	21
Blue Pear	**W Chester**	23
NEW Bobby's Burger	**Univ City**	-

Bonjung Japanese	**Collegeville**	26
Bourbon Blue	**Manayunk**	18
Brandywine Prime	**Chadds Ford**	22
Brauhaus Schmitz	**South St**	19
Bridget Foy's	**South St**	19
Brio	**Cherry Hill/NJ**	19
Broad Axe Tav.	**Ambler**	16
🖪 Buddakan	**Old City**	26
NEW Bull Durham	**W Chester**	-
Butcher/Singer	**Rittenhouse**	24
Cactus	**Manayunk**	17
Caffe Aldo	**Cherry Hill/NJ**	24
California Pizza	**Plymouth Meeting**	19
Cantina Caballitos/Segundos	**S Philly**	21
Capers/Lemons	**Wilming/DE**	22
🖪 Capital Grille	**Ave of Arts**	26
🖪 Catelli	**Voorhees/NJ**	25
Chickie's/Pete's	**multi.**	18
🖪 Chifa	**Washington Sq W**	25
Chima	**Logan Sq**	21
Chops	**Bala Cynwyd**	21
NEW City Tap House	**Univ City**	-
NEW Con Murphy's	**Logan Sq**	17
Continental	**Old City**	22
Continental Mid-town	**Rittenhouse**	22
Cooper's	**Manayunk**	22
Copabanana	**South St**	17
Creed's	**King of Prussia**	24
¡Cuba!	**Ches Hill**	16
🖪 Cuba Libre	**Old City**	22
Dalessandro's	**Roxborough**	23
Darling's	**N Liberties**	17
Del Frisco's	**Ave of Arts**	20
Derek's	**Manayunk**	22
NEW Dettera	**Ambler**	21
Devil's Alley	**Rittenhouse**	19
Dining Car	**NE Philly**	19
🖪 Dmitri's	**Rittenhouse**	24
Dock Street	**Univ City**	21
Doc Magrogan	**W Chester**	17
Dream Café	**Cherry Hill/NJ**	-
Earth Bread	**Mt Airy**	21
El Camino Real	**N Liberties**	21
El Fuego	**Rittenhouse**	19
NEW El Rey	**Rittenhouse**	-
Eulogy Belgian	**Old City**	19
Fadó Irish	**Rittenhouse**	17
Famous 4th St. Deli	**South St**	24

SPECIAL FEATURES

NEW Firecreek	Downingtown	20
NEW 500º	Rittenhouse	-
Fogo de Chão	Ave of Arts	24
Z NEW Fond	S Philly	27
Z Fork	Old City	24
NEW Garces Trading	Washington Sq W	-
NEW Gemelli	Narberth	23
Geno's Steaks	S Philly	18
Georges'	Wayne	22
Girasole	Ave of Arts	21
Golosa	S Philly	26
NEW Green Eggs	S Philly	26
NEW Harvest	Glen Mills	-
NEW Hawthornes	S Philly	22
Hokka Hokka	Ches Hill	23
Honey	Doylestown	26
Hymie's Deli	Merion Sta	19
Iron Hill	Lancaster/LB	19
Izumi	S Philly	25
Jake's	Manayunk	25
Z James	S Philly	27
Joe Pesce	Washington Sq W	21
Jones	Washington Sq W	20
José Pistola's	Rittenhouse	15
Kaya's	Havertown	19
Kibitz Room	Rittenhouse	21
Kite & Key	Fairmount	16
Knock	Washington Sq W	16
Z Lacroix	Rittenhouse	27
Langostini	S Philly	-
Le Castagne	Rittenhouse	25
Legal Sea	King of Prussia	19
NEW Leila Cafe	Washington Sq W	-
NEW Le Viet	S Philly	-
Limoncello	W Chester	23
Local 44	W Philly	16
London Grill	Fairmount	17
NEW Lucky 7	Fairmount	17
NEW Mac's Tavern	Old City	-
NEW MaGerks	Ft Wash	15
Maggio's	Southampton	18
MangoMoon	Manayunk	17
NEW Más Mexicali	W Chester	-
Max Brenner	Rittenhouse	19
McCormick/Schmick	multi.	21
McFadden's	S Philly	15
Mélange	Haddonfield/NJ	25
Melrose Diner	S Philly	15
Mémé	Rittenhouse	23
Memphis Tap	Port Richmond	23
Mexican Post	Logan Sq	16
NEW MidAtlantic	Univ City	20
Mirna's Café	multi.	22
Misconduct Tav.	Rittenhouse	19
Mission Grill	Logan Sq	18
Mix	Rittenhouse	17
Mixto	Washington Sq W	20
NEW MIXX	Villanova	17
Molly Maguire's	Phoenixville	16
Z Morimoto	Washington Sq W	28
Z Moro	Wilming/DE	26
Moshulu	DE River	22
NEW Munk/Nunn	Manayunk	-
Noble Cookery	Rittenhouse	20
Orillas Tapas	Wilming/DE	23
Z Osteria	N Philly	27
Paddock/Devon	Wayne	15
Palm	Ave of Arts	24
NEW Parker's Prime	Newtown Sq	21
Z Pat's Steaks	S Philly	21
NEW Percy St. BBQ	South St	20
Pietro's Prime	W Chester	23
P.J. Whelihan's	Blue Bell	16
Plate	Ardmore	14
Pod	Univ City	23
Ponzio's	Cherry Hill/NJ	20
Pop Shop	Collingswood/NJ	21
Z Prime Rib	Rittenhouse	27
Privé	Old City	21
Prohibition	N Philly	22
Pub	Pennsauken/NJ	19
Pub/Kitchen	Graduate Hospital	22
Public Hse./Logan	Logan Sq	14
Raw Sushi	Washington Sq W	25
NEW Resurrection Ale	S Philly	24
Rist. Panorama	Old City	23
Roberto's Tratt.	Erdenheim	19
Rouge	Rittenhouse	22
Royal Tavern	S Philly	24
NEW Ro-Zu	S Philly	-
NEW Sampan	Washington Sq W	21
Sang Kee	Univ City	23
Shiao Lan Kung	Chinatown	23
Sidecar	Graduate Hospital	23
Silk City	N Liberties	21
Slate	Rittenhouse	19
Smith/Wollensky	Rittenhouse	22

Smiths | **Rittenhouse** 16
Smokin' Betty | **Washington Sq W** 20
Snackbar | **Rittenhouse** 22
NEW Sonata | **N Liberties** 23
St. Stephens Green | **Fairmount** 18
Sullivan's Steak | **multi.** 23
Susanna Foo's | **Radnor** 24
Z Swann Lounge | **Logan Sq** 26
Swift Half | **N Liberties** 18
Sycamore | **Lansdowne** -
Table 31 | **Logan Sq** 21
Tango | **Bryn Mawr** 20
Tavern 17 | **Rittenhouse** 16
NEW Tavolo | **Hunt Vly** 21
Ted's Montana | **Warrington** 18
Teikoku | **Newtown Sq** 23
Z 10 Arts | **Ave of Arts** 22
Tequila's | **Rittenhouse** 25
Teresa's Next Dr. | **Wayne** 22
Time | **Washington Sq W** 20
Z Tinto | **Rittenhouse** 27
Tír na nÓg | **Logan Sq** 17
Tony Luke's | **S Philly** 26
Tria | **Washington Sq W** 23
Triumph Brewing | **Old City** 18
NEW Tweed | **Washington Sq W** -
Twenty Manning | **Rittenhouse** -
Union City Grille | **Wilming/DE** 22
Z Union Trust | **Washington Sq W** 24
Urban Saloon | **Fairmount** 18
Uzu Sushi | **Old City** 23
Valanni | **Washington Sq W** 24
Varga Bar | **Washington Sq W** 20
NEW Verdad | **Bryn Mawr** 19
Vesuvio | **S Philly** 14
NEW Village Whiskey | **Rittenhouse** 24
Vintage | **Washington Sq W** 20
Water Works | **Fairmount** 21
Xochitl | **Society Hill** 23
Yakitori Boy | **Chinatown** 19
Zacharias | **Worcester** 24
NEW Zama | **Rittenhouse** 26
NEW Zavino | **Washington Sq W** 22

POWER SCENES

Z Alma de Cuba | **Rittenhouse** 25
Z Amada | **Old City** 28
Azie | **multi.** 23
Z Barclay Prime | **Rittenhouse** 27

Bella Tori | **Langhorne** 18
Blackfish | **Consho** 25
Blue Pear | **W Chester** 23
Brandywine Prime | **Chadds Ford** 22
Z Buddakan | **Old City** 26
Butcher/Singer | **Rittenhouse** 24
Caffe Aldo | **Cherry Hill/NJ** 24
Z Capital Grille | **Ave of Arts** 26
Z Catelli | **Voorhees/NJ** 25
Z Chifa | **Washington Sq W** 25
Chima | **Logan Sq** 21
Chops | **Bala Cynwyd** 21
Continental Mid-town | **Rittenhouse** 22
Del Frisco's | **Ave of Arts** 20
NEW Dettera | **Ambler** 21
Doc Magrogan | **W Chester** 17
Z Estia | **Ave of Arts** 25
Famous 4th St. Deli | **South St** 24
Fleming's | **Radnor** 24
Fogo de Chão | **Ave of Arts** 24
Z Fountain | **Logan Sq** 28
Georges' | **Wayne** 22
Girasole | **Ave of Arts** 21
Green Room | **Wilming/DE** 24
Z Lacroix | **Rittenhouse** 27
La Veranda | **DE River** 22
Z Le Bec-Fin | **Rittenhouse** 27
Le Castagne | **Rittenhouse** 25
McCormick/Schmick | **multi.** 21
Z Morimoto | **Washington Sq W** 28
Morton's | **multi.** 26
Ms. Tootsie's | **South St** 25
Z Osteria | **N Philly** 27
Palm | **Ave of Arts** 24
NEW Parker's Prime | **Newtown Sq** 21
Phillips Sea. | **Logan Sq** 16
Pietro's Prime | **W Chester** 23
Ponzio's | **Cherry Hill/NJ** 20
Z Prime Rib | **Rittenhouse** 27
Privé | **Old City** 21
Redstone | **Marlton/NJ** 20
Rouge | **Rittenhouse** 22
Z **NEW** R2L | **Rittenhouse** 21
Ruth's Chris | **multi.** 23
Saloon | **S Philly** 24
Smith/Wollensky | **Rittenhouse** 22
NEW Square 1682 | **Rittenhouse** 21
Sullivan's Steak | **multi.** 23

SPECIAL FEATURES

Table 31 | **Logan Sq**	21
◪ 10 Arts | **Ave of Arts**	22
Time | **Washington Sq W**	20
Toscana 52 | **Feasterville**	20
◪ Union Trust | **Washington Sq W**	24
Water Works | **Fairmount**	21
William Douglas | **Cherry Hill/NJ**	24
◪ Zahav | **Society Hill**	25

PRIVATE ROOMS

(Restaurants charge less at off times; call for capacity)

Adobe Cafe | **Roxborough**	20
◪ Alma de Cuba | **Rittenhouse**	25
Alyan's | **South St**	24
America B&G | **Chester Springs**	18
August Moon | **Norristown**	20
Avalon | **W Chester**	25
Back Burner | **Hockessin/DE**	22
Barone's/Villa Barone | **Moorestown/NJ**	22
Bay Pony Inn | **Lederach**	21
Bella Cena | **Rittenhouse**	20
Bistro Romano | **Society Hill**	22
Bistro St. Tropez | **Rittenhouse**	19
Black Sheep | **Rittenhouse**	17
Blue Bell Inn | **Blue Bell**	20
Bourbon Blue | **Manayunk**	18
Brick Hotel | **Newtown**	16
Bridgetown Mill | **Langhorne**	24
Buca di Beppo | **Exton**	16
Byblos | **Rittenhouse**	18
Caffe Aldo | **Cherry Hill/NJ**	24
California Cafe | **King of Prussia**	20
◪ Capital Grille | **Ave of Arts**	26
◪ Catelli | **Voorhees/NJ**	25
Centre Bridge | **New Hope**	22
Chart House | **DE River**	20
Chez Elena Wu | **Voorhees/NJ**	22
Chophouse | **Gibbsboro/NJ**	24
Chops | **Bala Cynwyd**	21
CinCin | **Ches Hill**	23
City Tavern | **Old City**	19
Copabanana | **South St**	17
Creed's | **King of Prussia**	24
◪ Cuba Libre | **Old City**	22
Dark Horse | **Society Hill**	19
Dave & Buster's | **DE River**	12
Davio's | **Rittenhouse**	25
Derek's | **Manayunk**	22

Dilworth. Inn | **W Chester**	25
DiNardo's | **Old City**	19
Duling-Kurtz | **Exton**	25
Epicurean | **Phoenixville**	20
Feby's Fish. | **Wilming/DE**	21
Fez Moroccan | **South St**	19
Fountain Side | **Horsham**	20
Freight House | **Doylestown**	16
Gen. Lafayette | **Lafayette Hill**	18
Gen. Warren | **Malvern**	25
◪ Giumarello's | **Westmont/NJ**	26
Gracie's | **Pine Forge/LB**	-
Green Hills Inn | **Reading/LB**	-
Hamilton's | **Lambertville/NJ**	24
Hard Rock | **Chinatown**	13
Harry's Savoy | **Wilming/DE**	24
H.K. Golden | **Chinatown**	20
Il Portico | **Rittenhouse**	21
Iron Hill | **Newark/DE**	19
Italian Bistro | **NE Philly**	17
Jack's Firehse. | **Fairmount**	19
Joseph Ambler | **N Wales**	21
La Collina | **Bala Cynwyd**	22
◪ Lacroix | **Rittenhouse**	27
Lai Lai Garden | **Blue Bell**	19
Lamberti's | **Wilming/DE**	18
La Veranda | **DE River**	22
◪ Le Bec-Fin | **Rittenhouse**	27
◪ Lily's on Main | **Ephrata/LB**	24
Maggiano's | **multi.**	20
Mamma Maria | **S Philly**	22
Marg. Kuo Peking | **Media**	27
McCormick/Schmick | **Ave of Arts**	21
McGillin's | **Washington Sq W**	16
Meritage | **Graduate Hospital**	25
Morton's | **multi.**	26
Moshulu | **DE River**	22
Mrs. Robino's | **Wilming/DE**	14
Nectar | **Berwyn**	24
New Tavern | **Bala Cynwyd**	21
Newtown Grill | **Newtown Sq**	19
Osaka | **Wayne**	23
Pace One | **Thornton**	21
Palace of Asia | **Ft Wash**	22
Pho Xe Lua | **Chinatown**	24
Pietro's Pizza | **South St**	21
Plate | **Ardmore**	14
Pod | **Univ City**	23
Portofino | **Washington Sq W**	20
Primavera Pizza | **Ardmore**	19

Prime Rib | **Rittenhouse**	27	Gen. Lafayette | **Lafayette Hill**	18
Pub | **Pennsauken/NJ**	19	Girasole | **Ave of Arts**	21
Ralph's | **S Philly**	23	Gnocchi | **South St**	19
Rist. Positano | **Ardmore**	20	Golden Pheasant | **Erwinna**	23
Rist. San Marco | **Ambler**	26	Good/Plenty | **Smoketown/LB**	18
Ruth's Chris | **multi.**	23	Green Hills Inn | **Reading/LB**	-
Saloon | **S Philly**	24	Harry's Savoy | **Wilming/DE**	24
Savona | **Gulph Mills**	27	Haydn Zug's | **E Petersburg/LB**	23
Serrano | **Old City**	21	Kimberton Inn | **Kimberton**	25
Seven Stars Inn | **Phoenixville**	20	Lacroix | **Rittenhouse**	27
Shangrila | **Devon**	21	La Locanda/Ghiottone | **Old City**	24
Shiroi Hana | **Rittenhouse**	24		
Simon Pearce | **W Chester**	22	Le Bec-Fin | **Rittenhouse**	27
Smith/Wollensky | **Rittenhouse**	22	Lemon Grass | **Lancaster/LB**	20
Solaris Grille | **Ches Hill**	14	Little Café | **Voorhees/NJ**	24
Spasso | **Old City**	23	Little Marakesh | **Dresher**	-
Spring Mill | **Consho**	24	Majolica | **Phoenixville**	24
Sullivan's Steak | **Wilming/DE**	23	Mamma Maria | **S Philly**	22
Tai Lake | **Chinatown**	27	Manon | **Lambertville/NJ**	24
Tango | **Bryn Mawr**	20	Marrakesh | **South St**	25
Teikoku | **Newtown Sq**	23	Mendenhall Inn | **Mendenhall**	19
Ten Stone | **Graduate Hospital**	17	Meritage | **Graduate Hospital**	25
Tequila's | **Rittenhouse**	25	Mikado | **multi.**	23
333 Belrose | **Radnor**	22	Miller's Smorgas. | **Ronks/LB**	18
Tierra Colombiana | **N Philly**	24	Morimoto | **Washington Sq W**	28
Totaro's | **Consho**	24	Moro | **Wilming/DE**	26
Vesuvio | **S Philly**	14	My Thai | **Graduate Hospital**	22
Vietnam | **Chinatown**	25	Norma's | **Cherry Hill/NJ**	22
Wash. Cross. | **Wash Cross**	20	Nunzio | **Collingswood/NJ**	24
White Dog | **Univ City**	20	Paradigm | **Old City**	20
World Café | **Univ City**	16	Pattaya | **Univ City**	20
Yardley Inn | **Yardley**	22	Roller's/Flying Fish | **Ches Hill**	19
		Summer Kitchen | **Penns Park**	21
		Ted's/Main | **Medford/NJ**	26
		Thai Singha | **Univ City**	22
		Vetri | **Washington Sq W**	28

PRIX FIXE MENUS

(Call for prices and times)

Avalon | **W Chester**	25
Bay Pony Inn | **Lederach**	21
Black Bass | **Lumberville**	21
Bridgetown Mill | **Langhorne**	24
Bridget's Steak | **Ambler**	23
Caribou Cafe | **Washington Sq W**	21
Chez Colette | **Rittenhouse**	20
iCuba! | **Ches Hill**	16
Cuba Libre | **Old City**	22
Davio's | **Rittenhouse**	25
Devon Seafood | **Rittenhouse**	23
Drafting Rm. | **Exton**	16
Fayette St. | **Consho**	23
Fez Moroccan | **South St**	19
Fountain | **Logan Sq**	28

QUICK BITES

Alfa | **Rittenhouse**	17
AllWays Café | **Hunt Vly**	23
Almaz Café | **Rittenhouse**	21
Alyan's | **South St**	24
NEW American Pub | **Ave of Arts**	15
Aqua | **Washington Sq W**	21
Arbol Café | **N Liberties**	17
Ardmore Station | **Ardmore**	18
Auspicious | **Ardmore**	19
Banana Leaf | **Chinatown**	21
Bar Ferdinand | **N Liberties**	23
Bensí | **N Wales**	17
Bitar's | **S Philly**	25

Bobby Chez	multi.	22	Iron Hill	Lancaster/LB	19
NEW Bobby's Burger	Univ City	–	Isaac's	multi.	17
Bonté Wafflerie	multi.	21	Jake's Hamburg.	New Castle/DE	20
Brew HaHa!	multi.	17	Jim's Steaks	multi.	23
NEW Bull Durham	W Chester	–	Z John's Roast Pork	S Philly	27
Café Con Chocolate	S Philly	–	José Pistola's	Rittenhouse	15
Café Estelle	N Liberties	23	Kibitz Room	Cherry Hill/NJ	21
Café L'Aube	Graduate Hospital	25	Kotatsu	Ardmore	24
Cake	Ches Hill	20	NEW Kraftwork	Fishtown	–
Campo's Deli	Old City	23	La Lupe	S Philly	21
Cantina Caballitos/Segundos	S Philly	21	LaScala's	Washington Sq W	19
Charlie's Hamburg.	Folsom	23	Little Pete's	Rittenhouse	18
Cheeseburger/Paradise	Langhorne	14	Local 44	W Philly	16
Chickie's/Pete's	Bordentown/NJ	18	NEW Lucky 7	Fairmount	17
NEW City Tap House	Univ City	–	NEW Mac's Tavern	Old City	–
NEW Con Murphy's	Logan Sq	17	NEW MaGerks	Ft Wash	15
NEW Cooperage	Washington Sq W	–	Maggio's	Southampton	18
Cooper's	Manayunk	22	Manny's	multi.	20
Darling's	multi.	17	Maoz Veg.	multi.	23
Devil's Alley	Rittenhouse	19	NEW Más Mexicali	W Chester	–
Dining Car	NE Philly	19	Mastoris	Bordentown/NJ	20
Dock Street	Univ City	21	Max & David's	Elkins Pk	21
NEW Doghouse	Downingtown	–	Max Brenner	Rittenhouse	19
Du Jour	Haverford	18	Mayfair Diner	NE Philly	15
Earth Bread	Mt Airy	21	McFadden's	S Philly	15
Ekta	multi.	–	Melrose Diner	S Philly	15
El Fuego	Rittenhouse	19	Memphis Tap	Port Richmond	23
NEW FireStone	Wilming/DE	–	Mexican Food	Marlton/NJ	19
NEW fish	Graduate Hospital	25	Mexican Post	Logan Sq	16
Five Guys	multi.	22	NEW MidAtlantic	Univ City	20
NEW 500º	Rittenhouse	–	NEW MIXX	Villanova	17
Franco's Tratt.	East Falls	22	Mizu	multi.	20
Full Moon	Lambertville/NJ	18	Molly Maguire's	Phoenixville	16
Full Plate	N Liberties	19	NEW Momiji	Society Hill	–
NEW Garces Trading	Washington Sq W	–	Monk's Cafe	Rittenhouse	22
Giwa	Rittenhouse	23	NEW Munk/Nunn	Manayunk	–
Gold Standard	W Philly	17	Naked Choco.	Ave of Arts	24
Good Dog	Rittenhouse	22	National Mech.	Old City	18
NEW Green Eggs	S Philly	26	Nifty Fifty's	Turnersville/NJ	19
Grey Lodge	NE Philly	19	Paddock/Devon	Wayne	15
Ha Long Bay	Bryn Mawr	21	Z Pat's Steaks	S Philly	21
Han Dynasty	multi.	24	NEW Pizzeria Stella	Society Hill	22
Harusame	Ardmore	22	P.J. Whelihan's	Blue Bell	16
NEW Hawthornes	S Philly	22	Ponzio's	Cherry Hill/NJ	20
NEW HeadHouse	Society Hill	–	Pop Shop	Collingswood/NJ	21
NEW Healthy Bites	S Philly	–	Prohibition	N Philly	22
			Pub/Kitchen	Graduate Hospital	22
			Pura Vida	N Liberties	–
			Q BBQ	Old City	16

Reading Terminal Mkt. | **Chinatown** `24`

NEW Resurrection Ale | **S Philly** `24`

Royal Tavern | **S Philly** `24`

Sabrina's Café | **Fairmount** `24`

Sang Kee | **Univ City** `23`

Scoogi's | **Flourtown** `19`

Shanachie | **Ambler** `13`

Sidecar | **Graduate Hospital** `23`

Silk City | **N Liberties** `21`

Sketch Café | **Fishtown** `24`

Sláinte | **Univ City** `16`

SLiCE | **multi.** `22`

Smokin' Betty | **Washington Sq W** `20`

Snackbar | **Rittenhouse** `22`

South St. Souvlaki | **South St** `22`

Steve's Steaks | **NE Philly** `23`

St. Stephens Green | **Fairmount** `18`

Swift Half | **N Liberties** `18`

Tavern 17 | **Rittenhouse** `16`

Tierra Colombiana | **N Philly** `24`

Tiffin | **N Liberties** `25`

NEW Tiffin etc. | **N Liberties** `23`

Tony Luke's | **S Philly** `26`

Tortilla Press | **Pennsauken/NJ** `23`

Triumph Brewing | **Old City** `18`

Trolley Car | **Mt Airy** `16`

Urban Saloon | **Fairmount** `18`

NEW Village Whiskey | **Rittenhouse** `24`

NEW Zavino | **Washington Sq W** `22`

Z Zento | **Old City** `26`

Zorba's Taverna | **Fairmount** `20`

QUIET CONVERSATION

Aki | **Washington Sq W** `21`

NEW Amuse | **Ave of Arts** `-`

NEW Apollinare | **N Liberties** `-`

NEW Avenida | **Mt Airy** `22`

Bella Tori | **Langhorne** `18`

Z Bibou | **S Philly** `27`

Z Birchrunville Store | **Birchrunville** `28`

Bistro 7 | **Old City** `24`

Black Bass | **Lumberville** `21`

Blue Pear | **W Chester** `23`

Bocelli | **multi.** `20`

Braddock's | **Medford/NJ** `20`

Caffe Casta Diva | **Rittenhouse** `26`

Cake | **Ches Hill** `20`

Cascade Lodge | **Kintnersville** `20`

Chiarella's | **S Philly** `22`

Chinnar Indian | **Berwyn** `23`

Cochon | **Queen Vill** `26`

NEW Con Murphy's | **Logan Sq** `17`

Daddy Mims | **Phoenixville** `23`

Dilworth. Inn | **W Chester** `25`

Z Estia | **Ave of Arts** `25`

Z NEW Fond | **S Philly** `27`

Z Fountain | **Logan Sq** `28`

NEW Franco's Osteria | **Wynnefield** `-`

Full Plate | **N Liberties** `19`

Gaya | **Blue Bell** `-`

Z Gilmore's | **W Chester** `28`

Golosa | **S Philly** `26`

Gypsy Saloon | **W Consho** `22`

Honey | **Doylestown** `26`

Z Il Fiore | **Collingswood/NJ** `26`

Inn/Phillips Mill | **New Hope** `25`

King of Tandoor | **Fairmount** `23`

Z Lacroix | **Rittenhouse** `27`

La Famiglia | **Old City** `23`

Las Bugambilias | **South St** `24`

La Viola Ovest | **Rittenhouse** `23`

Le Castagne | **Rittenhouse** `25`

Z Le Virtù | **S Philly** `26`

MangoMoon | **Manayunk** `17`

Masamoto | **Glen Mills** `26`

Mi Lah Veg. | **Rittenhouse** `21`

Modo Mio | **N Liberties** `26`

NEW M Rest. | **Washington Sq W** `21`

Nicholas | **S Philly** `22`

Z Nineteen | **Ave of Arts** `23`

Novità Bistro | **Graduate Hospital** `18`

Parc Bistro | **Skippack** `23`

NEW Parker's Prime | **Newtown Sq** `21`

NEW Paul | **Washington Sq W** `22`

Pistachio Grille | **Maple Glen** `20`

PTG | **Roxborough** `23`

Rouget | **Newtown** `24`

Z NEW R2L | **Rittenhouse** `21`

Simon Pearce | **W Chester** `22`

Singapore Kosher | **Chinatown** `20`

Slate Bleu | **Doylestown** `23`

SLiCE | **multi.** `22`

NEW Sonata | **N Liberties** `23`

Z Swann Lounge | **Logan Sq** `26`

Sycamore | **Lansdowne** `-`

Z Talula's Table	**Kennett Sq**	27
NEW Tavolo	**Hunt Vly**	21
Ted's/Main	**Medford/NJ**	26
Toscana 52	**Feasterville**	20
NEW Très Elena	**Mt Laurel/NJ**	–
Trio	**Fairmount**	24
NEW Tweed	**Washington Sq W**	–
Umbria	**Mt Airy**	24
Z Union Trust	**Washington Sq W**	24
Water Works	**Fairmount**	21
William Douglas	**Cherry Hill/NJ**	24
Yalda Grill	**Horsham**	22
Yardley Inn	**Yardley**	22
Z Zahav	**Society Hill**	25
Z Zento	**Old City**	26

RAW BARS

Brandywine Prime	**Chadds Ford**	22
Caffe Aldo	**Cherry Hill/NJ**	24
Z Catelli	**Voorhees/NJ**	25
NEW Cooperage	**Washington Sq W**	–
Creed's	**King of Prussia**	24
Deep Blue	**Wilming/DE**	22
Doc Magrogan	**W Chester**	17
Feby's Fish.	**Wilming/DE**	21
Freight House	**Doylestown**	16
Z Gibraltar	**Lancaster/LB**	23
Harry's Seafood	**Wilming/DE**	25
Johnny Brenda	**Fishtown**	21
Legal Sea	**multi.**	19
Little Tuna	**Haddonfield/NJ**	19
Marsha Brown	**New Hope**	21
Z Nineteen	**Ave of Arts**	23
Osaka	**Wayne**	23
Oyster House	**Rittenhouse**	23
Pace One	**Thornton**	21
Snockey's Oyster	**S Philly**	21
SoleFood	**Washington Sq W**	20
Stoudt's	**Adamstown/LB**	19
Table 31	**Logan Sq**	21
Z Union Trust	**Washington Sq W**	24
Upstares/Sotto	**Ave of Arts**	23
NEW Verdad	**Bryn Mawr**	19
NEW Village Whiskey	**Rittenhouse**	24
Walter's Steak.	**Wilming/DE**	22

ROMANTIC PLACES

Aki	**Washington Sq W**	21
Alfa	**Rittenhouse**	17
Z Alma de Cuba	**Rittenhouse**	25
Anton's/Swan	**Lambertville/NJ**	22
NEW Apollinare	**N Liberties**	–
NEW Avril	**Bala Cynwyd**	14
Z Barclay Prime	**Rittenhouse**	27
Beau Monde	**Queen Vill**	23
Bella Tori	**Langhorne**	18
Z Bibou	**S Philly**	27
Z Birchrunville Store	**Birchrunville**	28
Bistro Romano	**Society Hill**	22
Bistro 7	**Old City**	24
Bistrot/Minette	**Queen Vill**	25
Black Bass	**Lumberville**	21
Blackbird	**Collingswood/NJ**	25
Blackfish	**Consho**	25
Butcher/Singer	**Rittenhouse**	24
Caffe Casta Diva	**Rittenhouse**	26
NEW Carluccio's	**S Philly**	25
Carversville Inn	**Carversville**	25
Cascade Lodge	**Kintnersville**	20
Z Catelli	**Voorhees/NJ**	25
Chlöe	**Old City**	26
Cochon	**Queen Vill**	26
Dilworth. Inn	**W Chester**	25
Divan	**Graduate Hospital**	20
Duling-Kurtz	**Exton**	25
Z Estia	**Ave of Arts**	25
NEW fish	**Graduate Hospital**	25
Z Fountain	**Logan Sq**	28
Franco's Tratt.	**East Falls**	22
Z Fuji	**Haddonfield/NJ**	27
Gaya	**Blue Bell**	–
Z Gilmore's	**W Chester**	28
Z Giumarello's	**Westmont/NJ**	26
Golden Pheasant	**Erwinna**	23
Golosa	**S Philly**	26
Honey	**Doylestown**	26
NEW Hoof + Fin	**Queen Vill**	–
Z Horizons	**South St**	27
Hotel du Village	**New Hope**	23
Il Portico	**Rittenhouse**	21
Inn/Phillips Mill	**New Hope**	25
Izumi	**S Philly**	25
Z James	**S Philly**	27
NEW Koo Zee Doo	**N Liberties**	25
Z Lacroix	**Rittenhouse**	27

Las Bugambilias | **South St**	24
La Viola Ovest | **Rittenhouse**	23
Z Le Bar Lyonnais | **Rittenhouse**	27
Z Le Bec-Fin | **Rittenhouse**	27
NEW Leila Cafe | **Washington Sq W**	–
Z Le Virtù | **S Philly**	26
Lilly's/Canal | **Lambertville/NJ**	21
L'Oca | **Fairmount**	23
Majolica | **Phoenixville**	24
MangoMoon | **Manayunk**	17
Marigold Kitchen | **Univ City**	24
Mendenhall Inn | **Mendenhall**	19
Modo Mio | **N Liberties**	26
NEW M Rest. | **Washington Sq W**	21
Z Mr. Martino's | **S Philly**	24
Ms. Tootsie's | **South St**	25
Z Nineteen | **Ave of Arts**	23
Novità Bistro | **Graduate Hospital**	18
Orillas Tapas | **Wilming/DE**	23
Z Osteria | **N Philly**	27
Paradiso | **S Philly**	25
Parc Bistro | **Skippack**	23
NEW Parker's Prime | **Newtown Sq**	21
Pietro's Prime | **W Chester**	23
Pistachio Grille | **Maple Glen**	20
PTG | **Roxborough**	23
Rose Tattoo | **Fairmount**	22
Z NEW R2L | **Rittenhouse**	21
Salento | **Rittenhouse**	23
NEW Sampan | **Washington Sq W**	21
Simon Pearce | **W Chester**	22
Slate Bleu | **Doylestown**	23
SLiCE | **multi.**	22
Southwark | **South St**	25
Spring Mill | **Consho**	24
Summer Kitchen | **Penns Park**	21
NEW Tavolo | **Hunt Vly**	21
Ted's/Main | **Medford/NJ**	26
Z 10 Arts | **Ave of Arts**	22
Time | **Washington Sq W**	20
Toscana 52 | **Feasterville**	20
Tria | **Washington Sq W**	23
Trio | **Fairmount**	24
Twenty Manning | **Rittenhouse**	–
Z Umai Umai | **Fairmount**	26
Umbria | **Mt Airy**	24
Valanni | **Washington Sq W**	24
NEW Verdad | **Bryn Mawr**	19

Z Vetri | **Washington Sq W**	28
Washington Hse. | **Sellersville**	–
Water Works | **Fairmount**	21
Yalda Grill | **Horsham**	22
Yardley Inn | **Yardley**	22
Z Zahav | **Society Hill**	25

SENIOR APPEAL

Abacus | **Lansdale**	24
AllWays Café | **Hunt Vly**	23
NEW Apollinare | **N Liberties**	–
Aqua | **Washington Sq W**	21
Aya's Café | **Logan Sq**	19
Bay Pony Inn | **Lederach**	21
Bella Tori | **Langhorne**	18
Ben & Irv Deli | **Hunt Vly**	19
Bird-in-Hand | **Bird-in-Hand/LB**	20
Bistro di Marino | **Collingswood/NJ**	23
Blackfish | **Consho**	25
Blue Pear | **W Chester**	23
Bocelli | **Gwynedd**	20
Bonefish Grill | **multi.**	21
Brandywine Prime | **Chadds Ford**	22
Brio | **Cherry Hill/NJ**	19
Broad Axe Tav. | **Ambler**	16
Cafe Preeya | **Hunt Vly**	21
Caffe Casta Diva | **Rittenhouse**	26
Cake | **Ches Hill**	20
California Pizza | **Plymouth Meeting**	19
NEW Carluccio's | **S Philly**	25
Cascade Lodge | **Kintnersville**	20
Cedar Hollow | **Malvern**	17
Cheesecake | **Willow Grove**	20
Chinnar Indian | **Berwyn**	23
Chophouse | **Gibbsboro/NJ**	24
iCuba! | **Ches Hill**	16
Darling's | **multi.**	17
Dining Car | **NE Philly**	19
Divan | **Graduate Hospital**	20
Doc Magrogan | **W Chester**	17
Du Jour | **Haverford**	18
Ernesto's 1521 | **Rittenhouse**	19
Z Estia | **Ave of Arts**	25
Fleming's | **Radnor**	24
NEW Franco's Osteria | **Wynnefield**	–
Franco's Tratt. | **East Falls**	22
Gaya | **Blue Bell**	–
Gen. Lafayette | **Lafayette Hill**	18

SPECIAL FEATURES

Georges' | **Wayne**	22
Girasole | **Ave of Arts**	21
Giwa | **Rittenhouse**	23
Gold Standard | **W Philly**	17
Good/Plenty | **Smoketown/LB**	18
Gypsy Saloon | **W Consho**	22
Ha Long Bay | **Bryn Mawr**	21
Hank's Place | **Chadds Ford**	21
Hokka Hokka | **Ches Hill**	23
Honey's Sit | **N Liberties**	25
NEW Hoof + Fin | **Queen Vill**	-
Z Horizons | **South St**	27
Z Il Fiore | **Collingswood/NJ**	26
Isaac's | **multi.**	17
Italian Bistro | **Ave of Arts**	17
J.B. Dawson's/Austin's | **multi.**	18
Joe Pesce | **Collingswood/NJ**	21
Kibitz Room | **Cherry Hill/NJ**	21
NEW Koo Zee Doo | **N Liberties**	25
Kuzina | **Cherry Hill/NJ**	22
La Fontana | **Rittenhouse**	21
Langostini | **S Philly**	-
La Pergola | **Jenkintown**	19
Las Bugambilias | **South St**	24
Legal Sea | **King of Prussia**	19
Z Le Virtù | **S Philly**	26
Little Pete's | **Rittenhouse**	18
Little Tuna | **Haddonfield/NJ**	19
Maggio's | **Southampton**	18
Majolica | **Phoenixville**	24
Manny's | **Wayne**	20
Marg. Kuo | **Wayne**	23
Marigold Kitchen | **Univ City**	24
Max & David's | **Elkins Pk**	21
Mayfair Diner | **NE Philly**	15
McCormick/Schmick | **Cherry Hill/NJ**	21
Melrose Diner | **S Philly**	15
Mi Lah Veg. | **Rittenhouse**	21
Miller's Smorgas. | **Ronks/LB**	18
Moonstruck | **NE Philly**	21
NEW M Rest. | **Washington Sq W**	21
Murray's Deli | **Bala Cynwyd**	18
Nifty Fifty's | **Turnersville/NJ**	19
Z Nineteen | **Ave of Arts**	23
Novità Bistro | **Graduate Hospital**	18
Old Guard Hse. | **Gladwyne**	22
Z Osteria | **N Philly**	27
Otto's Brauhaus | **Horsham**	19
Parc Bistro | **Skippack**	23

P.F. Chang's | **Warrington**	20
Phillips Sea. | **Logan Sq**	16
Pietro's Prime | **W Chester**	23
Pistachio Grille | **Maple Glen**	20
Plain/Fancy Farm | **Bird-in-Hand/LB**	19
Plate | **Ardmore**	14
Pop Shop | **Collingswood/NJ**	21
PTG | **Roxborough**	23
Pub | **Pennsauken/NJ**	19
Radicchio | **Old City**	25
Roberto's Tratt. | **Erdenheim**	19
Roller's/Flying Fish | **Ches Hill**	19
Rouget | **Newtown**	24
Z NEW R2L | **Rittenhouse**	21
Scoogi's | **Flourtown**	19
Simon Pearce | **W Chester**	22
NEW Sprig & Vine | **New Hope**	-
NEW Square 1682 | **Rittenhouse**	21
St. Stephens Green | **Fairmount**	18
Susanna Foo's | **Radnor**	24
Table 31 | **Logan Sq**	21
NEW Tavolo | **Hunt Vly**	21
Ted's Montana | **Warrington**	18
Ted's/Main | **Medford/NJ**	26
Toscana 52 | **Feasterville**	20
NEW Très Elena | **Mt Laurel/NJ**	-
Vesuvio | **S Philly**	14
Washington Hse. | **Sellersville**	-
Water Works | **Fairmount**	21
White Elephant | **Hunt Vly**	24
William Douglas | **Cherry Hill/NJ**	24
William Penn | **Gwynedd**	20
Yalda Grill | **Horsham**	22
Yardley Inn | **Yardley**	22
Z Zahav | **Society Hill**	25

SINGLES SCENES

Alfa | **Rittenhouse**	17
Z Alma de Cuba | **Rittenhouse**	25
Z Amada | **Old City**	28
NEW Amis | **Washington Sq W**	24
Azie | **Villanova**	23
Bar Ferdinand | **N Liberties**	23
Belgian Café | **Fairmount**	19
Beneluxx | **Old City**	20
Bensí | **N Wales**	17
Black Sheep | **Rittenhouse**	17
NEW Bobby's Burger | **Univ City**	-
Bourbon Blue | **Manayunk**	18
Brauhaus Schmitz | **South St**	19

Menus, photos, voting and more – free at ZAGAT.com

Broad Axe Tav. | **Ambler** 16
Cactus | **Manayunk** 17
Cantina Caballitos/Segundos | **S Philly** 21
Chickie's/Pete's | **Bordentown/NJ** 18
Chick's | **South St** 21
🗷 Chifa | **Washington Sq W** 25
NEW City Tap House | **Univ City** -
Continental Mid-town | **Rittenhouse** 22
Coyote Cross. | **Consho** 21
🗷 Cuba Libre | **Old City** 22
Darling's | **N Liberties** 17
Del Frisco's | **Ave of Arts** 20
Derek's | **Manayunk** 22
Devil's Alley | **Rittenhouse** 19
Devil's Den | **S Philly** 19
Dock Street | **Univ City** 21
Earth Bread | **Mt Airy** 21
El Camino Real | **N Liberties** 21
NEW El Rey | **Rittenhouse** -
Eulogy Belgian | **Old City** 19
Fadó Irish | **Rittenhouse** 17
Fergie's Pub | **Washington Sq W** 16
Field House | **Chinatown** 12
NEW Firecreek | **Downingtown** 20
Fleming's | **Radnor** 24
Good Dog | **Rittenhouse** 22
NEW Hawthornes | **S Philly** 22
NEW HeadHouse | **Society Hill** -
Jones | **Washington Sq W** 20
José Pistola's | **Rittenhouse** 15
Kisso Sushi | **Old City** 25
Kite & Key | **Fairmount** 16
Knock | **Washington Sq W** 16
NEW Kraftwork | **Fishtown** -
L2 | **Graduate Hospital** 19
Manayunk Brew. | **Manayunk** 17
Marathon/Sq. | **Rittenhouse** 18
NEW Más Mexicali | **W Chester** -
McFadden's | **N Liberties** 15
Memphis Tap | **Port Richmond** 23
Mexican Post | **Logan Sq** 16
NEW MidAtlantic | **Univ City** 20
Misconduct Tav. | **Rittenhouse** 19
Mission Grill | **Logan Sq** 18
Mixto | **Washington Sq W** 20
Molly Maguire's | **Phoenixville** 16
Naked Choco. | **Ave of Arts** 24
National Mech. | **Old City** 18

N. 3rd | **N Liberties** 23
Orillas Tapas | **Wilming/DE** 23
P.J. Whelihan's | **multi.** 16
Plough & Stars | **Old City** 20
Pod | **Univ City** 23
Privé | **Old City** 21
Prohibition | **N Philly** 22
Pub/Kitchen | **Graduate Hospital** 22
Public Hse./Logan | **Logan Sq** 14
Raw Sushi | **Washington Sq W** 25
Redstone | **Marlton/NJ** 20
NEW Resurrection Ale | **S Philly** 24
NEW Sampan | **Washington Sq W** 21
Sidecar | **Graduate Hospital** 23
Silk City | **N Liberties** 21
Slate | **Rittenhouse** 19
Sly Fox | **Royersford** 13
Smiths | **Rittenhouse** 16
Smokin' Betty | **Washington Sq W** 20
Snackbar | **Rittenhouse** 22
Standard Tap | **N Liberties** 22
St. Stephens Green | **Fairmount** 18
Sullivan's Steak | **multi.** 23
Swanky Bubbles | **Old City** 19
Swift Half | **N Liberties** 18
Tavern 17 | **Rittenhouse** 16
Tequila's | **Rittenhouse** 25
Teresa's Next Dr. | **Wayne** 22
Tír na nÓg | **Logan Sq** 17
Tria | **Washington Sq W** 23
Triumph Brewing | **Old City** 18
Twenty Manning | **Rittenhouse** -
Urban Saloon | **Fairmount** 18
Uzu Sushi | **Old City** 23
Valanni | **Washington Sq W** 24
NEW Village Whiskey | **Rittenhouse** 24
Xochitl | **Society Hill** 23
NEW Zavino | **Washington Sq W** 22

SLEEPERS

(Good to excellent food,
but little known)
Anthony's | **Haddon Hts/NJ** 22
Ariana | **multi.** 22
NEW Avenida | **Mt Airy** 22
Barnsboro Inn | **Sewell/NJ** 22
Bistro di Marino | **Collingswood/NJ** 23
Bomb Bomb BBQ | **S Philly** 23
Bona Cucina | **Upper Darby** 23

Bonjung Japanese | **Collegeville** 26	Kotatsu | **Ardmore** 24
Bridgetown Mill | **Langhorne** 24	Kuzina | **Cherry Hill/NJ** 22
Bunha Faun | **Malvern** 24	La Campagne | **Cherry Hill/NJ** 22
Café L'Aube | **Graduate Hospital** 25	La Esperanza | **Lindenwold/NJ** 25
Caffe Valentino | **S Philly** 22	La Locanda | **Voorhees/NJ** 25
Capers/Lemons | **Wilming/DE** 22	☒ Lily's on Main | **Ephrata/LB** 24
NEW Carluccio's | **S Philly** 25	Little Café | **Voorhees/NJ** 24
Carman's Country | **S Philly** 26	Mamma Maria | **S Philly** 22
Carversville Inn | **Carversville** 25	Manon | **Lambertville/NJ** 24
Catherine's | **Unionville** 28	Marg. Kuo Peking | **Media** 27
Cedars | **South St** 22	Marrakesh | **South St** 25
Centre Bridge | **New Hope** 22	Masamoto | **Glen Mills** 26
Charles Plaza | **Chinatown** 24	Megu | **Cherry Hill/NJ** 26
Charlie's Hamburg. | **Folsom** 23	Memphis Tap | **Port Richmond** 23
Chiarella's | **S Philly** 22	Mirabella | **Cherry Hill/NJ** 23
Chinnar Indian | **Berwyn** 23	☒ Mr. Martino's | **S Philly** 24
Clam Tavern | **Clifton Hts** 22	Ms. Tootsie's | **South St** 25
Coconut Bay | **Voorhees/NJ** 23	My Thai | **Graduate Hospital** 22
Core De Roma | **South St** 25	Nan Zhou | **Chinatown** 23
Culinaria | **Wilming/DE** 23	New Harmony | **Chinatown** 22
Dahlak | **multi.** 22	Nicholas | **S Philly** 22
DeAnna's | **Lambertville/NJ** 24	No. 9 | **Lambertville/NJ** 24
Eclipse Bistro | **Wilming/DE** 23	Norma's | **Cherry Hill/NJ** 22
Elements Café | **Haddon Hts/NJ** 22	Olive Tree | **Downingtown** 23
El Serrano | **Lancaster/LB** 22	Orchard | **Kennett Sq** 27
Four Rivers | **Chinatown** 26	Orillas Tapas | **Wilming/DE** 23
Funky Lil' Kitchen | **Pottstown** 25	Palace of Asia | **Ft Wash** 22
GG's | **Mt Laurel/NJ** 26	Parc Bistro | **Skippack** 23
☒ Gibraltar | **Lancaster/LB** 23	NEW Paul | **Washington Sq W** 22
Giwa | **Rittenhouse** 23	Pho Thai Nam | **Blue Bell** 23
Golden Pheasant | **Erwinna** 23	Pho Xe Lua | **Chinatown** 24
Golosa | **S Philly** 26	Pietro's Prime | **W Chester** 23
NEW Green Eggs | **S Philly** 26	Prohibition | **N Philly** 22
Green Room | **Wilming/DE** 24	PTG | **Roxborough** 23
Harusame | **Ardmore** 22	Rasa Sayang | **Wilming/DE** 25
NEW Hawthornes | **S Philly** 22	Ray's Cafe | **Chinatown** 23
Haydn Zug's | **E Petersburg/LB** 23	NEW Resurrection Ale | **S Philly** 24
HighNote Cafe | **S Philly** 23	Rib Crib | **Germantown** 24
Hokka Hokka | **Ches Hill** 23	Riverstone | **S Philly** 25
Hostaria Da Elio | **South St** 23	Robin's Nest | **Mt Holly/NJ** 22
Hotel du Village | **New Hope** 23	Sakura Spring | **Cherry Hill/NJ** 22
Izumi | **S Philly** 25	Sapori | **Collingswood/NJ** 25
Jasmine | **Wilming/DE** 23	Sazon | **N Liberties** 22
Jong Ka Jib | **E Oak Ln** 25	NEW Shank's Original | **multi.** 23
Kabobeesh | **Univ City** 26	Shiroi Hana | **Rittenhouse** 24
Kingdom of Veg. | **Chinatown** 25	Sidecar | **Graduate Hospital** 23
King of Tandoor | **Fairmount** 23	Sketch Café | **Fishtown** 24
Kisso Sushi | **Old City** 25	Slate Bleu | **Doylestown** 23
Knight House | **Doylestown** 23	NEW Sonata | **N Liberties** 23
Konak | **Old City** 23	Sweet Basil | **Chadds Ford** 23

Tai Lake | **Chinatown** 27

Taq. La Michoacana | **Norristown** 23

Teca | **W Chester** 23

Ted's/Main | **Medford/NJ** 26

Thai Singha | **Univ City** 22

Tierra Colombiana | **N Philly** 24

🆕 Tiffin etc. | **N Liberties** 23

Trax Café | **Ambler** 22

Trio | **Fairmount** 24

211 York | **Jenkintown** 22

2 Fat Guys | **Hockessin/DE** 22

Umbria | **Mt Airy** 24

Union City Grille | **Wilming/DE** 22

Uzu Sushi | **Old City** 23

Vientiane Café | **W Philly** 23

Walter's Steak. | **Wilming/DE** 22

William Douglas | **Cherry Hill/NJ** 24

Yalda Grill | **Horsham** 22

Zacharias | **Worcester** 24

🆕 Zama | **Rittenhouse** 26

🆕 Zavino | **Washington Sq W** 22

Zinc | **Washington Sq W** 23

TASTING MENUS

🖪 Amada | **Old City** 28

Arbol Café | **N Liberties** 17

🆕 Avril | **Bala Cynwyd** 14

Bistro 7 | **Old City** 24

Bridgetown Mill | **Langhorne** 24

🖪 Cuba Libre | **Old City** 22

Daddy Mims | **Phoenixville** 23

Devon Seafood | **Rittenhouse** 23

🖪 Distrito | **Univ City** 25

Dom. Hudson | **Wilming/DE** 24

🆕 Firecreek | **Downingtown** 20

🖪🆕 Fond | **S Philly** 27

🖪 Fountain | **Logan Sq** 28

Freight House | **Doylestown** 16

🖪 Fuji | **Haddonfield/NJ** 27

🆕 Gemelli | **Narberth** 23

🖪 Gibraltar | **Lancaster/LB** 23

🖪 Horizons | **South St** 27

La Campagne | **Cherry Hill/NJ** 22

🖪 Lacroix | **Rittenhouse** 27

🖪 Le Bec-Fin | **Rittenhouse** 27

Majolica | **Phoenixville** 24

Marigold Kitchen | **Univ City** 24

🖪 Matyson | **Rittenhouse** 27

Mercato | **Washington Sq W** 25

Meritage | **Graduate Hospital** 25

🖪 Morimoto | **Washington Sq W** 28

🖪 Moro | **Wilming/DE** 26

Norma's | **Cherry Hill/NJ** 22

Nunzio | **Collingswood/NJ** 24

Orchard | **Kennett Sq** 27

Privé | **Old City** 21

🖪 Rest. Alba | **Malvern** 27

Seasons 52 | **King of Prussia** –

Shiroi Hana | **Rittenhouse** 24

Simon Pearce | **W Chester** 22

Spence's Remedy | **W Chester** 21

🖪 Talula's Table | **Kennett Sq** 27

🖪 Tinto | **Rittenhouse** 27

Twenty Manning | **Rittenhouse** –

Upstares/Sotto | **Ave of Arts** 23

🖪 Vetri | **Washington Sq W** 28

🖪 Yangming | **Bryn Mawr** 25

🖪 Zento | **Old City** 26

TEEN APPEAL

Alyan's | **South St** 24

Brew HaHa! | **multi.** 17

California Pizza | **King of Prussia** 19

Charcoal Pit | **Wilming/DE** 20

Cheesecake | **King of Prussia** 20

Dave & Buster's | **DE River** 12

El Azteca | **Mt Laurel/NJ** 19

El Azteca I | **Washington Sq W** 20

Geno's Steaks | **S Philly** 18

Hard Rock | **Chinatown** 13

Hibachi | **multi.** 18

Italian Bistro | **Ave of Arts** 17

Jim's Steaks | **multi.** 23

Jones | **Washington Sq W** 20

La Lupe | **S Philly** 21

Marathon Grill | **multi.** 18

🖪 Pat's Steaks | **S Philly** 21

Red Hot/Blue | **Cherry Hill/NJ** 16

South St. Souvlaki | **South St** 22

Tacconelli's | **Port Richmond** 25

Tony Luke's | **S Philly** 26

Trolley Car | **Mt Airy** 16

TRANSPORTING EXPERIENCES

Anton's/Swan | **Lambertville/NJ** 22

🖪 Birchrunville Store | **Birchrunville** 28

🖪 Gilmore's | **W Chester** 28

Hamilton's | **Lambertville/NJ** 24

Illuminare | **Fairmount** 15

SPECIAL FEATURES

Jamaican Jerk	**Ave of Arts**	19
Kabul	**Old City**	21
☑ Krazy Kat's	**Montchanin/DE**	25
La Campagne	**Cherry Hill/NJ**	22
☑ Lacroix	**Rittenhouse**	27
☑ Le Bec-Fin	**Rittenhouse**	27
Le Castagne	**Rittenhouse**	25
Little Marakesh	**Dresher**	-
Manon	**Lambertville/NJ**	24
Marg. Kuo	**Wayne**	23
Marrakesh	**South St**	25
☑ Morimoto	**Washington Sq W**	28
☑ Moro	**Wilming/DE**	26
Moshulu	**DE River**	22
Penang	**Chinatown**	21
☑ Siri's	**Cherry Hill/NJ**	26
☑ Vetri	**Washington Sq W**	28

TRENDY

☑ Alma de Cuba	**Rittenhouse**	25
☑ Amada	**Old City**	28
NEW Amis	**Washington Sq W**	24
NEW Amuse	**Ave of Arts**	-
Auspicious	**Ardmore**	19
Azie	**multi.**	23
☑ Barclay Prime	**Rittenhouse**	27
Bar Ferdinand	**N Liberties**	23
Beneluxx	**Old City**	20
Bindi	**Washington Sq W**	24
Bistrot/Minette	**Queen Vill**	25
Brandywine Prime	**Chadds Ford**	22
Brauhaus Schmitz	**South St**	19
☑ Buddakan	**Old City**	26
Butcher/Singer	**Rittenhouse**	24
Cantina Caballitos/Segundos	**S Philly**	21
☑ Capital Grille	**Ave of Arts**	26
☑ Chifa	**Washington Sq W**	25
NEW City Tap House	**Univ City**	-
Continental	**Old City**	22
Continental Mid-town	**Rittenhouse**	22
☑ Cuba Libre	**Old City**	22
Darling's	**N Liberties**	17
Del Frisco's	**Ave of Arts**	20
NEW Dettera	**Ambler**	21
Devil's Den	**S Philly**	19
Dock Street	**Univ City**	21
Dom. Hudson	**Wilming/DE**	24
Earth Bread	**Mt Airy**	21
El Camino Real	**N Liberties**	21

El Fuego	**Rittenhouse**	19
NEW El Rey	**Rittenhouse**	-
Eulogy Belgian	**Old City**	19
NEW FireStone	**Wilming/DE**	-
NEW fish	**Graduate Hospital**	25
NEW 500º	**Rittenhouse**	-
Fleming's	**Radnor**	24
NEW Garces Trading	**Washington Sq W**	-
Girasole	**Ave of Arts**	21
Good Dog	**Rittenhouse**	22
NEW Green Eggs	**S Philly**	26
NEW Harvest	**Glen Mills**	-
NEW Hawthornes	**S Philly**	22
Izumi	**S Philly**	25
☑ James	**S Philly**	27
José Pistola's	**Rittenhouse**	15
Knock	**Washington Sq W**	16
NEW Kraftwork	**Fishtown**	-
Legal Sea	**King of Prussia**	19
NEW Le Viet	**S Philly**	-
Local 44	**W Philly**	16
NEW Lucky 7	**Fairmount**	17
NEW Mac's Tavern	**Old City**	-
MangoMoon	**Manayunk**	17
NEW Más Mexicali	**W Chester**	-
Max Brenner	**Rittenhouse**	19
Mélange	**Haddonfield/NJ**	25
Mémé	**Rittenhouse**	23
Memphis Tap	**Port Richmond**	23
NEW MidAtlantic	**Univ City**	20
Misconduct Tav.	**Rittenhouse**	19
Mission Grill	**Logan Sq**	18
Mixto	**Washington Sq W**	20
Molly Maguire's	**Phoenixville**	16
☑ Morimoto	**Washington Sq W**	28
Naked Choco.	**Ave of Arts**	24
Noble Cookery	**Rittenhouse**	20
Nunzio	**Collingswood/NJ**	24
Orillas Tapas	**Wilming/DE**	23
☑ Osteria	**N Philly**	27
NEW Parker's Prime	**Newtown Sq**	21
NEW Percy St. BBQ	**South St**	20
Pietro's Prime	**W Chester**	23
NEW Pizzeria Stella	**Society Hill**	22
Pod	**Univ City**	23
Privé	**Old City**	21
Prohibition	**N Philly**	22
Pub/Kitchen	**Graduate Hospital**	22

🆕 Resurrection Ale | **S Philly**	24
Rouge | **Rittenhouse**	22
Royal Tavern | **S Philly**	24
🆕 Sampan | **Washington Sq W**	21
Sidecar | **Graduate Hospital**	23
Silk City | **N Liberties**	21
Slate | **Rittenhouse**	19
Smokin' Betty | **Washington Sq W**	20
Snackbar | **Rittenhouse**	22
St. Stephens Green | **Fairmount**	18
Supper | **South St**	23
Susanna Foo's | **Radnor**	24
Swanky Bubbles | **Old City**	19
Swift Half | **N Liberties**	18
Table 31 | **Logan Sq**	21
🛛 10 Arts | **Ave of Arts**	22
Teresa's Next Dr. | **Wayne**	22
Time | **Washington Sq W**	20
🛛 Tinto | **Rittenhouse**	27
Tír na nÓg | **Logan Sq**	17
Toscana 52 | **Feasterville**	20
Tria | **Washington Sq W**	23
Triumph Brewing | **Old City**	18
Twenty Manning | **Rittenhouse**	-
Uzu Sushi | **Old City**	23
Valanni | **Washington Sq W**	24
Varga Bar | **Washington Sq W**	20
🆕 Verdad | **Bryn Mawr**	19
🛛 Vetri | **Washington Sq W**	28
Vietnam Café | **W Philly**	24
🆕 Village Whiskey | **Rittenhouse**	24
Water Works | **Fairmount**	21
Xochitl | **Society Hill**	23
Yakitori Boy | **Chinatown**	19
🛛 Zahav | **Society Hill**	25
🆕 Zama | **Rittenhouse**	26
🆕 Zavino | **Washington Sq W**	22

VIEWS

Ardmore Station | **Ardmore**	18
🆕 Avril | **Bala Cynwyd**	14
Bay Pony Inn | **Lederach**	21
Bistro St. Tropez | **Rittenhouse**	19
Black Bass | **Lumberville**	21
Café Gallery | **Burlington/NJ**	20
Cascade Lodge | **Kintnersville**	20
Centre Bridge | **New Hope**	22
Chart House | **DE River**	20
Chophouse | **Gibbsboro/NJ**	24

Cooper's | **Manayunk**	22
Dave & Buster's | **DE River**	12
Devon Seafood | **Rittenhouse**	23
DiNardo's | **Old City**	19
🆕 FireStone | **Wilming/DE**	-
🛛 Fountain | **Logan Sq**	28
Hamilton's | **Lambertville/NJ**	24
Harry's Seafood | **Wilming/DE**	25
Hibachi | **DE River**	18
Inn/Phillips Mill | **New Hope**	25
Jake's | **Manayunk**	25
Keating's | **DE River**	18
Kildare's | **Manayunk**	16
🛛 Lacroix | **Rittenhouse**	27
Lambertville Station | **Lambertville/NJ**	18
Landing | **New Hope**	18
La Veranda | **DE River**	22
Lilly's/Canal | **Lambertville/NJ**	21
L'Oca | **Fairmount**	23
Mary Cassatt | **Rittenhouse**	-
Moshulu | **DE River**	22
🛛 Nineteen | **Ave of Arts**	23
P.J. Whelihan's | **Medford Lakes/NJ**	16
Privé | **Old City**	21
Rembrandt's | **Fairmount**	19
Robin's Nest | **Mt Holly/NJ**	22
Rouge | **Rittenhouse**	22
🛛🆕 R2L | **Rittenhouse**	21
🆕 Shank's Original | **S Philly**	23
Simon Pearce | **W Chester**	22
🛛 Swann Lounge | **Logan Sq**	26
Swift Half | **N Liberties**	18
Trax Café | **Ambler**	22
Wash. Cross. | **Wash Cross**	20
Water Works | **Fairmount**	21
Yardley Inn | **Yardley**	22

VISITORS ON EXPENSE ACCOUNT

Azie | **multi.**	23
🛛 Barclay Prime | **Rittenhouse**	27
Bella Tori | **Langhorne**	18
Black Bass | **Lumberville**	21
Butcher/Singer | **Rittenhouse**	24
🛛 Capital Grille | **Ave of Arts**	26
🛛 Chifa | **Washington Sq W**	25
Chima | **Logan Sq**	21
Chops | **Bala Cynwyd**	21
Del Frisco's | **Ave of Arts**	20

Dilworth. Inn | **W Chester**	25
Z Estia | **Ave of Arts**	25
Fleming's | **Radnor**	24
Fogo de Chão | **Ave of Arts**	24
Z Fountain | **Logan Sq**	28
Il Portico | **Rittenhouse**	21
Z Le Bec-Fin | **Rittenhouse**	27
McCormick/Schmick | **multi.**	21
Z Morimoto | **Washington Sq W**	28
Morton's | **Ave of Arts**	26
Z Nineteen | **Ave of Arts**	23
NEW Parker's Prime | **Newtown Sq**	21
Phillips Sea. | **Logan Sq**	16
Z Prime Rib | **Rittenhouse**	27
Z NEW R2L | **Rittenhouse**	21
Ruth's Chris | **Ave of Arts**	23
Smith/Wollensky | **Rittenhouse**	22
NEW Square 1682 | **Rittenhouse**	21
Sullivan's Steak | **multi.**	23
Table 31 | **Logan Sq**	21
Z 10 Arts | **Ave of Arts**	22
Z Union Trust | **Washington Sq W**	24
Water Works | **Fairmount**	21
Z Zahav | **Society Hill**	25

WATERSIDE

Black Bass | **Lumberville**	21
Bourbon Blue | **Manayunk**	18
Centre Bridge | **New Hope**	22
Chart House | **DE River**	20
Chophouse | **Gibbsboro/NJ**	24
Dave & Buster's | **DE River**	12
NEW Firecreek | **Downingtown**	20
NEW FireStone | **Wilming/DE**	-
Golden Pheasant | **Erwinna**	23
Hamilton's | **Lambertville/NJ**	24
Harry's Seafood | **Wilming/DE**	25
Keating's | **DE River**	18
Lambertville Station | **Lambertville/NJ**	18
Landing | **New Hope**	18
La Veranda | **DE River**	22
Lilly's/Canal | **Lambertville/NJ**	21
Manayunk Brew. | **Manayunk**	17
Moshulu | **DE River**	22
Robin's Nest | **Mt Holly/NJ**	22
NEW Shank's Original | **S Philly**	23
Simon Pearce | **W Chester**	22

Water Works | **Fairmount**	21
Yardley Inn | **Yardley**	22

WINE BARS

Bar Ferdinand | **N Liberties**	23
Beneluxx | **Old City**	20
Chick's | **South St**	21
NEW Cooperage | **Washington Sq W**	-
Cooper's | **Manayunk**	22
NEW Dettera | **Ambler**	21
Dom. Hudson | **Wilming/DE**	24
Fleming's | **Radnor**	24
Z Horizons | **South St**	27
La Belle Epoque | **Media**	21
Newtown Grill | **Newtown Sq**	19
Penne | **Univ City**	18
Rist. Panorama | **Old City**	23
Seasons 52 | **multi.**	-
Teca | **W Chester**	23
Z Tinto | **Rittenhouse**	27
Tria | **multi.**	23
Vintage | **Washington Sq W**	20

WINNING WINE LISTS

Aki | **Washington Sq W**	21
Z Amada | **Old City**	28
Back Burner | **Hockessin/DE**	22
Bella Tori | **Langhorne**	18
Beneluxx | **Old City**	20
Blue Bell Inn | **Blue Bell**	20
Bobby Chez | **Sewell/NJ**	22
Brandywine Prime | **Chadds Ford**	22
Broad Axe Tav. | **Ambler**	16
Butcher/Singer | **Rittenhouse**	24
Z Capital Grille | **Ave of Arts**	26
Caribou Cafe | **Washington Sq W**	21
Chick's | **South St**	21
Chima | **Logan Sq**	21
Chops | **Bala Cynwyd**	21
Cooper's | **Manayunk**	22
Del Frisco's | **Ave of Arts**	20
NEW Dettera | **Ambler**	21
Dilworth. Inn | **W Chester**	25
Dom. Hudson | **Wilming/DE**	24
Fleming's | **Radnor**	24
Fogo de Chão | **Ave of Arts**	24
Z Fountain | **Logan Sq**	28
Georges' | **Wayne**	22
Green Hills Inn | **Reading/LB**	-

Harry's Savoy | **Wilming/DE**	24	Cherry Hill	
Haydn Zug's | **E Petersburg/LB**	23	La Campagne	22
Jake's | **Manayunk**	25	Collingswood	
Z Lacroix | **Rittenhouse**	27	Nunzio	24
La Famiglia | **Old City**	23	**Z** Sagami	27
Z Le Bar Lyonnais | **Rittenhouse**	27	Exton	
Z Le Bec-Fin | **Rittenhouse**	27	Duling-Kurtz	25
Le Castagne | **Rittenhouse**	25	Hockessin	
Z Le Virtù | **S Philly**	26	Back Burner	22
Meritage | **Graduate Hospital**	25	Kennett Square	
Mission Grill | **Logan Sq**	18	**Z** Sovana Bistro	27
Morton's | **Ave of Arts**	26	Kimberton	
Noble Cookery | **Rittenhouse**	20	Kimberton Inn	25
Z Osteria | **N Philly**	27	Lambertville	
Penne | **Univ City**	18	Hamilton's	24
Z Prime Rib | **Rittenhouse**	27	Marlton	
Rist. Panorama | **Old City**	23	Joe's Peking	22
Rist. Positano | **Ardmore**	20	Mendenhall	
Z **NEW** R2L | **Rittenhouse**	21	Mendenhall Inn	19
Saloon | **S Philly**	24	Mount Holly	
Z Savona | **Gulph Mills**	27	Robin's Nest	22
Sullivan's Steak | **multi.**	23	New Hope	
Table 31 | **Logan Sq**	21	Hotel du Village	23
Tavern 17 | **Rittenhouse**	16	Inn/Phillips Mill	25
Z 10 Arts | **Ave of Arts**	22	Pine Forge	
Z Tinto | **Rittenhouse**	27	Gracie's	-
Tria | **Washington Sq W**	23	Reading	
NEW Tweed | **Washington Sq W**	-	Green Hills Inn	-
Z Union Trust |	24	Southampton	
Washington Sq W		**Z** Blue Sage	26
NEW Verdad | **Bryn Mawr**	19	Voorhees	
Z Vetri | **Washington Sq W**	28	Little Café	24
Vintage | **Washington Sq W**	20	West Chester	
William Douglas | **Cherry Hill/NJ**	24	**Z** Gilmore's	28
Yardley Inn | **Yardley**	22	Simon Pearce	22
		Wilmington	

WORTH A TRIP

		Z Moro	26
Birchrunville		Toscana Kit.	24
Z Birchrunville Store	28	Yardley	
Carversville		Yardley Inn	22
Carversville Inn	25		

SPECIAL FEATURES

Wine Vintage Chart

This chart is based on our 0 to 30 scale. The ratings (by U. of South Carolina law professor **Howard Stravitz**) reflect vintage quality and the wine's readiness to drink. A dash means the wine is past its peak or too young to rate. Loire ratings are for dry whites.

Whites

	95	96	97	98	99	00	01	02	03	04	05	06	07	08
France:														
Alsace	24	23	23	25	23	25	26	23	21	24	25	24	26	–
Burgundy	27	26	23	21	24	24	24	27	23	26	27	25	25	24
Loire Valley	–	–	–	–	–	23	24	26	22	24	27	23	23	24
Champagne	26	27	24	23	25	24	21	26	21	–	–	–	–	–
Sauternes	21	23	25	23	24	24	29	25	24	21	26	23	27	25
California:														
Chardonnay	–	–	–	–	23	22	25	26	22	26	29	24	27	–
Sauvignon Blanc	–	–	–	–	–	–	–	–	25	26	25	27	25	–
Austria:														
Grüner V./Riesl.	24	21	26	23	25	22	23	25	26	25	24	26	24	22
Germany:	21	26	21	22	24	20	29	25	26	27	28	25	27	25

Reds

	95	96	97	98	99	00	01	02	03	04	05	06	07	08
France:														
Bordeaux	26	25	23	25	24	29	26	24	26	24	28	24	23	25
Burgundy	26	27	25	24	27	22	24	27	25	23	28	25	24	–
Rhône	26	22	24	27	26	27	26	–	26	24	27	25	26	–
Beaujolais	–	–	–	–	–	–	–	–	24	–	27	24	25	23
California:														
Cab./Merlot	27	25	28	23	25	–	27	26	25	24	26	23	26	24
Pinot Noir	–	–	–	–	24	23	25	26	25	26	24	23	27	25
Zinfandel	–	–	–	–	–	–	25	23	27	22	22	21	21	25
Oregon:														
Pinot Noir	–	–	–	–	–	–	–	26	24	25	26	26	25	27
Italy:														
Tuscany	24	–	29	24	27	24	27	–	25	27	26	25	24	–
Piedmont	21	27	26	25	26	28	27	–	25	27	26	25	26	–
Spain:														
Rioja	26	24	25	–	25	24	28	–	23	27	26	24	25	–
Ribera del Duero/Priorat	26	27	25	24	25	24	27	20	24	27	26	24	26	–
Australia:														
Shiraz/Cab.	24	26	25	28	24	24	27	27	25	26	26	24	22	–
Chile:	–	–	24	–	25	23	26	24	25	24	27	25	24	–
Argentina:														
Malbec	–	–	–	–	–	–	–	–	–	25	26	27	24	–

Menus, photos, voting and more – free at ZAGAT.com

Take us with you.
ZAGAT Mobile

You choose the phone and we'll help you choose the place. Access Zagat dining & travel content on your **iPhone, BlackBerry, Android, Windows Mobile** and **Palm smartphones.**

Text **EAT to 78247** for more information or visit us online at **www.zagat.com/mobile**

ZAGATMAP

Philadelphia Transit Map

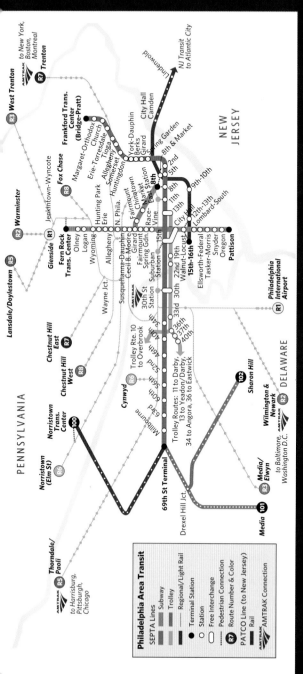

to New York, Boston, Montreal

R7 Trenton

R3 West Trenton

NJ Transit to Atlantic City

Lindenwold

Frankford Trans. Center (Bridge-Pratt)

Fox Chase

R8

City Hall Camden

Margaret-Orthodox
Church
Erie-Torresdale
Tioga
Allegheny
Somerset
Huntingdon
Somerset
York-Dauphin
Berks
Girard
Spring Garden
8th & Market
2nd
5th
8th

R2 Warminster

Jenkintown-Wyncote

Glenside R1   Fern Rock Trans. Center R1

R5

Lansdale/Doylestown

Olney
Logan
Wyoming

Hunting Park
Erie
N. Phila.

Fairmount
Chinatown
Market East
Race-Vine

9th-10th

Allegheny

Susquehanna-Dauphin
Cecil B. Moore
Fairmount
Spring Gdn.
Girard
15th

11th
13th

City Hall

12th-13th
Lombard-South

NEW JERSEY

Wayne Jct.

30th St Station
Suburban Station

15th

19th
Walnut-Locust

15th-16th

8th

Thorndale/Paoli R5

to Harrisburg, Pittsburgh, Chicago

Chestnut Hill East R7

Chestnut Hill West R8

Cymwyd R6

Norristown Trans. Center

Norristown (Elm St)

100

Trolley Rte. 10 to Overbrook

33rd
34th
36th
37th
40th

40th
49th

30th
22nd
19th

Ellsworth-Federal
Tasker-Morris
Snyder
Oregon
Pattison

Philadelphia International Airport R1

Trolley Routes: 11 to Darby, 13 to Yeadon/Darby, 34 to Angora, 36 to Eastwick

52nd
56th
60th
63rd

Millbourne

Sharon Hill

102

Wilmington & Newark R2

DELAWARE

PENNSYLVANIA

69th St Terminal

Drexel Hill Jct.

Media/Elwyn R3

to Baltimore, Washington D.C.

Media 101

101

Philadelphia Area Transit

SEPTA Lines
- Subway
- Trolley
- Regional/Light Rail
- Pedestrian Connection

● Terminal Station
○ Station
◯ Free Interchange

R7 Route Number & Color

PATCO Line (to New Jersey)

AMTRAK Connection
Rail

Philadelphia's Most Popular Restaurants

Map coordinates follow each name. For chains, only flagship or central locations are plotted. Sections A-G show places in the city of Philadelphia (see adjacent map). Sections H-N show nearby Delaware, New Jersey and Pennsylvania (see reverse side of map).

1 Amada (D-8)

2 Buddakan (D-7)

3 Le Bec-Fin (E-5)

4 Osteria (B-5)

5 Vetri (E-5)

6 Zahav (E-7)

7 Prime Rib (E-4)

8 Alma de Cuba (E-5)

9 Capital Grille (D-5, L-6)

10 Fountain Restaurant (C-4)

11 Morimoto (D-7)

12 Parc (E-4)

13 Tinto (D-4)

14 Chifa (D-7)

15 Barclay Prime (E-4)

16 Lacroix (E-4)

17 Fork (D-7)

18 El Vez (E-5)

19 Bibou (G-6)

20 Estia (E-5)

21 Distrito (D-1)

22 Gilmore's (L-3)

23 10 Arts (D-5)

24 Matyson (D-4)

25 Cuba Libre (D-8)

26 Pat's Steaks (G-6)

27 Yangming (K-5)

28 Savona (K-4)

29 Dmitri's † (E-3)

30 Devon Seafood (E-4)

31 Palm (E-5)

32 Davio's (E-5)

33 Butcher & Singer (E-5)

34 Continental Mid-town (D-4)

35 Blackfish (K-5)

36 Melograno (E-4)

37 Sabrina's Café (C-4)

38 Fogo de Chão (D-5)

39 Kanella (E-6)

40 Birchrunville Store (J-3)

41 White Dog Cafe (E-2)

42 Sang Kee Asian (K-5)

43 Reading Terminal Mkt. (D-6)

44 Modo Mio (A-8)

45 Morton's (E-5, K-4)

46 Jim's Steaks † (F-7)

47 Tony Luke's (L-6)

48 Monk's Cafe (E-5)

49 Cheesecake Factory † (K-4)

50 Honey's Sit n Eat (B-7)

† Indicates multiple branches